7

THE ISLAND

THE
NOVELS OF
FRANCIS BRETT YOUNG

THE ISLAND

BY

FRANCIS BRETT YOUNG

Vouchsafe to those that have not read the story,
That I may prompt them; and of such as have,
I humbly pray them to admit the excuse
Of time, of numbers, and due course of things
Which cannot in their huge and proper life
Be here presented . . .

SHAKESPEARE. HENRY V.

WILLIAM HEINEMANN LTD
LONDON   ::   TORONTO

FIRST PUBLISHED NOVEMBER 1944
REPRINTED JANUARY 1945
JANUARY 1946

THIS BOOK IS PRODUCED IN COMPLETE
CONFORMITY WITH THE AUTHORISED
ECONOMY STANDARDS
—
PRINTED IN GREAT BRITAIN AT THE WINDMILL PRESS
KINGSWOOD, SURREY

FOR

JESSICA

1904—1944

Dearest, in all my life I have known but two
Unwavering loves: for England, and for you:
What then more just than that this tribute paid
To one should at the other's feet be laid?

AUTHOR'S FOREWORD

THE idea of attempting a work of this kind and scope first came to me in South Africa in 1920, when a few of the lines now incorporated in the *Invocation* were written; and, from E. G. Twitchett's critical study of my work*, it appears that I was still talking about it in 1930, ten years later. In the years between, the long series of Mercian Novels had engrossed me, and it was not until 1939 that the composition of *The Island* was begun. In those distressful days, when the very existence of Britain was imperilled, the writing of anything so flimsy as fiction seemed out of tune with the times; and since no Government Department appeared to have much use for my services, I resumed the discarded project of trying to give shape in verse to my thoughts and feelings about my native land. It was not an easy task: for the Muse does not smile on a neglectful lover; my ear had been attuned too long to the rhythms of prose and conformed with difficulty to the more stringent discipline of verse; and the amplitude of the work which Youth had envisaged so light-heartedly appalled me. I have not (as any scholar who reads this work will perceive) any pretensions to being a historian. However, my own vision of what I desired to create was still clear to me; and in spite of inadequate powers and equipment, I have tried to fulfil my original plan. Indeed the writing of *The Island* has absorbed all my energies of thought and feeling for more than four years. It would never have been accomplished but for the sympathy and encouragement of others: of Edward Marsh, the sponsor of my earliest essays in Poetry, who has read and 'diabolized', as he calls it, every section of the Poem as it was produced; to C. P. Snow, who has borne the infliction of hearing it read; and, above all, to my wife, who has shared the strain of its protracted parturition.

F. B. Y.

* *Francis Brett Young* by E. G. Twitchett (Wishart, 1935)

CONTENTS

CONTENTS

INVOCATION

To you, dear brethren of the Seven Seas
And the Five Continents, strong progeny
Of one earth-girdling brood—to you, whose Hopes,
Wills, Visions, Aspirations, are moved as ours
By living memory or the more profound
Surge of the unremembered; you, in whose ears
Words of a common stem and heritage
Waken the self-same echoes; you, from whose lips
High-syllabled names of legendary scenes
Fall neither more beloved nor less familiar
Than those of shires, cities or villages,
That gave your forbears birth and burial—
To you, from her wave-battered, war-swept shore
The Muse of Britain calls.

First unto you,
Wielders of axe and plough, who in midmost West
Patiently watch your wheat-sown prairie quicken
With fledgeling green, warm to red wealth of harvest
(Before your phœnix maple flames in death),
Then whiten with the powdery incandescence
Of Arctic snowlights, till, at a milder waft,
Their frozen sap shatters the living trees
In loud reverberation, and ice-locked lumber,
Loosened from glassy fetters, yields to the undertow
Of snow-fed cataracts falling
To lakes that swim like seas, and torrents lashed
By shoals of spring-run salmon—till, once again,
The axe rings in the sodden woods, the mould
Turns from your cleaving share in corduroy
Of tawny velvet, and Autumn's ivory grain
Once more is drilled or scattered on the fallows.

Next you, whom that old sorceress Africa
Bewitched with her hot potions of welling light
And airs pellucid: you, twixt veld and sky,
Long-stirruped, falcon-eyed, riding for ever Northward
From pinnacled dolomite of stark Drakensberg
Trembling against the inviolable blue
To where Zambesi's smoke
Rolls from his thunderous chasm: you, that in galleries
Torrid with neighbourhood of Earth's radiant core
Blast grains of gold from niggard quartz to slake
The greed of cities; you that, saddle-propped
Beneath your trinket cross and old Magellan's
Star-cloudy galaxies, hear in the breathless night
The whine of fever's wings; the leafy rustle
Of stealthy-treading paws, or grosser wallowings
Of monsters that once ruled the wild, but now
Quail at the scent of man . . .

Then you, my brothers,
Who, ceiled by selfsame stars, but in a clime
Less terrible for aught beside its silence,
Deep in smooth-pillared eucalyptus, hear
The brittle chatter of bark, like cobra-casts
Sloughed from the living tree;
Or startled scream of halcyon parakeets
Splashing the blue-green twilight—you who, poised
Between parched earth and salamander sky,
Range the dun Austral sheepwalks, choked with dust
Of myriad-pattering flocks and the hot reek
Of burdened fleeces; you who, more venturous
Through thickset tropical tangles penetrate
The trackless Never-Never Land, or Northward
By Carpentaria and the Coral Sea,
Through hyaline glooms
Watch the sleek Philipino grope for pearls:
You, harlequin crowds,

INVOCATION

Who, on loud ocean-beaches, lazily
View the Pacific gather in indigo deeps
His cumulative surges, where, rank on rank,
His shuddering rollers break, plunge, pound, and seethe
Over the hissing sands to kiss your feet
With warm, sun-dazzled fringes of faint foam . . .

You, Eastward of the stormy Tasman housed,
Youngest in heart and blood,
Most distant yet most near;
Islanders, like ourselves, braced by the breath
Blown from another Pole—who hear, as we,
Dawn-song of lark and ousel and homely rooks;
Who, from your ferny mountain corries, see
The red stag toss his antlers, and far beneath,
Sheep-dappled downs and comfortable farms
Where, when the South whitens your hills with snow,
And timber-fires burn bright,
The old songs are sung, the old tales re-told . . .

To you, more lonely,
Who, on blanched coral beaches, where man's blood
Grows thin with tropic languors, from Antilles
To hot Malacca, see the identical fringe
Of leaning palm-fronds seaward, landward, sway
On tides of tepid air diurnally
Ebbing and flowing; you, who by steamy estuaries
Of mud and mangrove gloomed with melancholy
Thickets that neither Spring nor Autumn know,
Swelter and languish; you who in jungle-clearings
Watch viscous rubber from the wounded bark
Drip and congeal;
You, who on orient uplands, holly-green
With kempt plantation, raise flinching lids to meet
The dazzle of heaped Himalaya's glaciers
Taunting dry lips; you, who in shuttered chambers

Above the babel of murmurous bazaars,
Lulled by the lazy punkah and the shuffle
Of bare or sandalled feet, must chain your wits
To tallies, files and ledgers, checking bales
Of musky merchandise—yet often pause,
Pen in mid-air, closing your eyes to see
The king-cup watermeadows and dewy lawns
Hushed in bird-haunted twilight . . .

You, no less,
Whom a crazed king and his crass minister
With feeble mercenary arms provoked
Affronted and estranged (but in a struggle
Less bitter than the later feud that reft
Your brotherhood) and thereby sealed those freedoms
Of thought and speech ungrudged and unafraid
Which are our common pride in kinship deeper
Than that of blood or tongue—whose eager brains
And tireless thews have wrested from the soil
Of an unpeopled continent such wealth
And power as never Empire yet on earth
Has known, casting the mantle of your might
In three short centuries from the frozen shores
Of Massachusets and the pinnacles
Of many-towered Manhattan to far sands
Where the Pacific thunders—and from the ice
Of our unguarded frontiers to the warm seas
Where New Orleans swelters and the silt
Of Mississippi clouds the steamy gulf
Of Mexico—you, whose most noble spirit,
Re-minting the rough ore of Runnymede
At bloody Gettysburg, stamped on it the shape
Of a new currency that rings as bright
In our ears as in yours, for ever honoured
By them that stand for liberty and prize
The rights of the defenceless . . .

INVOCATION

Unto you all,
Now, in this awful hour, when earth's foundations
Quaver as when, long since, her cooling crust
Wrinkled in slow convulsions, overwhelming
Oceans and lands—now, when the patient flesh
Of frail, brief-sojourning man sustains anew
Fate's most barbaric insults, let us remember
How that our heritage was ever rooted
In stress and turmoil—nay, how the very soil
We cherish, our sovereign isle, was born of tumult:
Vexed by titanic forces, blasted, riven,
Torn from her mother-continent, then moulded
By mortal drift of long-forgotten seas;
Her basalt core by frost and torrent fretted,
Her mountains etched with ice.

      Let us remember
What fierce and gentle strains war in our blood,
Colour our eyes and hair; the innumerable richness
Of entropy that gives our chequered race
Its greatness. For Britain is not one, but many:
She is Brython and Saxon and Norse; she is Brennus, twin
            son
Of the Gaul Dunwallon, who cast
His Celtic sword in the ransom-balance of Rome:
She is Shakespeare and Burns, Jane Austen and Jonathan
            Swift;
John Brown and Abraham Lincoln, Pitt and Washington;
Gloriana, and Florence Nightingale—and Nell Gwynn.
She is rude Stonehenge and ageless Avebury no less
Than Hadrian's rampart and Durham's Norman Keep;
Paul's guardian dome and Lincoln's aery Gothic.
Hers are the Pennine scarps; the stormy summits
Of Grampian and Cader Idris and helmed Blencathra;
Smooth Sussex downs, dappled with shine and cloud;
The patient central ploughlands; the cherry-blossom
Of Teme and Medway. Hers are the silent rivers

And singing streams we love: strong-flowing Severn,
Spey's snow-fed torrent; Test's pellucid slides
And emerald-weeded stickles; those dimpling rivulets
That, born of Cotswold, feed the lordly flood
Of many-masted Thames. All these are hers;
Yet the core of her coasts is granite; the salt in her blood
Is drawn from no mediterranean puddle, foul
With the ordure and deliquescence of dead dynasties,
But from ocean's running surges, the fury that beats
On iron-bound cliffs from Cornwall to Cape Wrath,
Rimed with Atlantic spray: the seas that sever:
The seas that make us one! Come then, my brothers,
Hear, and behold!

II

PANORAMA AND CHANTS OF THE AGES

From an exalted station upon the confines of stellar space, the terrestrial globe is seen. The view-point is sufficiently low for certain general features of the planet's surface to be vaguely discernible; yet so high that the curved outline of the Northern Hemisphere, immediately beneath our eyes, can be marked as it rolls over, within its enveloping atmosphere, against the background of space, through which it is travelling, and in which it revolves. The turning of the globe becomes appreciable not so much through any details in the variation of its surface (which indeed are but dimly seen) as through the manner in which it appears to heave its bulk out of darkness, and, as day succeeds night, into sunlight which suddenly quenches those volcanic coruscations that, like the glow from the flank of a smouldering pit-mound, or sparkles of ignited carbon amid the soot of a fire-back, break out in a series of quick pin-points and serpentine lines of flame. From this contemplation the voice of the First Age summons us.

Come then, and from this breathless height,
Where, through the silent stratosphere
Dead planets blaze with borrowed light
And live suns sparkle doubly clear;

Where the cold moon, but lately torn
From her parent's riven sides,
Circling, captive and forlorn,
Drags at the lava-tides;

Where, in an incandescent dust,
Meteorites, like Lucifer
Falling, burst their iron hearts,
Sputter, and disappear:

See the lumbering Earth upthrust
Out of darkness into day
One segment of her cooling crust,
Gleam for a while, then roll away

From out the creeping sickle of light,
To sink beneath night's blinding veils,
Flecked with spurts of flame and bright
With red serpiginous trails;

Where, piercing Earth's integuments,
The flux of molten magma spills
Through fissures and red-throated vents
Of domed volcanic hills:

Till seas go up in plumes of steam,
Threshed by the fiery flail
Of spent lapilli, and ocean-beds
Lie choked in pumice hail;

Till new-formed plains are rent again
By fiercer shocks and quakes,
And sands are strewed with lava spewed
From out the heaving lakes;

Till the last cooling crater spends
Its last Titanic ire,
And a cold quietude descends
On the First Age of Fire!

As the tempestuous chant of the Archæan Age dies away, the Earth is seen to be wrapped in vapours condensed from her seas during these phlegræan convulsions: a shroud of dazzling whiteness defines and magnifies the invisible sphere. By degrees, the mist thins and dissipates, and through its vestiges, faintly at first, the calmer chant of the Second Age is heard.

No more, no more, tormented planet
Suffer birth-pangs such as these!
Earth's cold heart shrinks; her limbs of granite
Sprawl to embrace the Cambrian Seas.

Bemused she sleeps; if she be shaken
'Tis by the swell of earth-storms spent
That heave her bulk but cannot waken
The new Atlantic continent.

No sound her slumber breaks; naught changes
Her form but fretting of the tides,
Or polar winds that scour the ranges
With grits from their dead crater-sides.

Lifeless the lands, and deathlike-seeming
The mask of ocean; yet beneath
That crushing weight of water teeming,
A myriad lives grapple with death:

Dreamy Medusa trails her springes
For floating prey, and Trilobite
Gropes eyeless through the coral fringes
Blanched by the deep sea's timeless night;

And carrion of that carnage, drifting
With land-born debris swept from shore,
Death's silt, perpetually sifting,
Settles in slime on the sea-floor,

A new, dim continent devising—
Till, a chained monster, ill at ease,
Earth burst her granite bonds uprising,
And shook the oceans from her knees;

Till, mountain-high, the waters, helmed
With emerald spindrift, surged and tossed;
And, in white fury overwhelmed,
Atlantis foundered and was lost . . .

Was lost, for ever lost . . . And yet,
See, where the patient corals built
Their galleries, a domed island set
On slimes of powdered shell and silt.

That dome (whose brittle matrix shrank
To bone of Malvern, yet to be,)
Loomed for an age; then slowly sank
In a tumultuous sea

That seethed and simmered as when schools
Of whales in polar waters sport,
Or grey amphibians, in the pools
Of green Limpopo wallowing, snort—

Heaving their leaden sides to shake
The river from their streaming flanks,
And, sounding, spread a wave to wake
The saurians basking on her banks.

So, from that sea, emergent shapes
Of mountain sent a great wave forth
That lashed the Hebridean capes
And woke the craters of the North

To frenzies of a second birth
In sheeted flame amid the roar
Of waters. And bewildered Earth
Is lost to sight once more.

Birth and Destruction . . . So they run;
Yet each is granted little room:
The new theme, tenderly begun,
Fades, silenced by the drums of doom;

Buds, cheated of their blossoming,
Fall to feed the common mould;
And ever new creations spring
From the dust of the old.

So, recking neither toil nor waste,
Creative Earth's indifferent eye
Sees each new chronicle erased
Before the ink is dry—

As when some eager poet, swayed
By exaltations of fierce thought,
Pores on the music he has made
And knows it for a thing of nought,

Then, challenged by that mocking gage,
Crumples the paper, lifts his pen,
And pondering on the vacant page
Fashions his faulty dream again.

In this cataclysmic scene we have witnessed nothing less than the birth-pangs of Europe. Again and again the amphibian ranges lift their whale-backs and subside; until, at last, land and sea appear to have reached a state of equilibrium, and the monsters emerge as a series of mountain chains of an Alpine magnificence—resembling the fingers of a prone hand, in the intervals between which lie a number of diagonal firths and elongated lakes of fresh or brackish water: the obverse, as it were, of the Caledonian orograph. But though the ranges gather clouds from the sea, and torrents, born of these, eat into their flanks with deep erosions, draining into the Devonian lakes and friths, at their feet lie thirsty steppes swept by pillars of dust and veiled in sandstorms—the earth caked and cracked with heat, or pitted with infrequent rain; and though the bases on which this continent rests may seem to be built for eternity, the forces of subsidence and destruction are already at work; and lo, before the volcanic fires have flickered out, this new continent collapses—volcanoes and peaks, firths, lakes and inland seas commingled in what is neither wholly sea nor land: a vast swamp of black pools and crevasses, and one immense delta, where conterminous rivers, wider than Mississippi or Amazon, discharge the silt and debris of that destruction. Through warm, moisture-laden air, the chant of the Third Age is heard.

[11]

Yet mark how from this waste of fire and mud
Steaming and seething with mephitic gases
That break in bubbles from its black morasses,
Wells, with incontinent haste, the living flood
Of high, impetuous growth: how root with root,
In subterranean struggle for survival,
Wrestles to overwhelm its bitterest rival;
How leaves with predatory leaves dispute
The ambience of moist air, that, like a lens
Gathers and concentrates upon the fens
Rays fiercer than our planet's denizens
Have ever known. See, in this carnival
Of lush proliferation, how the tall
Lycopod drinks the light and steals the breath
Of humbler creatures stifling underneath
Her dome of shade; and how the gorgon hair
Of Sigillaria with aerial tresses
Sucks moisture from the sodden swamp's recesses,
Then droops to earth to find new foothold, where
Fanwise the fern-frond sways, and epiphyte
In crevice of bark or mossy fork entreed
Drains the sap blindly creeping toward the light;
How, in this world that knows nor flower nor seed,
The sexless spores shed from green leaves and breed,
Unravished by wantoning of breeze or bee!
Yet wingéd life there is: from tree to tree
Bright Archeoptilus, like a dragon-fly
Rustling his gauzy pinions, quivers and flits,
And clouds of locusts darken pools of sky
Reflected in the coal-swamp's inky pits;
While spider, roach and cricket grave their trails
On the smooth mud-bank's palimpsest, and scales
Of armoured ganoids gleam as each pursues
His prey of shrinking molluscs in the ooze.

So, on that dreamlike world, deep silence broods
For all its restless vehemence—save when floods
Of swollen sea, bursting its bars of sand,
Surge through the estuaries and drown the land,
Through creek and channel curiously creeping,
Brimming the lone lagoons with brine, and seeping
To rot each rootlet with a salty kiss,
Till the whole forest wilts and perishes!
And see how, revelling on that poisonous tide,
The plunging shapes of sea-born creatures ride;
Shoals of lean sharks, with crushing pavement-teeth
Explore their new-found pastures, and beneath
Ridges of shell-bank delve with routing heads
To crunch the blind crustaceans on their beds!
Time and again, the inflowing salty tide
Sickened those forests, and the green trees died
And fell and rotted; in the age between,
Time and again, they quicken with new green,
And coldly by their chlorophyll, encage
The sunlight that shall warm a distant age.

*And now (it is almost as if the Earth herself grew intolerant of
these endless alternations of growth and decay that seem to lead
nowhere) a new cataclysm shakes those regions of drowned Atlantis
from which the bastions of Armorica still tower unsubmerged. From
their bases an earth-wave spreads Northward, rippling the ocean-floor,
and breaking, at last, on the rudimentary ridge of the Malverns, which
it overrides with so great a pressure that their basalt is buckled and
curled over to enfold the verges of the coal-swamp. And now that this
barrier has been lowered, torrential floods, charged with alluvium from
the flanks of the quiescent Western volcanoes, pour into the swamp and
seal it; and later, amid these flats of solidifying sand, which resemble
those that surround the Dead Sea and the Caspian, there is born a
pellucid lake; and the water sucked up from that lake in innumerable
summers descends as rain, so that the basin, extending its margins by
constant erosion, at length breaks its banks and lets in the Sea of the*

Oolite, warm from the tropics and rich with new forms of life. From the borders of that sea the Chant of the Fourth Age is heard.

Beneath my corals, locked in death
Of ebony, the coal-swamps lie;
And, for an age, no living breath
Ruffles my tepid air or wakes
The slumber of my silken sea—
Till, sudden from the silence, breaks
The Scherzo of Time's Symphony!

Now behold the labouring Earth
Delivered of a monstrous birth,
As from creative fancy swarms
A welter of fantastic forms:
See, where the fruitful sea impinges
Upon my sands, the palmy fringes
Of cycads thrust their clustered spears,
And forests of flowered conifers
In myrtle and magnolia mingle
Honey and resin. On slopes of shingle
The crocodile with languid eye
Stares into a steamy sky,
And wandering through cypress-groves
Nightmare creatures of this age
Make their gigantic pasturage
Or celebrate their monstrous loves:

Here, with deliberation, moves
Bird-footed Iguanodon
To curve his slender neck and slake
His thirst within the Wealden Lake
Or pools where Ichthyosaurs and lithe
Water-serpents swarm and writhe,
And through the blue-green opal gleams
The moon-pale radiance of the chalk;
Or sprawls where Pterodactyls stalk

[14]

And, lighting, furl their bat-like wings
To stamp upon the forming cliff
Their footprints' feeble hieroglyph.

Inland, ravening forest plains,
Hear the more formidable brood
Of Dinosaurs crash through the wood,
Rending their unsuspicious prey
With sabred fangs and vulture claws,
Or, if a rival bars their way,
Engrappled with ferocious jaws;
While, at the first loud challenge flung,
Fleet marsupials pouch their young
And scatter, like the animate spray
Of flying-fish when dolphins play;
And every beast that feels the ground
Shudder with clash of armoured sides,
And heaven shaken by the sound
Of those tremendous battle-cries,
Cowers in the trampled fern and hides
Until the deadly work is done,
As the vanquished roars and dies
And the dazed victor stumbles on.

So, in those resinous woods, and glades
Of honey-sweet magnolia, fades
This pageant of fantastic Time:
The mailed reptiles sink to slime:
Dinosaur, Iguanodon
And Pterodactyl, all are gone,
And o'er their unrecorded grave
Shimmers again the lustral wave.

*This is indeed the greatest deluge of all. Unceasingly the chalky
seas pour out of the Asian tropics through the gulf of Greenland, until
all that remains of the British lands, over which the great reptiles
roamed, is an archipelago of islands—the greater of which are based*

on the Grampians, the Snowdon massif, the Brecon Beacons and the Carmarthen Vans. In the strait between these and the perdurable Armorican granite, the white dome of the Weald uprises, then sinks, and then reappears as part of a promontory jutting Northward from what is now the European mainland, presenting the profile of a human head in a peaked hood, and vaguely foreshadowing the shape of the British Isles.

But this promise, too, fails of fulfilment. Fire's last and most violent protest, launched from the volcanic chain that bounds the North from Antrim to Hecla, overwhelms this rudimentary Britain in a flow of lava—and all that can be seen is an inferno of fire and water fiercely contending. When the lava-flow cools and sets, rains furrow its slaggy surface, and, streaming Southward, carve out of the silt left by the last sea, the courses of two great rivers. One, impeded by Pennine, sweeps over the bed of the Irish Sea and flows into the Atlantic; the second shies from what remains of the Malvern ridge to break through the Southern Cotswold and join the Channel. Though it is still part of Europe, the shape of Britain begins to define itself and the Chant of the Fifth Age is heard.

> From Ushant unto Orkney spread
> Green lies my land, new-forested
> With oak and ilex, birch and ash,
> Made musical by streams that splash
> To silence in their river-bed.
>
> Green lies my land: a temperate air
> Wavers and wanders everywhere
> Through wood and marsh and water-meadow.
> To dapple with a moving shadow
> Of cloud the downland bare.
>
> Green lies my land: from dusk to dawn
> Peace broods upon the forest lawn,
> And ever mistier starlight spills
> Its silver on sleep-folded hills,
> Till darkness be withdrawn,

And my bird-nestling woodland wakes
In tender tremolos and shakes
And muted whimperings that fill
Its leafy clerestories, until
Morning's full music breaks.

Hear my woodlarks, tossed in bright
Fountain-jets of sheer delight,
From their palpitating throats
Let fall a shower of limpid notes
Like raindrops sprayed with light,

And sinking on extended wings
Bestir the thrush to murmurings
Of sweet, reiterated phrases,
While the bolder blackbird raises
His orange bill, and flings

Reveille through the echoing wood
Waking the drowsy multitude
That through the tapestry of leaves
A web of tenderer music weaves
Till noonday silence brood

Unruffled on that leafy sea
Save for the drone of honey-bee,
Or doves that croon, or whispering
Of branches where the squirrels spring
Nimbly from tree to tree.

Yet ever, from the whirling snows
Of deserts where the ice-wind blows
Cutting the tundras like a knife,
A slow tide of warm-blooded life
Into my pleasance flows:

See the light-stepping reindeer nip
Young lichens with a velvet lip,
While herds of roes and dappled fallows
Pause to drink from minnowed shallows,
Where hare and marmot sip

Dew from blades of springing grass,
And in the bittern's moist morass,
Knee-deep, with antlers tossing high,
The red stag roars his rutting-cry,
And droves of lemmings pass:

Like calm thoughts in a dream they roam,
Seeking an unimagined home;
And the brown bear's inquiring snout
Snuffles and sucks the sweetness out
From the wild-bee's honeycomb,

Where, deep in sunless forests, grey
Rhinoceros and mammoth stray,
Brushing bent saplings from their knees,
And through the wrack of shattered trees
Forging their ruthless way.

And when the pride of day is done,
Creatures that in the friendly sun
Browsed without terror, rise and slink
To reedy waterpools and drink
Timidly, one by one.

Beneath the dark's protective shield,
In thicket, bush and brake concealed,
They sink and cower out of sight,
When the fierce hunters of the night
Breathe fear upon the field;

When, from her caverned resting-place,
The tigress, with deliberate grace
Steals, and the lion licks his jaw
And yawns, or with a curving paw
Washes his golden face,

When startled on the darkening plain
The wary aurochs shakes his mane,
And stamps and snorts and sniffs the airs
That eddy from the charnel lairs
Wherein their cubs have lain.

Through wood and weald and waving grass
The hunters and the hunted pass;
And mingling in this carnival,
A shape more terrible than all,
Deadliest that ever was,

Man, with soft skin and brittle bone
And puny sinew, hunts alone,
In his brain's many-shuttled looms
Weaving more complicated dooms
Than life had ever known;

In his dim armoury of wit,
By fear's imaginations lit,
Fashioning pikes of wood and bone,
Flint-headed lance and throwing-stone,
And thongs for axe-heads split:

Man, who in loops of springe and snare
Trammels the heron and the hare,
And with stone axe or bludgeon clubs
The litters of blind tiger-cubs
Mewling within their lair:

[19]

Whose mind, more swift, can overtake
The fleetfoot reindeer herds, and break
In sunken pits the mammoth's pride,
Laughing to see that shaggy hide
Pierced by the pitfall stake.

Man, whose inventive fingers crave
Perpetual artifice, and grave
The imaged victims of his sleight
On ivory, or the stalagmite
That glazes his dark cave;

Ever, with cumulative skill
Sharpening his wits and flints, until
Hunters and hunted wince to hear
His voice, and sniff his scent with fear,
And perish at his will,

Or, like the wild dog, cringe and cower
To serve. Yet, even in this hour
Of man's first mastery, he and they
Together quailed beneath the sway
Of a more pitiless power,

When flying flakes of owl-soft snow
Whirled from the fields of Arctic floe
Weighed on the forest's sagging crown
And sent the green vault crashing down
On the warm life below;

And, winging these, an icier breath,
Foretaste of a crystal death,
Sealed the lakes in sheeted glass
And froze the lemmings to the grass
They nibbled underneath;

And crept into foul caverns where
Man, with the tiger and the bear
And cowed hyæna, huddles near
Fires whose very flames appear
To freeze upon the air,

Till, mustering his numb wits, he sees
How blue-green glaciers lap the knees
Of mountains, and the glacial wave
Sets on the threshold of his cave,
And, cold with terror, flees.

Southward, to where the blood-red sun
Sickens at noon in vapours dun,
He stumbles with the fear-tamed herds
Of savage beasts, while homeless birds
Waft over, one by one.

So, in dumb fellowship of pain,
Man, with his victims, limps the plain;
And he that lags or falters feels
Ice-cold fingers clip his heels,
And staggers on again,

Or falling, crushed beneath the tread
Of starved hordes trampling overhead,
Stiffens, and still for ever lies
Under the glassy shroud of ice
That ceres those frozen dead.

Thrice the grey glaciers melted—thrice
They clamped the mammoth in a vice,
Moulded the fell and scoured the plain
With boulder-drift and sharp moraine,
While, lost beneath the ice,

Their voiceless waters patiently
Furrowed new river-bed and sea,
And chiselled under moving floe
The lineaments of the land we know,
Peerless epitome

Of all sweet shapes and tender hues;
Land that the girdling sea imbues
With misty radiance, clothing green
Mountain and meadow with the sheen
Of its pellucid dews.

Yet, year on year, the greedy tide
Swelled from the West, unsatisfied,
And ever, with impatient fret,
Gnawed at the bridge of land that yet
Bound her to Europe's side;

And currents of the hungry Rhine
Rifted that bridge with creek and chine,
Crept to the base of every baulk
That propped the flint ribs of the chalk
And rotted it with brine;

And undermined the chalky lea
Till, in a foaming ecstasy
The twin tides kiss—and, like a ship
That shudders from the launching-slip,
An Island takes the sea!

III

Through years unnumbered now the Western tide
Boring and fretting has poured into the breach
And scoured the crumbling funnel of the chalk.
And now, behold, the Kentish cliffs, clear-cut
Above their hissing beaches of chesil, frown
Upon a sea that knows its continents.

Mark, on the Gallic shore,
Two bony promontories, Blancnez and Grisnez,
Resistant remnants of that broken causeway,
Gape to engulf a shallow crescent of sand
And one precarious roadstead: *Portus Itius*,
Where, rocking at their anchors, or careened
Above the driftwood tidemark, see assembled
Cæsar's diverse armada: high-pooped carracks
With leather lugsails and thonged rigging, reft
From the vanquished Veneti; Gaulish coracles
Of hide and wattle, that like water-spiders
Skim between shore and ship; lean Roman galleys,
Iron-rammed and beaked, fitter for tideless waters
Than these capricious surges: an ominous throng
Of eighty ships and more.
                 Here, on the crown
Of Grisnez's thrifty turf, it is so calm,
So still, this breathless evening, you can hear
Voices of seamen in the anchored fleet
Crying from ship to ship—and from inland dunes,
Where the two legions lie, an undertone
Like noise of babbling water or starling-flocks
Roosted in reed-beds; see, from their bivouac-fires,
A dove-grey smoke-film dim the harbour's glass
Like a breath-misted mirror; smell the pungency
Of woodsmoke wavering where the breath of thyme

[23]

Mingles with salt marsh savours . . . It is so clear
That the silken channel, shot with the iridescence
Of a pigeon's throat or milky mother-of-pearl,
Swims like a tide-brimmed estuary, and the downs
Beyond the cliffs of Kent float unsubstantial
As layered cloudbanks.

                      Here, set upon the summit,
A group of reed-thatched hutments, ragged by the wind,
Shelter headquarters; and here, that evening,
Three men bareheaded walk: First, Titus Labienus,
Stocky and shaggy as a moor-fed colt,
Gruff-voiced, short-spoken, with decisive gesture,
And a skin tanned as leathery as his tunic
By three years hard campaigning in the hungry
Winters of Gaul. Next, Quintus Cicero,
Thin-lipped, dark eyed, and elegantly-fashioned
With more Greek subtlety than Roman iron,
Mocks, with the indolent flicker of a smile,
The old campaigner's earnestness, interjecting
The lancet of a finely-pointed phrase
That makes the elder pause suspiciously,
Knitting his brows in doubt whether the word
Be bitter jest or earnest,—then laugh to hide
His solemn mind's perplexities. Last, Julius Cæsar,
Triumvir and Proconsul of Transalpine Gaul,
A spare man, taller than either of these, whose mien
Combines both qualities—the literal pragmatism
Of Labienus, and Quintus' Attic subtlety:
Master of word and deed, and yet the slave
Of single-minded purpose; soldier and orator,
Schemer and dreamer. His furrowed face betrays
Anxieties unshared; the firm mouth, faintly drooping,
Ruthless self-confidence; that width of brow
From which fair curls retreat untimely, carries
The vision of a widening world unguessed

By lesser minds; and, though he seems to heed
The chaffering of his legates, and sometimes smiles
When Cicero's lazy wit pricks at his humour,
His eyes, chained to the master brain behind,
Brood on the silken straits, and probe incessantly
The darkening shores of Cantion. He speaks:
"It seems so near," he says . . .

                        Labienus stiffens:
"So near? The width of water has been computed
At thirty thousand paces—or, by the reckoning
Of the barbarians, eleven leagues."
Cicero laughs: "Too wide, too far, for me!
If Balbus and his engineers could bridge it
As once they bridged the Rhine, I'd like it better.
Give me firm land! There's width enough in Gaul
To keep my legion tramping, and enough
Booty to gild the spectacle of a triumph
Would make Rome yell with rapture. Why go to Britain
With Gaul but half subdued? This gentle sea
Fawns like a leopardess, whose very velvet
Sheathes iron talons. Listen how she purrs,
And licks the shingles with a rasping tongue;
But when she rises, your flat-bottomed craft
May feel her teeth. Why, even her monstrous tides . . ."
"The tides, too, have been measured," snaps Labienus.
"At Springs, with the full moon as now, they rise
To twenty Roman feet, two palms, one digit,
Varying, of course, with the wind's strength and quarter;
And now there is none." Cicero spreads his hands
In a gesture that is all Greek. "No wind to-night:
But what of winds to-morrow? I'm neither augur
Nor seaman, and Poseidon never smiled
Upon my stomach. He may have dark designs
In store for us, and, speaking with respect,
Cæsar, your obstinate phantasy . . ."

                        The black eyes burn.

Then smile on him. "Phantasy, Quintus, phantasy?
That word is Greek. Imagination
Is better Latin; and, if Imagination
Set my feet on a path, nothing but reason
Will ever keep them there. It's an old tale
(Your brother knows it well)—how this one image, Britain,
Has lured me like a marsh-fire, ever since,
Flying from Sulla's tyrannies, I sailed
For Rhodes; how, leeward of Pharmacuse, the wind
Failed us, and as we rocked with flapping canvas
Becalmed, a pirate galley of Cilicia
Swooped, like a famished falcon on a quail,
And held our souls to ransom. In that hulk,
Stinking with bitumen and sun-dried fish,
There was one man (or monster) whom our captors
Favoured as their familiar laughing-stock:
A wizened bow-legged antic, that swarmed the mast
With half-articulate cries and fierce grimaces.
Naked he swung, but for a leather loin-cloth
And torque of iron forged about his neck;
And from that torque there hung an amulet,
A disk of graven metal. A hundred times
With scraps and blandishments I tempted him
To let me touch his trinket; and, when at last
I tamed him—lo, a coin of gold, resembling
A stater of Philip of Macedon as rudely
As he resembled Man. Oft and again
(For the time hung heavy on my hands) I pressed him
To tell me whence that relic came, until
One day, unasked, he blurted out my answer
In bastard Greek: "From the Pretanic Isles . . ."
"The Pretanic Isles," he said, "the Pretanic Isles . . ."
A name and nothing more . . .
Now mark the sequel: when, our ransom paid,
I landed at Piræus and made my way
To the house of your wife's brother, Atticus,

There, in his library, I found an inky slave
Squatting among his parchments. The work he copied
Was the geography of Posidonius:
And, once again, the name of Britain flashed
Into my mind and stirred it. Greedily
I snatched the rolls, and read them to the end:
They told of a great island, forested
With green woods, under skies for ever veiled
In ocean mists, whose ultimate cliffs divided
The Frozen Sea; of painted men who wrought
Weapons of curious bronze, and threshed their grain
In barns, and brewed of it a honey-wine;
Of a cragged promontory, Belerium,
Where troglodytes on breathing embers smelted
The tin they dredged from rivulets or delved
With uncouth hands from crannies of the rocks;
And there were grains of gold, and pearls . . ."
                                        Cicero started:
"A pearl, a pearl," he thought. There is the simile
For which I laboured. There it lies, an island
Luminous as a pearl born from the nacre
Of the sea's iris. I must remember this."
Once more Cæsar's eyes held him: "Gold and pearls . . .
When one is young, my friend, intangible treasure
Dazzles our sight, our fingers itch to clutch it;
Yet ageing eyes see not the thing itself
But what it buys—the wills of other men,
With power to bend or use them; and, in the play
Of restless wits that, like corpse-candles, flickered
Over dead Athens, that island-image faded—
While Rome, the richer treasure, dazzled me,
And might have led me, blinded, to calamity
Had I not found that neither birth nor eloquence
Nor wealth (as witness Crassus!) can tip the beam
Against the naked sword. And I had none.

Therefore I left the wine of young ambition
To season; sailed for Spain, and nursed my legions,
And learnt the weightier art of War. Yet even in Spain
Reminders of that lost image came to me,
In ships that nosed the wharves of Gabes, captained
By slim Phœnicians (friends of our good Balbus)
Men who had seen Belerium, and trafficked
Made wares for British ingots. So the vision
Grew nearer and more real. And when I marched
My legions into Gaul and broke the Veneti,
I found their fleets were fed and manned from Britain,
And that their chiefs sought sanctuary in Britain
To brew rebellion. I am no mystic, Quintus,
Nor Platonist; Aristotle is my master:
Yet I believe my destiny is linked
With Britain's; and, to purge my mind of Britain,
I must subdue it—not pursuing any phantasy,
Nor slaves nor gold nor commerce, but compelled
By the cold logic of necessity.
Listen: To-night I hold Gaul in my hands,
But as a fluttering eaglet; if I unclasp
My fingers she escapes me. Beyond the Rhine
Enemies far more formidable and fiercer,
The bloody German horde, shadow my flank,
And know (for they are cunning) I cannot venture
Beyond their marches and crush them in their forests
With Gaul, unfettered, rising in the rear;
And Gaul I cannot wholly break while Britain
Remains her arsenal: my Gallic enemies
Gather the threads and weave their plots unseen
In that veiled island. Gaul can never know
Peace, with those German savages untamed;
Yet, if I turn to tame them, I must risk
War on a double front . . .

                   This is the strategy
Of all Transalpine Europe, as I read it,

[28]

Now and for ever: No power that hath not gained
Mastery of Britain and her seas can hold
Gaul and the frontier of the Rhine. No other power,
Lacking the mastery of those narrow seas,
Can long hold Gaul or Britain in subjection."
He smiled. "I think you have your answer, Quintus.
The sea is calm; the land-breeze stirs. At midnight
We sail for Britain. The Gallic cavalry,
Embarking at the nether port, will join us
Tomorrow. You, Cicero, will go with me;
You, Labienus, stay."

And now, before late moonrise, see the dunes
Flicker with marsh-fire lanterns. On the shore
Two legions stand to arms, the Seventh and Tenth,
With complement of swart Numidian bowmen
And Balearic slingers. Hear, as they muster,
The trumpet-calls and sharp words of command,
And, as each cohort forms its ranks and marches,
Methodical plod of hobnails pounding shingle
Or shuffling through soft sands to plunge knee-deep
And launch the galleys. Hear the metallic clink
Of javelin and sword on iron-banded corselets;
The creaking of taut halyards in the tackle;
The shudder of rowlocks and the measured plash
Of sweeps that dip as one. Now, as the full moon rises,
See the whole fleet afloat, and all the roadstead
Rippled with broken moon-flakes: galley and carrack
Burnished alike with clustered helms and eagles.
Then, as the land-breeze freshens, watch them steal
Seaward, between the headlands—till the chuckling
Waters are silent, and the moony wakes
Lost in the outer channel.

                        Labienus,
Lonely on Grisnez, saw them out of sight;
Then wrapped his cloak around him, and turned, and slept.

And, as he slept, the foremost galleys, clearing
The windward headland, led the fleet of sail
West of the Lodestar's bearing, like pilot-fish
Guiding a shoal of sharks; but with the dawn
(Dawn ominous for Britain) the land-breeze freshened,
Veering into the sun, and held the transports
Floundering a league astern. On the larboard bow
Unscalable scarps of chalk loomed through the mist
And drove the galleys northward to a breach
Where the cliffs fell away, and running surges
Crashed on a shore of shingle. It was a landfall
To quell the most adventurous. But time pressed:
Already watchful eyes, piercing the mist,
Had spied the straggling flecks of sail. Already
The brazen wail of war-horns drifted inland
To wake the hornets' nests; already the beaches
Swarmed with blue-painted warriors and rang
With battle-cries.
                          Two galleys of the Tenth,
Urged by swift strokes, shot forward, and shuddering
Grounded in shelving sand. Swept by a hail
Of slingstones and a whirling sleet of spears
They stopped. A hoarse cry broke: "All overboard!
Charge for the shore!" But not a soldier stirred.
"What, would you shame your leader and your eagles,
Men of the Tenth?" The legion's signifer
Clambered the bows and plunged in, shoulder-deep,
His eagle held on high. Another followed
And soon the shallows frothed with half a cohort
Floundering and staggering shoreward up the shelf,
Tripped as the undertow dragged back the shingles,
Yet ever stumbling on, until firm foothold
Gives purchase for the javelin-fling. And soon,
Before that inexorable wave of iron
Creeping from out the wave of sea, the British
Quaver and break, leaving their dead awash

In blood-stained foam—yet never lessening
Their hail of taunts and missiles.
                                        See that drenched cohort
Straggle ashore and stamp and shake themselves
Like water-spaniels, laughing as they press
Salt from their smarting lids and curse the plague
Of gadfly missiles—yet each no sooner set
Foot on firm sand than the iron habit of discipline
Led him, unthinking, to his appointed place
In the fixed battle-order. Now, with locked shields,
The armoured tortoise crawled, when, suddenly
Launched from the woods, a formidable host
Fell on their flank: a charge of chariots,
Fierce as a breaking coamer helmed with fury,
Smote on them and surged over. Dazed and deafened
By wild cries, thunderous hoofs, and the shrill whinnying
Of horses maddened by lash and spearprick; blinded
With clouds of javelins and spatters of sand
And rattling chesil thrown from rapid wheels;
Shorn from their severed feet by blades that flashed
From every spinning felloe, the dwindled cohort
Still held its ground—but, from the foremost rank,
The maimed and dead lay strewn like corn in swathes
Shed from the mowers' scythes. And, even before
The rearward files sprang forward, sword in hand,
To mend the ranks and close the riven carapace
Of shields, the charioteers had whirled away
And wheeled behind them—and the bloody scythes
Swung through the second cohort, straggling forward
Knee-deep to aid its fellow!
                                        Thrice the wheeled fury swept
On the linked lines of shields, and thrice it shore
Through them and shredded them to particles
Of stubborn valour, fighting back to back,
Broken, but still unvanquished: till the British,
Drunken with pride and blood, and over-eager

B*

To clinch their triumph, leapt from their running chariots
And rushed, incontinent, to make an end
Of the shorn fragments, battling, hand to hand,
In single combat. Then the iron of Rome,
Forged in the furnace of wild Gaul and tempered
On battle's anvils, proved its mastery
O'er mere impetuous courage, stroke by stroke
Hacking a pathway through the light-armed rabble
Of Britain—till their Celtic fury spent
Its vehemence, and the painted warriors
Confused, ran for the chariots and scattered
To shelter of their woods . . .

                        It was a moment
When, in the tilting balance, victory
Lay for the taking, could but the fingers grasp it.
"Pursue, pursue!" men cried: but what pursuit
Of plodding foot could hope to overtake
Wheeled chariots? "Where are our cursed cavalry?"
The old centurions swore, straining their eyes
For sight of nearing sails, but seeing only
Blank waters lashed by ever-rising wind
And not a sail in sight.

                      That night, the legions
Dug fosse and vallum, and entrenched a camp
Foursquare above the beach, hauling their galleys
High on the shingle, while the transports rode
At anchor, where they had grounded.

                          On the morrow
There came an embassy from the chiefs of Kent
Entreating Cæsar's pardon for the hot-headedness
Of their impetuous youth; offering hostages
With full submission; humbly beseeching
The grace of an alliance and protection
Against more savage neighbours. Cæsar listened
Gravely, and granted all. It was the story

[32]

Of Gaul again: for every word betokened
That malady of which the Celtic spirit
Sickened—those jealousies of tribes and feuds
Of princes which had lately rotted Gaul
And, shrewdly fostered, might soon deliver Britain
Into his hands with even scantier shedding
Of Roman blood. Therefore he frowned, and bade them
Bring in their hostages, fencing, with words, for time
And kindlier winds, knowing (as they knew not)
That, without cavalry, he could neither master
Their chariots nor keep what land he held.
But, on the third day, when the tardy convoy
Dipped like a flock of kittiwakes in the troughs
Of off-shore waves, he saw the reefed sails suddenly
Gybe, put about, and scatter, till all were hidden
In white spume shredded from the outer sea;
And, that same night, the risen North Easter, stiffening
To a full gale, drove the full moon's spring-tide
Over the roaring chesil, to brim the fosse,
And breach the parapets, till the camp was drenched
Knee-deep in icy brine—while wind and tide,
Rioting together, snatched at the grounded galleys
With fierce teeth, tossing them like windlestraws
To crash on grinding shingle; and half the carracks
Carried away their anchors and were spewed
Out of the channel's throat or, caught abeam,
Flung through mid-air and cast above the tidemark.
So, through the dusk
Of stormy dawn and moonset, Cæsar saw
Only grey desolation: half the fleet
Vanished or stove or floundered, and, of the rest,
Not a third seaworthy. Shivering in their camp,
Amid salt-sodden victuals and quenched embers,
The legions murmured: "Better we had stayed in Gaul
Where, at the worst, an army can draw back
Upon its bases, than have hazarded

Starvation on this barren shelf of sand,
The impassable sea behind us, and before
The bloody chariot-scythes!'' And others cried:
"We are lost: the unpropitiated gods
Of these barbarians scourge us. How should we
Who are mortal match our valour against mysteries
Of air and water? Ay, and where is the plunder
With which we were lured: the vaunted gold and pearls
Of Britain; the rich pastures, the sleek herds,
The white-armed captives? There is more tangible loot
In one square league of Gaul than in all Britain!
Say what you will, our leader's wits have erred,
Tricked by the malice of some jealous god
Who grudged his easy triumphs—and we, chained
To the falling star, fall with it.''
                                        So the camp
Seethed like an ant-nest, till the centurions
Brought word to Cæsar's tent: and he, straightway,
Summoned the mutinous troops with trumpet-call
To stand to arms, and held the murmurers clamped
In rigid ranks of discipline. Some of the Tenth
He set to salvage of the wrack, and gathering
Of broken flotsam; shattered spars and timbers
Tumbled in the waves' wash, and floating sweeps
And nests of tangled tackle. Others, more skilled
In the shipwright's craft, caulked bulging seams and botched
The riven hulls with bolts of copper hammered
Out of the driftwood—till the beaches rang
With busy adze and matchet and the blithe voices
Of men heartened by toil. The Seventh Legion,
Screened by a single maniple, marched inland,
Scouring the woods for fuel and seeking grain
To eke their ruined rations; and now the sun,
Which had withheld his blessing from that scene
Of comfortless frustration, broke through and flooded
The mournful land with light, and every heart

Quickened to feel his warmth and see the fleets
Of dazzling cumulus scud through a lightened sky
And a sea no longer sullen-faced, but dancing
With gay sapphire and crisped by wavelets capped
With joyous foam. Even those sombre woodlands
Of oak no longer boded ill, but showed
Through sunlit glades the green of pastures, misted
With ivory of meadowsweet, traversed by streams
Winding through minty marsh-land, and the gleam
Of cornfields ripe for harvest but unreaped
That rippled like the sea. Then, as a flock
Of noisy daws swoops on a stubble, the Seventh
Broke ranks and scattered, and fell upon the corn
With swords for sickles, boisterously calling
And laughing as they reaped. Some, faint with hunger
And lack of sleep, sprawled on the headlands, lazily
Watching their comrades toil; others, who reaped,
Stripped to their woollen tunics, shed their armour
And piled their shields and javelins in the shade,
Unwary, not unseen . . .
                        For this fair day
Had brought new hope to Britain. From the downs
Above the ravaged cornfields, and from the cliffs
That frowned upon the beaches, watchful eyes
Marked the wrecked fleet of Rome, and saw their enemies,
Disarmed and unsuspicious, pillage their harvest.
And, swarming to their camps, the headier youth
Called on their faint-heart elders to send no more
Hostages, but rather, summoning strength and courage,
Fall on the crippled foe and hurl him, broken,
Into the sea. So, in the heat of noon,
When broom-pods crackled and the slumbrous crooning
Of stock-doves in the drowsy woodlands lulled
The harvesters to stretch their limbs and sleep—
Deep in those silent woods, their footfalls muted
By felting of soft leaf-mould, horse and chariots

[35]

And spearmen mustered; all the armed might of Kent
Waiting upon a word; and, that word spoken,
Whirled through the hapless reapers like the wind
That wakes a thunderstorm. But that storm broke
Before they knew it near . . .

               A mile and more away
On the busy beaches, deafened by the sullen
Pounding of the spent sea and the perpetual
Brisk clatter of adze and hammer, Cæsar heard
Naught of this sudden onslaught—yet, forearmed
By that taut wariness which is the instinct
Of the tried soldier, and ever glancing inland,
Suddenly saw the dark woods topped with clouds
Of turbulent dust churned from the chariot-wheels
Of the invisible battle, and instantly
Called out the guard, two cohorts of the Tenth,
And bade the rest equip themselves and follow
As swiftly as they could. Another moment,
And he had been too late! Even as he reached
The trampled corn, reft fragments of the Seventh,
Like empty husks whirled from a threshing-floor,
Streamed back to meet him—nor could he hope to stay
The rout, but opened ranks to let them pass
Through his advancing cohorts—then closed the ring
Of iron shields behind them, and stubbornly
Fighting a rearguard action, foot by foot,
Withdrew within the camp.

               That night, two ships,
The remnant of the storm-tossed fleet of transports,
Made land, and disembarked a single squadron
Of sick, bedraggled cavalry, but not a bale
Of stores, and only scanty, salt-spoilt forage.
And now, the long storm spent, motionless clouds
Drank up the moonlight and, in darkness, drenched
The huddled legions: two days, unceasingly,
A pitiless rain came down, and fouled the camp

With trampled quagmire—and still the tattered sky
Hung black with unshed water . . .

                               "Autumn has come,"
The old men murmured. "Ay, and if this be Autumn,
What danker misery faces us? What of Winter,
When, as they tell, the sun is hardly seen
And the rain never ceases, and the waves
Are never still? If we must die," they cried,
"Then let us perish in Gaul among our comrades;
Or, at the worst, go forth and fall like men,
Fighting, rather than perish like clemmed rats
Drowned in their holes!"

                        Hearing these murmurs, Cæsar
Held conference with his legates—more to test
The legions' dubious temper than to take
Counsel—and, in cold judgement, struck a balance
Of loss and profit: First, twelve ships destroyed
Or wrecked beyond repair; of men,—two cohorts
Lost or put out of action, and the rest
Weakened by want of food; of booty—nothing;
Of captives—but a handful of ragged hostages
Unfit for sale or triumph. Against these
Debts of misfortune, he set some solid gains:
Much bitter knowledge of the island's crags
And hazardous landings; more of its evil tides
And freakish climate; most, of its natives' mettle,
That breathless valour which gave the British chariot
(A weapon old as Troy!) the mastery
Of men who fought on foot; something, again,
Of Britain's weaknesses—her lack of leadership,
Divided will, and dim-witted neglect
To man her invulnerable moat and stem
Invasion on her seas; enough, in all,
To make the prospect of a second landing,
With stronger force of cavalry and more propitious
Season, secure of victory. This year

[37]

He could not conquer Britain; but, lest his men
Should carry back to Gaul the bitter aftertaste
Of failure, and the enemy reap unmixed
Glory from their retirement, he determined
To offer battle.

               No bloodier day than this
Had ever dawned on Britain. Hour after hour,
Gigantic in white sea-mist, wave on wave
Of British chivalry, their horses spattered
With flakes of blood and foam and terrified
By fierce cries, cast themselves on the locked shields
Of Rome—to be tossed forth like broken water
Spewed from a basalt cliff, and then sucked seaward
To gather from the deep new spite and strength
To charge and charge again. But still, at sunset,
The iron wall held firm—and at its feet,
Like a fringe of driftwood lodged upon a tidemark,
Lay wrack of horse and horseman, broken chariots,
Cleft helms and twisted weapons—all the bronze panoply
Of Britain dashed to pieces! And in the night,
While the bruised Britons licked their wounds and wrangled
Over new means to breach the wall of shields
Or sap its stubborn bases, the worn legions
Hoisted full sail and manned the galley-sweeps;
So, in the darkness fading like a ghost,
The fleet set course for Gaul, leaving their fires
To burn out, and their very dead unburied
In the deserted camp. And when the sun
Rose on the reddened beaches, all were gone.

IV

On Bredon Cloud the starveling grass
No echoes made
To hooves in loose-reined canter threading
The firwood's needly shade

To where an earthen rampart, ledged
Like a peregrine's nest
High on the badger-scrabbled scarp,
Brooded on the West.

Statue-still at the falling brink
My horse and I
Paused, in an element that seemed
Neither of Earth nor Sky;

While downward-plunging sight, through glaze
Of denser airs,
Marked tower and steeple blossom-misted
In Avon's steely snares:

All that dry firth where salty tides
Once inward swirled,
Breaking on basalt barrier-cliffs
Of an old western world.

So still that air, so mute that hour
Rapt and sublime,
The solitary mind must turn
To thoughts of Life and Time;

Yet, meditating, never guessed
How near beneath
The rabbit-nibbled sward lay strewn
A hecatomb of Death;

Herdsmen, who on that airy dome
(Alas, in vain!)
Sought refuge from the treacherous woods
Of Severn's firth and plain,

Pastured their lank-ribbed beasts and wrought
With pick and spade
Rampart and fosse and guarded gate,
And dwelt there, unafraid;

Yet woke, one startled midnight, blinded
By fire and blood;
Swarmed to their broken gates in panic,
And perished where they stood.

Axe-cloven skull and splintered thigh,
Those dead lay prone
Till kites had pecked the marrow out
And wolves gnawed flesh from bone;

Till greedy beak and claw had stripped
Their carrion prize,
And wood-wolves sniffed in vain to sate
The hunger in their eyes;

Till blistering sun and icy wind
Bleached the bones dry,
And only brittle fragments crumbled
Beneath the empty sky;

Till wind-blown dust and sailing seed
Silted between,
And wove about the mortal wrack
A soft shroud of green;

Till, a palm's depth new sward beneath,
Those dead men lay
Flattened, like shapes of Pleistosaurs
Locked in the Lias Clay . . .

Two thousand years the missel-thrush
His challenge loud
Flung in the teeth of Winter riding
On banks of snow-black cloud;

Two thousand Springs the risen lark
In twittering flight
Rained there on hand-clasped lovers' ears
His ripples of delight.

Lirra, lirra, trills the lark,
While lovers list,
Finger to lip, that silvery shower
Filtering through the mist . . .

That day I rode on Bredon Cloud
Loud sang the lark;
Yet a shadow of undiscovered dooms
Made my mind dark;

My horse, too, trembled and snatched the rein,
Restless to depart,
And the shiver that spread from his body to mine
Troubled my heart.

So I turned his head from the hidden death
And rode like the wind,
Galloping back through the firwood shade,
But dared not look behind.

What was it plucked at my heart that day
With fingers cold?
I cannot tell . . . I only know
That Man's mind is old,

And the memory of Man a mystery:
That in my veins
There may run, (who knows?) the blood of one
Who fled that night to the plains;

That, in my brain, some timeless cell
May still be endowed
With a dim dream of the massacre
That reddened Bredon Cloud.

V

EPISODE OF THE GARRULOUS CENTURION

Middle England, A.D. 78. The Scene is on the Southern boundary of the country of the Cornavii, fifteen miles North of the settlement of Glevum (Gloucester). To modern eyes the landscape would be almost unrecognizable; for the shrinking Severn Sea still retains its estuarine character, and the Hams of Severn are huge mud-flats, submerged, at Spring-tides, by the Bore, and scattered at low water (as now) with flocks of waders and other water-fowl.

On the left bank of the river, a dense bush of dwarf oak and ash and holly covers the triangle between Severn and Avon; but West of the greater river the woodland lies more open, with grassy slades, in which herds of roedeer are grazing, interspersed with vivid green patches of swamp. The only familiar features in this countryside are the summits of the hills that bound the plain: the wide dome of Bredon, with the ramparts of a deserted camp crowning its escarpment, and the serrated outline of the Malverns rising stark from a sea of forest which overflows their Northern prolongations, the Ankerdine and Abberley Hills.

On the Southern slope of Bredon, in the midst of a considerable clearing, stands a solitary white habitation: a small, half-timbered villa, consisting of a long, low range of rooms facing South, with a covered terrace in front of it, an entrance in the middle of the façade, and two wings protruding at right-angles to enclose a courtyard (or farmyard), in the midst of which stands an ornamental well-head, with a wrought-iron pulley and tackle for hoisting water.

On this terrace, enjoying the air of the early autumn evening, walks the owner: a small, spare, rustic figure, with a round head still covered by a close crop of white hair—a time-expired centurion, named Caius Petronius. He is shod with laced sandals of ox-hide, home-made, with the hairy side outward; and wears strips of wool wound round his legs like puttees, and, above these, a short-sleeved coarse woollen tunic, open at the neck and loosely girt about the waist by a belt of leather. As he walks to and fro, like a ship-master pacing his quarterdeck, his eyes

[43]

rest idly on the moss of rank forest that clothes the plain at his feet;
but, at the end of one turn, he stops and shades his eyes to focus a trail
of dust which he has seen slowly rising and creeping forward above the
treetops. After a moment he hurries to the door of the villa and
shouts instructions in Latin to the slaves at the back of the building.
Then he tucks up his tunic, tightens his belt, and sets off, with an
agility remarkable in a man of his age, down a steep path which,
judging from the direction of the dust-trail, seems likely to intercept
its course at the foot of the hill. And indeed, as he reaches the level,
well in front of the advancing dust, he steps out on to a rudimentary
road, which has once been metalled but is now overgrown with grass.
Here he stands waiting, slightly out of breath from his rapid descent,
until he hears the sound he has been expecting, the rhythmical plodding
of hobnails, and sees, in front of the dust, the head of a column of
soldiers slowly advancing and led by a tall young man, more lightly
and elegantly clothed: a subaltern commanding a vexillation of the
Twentieth Legion. The young officer wears a plumed helmet of bronze
and carries no shield; and his sword, longer than those of his detach-
ment, is slung from his girdle. As he approaches, the old centurion
hails him cheerily, and holds up his hand; and the optio, returning his
salute, calls his men to a halt. Caius Petronius speaks.

Hail, comrade! Welcome, and welcome again! Do you know,
When I saw your dust topping the woods by Severnside
I said to myself: "By Hercules, there's a draft
Coming up from Glevum!" And that's a rare thing nowadays—
Though thirty years ago, when we made this road
In the time of Caratacus, it wore out some shoe-leather
And no grass ever grew on it! Why, not a day passed
Without troops on the march; while now . . . But bless my soul,
You don't know who I am! My name's Caius Petronius,
Centurion of the Third Cohort of the Second Augusta,
Time-expired these many years. And yours? Claudius
Terentius?

Terentius . . . Yes, I remember a man named Terentius;
But he was a Thracian horseman, while you are Italian:

That's easily known from your speech, and damned good to
hear
In these days, when the legions are stiff with barbarians
Who can't speak articulate Latin. So you're in the Twentieth,
Valeria Victrix? Oh yes, *I* know the Twentieth:
They're old comrades of ours: came over from Gaul with us
And the Fourteenth Gemina in the year of the big invasion
Under Aulus Plautius—but the Fourteenth Gemina,
Or all that was left of them, were transferred to Armenia
Soon after the trouble with Boudicca. That's a long time ago,
And you've probably never heard of it. Still, ours and the
Twentieth
And the poor old Ninth are regular British legions:
And I always say, no man who hasn't done service
In Britain has any right to call himself soldier.
Well now . . . We'd better step to it. The sun's nearly down.
The best thing you can do is tell your lads to fall out
And bivouac here. They'll find plenty of dry wood about
For a fire to keep off the wolves, and excellent water.
You, of course, will come up to my farm and drink something
better.

Vile potabis modicis Sabinum cantharis. What?
Do young soldiers ever read Horace nowadays?
I don't suppose so. I'm not much of a reader myself;
But it happens that I was born in the Sabine Hills,
And the poet's farm—the one Mæcenas gave him,
To keep him out of the way as I always think,—
Was near my grandad's; and he used to drop in of an evening
And spout verse by the hour, for lack of a better audience,
Though the old man was deaf as a post. Flaccus must have been
An odd fellow by all accounts; yet his verse has a way
Of sticking in one's head—not the odes in which he buttered
Mæcenas and Augustus, but those that remind me
Of the country I knew as a lad and haven't set eyes on
Since long before you were born. *Eheu fugaces* . . .
Yes, they shoved me into the army when I was eighteen,

[45]

Being a younger son with a taste for women and gladiators,
And because a neighbour of ours, Vespasian,
Commanded the Second in those days, and promised my dad
He'ld keep an eye on me.
                                                    I can't say I've ever regretted it,
Nor yet that Fate took me to Britain. Let me tell you something
For the good of your soul: When first I came here, I felt
I'd slipped over the edge of the world. It was the light, or the
                                                    lack of it,
And the endless rain that made my heart sink to my boots;
But after a while, when my eyes grew used to the change,
I found this light kinder to them than the glare that beats back
From Apennine rocks or the black dust of Campania;
And the older I grow, the better I like it. You know,
Many's the time, when I was a lad, I used to think
Summer was the only season worth living in: how good it was
To wake in the cool of the morning and pick black mulberries
Or figs when the dew was on them, and lie all day
Under a pinetree, watching the lizards, and snaring them
With a noose of grass—ay, and listening to the crickets
Trilling in the ilex-woods or the wind-blanched olives
Till the very sky seemed to simmer—and sometimes a serpent
Swarmed over your legs and blinked with little flat eyes
Before he dared put out his flickering tongue to sip
At our fountain . . . Yes, yes, but when you are middle-aged
And glad to loosen your belt, you begin to feel
The sun a torment and Summer too long—while here
It's never too hot nor too cold. Of course there are things
One can't help missing at first. It's no use pretending
This clammy soil's as fertile as the red Tuscan earth;
And you haven't the sense of space you feel when you see
The foothills falling away from the knees of Soracte
To the Tyrrhenian shore. And yet there are compensations
And even likenesses . . . Do you mind if I halt a moment?
Of late years I have found it wiser to take things easily
Up a stiff pitch like this: the old bellows aren't what they were.

That's better . . . What was I saying? Ah, yes, likenesses . . .
Observe how the land slopes downward from here to the ford
By the fifteenth milestone from Glevum—in your itinerary
They call it *Ad Antonam*. Now half-close your eyelids.
Remark that undulant mountain-line in the West,
And tell me, candidly, if it doesn't resemble
The Alban Hills where they bar the Appian Way?
Now look half-left, where you see my vineyard reddened
With Autumn (the vines change colour earlier here)
And imagine those thorn-trees olives, which isn't difficult
In the fading light. Now doesn't that remind you
Of Latium as it did me when first I saw it?
No? Well, you're honest enough. Perhaps I've forgotten
What Latium looks like—and I shan't ever see it again;
But that's how it struck me, all those years ago,
When my gang was at work on the road, and I built a hut
Just where we're standing now. I remember, that evening,
I said to myself: "Why keep on hankering after Rome
When you know very well, by the time your service is over
There won't be a living soul left there to remember you,
And everything will have changed?" And not only that.
During all those years of soldiering with the Second
I'd seen a good bit of Britain, from Vectis, the island
That guards the Great Port, to the moors of Belerium
And then north again to Isca, where the legion was stationed
To keep the Silures quiet; and during that time—
Though it may seem odd to you—I'd taken a fancy to Britain.
Why? That's not so easy to answer; but I think the first thing
That attracted me was its quietness. Of course we had fighting
Now and again; but war is a soldier's duty,
And fighting's what he's paid for. Yet, here in Britain,
Our life was secure and placid beyond measure
Compared with life in Rome or even in Gaul.
Consider a moment; during my forty years' service
There have been four Cæsars—and every jack man of them
Has died by violence! Claudius, Caligula, Nero,

[47]

And Galba. And every time an emperor's died
He's dragged his friends to the grave with him, and left
Our poor distracted Italy to be vexed
By plots and jealousies, persecutions, portents
And judgements of the gods: Rome burnt to ashes,
Pompeii buried in pumice—while here—in Britain,
Year stole on year unvexed by any violence
But of our changing seasons, and not a ripple
Of the storms that lashed the empire ever reached us
Across the blessed sea. And, since man lives but once
I think he may as well live peaceably,
And no land is more peaceful than Britain to-day.
Now here's another thing that may surprise you:
I like the Britons as much as I like their island.
Of course you are bound to have heard a lot of nonsense
About them at home, where nobody sees any farther
Than Mons Albanus or Tibur; but when you've travelled
As I have, you'll find that (but for the Germans and Scythians,
Who are utter barbarians) men are much of a muchness,
And one people as good as the next. These Gauls and Britons
Have ancient virtues that have grown old-fashioned in Rome,
More's the pity. As slaves they may not be so intelligent
As the Greeks—but who wants to be a slave or a Greek?
While as for calling them 'bloody savages'
'Brutal barbarians' and all the rest of it—
That's just the flattering writers' way of saying
What fine fellows we were for licking them—just as if
We'd fought them on equal terms and with equal weapons;
While, in fact, they faced us without any body-armour
And with swords of untempered iron, ay, and gave us a run
For our money too! If you could only have seen—
As, thanks be, you probably never will now—a British host
With their waving plumes and blue-painted chariots;
Their rainbow-coloured kilts of saffron and emerald,
Azure and Tyrian, and their helms of bronze,
You'ld think you were back in the age of Troy, and wonder

[48]

How anything so brilliant could have happened
Under these Boreal skies. The shield of Achilles
Was not more finely wrought than those which Caradoc
And the Silurian chieftains bore in battle.
They died like heroes too . . . No, Britons, take my word
for it.
Are neither better nor worse than you or me.
They have their own way of life; their own dignities;
Their own strait standards of honour; their own religion—
Which is much like ours, by the way, though the names of
their gods
May be different. And when it comes to the arts of peace,
Their craftsmen can teach us a lot. When we reach the farm,
The wine you drink may be tart, but the cups you'll drink from
Are choicer in shape than Samian. Our greatest mistake
Is our arrogance in forcing these Britons into the mould
Of Rome, and sneering at all they do or make,
Not because it's worse than ours, but simply because
It's British and different . . .
Suppose we quicken
Our pace a little? I should like you to see
The view from my terrace before we lose the sun
And recline for supper. I've told you what I think
Of the British men. But what of the British women?
You've been warned against them, no doubt; but take no heed
Of that, my boy. Should you go ramping round
Like a randy young bull, it's possible you will get
More than you bargained for. If your hand is heavy
You may find you are fondling a tigress. Boudicca was one;
And Cartimandua, the Brigantine witch
Who betrayed Caradoc another: and both were queens!
But tell me: were there never such queens in Rome?
Even we, in dim, benighted Britain, have heard
Of Messalina's poisons, and how she played
With her poor cuckold Claudius—while Agrippina
Was handy with the same medicine—as Claudius

[49]

Found to his cost, and Nero might have found
To his, had not another queen (and poisoner),
His sweet Poppæa, taught him matricide!
Yet I will tell you of one British woman
Who was no queen, yet queenly in all graces
And dignities. Her name was Placida,
And placid was her spirit. We lived together
For more than thirty years, and she is dead;
(Gods of the Shades, be gracious!) but no woman
Of any race could have been wiser, stronger,
Or tenderer than she—ay, or more beautiful
In her clean, swift youth—though beauty is a thing
The memory cannot hold for long. My wife
Bore me three sons. I wish they were here this evening.
One is a signifer of the Fourteenth,
Now on the Danube; the second a centurion
In my sister legion, Adjutrix, stationed at Deva;
The third, alas, had little taste for soldiering,
But may go farther than either of his brothers
In this long peace: he's a decurion
Of Verulamium—a coming man
By all accounts, although I never see him,
Being a rough old farmer. But all three
Have half of Britain in their blood, and that
Seems good to me. You think I'm talking treason?
But then, an old man as lonely as myself,
Browsing on memories, has much time for thought;
And I have often wondered why this empire
Of ours should have more permanence than those
Which rose and fell before us: Athens, Macedon,
Carthage and Egypt . . . Rome will not last for ever;
And if she withers like a stricken oak,
Maybe—who knows?—that which was best in her
May live in lands where the acorns were scattered
In her green prime—perhaps even in this Britain
Which she despised. Sometimes I think I see

This Island as the ultimate sanctuary
Of ordered life—in which a new Deucalion
Shall ground his Ark upon a new Parnassus
To populate a world that has been drowned
Beneath barbaric floods with the old stock
Of homely, civil virtues. A new Parnassus . . .
Why not? Who knows but that the Muses may find
Foothold in Britain?

                  Enough . . . This is sober talk
For a lusty lad like you. Old minds are prone
To meditate upon the past and probe
A future they will never know—while Youth
Has far too much to think of in its present,
Too much to grasp, to worry about either.
And here's my villa! Note how I have placed it
To catch the light from dawn to dusk. You may think
The scale ambitious for a humble veteran;
But old bones covet comfort. Let me tell you
What fortune made me master of it. We will sit here
A moment while we talk; this tawny stone
Drinks in the sunlight and dispels its warmth
Slowly . . .

             I left the legion, time-expired,
Ten years ago. The Second had gone West
To permanent quarters in Isca of the Silures;
And we, its veterans, had been granted holdings
In our old station, the new city of Glevum,
To drag out our declining years—and many
Were grateful. But not I. I'm a born countryman
And hate the smell of towns: the city life
Irked me unbearably. It was about the time
Of Nero's murder, when the Spanish legions
Had lifted Galba on their shields. No sooner
Had he assumed his honours than we, in Britain,
To whom his name meant next to nothing, heard
That he, too, had fallen: Otho and Vitellius

Were scrabbling for the purple like a couple
Of curs worrying a bone. We only shrugged
Our shoulders—for it mattered little to us
Who ruled in Rome so long as we enjoyed
The peace of Rome in Britain. Then, of a sudden,
Great news for me! My old friend and commander
Vespasian had left Judæa to his son Titus,
And marched on Rome. It seemed the time had come
When quarrelsome rogues were silenced, and honest men
Might get their dues. Next year he came to Britain,
And halted at Glevum on his way to inspect
His old command at Isca. That was a day
Worth waiting for! Ha . . . I can see it now:
The great brand-new forum densely lined
With files of cheering veterans; the Prætorium
Thick-set with spears and trumpeters—and, in the midst,
That spare old figure in the faded purple
Limping along the lines, his wrinkled eyes
Bright as a bird's, searching the ranks to find
The face of an old comrade. When he came
Abreast of me, he halted; and the old smile
Lightened his leathery face: "What, you, Petronius,
Old friend? I hardly knew you; for your head's
White as Soracte in Winter! Many snows
Have fallen and melted there since last we met.
So come this evening: we will sup together
To talk of Tibur and the Sabine Hills,
And make the lost years live again."

       That night
We talked and laughed till daybreak, happily
Recalling the small things old men remember,
And joking in the rough mountain dialect
We spoke when we were boys—a saltier tongue
Than your smooth Latin, which was the mean language
Of plebs and plain-dwellers! And, in the end,
He tempted me: "Petronius," he said,

[52]

"Why not come back with me to Rome? I shall have need
Of men whom I can trust—and they are rare."
And when I shook my head, and told him frankly
My roots were deep in Britain, he only laughed
And wrinkled his bright eyes: "Perhaps you are right.
My friendship may prove dangerous. But tell me,
Before we part, if you are so determined
To die in Britain, what can I do for you
In token of our comradeship?"

                              I had no shame
In taking what he offered: I think I had earned it
By solid years of service, better than many
Who fawned on him like dogs begging for scraps.
So, with the gold he gave me, I built this house
And cleared the forest, and broke up the fields
With a wheeled Gallic *caruca* whose iron coulter
Bites deeper than the share of the *aratrum*
With which we plough in Italy; and here
I set my vineyard with soaked vine-shoots packed
In moss that Cæsar sent me by his couriers
From our old Sabine Hills, and trained and pruned them
With my Calenian knife: no Britain knows
The vine, or ever will. And here I have lived
Eight lonely years since my wife Placida
Left me. You see her tablet: DIIS MANIBUS
PLACIDA ANNORUM QUINQUAGINTA
CURAM AGENTE CONJUGE ANNORUM
TRIGINTA. Yes, thirty years . . . The lettering
Was chiselled by my foreman. So were these altars
To our Lares and Penates and Mars, my patron.
Nodens—that puzzles you?—is a British deity
Of my wife's country, the March of the Silures:
She had great faith in Nodens . . .

                            But sit you down.
Let the dogs sniff your knees: you need have no fear of them
For all their snarling looks—they know the difference

Between master and slave without my telling them,
And keep their fangs for wolves. These British hunting-dogs
Are famous the world over. Ay, sit you down,
While the girls light the lamps and cool your wine,
The *vile Sabinum* of which I spoke to you.
It's no choice vintage, but you'll find it wholesomer
And far less heady than the honey-wine
The Britons brew, or even the barley-beer
Which they call *Courmi*—not a headache in it!
And now let your mouth water: we will dine
On a fish more tasty than any bearded mullet
That ever floundered in the porphyry fishponds
Of the new-rich at Baiae: a noble monster,
With succulent flakes as pink as rosebuds, netted
By coracle-fishers in the foamy stickles
Of clear Sabrina this very day. The salmon
We call it. *Salmo*—the fish that leaps. You'ld know
The reason for the name if once you'd seen them
Hurling themselves in the air, again and again,
With the curve of a Parthian bow. And after that
You shall eat well-spiced venison, which that fine fellow
Who licks your hand bowled over in the woods
A week ago—and then a roasted pheasant
Fattened in my pens. We do not fare so badly
In our outlandish back-of-beyond. In Rome
Such living as ours would cost a poor pensioner
A mint of money; nor is my house so comfortless
As the farm in which I was born. This pavement, bright
With tesseræ of marble, is cool to the feet
In Summer; but later in the year, when Boreas
Howls in the thatch and snatches at the shutters,
The hypocaust, fed with logs of seasoned oak
And crackling brushwood, warms it so thoroughly
That a man may walk bare-footed. I love our Winters
As well as any season, though now, alas,
My nights are long and lonely, and the days

[54]

Seem shorter than they used to be. That is why
I welcome visitors, and probably,
Being old and prosy, bore them with a spate
Of inconsequent garrulousness. I ask your pardon,
Claudius Terentius, and will talk no more.
I lift my cup to you! Dinner is served!

c

VI

HIC JACET ARTHURUS REX QUONDAM REXQUE FUTURUS . . .

Arthur is gone . . . Tristram in Careol
Sleeps, with a broken sword—and Yseult sleeps
Beside him, where the westering waters roll
Over drowned Lyonesse to the outer deeps.

Lancelot is fallen . . . The ardent helms that shone
So knightly and the splintered lances rust
In the anonymous mould of Avalon:
Gawain and Gareth and Galahad—all are dust!

Where do the vanes and towers of Camelot
And tall Tintagil crumble? where do those tragic
Lovers and all their bright-eyed ladies rot?
We cannot tell—for lost is Merlin's magic.

And Guinevere—call her not back again
Lest she betray the loveliness Time lent
A name that blends the rapture and the pain
Linked in the lonely nightingale's lament,

Nor pry too deeply, lest you should discover
The bower of Astolat a smoky hut
Of mud and wattle—find the knightliest lover
A braggart, and his Lily Maid a slut;

And all that coloured tale a tapestry
Woven by poets. As the spider's skeins
Are spun of its own substance, so have they
Embroidered empty legend. What remains?

This: That when Rome fell, like a writhen oak
That age had sapped and cankered at the root,
Resistant, from her topmost bough there broke
The miracle of one unwithering shoot

Which was the spirit of Britain—that certain men,
Uncouth, untutored, of our island brood
Loved freedom better than their lives; and when
The tempest crashed about them, rose and stood

And charged into the storm's black heart, with sword
Lifted, or lance in rest, and rode there, helmed
With a strange majesty that the heathen horde
Remembered after all were overwhelmed;

And made of them a legend, to their chief,
Arthur, Ambrosius—no man knows his name—
Granting a gallantry beyond belief,
And to his knights imperishable fame.

They were so few . . . We know not in what manner
Or where or when they fell—whether they went
Riding into the dark under Christ's banner
Or died beneath the blood-red dragon of Gwent;

But this we know: That, when the Saxon rout
Swept over them, the sun no longer shone
On Britain, and the last lights flickered out;
And men in darkness murmured: Arthur is gone . . .

VII

NIGHTFALL BY WANSDYKE

Wessex, A.D. 878. The Scene is the western edge of the limestone escarpment of Mendip. It is a frosty winter evening, and the air is so dry that from this point of vantage the greater part of the swamp of Somerset can be seen outstretched from the foot of these hills to the muddy waters of the Severn Firth. At this season, indeed, the colour of the land is hardly distinguishable from that of the tidal flats; and the seaward prolongations of the Mendip range—Wavering Down, Brean and Bleadon, together with its detached outliers—Brent, Glastonbury Tor, the knoll of Athelny and the little hill of Nyland, appear as insular in character as the two veritable islands—the Steep Holme and the Flat Holme—whose dim shapes are seen in the distance of mid-channel. Apart from these elevations, the whole of the Somerset plain, from Mendip to Quantock, is an undrained morass— a vast sponge of land, over which the tributaries of Axe and Brue and Parret spread a network of stagnant water, made brackish at spring tides by the invasion of the Atlantic.

For melancholy, this landscape would be hard to match in any part of Britain save the East Anglian fens or the mosses of Solway; and this sense of desolation is increased by the presence, in the middle distance, of the ruins of what must once have been a human habitation, now fallen to waste, which would have been covered long since by brushwood and weed had the site been less exposed to the violence of the South Wester, and, near this, a reed-thatched hovel shaped like a bee-skip, from the apex of which a thin spiral of pale blue smoke now rises into the still air filling it with the reek of smouldering turves. Outside this hovel there burns another fire of sticks, and two shaggy men are sitting by it, with thick woollen cloaks wrapped over their byrnies of chain-mail. They are, in fact, two of the King's Thegns, or bodyguard, of Ælfred of Wessex. The elder is Ælfric, an atheling of the royal house and of the blood of Cerdic. The younger is Edred, son of the Ældorman of Wilsætan. Both are weary with their long flight from the defeat of the fyrd of Wessex at Chippenham

*at the hands of the Danes under Halfdene; but Edred, who sits huddled
close to the fire, appears to feel the cold more keenly than his grizzled
companion.*

EDRED:

How far are we from Athelny?

ÆLFRIC:

Another night
Of stiff plodding over the hills, and then
We drop to Glastonbury. Look . . . there it lies.
The high tor marks it. If we took to the fen
In these dank winter days we might well flounder
Knee-deep another week before we reached
Our bourne.

EDRED:

Yet how I hate these hills: They smell
Of death. See how those barrows on the down
Brood over us! I have seen the like before
Where I was bred, and heard the old men tell
How, at midnight, dry bones that moulder in them
Take flesh, and withered fingers clutch their weapons,
And ghosts of dead men gibber at the doors
Or sit in awful dumbness. And these stark walls
That crumble behind us . . . Who knows what witchery
Clings to their stones? There is a haunted chester
Hard by my home at Wilton that has lain waste
Years beyond reckoning—a wilderness
Of dust and nettles. None of our churls dare dwell
Beside it or draw near it, even in daylight;
But when night falls in winter, and the wind
Howls through its empty streets, the stones awaken
To shrieks of woe and the loud clashing of shields,
And panic clatter of hurrying feet that run
This way and that in shiftless dread. . . .

ÆLFRIC:

They hear
The rattle of driven leaves, or pads of wolves
Hunting for conies, and shrieks of night-owls harrying
Their small game. Stones are speechless; and the dead
That walk the night, sad souls, grow dim and falter
If but you sign yourself.

EDRED:

Yet these hills fright me.
I think we must have come to the world's end,
And this bank be the brink of it. Have you ever seen
A waste more threatening than this soaked marshland
That lies beneath us—its net of waterways
Brimmed by the red of sunset—as though they ran
With the blood of an old slaughter, or foretold
Slaughters to be? Why need our lord have chosen
A halt unhallowed as this?

ÆLFRIC:

The king was sick,
And held till his strength dwindled. This is the ill
That smote him first upon his wedding's morrow
And lies in wait—so that he never knows
What time the blow may fall. You have seen the swiftness
With which it sets on him. First his eyes dazzle;
Then his head swims, and he must stagger, blind
As Paul upon the road to Philippi;
And eft an arrowy ache bores through his skull
And splits it like an axe, and numbness wilts
His thews to watery weakness, so that he halts
Like a foot-rotted wether. It is a mischief
That neither prayers nor leeches can allay;
So lie he must until the evil lifteth,
And we must tarry with him. It ill becomes
A king's thegn and thegn's son to show such scant
Forbearance. Asser, the Welch priest, will warn us

When the pain's fetters slacken. Better snatch
What sleep you can, as I do; for when he rises
We must plod on to Athelny.

EDRED:

Forgive me,
But I am overdone. This homeless faring
Through the mired ways of Winter quenches all hope
That ever was in me. It would not irk me, Ælfric,
If we could see an end to it.

ÆLFRIC:

It is not for us
To plot the end or seek it. That is work
For wits more cunning than yours or mine. Enough
For us that Ælfred leads, and that we follow
Our king.

EDRED:

A landless king of waste and water!
There are no kingdoms left in England now.
See how the wave of heathenesse overflows
And whelms them one by one! Bernicia,
Northumbria, Mercia . . .

ÆLFRIC:

Mercia has always played
Loose with her neighbours. Mercia is English—
Which is to say half-Dane, more than half-heathen.
There's not a Mercian but would gloat to see
The doom of Wessex, and the Danish ravens
Fattened on her torn flesh!

EDRED:

There your teeth grit
Upon the gall of truth. Our house is cleft
Within itself; and how shall we of Wessex
Tauten the sagging timbers—our king in flight,
His fyrd dwindled and scattered? I may seem to you

[61]

Redeless and callow; yet I see the years
That stretch before us yawn as emptily
As those drear marshlands. I think we have been born
Beneath a creeping shadow, ruthless as that
Which erstwhile swallowed up the morning sun
And made noon midnight. We are the ill-begotten
Brood of a thriftless fatherhead who, while we lay
Like a litter of blind whelps, besotted with milk
And sleep, gave up our birthright and let us wake
To meet their reckoning. If they had stopped
The first cracks in the dyke—if they had shown
Their spunk and driven the first Danes from Sheppey,
Or drowned them on the seas before they fastened
Deep roots in Kentish earth, we might have hoped
To stem the seepage. First they were only flighted
Like woodcock on the North wind driven: now
There is no tide nor airt that does not bring
The winged helms and the red sails bearing on us
From East or South or West: white Danes of Norway,
Black Danes of Ireland—we are meat for all.
And now it is too late . . . They have horsed themselves
On the wild hengests of the Anglian woods,
And sweep the land, swift as a swaling fire
In a high wind. There is no inch of England
From Lindisfarne to Exeter unreddened
By fire and blood; there is no hidden creek
But the oared dragons have thrust their greedy snouts
Within it, snuffling for flesh and plunder.
And God is blind or deaf . . . Minster and chantry
Topple their spires together; the holy images
Are hacked and hewn; Christ's very roods now feed
The fires that roast His ministers! How could this be
If He had not forsaken and foredoomed us
To utter loss? Why, there is nothing fair
Or seemly but these heathen run to wreck it;
No learning that they loathe not, and no law

But they must trample on. Within their pack
No man has any rights but what he can wrest
Wolflike from weaker wolves than he. What boots it
That our king, or another, and his wise men
Have set down dooms to bind us, if the writ runs
Unheeded? There is neither law nor learning
Alive in England now—nor ever will be,
From what I see of it. This is the end
Of all our civility: Egyptian night
Smothers the land; no spark will wink in it
But one thin taper flickering like a marsh-light
In Athelny so long as Ælfred lives,
And, after that, the darkness . . .

ÆLFRIC:

                    I am neither learned
Nor over godly—but if my eyes were as yours
I would liever have left them on the field at Chippenham
In the last folk-fight to be pecked from their sockets
By Thor's ravens! This is a nithing's talk.
I'll hear no more of it. If we must die,
What then? Do we not know that God still whets
The keen sword of vengeance on the behalf
Of those who bleed for Christendom, and for a king
Whom Christ's own vicar has aneled? Our meed
Is bliss in heaven or freedom on British earth.
I ask none other. Whist . . . I hear footsteps.
Hand to your hilt!

*From the ruins of the waste villa a gnomish figure emerges furtively.
It is that of a small, dark man, with a bristling grey beard. He is
clothed in a leather smock, and his bow-legs are clumsily strapped with
bands of the same material. Over his shoulder he carries a bundle of
nets. At the sight of the two Saxons he hesitates and halts, looking
around him nervously for a way of escape. The loud laugh with which
ÆLFRIC greets his appearance seems to reassure him. He changes*

                                                   c*

his mind and comes nearer. There is a look of shy curiosity in the
black, humorous eyes that shine through his unkempt thickets of hair.
EDRED, *too, laughs uneasily, and releases the sword-hilt he has grasped.*

ÆLFRIC:
Who are you, churl? What do you here?

THE MAN:
What do I here? So said the cuckoo's brat
To the wagtail that hatched him! This is my own toft—
Or so I thought it. I am a groovier,
And delve for lead in Mendip; and now I go
To snare my morrow's meat.

ÆLFRIC:
                    Who is your lord?

THE MAN:
The first that feeds me. We have no lords in Mendip
But cold and toil and hunger. We fend for ourselves,
And ask no leave of any man for the right
To bide where we were born.

ÆLFRIC:
Tell me your name, then.

THE MAN:
My name is Maccus, son of Rum of the Holloway.

ÆLFRIC:
That is no Christian name! You are a Welchman,
Or kin of Welch.

THE MAN:
I am a man of Mendip:
We have no kinship with any other folk,
And need none. Have you done with me?

ÆLFRIC:
                                Wait a while!

Tell me: have any Danes been seen of late
About your hills?

THE MAN:

    Danes? Danes? You mean Redshanks?
Ay, there was a deal of that fair-headed devilry
Came to the marshes back of Parret-mouth
Last harvest, filching corn. You could see their fires
Specking all Somerset to the fords of Severn;
But none set foot on Mendip, and we took
No heed of them.

ÆLFRIC:

    You would heed them sore enough
If once you met with them!

THE MAN:

    What should we fear?
There is naught for them to take and naught for us
To lose but our lank bones—and them they would never
Set teeth on, for the hills are riddled with dens
And grooves and swallet-holes where we could lurk
As our fathers hid before us till they were gone.
No outland folk ever abode in Mendip
Longer than snow on Mayday—though, in old time,
Many have come and gone again. Once, they say,
Came web-foot men who propped their nests like dabchicks
On eyots in the meres, and lived like herns
On fish they jagged—but these were over-nesh
For Mendip winters, and soon trickled back
Starved to their fens. They were a sorry folk,
And baneless. Next, out of the sunrise, came
An angrier breed, red-maned and horsed in war-wains,
Who bore the grinning heads of boars and wolves
And dyed their bodies with woad. These men were tall
As gods that ride on clouds above a field
Of slaughter; but when our fathers hid, they fell
To fighting with one another, and so dwindled
Till the Romans drove them westward. These same Romans

Were a cunning folk, of our own hue and kidney,
Who knew the groovier's craft, and cast the ore
Our fathers found in shapes of sand and stamped it
With their king's runes. They brought their gods with them
And built stone housen, and a shallow pit
Where cocks and men were set to fight. Long ages
They dwelt with us; then, like the swallows, packed
And flew from Mendip, leaving their gods to crumble
In the waste chester; and a guileless brood,
Skirted like women, with close-shaven heads,
Sailed over Severn from Gwent and broke their altars,
Bidding us worship a man the Romans slew,
Yet found us and our hills too cold, and took
Their god to Glastonbury. Next came King Ceawlin,
With a wild host flaxen-haired, who swung the axe
And guzzled ale like swine . . .

ÆLFRIC:

        Now heed your words!
This Ceawlin was a Saxon, and those stout drinkers
Were our forefathers!

THE MAN:

        Time has ripened their sons
And made them milder. It has been so with all
Who ever dwelt in Mendip but us, whose roots
Are tough as those of hews bird-sown in clefts
And cracks of thirsty stone, and have no pride
Of branch but the brine burns and the wind lops it,
Keeping us hard and lowly. Your folk will last
No longer than the Roman. Now come these Redshanks.
They, too, will bide their while and go their ways
As Merlin's rede foretold.

ÆLFRIC:

        Who was this Merlin?

THE MAN:

What? Know you not Merlin? He was the wisest druid
That ever wont in Britain, and this his weird:

"Woe to the Red Dragon," he said—and that was Rome—
"The White Dragon shall seize his lurking holes"—
That was the Saxon—*"and Britain shall lie wet
With night tears. Then shall the Danish wood be stirred.
And cry, on a man's speech: 'Come, Cambria!
Bind Cornwall to thy side; tell Winchester
The earth shall swallow her!' Usk shall burn seven months
And Badon's baths grow cold. The bones of Kings
Shall bleach upon the waste. The floors of harvest
Shall turn again to forest, and evil weeds
Riot within the City of the Legions
And all men starve—till, out of Winchester,
Three streams shall break, and these three sunder Britain
Into three shares, and the twelfth Bretwalda
Shall build a fleet of ships . . ."*

ÆLFRIC:

      Enough, enough
Of this rambling. I see no wisdom in it.

THE MAN:

It has this wisdom: that, when you are gone
And those that follow you, Britain will still be Britain
And Mendip ours . . . till the King come again.

ÆLFRIC:

Your king is come.

THE MAN:

    What? Arthur?

ÆLFRIC:

      He is named Ælfred
Of the West Saxons.

THE MAN:

   I never heard that name.

ÆLFRIC:

Nor yet I Arthur's. Who is this king of yours?

THE MAN:

Arthur is gone . . . But he will come again
Riding to Camelot on a May morning

When hawthorn-buds are swollen, and the dykes
Golden with water-blobs and fringed with spears
Of yellow marsh-flags; and a glittering host
Will ride behind him—Tristram and Lancelot
And Gawain—to give back freedom to the earth
And Britain to her own . . .

ÆLFRIC:
Quick! On your knees!
Here comes the King!

(*Two figures emerge from the hut. The first is a cleric,* ASSER, *the Welchman, newly appointed Bishop of Sherborne. He is a dark little man, hardly taller than the groovier, with eager, intelligent features and a Roman tonsure. The second is* ÆLFRED *himself: a fair man of slender build and middle height. His face, clean-shaven but for a reddish moustache, is still pale and pinched with pain, and his blue eyes are narrowed, as if they still feared the light, though it is now dusk. When he sees the two thegns he raises his hands and smiles.*)

ÆLFRED:
I have kept you a long while; but now it is over
And I am myself again. Who is this knave?

ÆLFRIC:
A man of the hills. He has whiled away our waiting
With his silly talk.

ÆLFRED:
Better let him be gone.
I have much to tell you of what ran through my mind
While I lay gripped with anguish: At such times,
Though outwardly I be blinded, the inward eye
Sees sharper in grief's night, than in health's noon;
And, when pain dims the sight, that which was clouded
Takes hopeful shape. And even as the burdock
That soothes the nettle's sting grows next the nettle,
So, next the mischief of to-day, I have seen

[68]

The healing of tomorrow. Britain is broken
Beyond mending—there's not one kingdom can boast
Strength greater than another's: therefore should those
Who grudged their neighbours' might take heart from it,
Old wrongs forgotten, and clasp hands to stay
The ill that threatens all. This is the time
When one strong will may weld all broken folk
Who share our blood in Britain—from Hadrian's dyke—
Ay, and beyond it—to the Exe, to stand
By their lost brotherhood. One land, one folk
Forged in war's smithy . . .

ÆLFRIC:
                    None will ever bring
Mercia to stand by Wessex, or Northumbria
To stand by either—and the East English love us
As little as the West Welch.

ÆLFRED:
                    Your eyes are bleared
By an old, backward-looking bitterness.
What say you, Edred?

EDRED:
                    Mayhap mine are too young
To see beyond to-morrow. I can say nothing
But that the King's sight flies too far for me
To follow.

ÆLFRED:
                    Yet you may be young enough
To see the end I have dreamed of. Here's a vision
For shorter-sighted eyes. Your fathers and mine
Were erst sea-faring folk who sailed to Britain
Over salt water, but found so fat a living
That they forgot their seacraft. Now we are tied
To the plough's tail, and dread to dab our feet
In the brine that we were born to; while these Danes

[69]

Fare where they will and flick at us like gadflies
From every wind. Therefore, if we would thwart them,
We must turn seamen. Our flat-bottomed hoys
Of Frisian build can never match their longships
In speed or handling—but there's no lack of oak
Nor yet of shipwright's cunning in the coves
And creeks of Britain. Our first need is ships
More speedy and more heavily-oared than theirs
And loftier in the bulwark, so that they loom
Above their benches and they cannot board us.
Such is the work that I have set myself
While we lie lost in Athelny, gathering
Our dwindled strength. I will build such a fleet
Of ships . . .

ÆLFRIC:

Hearken, Edred! This is the weird
Of Merlin. Do you mind it? *The twelfth Bretwalda*
Shall build a fleet of ships . . .

ÆLFRED:

Who is this Merlin?

ASSER:

That I can tell you. He was a devilish wizard
Of Gwent, who cast so many haphazard prophecies
Into the winnowing wind that some few grains
Of sooth still settle from his clouds of chaff
And make the credulous gape. I would have burned him
And all his prophecies!

ÆLFRED:

Yet he spoke truth:
For I am Bretwalda—and, by the Grace of God,
I will build my fleet. So, on to Athelny!

VIII

THE BALLAD OF ST. KENELM

In our sweet shires of Mercia
Five blessed Saints we had;
Four were proud Princes of the Church,
And one was a little lad.

Wistan, Wulstan, Oswald, Chad:
Each hallowed Mercia's realm;
But the saint we love all others above
Is little Saint Kenelm.

Kenelm was but a child of seven
And his father seven weeks dead,
When in Lichfield town they set the crown
Of kingship on his head,

And hailed him as their anointed king,
While all the Mercian lords
Took oath to stand at Kenelm's hand
On the cross-hilts of their swords;

And the bronze bells of Lichfield clanged
And rocked their towers of stone,
That God had sent an innocent
To sit on Offa's throne;

While folk that laboured in the fields
Heard the bells clang with joy,
And thronged the ways to cheer and gaze
On the beauty of the boy.

But his sister Quendryth in her bower
Brooding stayed apart;
Alone she sate, with naught but hate
And black gall in her heart,

And a sour face thrawn with bitterness
That this weak child should own
The shining prize for which her eyes
Most lusted: Mercia's crown.

So sent she for her paramour—
Lord Escebert was his name—
And whispered near his willing ear
These words of dark shame:

"We twain are one in will and flesh,
And but for one small thing
I should have been thy crowned queen
And thou my wedded king;

"And that small thing is but the breath
Of my father's brat, Kenelm.
Give me his life, and wed me wife,
And we will share this realm!"

Then Escebert, her paramour,
Pondered Quendrytha's rede,
And searched his mind some way to find
To compass that dark deed.

And as it chanced, that very month,
The Lords of Mercia went
To hunt the wolf in Offa's Wood
That shags the hills of Clent:

A deep wood and a dark wood,
For black deeds meet, where grew
A brambled brash of oak and ash,
Hazel and holly and yew.

And when into the wood's green heart
He saw the hunters ride,
Then Escebert slipped behind, and clipped
Himself to Kenelm's side.

"Good Escebert, they ride too fast:
Forsake me not, I pray,
When through the thorns the wail of horns
Shivers and dies away!"

"Let them ride on, my little king:
No matter how far they go,
You need have no fear of wolf or bear
With me at your saddle-bow."

"Good Escebert, a thorn has hurt
My pony's hoof, I fear:
The dusk now broods on these wild woods
And the black of night draws near."

"Content thyself, my little king,
Nor dread the fading light:
Full well I wot of a woodward's cot
Where we may bide this night."

"Good Escebert, I am athirst,
And my tongue cleaves to my mouth."
"I know of a spring, my little king,
To slake and quench thy drouth."

But when they came to a woodland brook,
And the child, unaware,
Knelt by the brink and bent to drink,
A sword flashed in the air;

And the shorn head of little Kenelm
Reddened the brook with blood,
While Escebert leapt to his saddle and crept
Like a wolf from Offa's Wood.

Loose-reined he rode through the dark night
Till he came to the hall of a thane
Where the huntsmen rolled with ale and told
Of the fierce wolves they had slain.

[73]

"Ho, Escebert, good lord," they cried,
"Come join our wassailing!
For you have missed our drinking-tryst
To ride with the little king."

Then Escebert's false cheek grew wan:
"God witness what I say!
I have not seen Kenelm, I ween,
Since noon of yesterday,

"Nor can I guess what ways he strayed:
So quit your wassail-board,
That all may search oak ash and birch
To find our little lord!"

A weary week those woods they searched
By holt and holm and glade;
But neither eye nor foot drew nigh
The place where he was laid;

And never a single whisper woke
Those brambly solitudes
But the rustle that spreads from the wind-stirred heads
Of wild trees in the woods.

(Hazel, hazel, bend your boughs
Over the streamlet's bed,
And with your primrose pollen gild
A halo for his head!

Holly, holly, shake your branch
Till the brittle leaves rain down,
And weave about the dead child's brow
A martyr's thorny crown!

Cherry, cherry, shed your snow
Of petals in a cloud,
And on the little limbs below
Spread a soft shroud!

Yew tree, yew tree, over him
Your funeral pennons wave;
But let not your bright berries drip
Their blood upon his grave,

To fleck the whiteness of the shroud
That the wild cherry strewed
On the gentlest fawn that ever was torn
By wolf in Offa's Wood!)

So home the hunt to Lichfield rode
And the bronze bells clanged again
A muffled toll for the innocent soul
Of the child that had been slain;

And folk who heard the tolling wept,
For they knew what it must mean;
And the Mercian Lords swore on their swords
To hold Quendrytha queen.

Now far away in Italy,
Under Peter's dome,
Frail and old on his throne of gold
Slept Paschal, Pope of Rome.

A weary man, an aged man
Of four score years and seven;
And in his listless hands he held
The Crossed Keys of Heaven.

Holy, Holy, Holy!
The children's voices swell,
While sweet and loud, through the incense-cloud
Shivers the Sanctus Bell;

And as they heard the silvery chime,
From the clouded vault above
Like a falling flake of cherry-bloom
Fluttered a milk-white dove

That held a quill in his golden bill
And laid it on the Host,
And all the people rose and cried:
"See, see: the Holy Ghost!"

"A miracle . . . A miracle!"
So loud a cry there broke
That the old Pope rubbed his rheumy eyes
And dropt his keys, and woke!

And he called three scarlet cardinals
To read out what was writ
On the parchment folded within the quill,
But they could not fathom it.

"These words are writ in rhyme," they said,
"And the tongue of a far land
That none in Rome or Christendom
Is like to understand.

"Yet all strange peoples come to Rome,
So let the rhyme be heard;
Some ear may catch the sound and match
The sense to fit the word":

*In Clent coubethe Kenelm Kynebear lith
Under thorne hævedes bereaft.*

Then up spoke an old Saxon clerk:
"Sirs, you have given news
Of the bloodiest deed that ever was done
Since Christ was slain by the Jews:

"That in Cowbeath, which is by Clent,
Midmost in Mercia's realm,
Beneath a thorn, his head off-shorn,
Lieth our king, Kenelm."

So the Pope blessed that screed, and with
The ring of Peter sealed,
And bade that Saxon carry it
To his Bishop, in Lichfield.

Then, once again, from Lichfield towers,
The bells boomed overhead;
And the Mercian thanes rode out again
To search for Kenelm's head;

And when they came to the woods of Clent
And rode into the shade,
Behold—a shaft of blinding light
Fell where the child was laid!

So, tenderly, they lifted him
And bore him to his tomb
In Winchcombe, where our Mercian kings
Lie till the Day of Doom;

But as through Winchcombe's mourning street
They passed by slow degrees,
Quendrytha at her window sate
With the Bible on her knees.

She read of false Queen Jezebel,
And when they spied the hearse
That carried Kenelm, her wicked eyes
Spat blood upon the verse.

And the common folk, who saw this thing,
Knew what it meant full well,
And flung her down into the street
To lie like Jezebel;

And Escebert, her foul paramour,
They slew him where he stood;
And those twain lay for a week and a day,
And the dogs lapped their blood.

But the king's lords buried little Kenelm
With pomp in Winchcombe's fane,
And built a chantry for pilgrim-folk
By the brook where he was slain;

And the waters that well from where he fell
All mortal ills assuage—
Not even Saint Thomas of Canterbury
Hath greater pilgrimage

Than the innocent king of Mercia
That his sister's leman slew
And hid in the brash of oak and ash,
Hazel and holly and yew!

Wistan, Wulstan, Oswald, Chad:
All pray for Mercia's realm;
But our loveliest saint was a little lad.
King Kynewulf's son, Kenelm.

IX

THE TALE OF ÆDWULF THE DISPOSSESSED A.D. 1080

It was the black year when King Edward died,
And the Octave of Easter in April, that Wulfgeat, my father,
Dragged me forth from deep sleep and flung wide the window-
                               shutters
Bidding me gaze at the heavens, and, therein hanging
Bright over Bredon, the star men called the Comet
Trailing its horrid tresses with such fierceness
That lesser lights grew wan, as when the moon
Quenches their shine. And my father said to me:
"Son, this is no mean portent, but one that foreshadoweth
Dooms that we dream not. No living eye hath seen
The like of it since the time when Swegen and Olaf
Reddened the reign of Ethelred the Redeless;
And let none doubt but that God's sword is unsheathed
To flash and fall on England. Wherefore, at daybreak,
We will ride to Evesham and make our peace with heaven
Ere worse befall. Our kinsman, Ælfwine the Abbot,
Shall shrive our souls; and I will give his Abbey
The lands by the Whitsun brook and the watermill
Which was your brother's portion before he turned monk
And left us."
           So I, Ædwulf, arose, sore in heart,
And rode with him sullenly—for, being the eldest,
I grudged to see those fair fields and the watermill
By the pools where I had fished for perch as a lad
Go to feed the fat Abbey of Evesham. Yet was I dutiful
As became my father's son—and in aftertime
Have had cause to bless the cold hand that robbed me then
Of my rights; since now I would rather see them sealed
In the Abbey's honour than wrung from me like the rest
By the Norman Urse and his bear-cubs!
                     A full week
The comet shone in the sky; and many were driven

By dread to shiftless penitence; yet the doom
Betokened fell not on them—though many rumours
Ran through the shires: how that Duke William, the Bastard,
False kinsman of our new King, Harold Godwineson,
Denied his right, boasting he had sworn away
That heritage in his favour; how William stayed
Gathering sails in Normandy to swoop
On England unawares, and had suborned
Pope Alexander to hallow his enterprise;
How that King Harold, stedfast in the certainty
Of his chrismed kingship and the inheritance
King Edward, dying, gave him, now swept the channel
With such a well-found fleet as had not furrowed
The waves since Alfred died, and his weak heirs
Left half his ships to lie with rotting ribs
In the Cornish creeks. Neither did these tales fright us
(Mayhap King Edward's peace had sapped our wits)
Nor had we dread of foreigners: many such
Had dwelt long time among us: some thanes of Denmark,
Old servants of King Cnut, and some few Normans—
Earl Ralph of Hereford, Richard son of Scrob,
Who, riding from their towers on Offa's Dyke
(That now sprang up like mushrooms in an orchard
Grazed by a stallion,) and keeping the March of Powys,
Clipped the Welsh dragon's claws and stayed his ravaging
Of Severnside. Nor had we any fear
Of William and his barons; since we knew
Harold a proven warrior, and his housecarls
Unmatched in battle. So, shriven, we slept sound
While the doom-star flared beneath a waxing moon
And waned to a snuffed candle-wick, and went out,
And the mild, familiar stars stole over Bredon
Once more from dusk to dawn.

                                        That was a season
Of kindliest showers and warm sun, promising
A plenteous harvest; but, when the bearded grain

[80]

Bent its ripe ears for reaping, there came word
That Harold Hardrada had broken forth from Norway
And fallen on Northumbria, while Harold of England
Now rode loose-reined to meet him. And my father,
Being a king's thane, and bounden by that honour,
Took down his rusty mail and whetted the bite
Of his double-handed battle-axe. Hotly I pleaded
To ride with him; but he denied me, saying:
"This is no stripling's play. You are over-young
For such stern service. See, I have but two sons,
And one vowed to the cloister. Should you fare with me
And we two fall together, who would fend
For your mother and sisters? Nay, if I take the sword,
Take you the sickle and tend the fields and see
Our harvest reaped and garnered. If I should die
In the King's battle, then will he care for you
As the son of one who served him. But if fortune
Turn against Harold, remember: you are his man,
And owe him a thane's fealty till your death."
Then he spoke darkly: "These are but the first-fruits
Of the dooms that star foretold. Let no man doubt
That our fyrd can crack the Northmen; for we are swift
In movement, and our Saxon battle-axes
Bite deeper than theirs, I reckon. But if news travel
By any traitorous tongue to Normandy
Whispering Duke William that the English fleet
Keeps not the southern sea, and that our King
Speeds to the North to grapple with Hardrada
A hundred leagues away, then may he catch
His moment, and hurl his host on the naked shores
Of Kent and Sussex—and, if that befall,
Then God help England!—for no lesser hand
Can save our necks from the dominion
Of a foreign yoke. Such ills could never have been
Were we but one in spirit; but the King's realm
Is riven by bitter jealousies and sapped

By treasons that have burrowed underground
Like oonts since Edward's faltering hand forsook
The sceptre for the breviary, and, fumbling
For a heavenly diadem, left the crown of England
Fallen in the dust while subtle foreign priests
Battened on English bishoprics: Robert of Jumièges
Sat throned in Canterbury, and William, the king's chaplain,
Still holds the see of London; and other strangers
Have Wells and Hereford. Nor can the sons
Of Godwine, the King's blood-brothers, be fully trusted
To take his part: Tostig has ranged himself
With Harold Hardrada; and the Northern Earls,
Edwin and Morcar, sit lightly in their saddles,
Unstirrupped, to leap which side they list should Harold
Falter or fall. Now all our loyalties
Lie in God's hand; and you, lad, should be grateful—
Though you looked crabbed about it!—that I gave
The Whitsun lands to Evesham."

                                        So he blessed me,
And spake no more, but smiled, and bade me follow him
To the Manor, where my sisters Eadhild and Eadgyth
Scrubbed his chain-shirt and burnished it with sand
From the Whitsun brook's bright shallows, laughing, child-like,
And vying with one another for the prize
Of polishing his head-piece. And my mother
Laughed with her lips to see them; but her eyes
Though tearless had no brightness, and I guessed
Her heart was emptier than mine. And once
I saw my father look at her, and her lips
Trembled, yet smiled again; and she turned away
Hurriedly, calling on the maids to bring
Meats from her store to stuff his saddlebags
With provender for the journey. Then little Eadhild
Chirped like a wren: "Father! Come, father! See
How silver-bright your helm is burnished. Look!
You must put it on and see yourself in the mirror!"

[82]

But Eadgyth sulked: "It is no better burnished
Than the ugly shirt I scrubbed. See how the rust
Reddens my finger-nails!" And he, to please them,
With a grave mien armed himself, cap-à-pie,
As the Normans say, turning this way and that
To show his glory—while our great hound Bran
Gazed at him with anxious eyes and thrashed his tail,
Not knowing what mood could have moved so grave a man
As his master to play; and the two children danced
About him, boasting of their handiwork,
Crying: "Rode there ever a king's thane out of Mercia
More knightly than our father? When the King sees him
His eyes will dazzle! Ay, and father will tell
How two small maidens in Worcestershire, Eadgyth and
                                                    Eadhild,
Thus preened him for the fight. But now," they said,
"We must burnish sword and axe." And when she heard them
My mother's brows were knitted, as though her eyes
Were hurt by the fancy that such gentle fingers
Should handle such grim tools. So she forbade them.
And now came Cerdic—he who first taught me to ride,
And was our staller, a halting, bright-eyed old man
With a slant mouth and a shrewd face as warty
As a notched crook cut from a blackthorn thicket, leading
Two saddled horses: one was my father's grey,
A Picard stallion with hot blood of Aragon
Lightening his bone to fleetness, and the other
Our plodding thill-horse, Grim, that was twelve year old,
Slow-paced and patient-natured, having been wont
To plough in the yoke with oxen—yet wise enow
To guide the furrow straight if the ploughman nodded;
And Cerdic held both of them dearer than his wife
(Who was a shrewish body) and they, in return,
Loved him as rarely, though when the grey was younger
And mettlesome in mating, it had cracked a leg for him
And made him limp for life!

                                        I reckon my father
Was loth to tarry longer; for he kissed the two maids
And swung himself to the saddle nimbly, for all
The weight of his harness. But when my mother drew near
He stooped, and took her face in his hands, and kissed her,
But spoke no word; and she kissed him again, with closed eyes
Now I knew naught of love, being but a boy
And simple in all such ways; yet I think no kiss
Spoke ever deeper of love than theirs, being given
Not in the heat of desire but in pure tenderness
To a woman whose beauty had waned long since in the bearing
Of children and homely labours. And she laid her fingers,
That were roughened by toil, on his hand that held the rein,
Till the tall grey tossed his head and moved on,
And her hand fell limp to her side, and she turned and went
With downbent eyes to her bower . . .
                                        But the great hound, Bran, who had stood
With head on one side, in doubt of what was afoot,
When he saw the two riders move to the verge of the woods
Threw back his jowl and bayed for joy, for he thought
They were going a-hunting wolves, and leapt after them eagerly
With his long loping stride, till my father swerved in his saddle
Halloaing 'Home, Bran! Home!'; and the hound, for a moment,
Stood still with one paw uplifted, gazing after them,
Then trotted back, cowed and puzzled; nor would he heed me
Howsoever I petted and called him . . . So they rode Northward;
And I, with a dreary heart, betook myself
To the fields of harvest and toiled there, thinking thereby
To lighten my load of gloom—but all in vain.

Now this was the twentieth day of September, the feast
Of Saint Matthew Evangelist, and a week and a day to go
To Michaelmas. Never in all my life have I seen
An Autumn more richly dight; for early frost
Had touched the elms, and the corn-lands of Avon
Lay floored with golden stubbles. The apple-orchards

Drooped with their bounteous burdens, and the wild pears
Robed with vermilion flared in pyramids
Of flame against the darkening woods. By night
The brown owls swooped across the stars and filled
The sky with whinnyings and hag-like scritches,
Hunting for shrews and flittermice, so that none
Could sleep for their shrill carnival. One such night
When Bran was couched beside me—for since the hour
That my father went he had moped all day in the hall
Miserable of mute bereavement, more like a Christian
Than a dumb brute, for ever cherishing
A cast clout of his master's that still kept
The smell of him—on one such night, I say,
In the dark of the moon, Bran started to his feet
And opened his fanged throat in such a bellow
As made the rafters shake; nor could I calm him,
For the dog was distraught, and panted and paced the hall
Like a sad soul in purgatory, dismally howling
As one that bays the moon. But there was no moon . . .
So at dawn my mother stole to my side and said:
"What was amiss with Bran?" And I lied to her,
Saying he was angered by the pattering feet
Of rats in the thatch, and that bats had flown into the hall,
Chased by the owls, and fluttering in aimless circles
Had maddened him. Whereat the maidens, hearing
My tongue stammer of bats, screamed out in fear
Of the foul mice tangling their unbraided tresses;
But my mother sighed and gazed and shook her head;
And I ran afield rather than face her, knowing, as she did
That my father had fallen . . .

        There were partridges in the stubble
Pecking for ungleaned grain; but I never thought
To set a springe for them; and the grey fisherman
That pored on the minnowed shallow flapped his wings
And flew unscathed to his heronry—for I had no heart
To fly my falcons, though the young peregrine

[85]

Was a fierce hearner. And a week passed.
                                    It was Michaelmas
When the ill word came by old Cerdic, limping home
With the lamed thiller, and, slung from his saddle-bow,
My father's sword and helm and the shirt of mail
They had stripped, at my father's behest, from his warm body
Before they buried him. "Take these," he had said,
"To my son Ædwulf. Tell him that Harold Godwinson
Hath utterly broken the host of Harold Hardrada
At Stamfordbridge on Derwent, and his king
Now hastens southward to uphold his rights
Against his cousin of Normandy, disembarked
At Pevensey. And tell Ædwulf that his hand
Must grasp this sword that has dropped from mine, and wield it
In Harold's service and in the honour of England
Unto his death. And so God help him!" Then I
Took the sword from him, kissing the hilt, and swore
To serve as my father had bidden me, and put on
My father's helm and byrnie, and strode to the bower
To tell my mother; and she, first seeing me
Loom in the doorway with the light behind,
Thought it had been my father, and stretched out her hands
To clasp me, crying: "Dear love, art thou come indeed?
I had thought thee lost for ever and my heart was broken."
Then little Ædhild laughed: "This is not my father,
But brother Ædwulf. I know him by the brown mole
At the side of his nosepiece." And I cried: "Mother,
It is I . . ." But she thrust me from her in anger. I think
She never forgave me the trick I played that day,
Though indeed it was no trick, but the thoughtless vanity
Of a youngster pranked in armour.
                              She was a strange woman,
Kin to that lady Godiva, wife of Earl Leofric,
Who rode stark-stripped through Coventry; and I never knew
As a son should know his mother; for all her love   [her
Had been given to my father, and none left for her sons,

And I never saw tears in her eyes but on that one day.

Thus, on the morrow, I went from my home, ill-mounted
For a thane and a thane's son, on the halting thill-horse,
And Cerdic behind me, riding on a shaggy pony
That was half-Welchman and barely broke. Old Bran
Watched me go listless; for his spirit was gone, and the ribs
Stared through his brindled hide. One look he gave me
Of neither joy nor pain; then dropped his head
On his paws and blinked his eyes. Four days we rode
Clean over Cotswold to the cold clay stubbles
Of Essex, where Harold lay gathering his powers
At Waltham Holy Cross. And though doom still darkened
My mind, yet must I grant that this sudden journey,
With the glory of battle before it, quickened the blood
Of a youth who had never ranged farther than Worcester, and
Beheld the world opened wide, and had come to manhood [now
And the pride of arms in a single hour, and for copper
Bore gold in his purse. So, when I rode through the city
Of Oxford, it seemed to me gowned merchants gaped
To see so gallant a warrior, and maidens stared
At my tall helm, smiling kindly—though, like as not,
They were wondering in what outlandish wood or waste
Of uttermost Mercia this uncouth stripling-in-arms
Had gotten his horse from the tail of the plough and dragged
His shaggy hind to follow him!

                    On the fifth day we came
To the new Abbey of Waltham, where I did homage
To Harold of England; and the King, in requital
For my father's blood, gave me, by writ and seal,
Seizin of all his lands, free of redemption;
Yet he hardly looked at me—and I who had yearned
To see him royally robed in ermine with a gold crown
On a high throne, saw a plain man, no taller than myself,
Wan-featured, haggard-eyed, and garbed not in gold
But in a woollen shirt, such as my mother wove,

[87]

D

Bearing no token of kingship: and I felt I was cheated,
Like a child, when minstrel and mummer come not at Christmas,
Being mired in mud or snowdrift.

                      But two things I saw there
Bide with me yet: how, first, in the hush of evening
I saw the King walk with a woman in the closed garth
Of the Abbey cloisters. Never had I dreamt such rareness
In shape or hue as hers—for her hair, unbraided
Shone like wind-rippled barley, and her throat
Showed moonpale in the dusk as doth the wild cherry
Or March windflower in Werewood; and when she bent
Her lissom body toward him she swayed like a birch-tree
Or aspen puffed by a gust of April, that curtseys
But to recover; and when they walked more swiftly
She seemed to feather the earth rather than tread it,
As doth the lightfoot plover that skims to her landing
And runs before she lights. So, when I stood ravished
By her beauty, and asked her name of a man-at-arms
Who stared beside me, he laughed: "What? Have you not heard
Of Eadgyth Swan-neck, the King's paramour? It is she—
And a tastier morsel, I reckon, than the Welch King's widow,
Who is his lawful wife! See what it is
To be a king, and gobble the first dainty
That whets your fancy!" And I, having been nursed
In the rustic modesty of my mother's ways,
Felt shamed by the King's lightness, yet, no less, stirred
By the warmth of his dalliance.

                      Next, I remember
How, on the morrow, Harold, with kingly pomp
And lordly company, paid his last penance,
Laying upon the high altar a rich oblation
Of treasure, and holy relics reft from the shrine
Of King Edward in Westminster. Humbly he prayed
For the grace of victory, vowing, if that were granted,
To be God's ransomed servant all his days.
Then turned he to depart; and the black-robed canons

Slow-footed followed him under the new-cut ashlar
Of their pillared nave. But when he came to the galilee
Where the Holy Rood of Montacute fronts the West,
He flung himself down in the dust, and lay abased,
Flat on his face; and the thorn-crowned head of Christ
Bowed sorrowfully above him and bent downward,
As though the carved lips murmured: "It is finished . . ."

But this omen the King saw not, though Thurkill, the Sacrist,
Marked and remembered it; and Harold, for sure,
Thought that his prayer had been granted; for now his face
Like that of a saint in glory, and the splendour   [shone
Of its majesty overbore me through all that day
While we rode to the city of London, and crossed the bridge
Where grim heads of traitors grinned from the parapet
Of the gatehouse, and a gay throng babbled about us,
Noisy as crows at Craycombe in their nesting
When the twigged trivets are tossed, and the March wind
Roars through the naked wood.
                                    Six days we tarried
In London, undetermined; for Gyrth, the King's brother,
Earl of East Anglia, withstood his purpose
To fall on William with that dwindled host,
Hard-ridden and battle-weary. "Rather," he said,
"Let me ride forth short-handed, and call the Norman
To single combat, seeing I am not bounden
By any oath of homage, however given,
So risk no charge of perjury; and if he disdain
To lift my gage, then let me harry the shires
From London to the sea, and burn the harvest
So that he starve in the waste!"
                                    And the court cried
This was good counsel; but Harold would have none of it.
"Never," he swore, "will I burn an English village
Or an English house! Never will I hurt the lands
Or goods of any Englishman! How should I plunder

The folk who are put under me to govern
As their just King?"
                Thus, on the seventh day,
He led us forth from London over the marshes
To the white-scarred Kentish downland, pied with cloud
And crisped with crinkling hoar-frost—a rare field
For falconry; but by sunset we were swallowed
By the forest of the Weald, where the shy roebuck
Scattered like ghosts (and I wished old Bran were with me!)
Till night fell, and the charcoal-burner's fires
And gleed of smelting-hearths winked through dim glades
Wreathed in sweet-smelling woodsmoke. Darkling we rode
Till we came at dawn to the Andrædasweald,
Where a waste chester crumbles, that was once
A city of the Romans, and from the verge
Of smooth downs stared upon the glassy sea
Where the fleet of Normandy bobbed like a flight of mallard
Floating upon a mere, and their sprinkled sails
Scudded this way and that as when the breast-feathers
Are plucked from a goose at Michaelmas.
                      It was the Eve
Of Saint Calixtus (though who Calixtus was
Or why Rome hallowed him I know not) when,
On the long ridge called Senlac we pitched our camp
By the hoar apple-tree. Many have asked me
What force we had at Hastings; and the Normans,
To gild their own glory, have magnified our number
Beyond belief or measure. Yet this I know:
There were nigh three thousand housecarls, sorely-tried
In the battle with Harold Hardrada, and besides
Eight or nine thousand more, free men, such as I,
Who had ridden from far shires alone, and many
Who brought their followers: Breme of East Anglia;
Esegar the Staller, Sheriff of Middlesex,
Who led the fyrd of London; Ælfric of Huntingdon;
Godric of Fifhide; Thurkill, the Dane, a Lord

Of Berkshire; two mitred Abbots—Ælfwig of Winchester,
Who was the King's own uncle, Earl Godwine's brother,
With twelve monks from his Abbey, and Leofric
Abbot of Peterborough, with his own chaplain
Easric the Deacon—ay, and a dozen more
Whose names I disremember. But there was none
Rode from Northumbria, where the earls Edwin and Morcar
Still waited on the issue. It was the East
And the South that fed us with a multitude
Of homespun folk who had dropped their sickles and flocked
From Wessex and East Anglia, armed with few weapons
But the tools of their husbandry—pikels and flails,
Hayforks and blackthorn staves hacked from the hedge—
And had no body-armour and no buckler
But their lust for freedom and their fixed intent
To rid their land of strangers.

                       On that night
Few slept, for all their weariness. I have been told
The Normans kept vigil on their knees and were shriven
By the fierce Bishop of Bayeux—who had better
Repented his own deeds of blood than pardoned
The sins of others—but we were a merry folk
By nature—and the merrier that our consciences
Were lighter than theirs; so, while the watchfires flared
And the harps twanged, we gathered round them, roaring
The battle-song of Brunanburh, and sang
Of the three who kept the bridge against the Dane
When Byrhtnoth fell at Maldon; and every heart
Waxed great with courage of our right. So dawned
The day of Saint Calixtus . . .

                       Harold had set
Our line of battle cunningly. Behind us
Lay the woods of Anderida; on our right
We were girdled by a sluggard stream that wound
Through a sogged marsh, while on the other flank
And the full front, the slope fell to the plain

So steep, no charge of cavalry could breast it
With wind unspent. On our right, where the brook guarded
He had ranged his right-armed levies; in the centre [them,
Set the main battle—the iron of his housecarls
Locked in three ranks of shields so densely knit
There was bare room to sweep and swing the axe
That had cracked Hardrada's pride; and at their feet
We had dug a fosse to cast the floundering cavalry
Into confusion. Behind this triple barrier
Of iron, where the thrawn crabtree stood, he raised
His banners: first, the ancient Dragon of Wessex
That Ælfred bore to victory at Ethandun
And Æthelstan at Brunanburh, and beside it
Flaunted the standard of the Fighting Man,
A gonfanon of gold, broidered with gems,
That drooped of its own richness. There, between them,
With axe slung from the shoulder and spear in hand,
Stood Harold the King, and his own kinsmen: Hakon,
Son of his brother Swegen, Gyrth and Leofwine,
And his uncle Æthelwig, Abbot of Winchester,
The monk's cowl tucked within his helm—the pride
Of the great house of Godwine.

       This was the charge
The King laid on us: that all should hold their ground
And let the horsed Norman fury spend itself
On spear and shield, until the terrible axe
Had tamed it; and that none, however tempted
By triumph or wrath of battle, should break his ranks,
Or we were lost; for, if the shield-wall held,
He knew there was no earthly power could break us,
And Heaven fought on our side.

        It was the hour
Of Prime, three before noonday, when the battle
First broke. Well I remember how we had waited
Gazing across the valley to Telham Hill
Where they had trenched their camp, with a tower of wood

[92]

In the midst; how, in the steely light of morn,
Their lifted lances glinted like icicles
Dripped from a thatch; how the sea-breeze, arising
Wafted the smoke of camp-fires and the hoarse challenge
Of their battle-cry 'Dex aie!', and we roared back
Our own cries: 'Holy Rood!' and 'God Almighty!';
How next the glinting lance-icicles melted
Into an iron-grey wave that slowly crept
Across the sere grass of Autumn; and how there passed
Suddenly a sleet of arrows, whispering
Like the wing-beats of packed starlings when they wheel
Over a reed-bed—but these wings whispered Death,
And one glanced from my father's byrnie, splintering
The shaft to fragments; yet I felt the blow
As though a mailed fist had smitten me: an inch higher,
And I had not lived to tell this tale! But now
My heart, that had been drunk with the fumy wine
Of war's adventure, halted, and grew cold
As that of a partridge flattened in the stubble
When my falcon stooped; and I knew I was afraid
Of a sport in which I was quarry; the next I knew
That the grey wave I had watched was made of men
Ready to slay me, who had done them no wrong,
And there was kindled in me a hot anger
Against these men I knew not; and its flame, rising,
Consumed both fear and anger in one desire—
To have at him who would hurt me; and this, I reckon
Was what most men call Courage, though I was a boy
And did not stop to question, only knowing
I would liever slay than be slain. So I grit my teeth,
That were chattering of themselves like knuckle-bones,
And laughed at the splintered arrow-shaft—though verily
My laugh had no mirth in it, and my lips bivered
Like a child's when the trumpet blared, and under the sleet
Of bolts and arrows the Norman foot rolled forward
To fall on us.

Now a strange thing befell:
For, through their opened ranks full-tilt, there rode
An antic horseman, who threw his sword in the air
And caught it like a juggler when it flashed
Before him. This was the minstrel Taillefer;
And, as he charged, he stood in the stirrups, singing
The high song of Charlemagne, Roland and Oliver
And the vassals that died at Roncesvalles. When we saw him
Hurl himself single-handed on all our host,
We laughed—but the fool was bolder than we reckoned,
For ere the axes felled him in the fosse
He had spitted one housecarl on his lance, and cleft
A second with his sword. And the heavy footmen,
Spurred by this crazy valour, cast themselves
Reckless upon the shield-wall. Then I saw
A sight of terror: the line of great axes rising,
Flashing, and falling as one, and the mortal wrack
Mown down before them till the fosse was cluttered
With maimed and dead—and I heard the housecarls roaring
"Out! Out!!" with every stroke; and the axe-heads clanged
On cloven helms like hammers in a smithy
Smiting on anvils; but the shield-wall, unbreached,
Still fronted the broken remnant, and they fled.
Then were we itching to pursue, but minded
The King's strict counsel that we should not swerve
But hold our ground: and it was well we heeded him;
For now, through the rout of flying foot, Duke William
Launched the full pride of Normandy, lance in rest,
To crash through the iron barrier by sheer weight
Of metal and maddened horseflesh. Four thousand knights,
Choicest of Europe's chivalry, hurled themselves
Upon us like a thunder-wind; and the dust
Was churned from their thudding hooves, so that they rode
Wrapped in the heart of a storm-cloud. And before them
Came William and his brother, the black-hearted
Prelate of Satan, bloodier than he,

[94]

Odo of Bayeux, armed not with sword or lance
But with maces of iron, heavier than the battle-axes
The housecarls swung two-handed, yet these men whirled them
With one. And round his bull-neck William wore
The relics on which King Harold had sworn away
(As he said) the crown of England; and behind them
Billowed the banner of the Apostle, blessed
By their pander, the Pope of Rome. Now in the clash
Of the main battle I could see naught but a mellay
Of helms that rose and fell and arms that flashed
Through the dust the wind blew over them. Yet I saw
That the Dragon of Wessex still flew, and the Fighting Man,
Which had drooped of its weight of gems and gold, now
streamed
On the wind; and though there were times when the wall of
shields
Seemed bent or buckled, it straightened itself, and the knights
Of Normandy were rolled backward down the long slope
To form and charge again till their spent steeds panted
For lack of breath. And once I heard a great cry
Rising above the tumult, that William was down,
And the shaken cavalry snatched at their reins to turn
Their horses and flee; but out of the fosse's carnage
I saw a tall man arise and tear the helm
From his fiery face. "Madmen," he cried, "Why flee ye?
There is death behind you, and victory before.
I am living—and by the grace of God I will conquer!"
So he snatched a spear from a fallen hand to rally
The fugitives, and they turned; and once again
His tall bare head and flushed face were lost in the dust
Of battle. No doubt but the Bastard bore himself well;
For, now the black destrier that the Spanish King
Had sent him was fallen, he called on a knight of Maine
To give him his horse, and when this knight refused it
He felled him with one fierce blow of the mace and leapt
To the empty saddle; and when this horse, too, fell pierced

D*

By the thrust of an English spear, he called on Eustace,
Count of Boulogne, for his. Three times in all
Was William unhorsed, and twice mounted; and with his own
hand
He slew Gyrth, the King's brother; and Odo the Bishop slew
Leofwine:
So that now, of the sons of Godwine, was only one left,
And that Harold of England; but him the Duke could not reach,
For the King was hedged by the shield-wall of his housecarls
And the swinging axes that none could pass; and the flag
Of the Fighting Man still flew. So, at last, the Normans,
Having had more than a bellyful, thundered back to their camp
And gave us breathing-space.

                                    God knows we needed it:
For the fight had been joined at the house of Prime, and now
The hour of Vespers drew nigh, and the sun that had crept
Westward over the sea, now slowly sank,
Staining the bloody field with a baleful light.
Six hours had we fought, and the battle hung still in the balance
Though the beam seemed to tilt in our favour. So I drew breath
And gulped a mouthful of muddy water old Cerdic
Had cupped from the brook in the helm of some dead Breton;
And as I moistened my throat, I became aware
That blood dripped in the cup from my brow where a bolt had
grazed it,
And my tunic-skirt was stiff with caked blood that had run
From a wound that ripped my flank, but I had not heeded it
In the heat of battle. And I thought how strange it was
That I, Ædwulf, a country lad with no care
For aught but my hawks and hounds and the simple ways
Of husbandry, should be sitting there on the brow
Of Senlac, weary and bleeding, with the wide sea
Before me, and the dark woods behind, and never a soul
I knew, save Cerdic, near me. Yet before I had wiped
The blood from my cheek, I heard men crying: "Ware. Ware!
They are on us again!" So I dragged myself to my feet

[96]

And gripped my father's sword, though its weight seemed the
double
Of what it had been when the fight began, and my fingers
Felt numb and nerveless.
Now this, though I knew it not,
Was the turning-point of the fray; for when William saw
That no spite could breach the shield-wall, he contrived
A subtler stratagem, and sent forth the levies
Of Maine and Poitou, with the Welch of Brittany
Led by Count Alan, and flung them on that flank
Where the low sun beat in the eyes of the light-armed fyrd
Of Wessex—but bade them let their onslaught seem
Half-hearted. And when these simple country-folk
Saw the French falter, they straight forgot the charge
Harold had laid on them, and broke their ranks
To rush upon them with their pikes, pursuing
The feigned flight in a rabble. And now the Bastard,
Having gotten his end and cracked the line that held
The hilltop, launched his lances in a wedge
That split the scattered fyrd of Wessex, and gained
The vantage of ground to smite us on the side
Their reckless zeal had breached.
Then, then indeed
Were we hard beset: for though the shield-wall swung
Westward to meet them, now we faced two fronts;
And the horse that swerved between us and the woods,
Drove in upon our rear—so that the housecarls,
Girdling the standard of the Fighting Man
With steel, rose like a spray-stripped island crag
Or an eyot in a mill-race; and though they wielded
Their axes in the same awful unison,
The shield-wall shrank and the narrowing ranks were pressed
Inward upon the standards, where Harold towered
Above his two slain brethren. One desperate knight,
Robert Fitz-Erneis, kin to Ralph of Tesson,
Shore through three ranks of housecarls, only to fall

[97]

As his hand clutched the standard, and the wave
Of the heaving mellay broke on him and covered him
With swathes of newly-slain, and the breach he had made
Was healed anew with flesh and steel, and rivetted
By the valour of Harold's housecarls, and held fast
By the grace of a miracle. So we fought on; but ever,
Above that changing battle, I saw two faces:
The Bastard's fiery jowl, grown black with rage,
And the fair head of Harold, streaked with blood
And sweat, yet ever kingly. And once again,
Foiled of their purpose, the Norman horse fell back,
While a crimson sunset, barred with black cloud, dyed
That dreadful hill with the hue of blood and dazzled
Our blinking eyes—and I prayed it would set soon
And twilight bring us respite.

       William no less
Saw how the dark might save us, and summoning
His knights to a last onslaught, bade the archers
Shoot to the sky, so that their arrowy sleet
Beat on us from above, unseen, and centre
This falling terror on that one small space
Where Harold and the remnant of the housecarls
Ringed the two standards. Thus, when the trumpets wailed
And his knights charged on us, the air was threshed
By a winged storm that smote us unawares,
Soundless and shadowless, falling ere we knew
That death was on us. Many a helm was pierced
By shafts that dropped as plumb as a falcon stooping
To kill his quarry. Many lifted their shields
For shelter, and so laid their bodies bare
To thrust of lance or sword-stroke. Some, dismayed,
Threw back their heads to see whence the winged fury
Fell, and were smitten as they stared. Three times
I plucked away three glancing arrows caught
In the chain-links on my shoulder; and as I turned
To pluck the last I saw King Harold topple

Like a tree struck by lightning, and he fell
At the standard's foot with an arrow in his eye,
Pierced to the brain. And a cry came to my lips,
But I could not utter it; for, as I gazed at him
With eyes distraught, a lance-point ripped my ribs
And flung me flat and senseless, where I lay
Sprawling amid the dead. . . .

                        Full night had fallen,
When a whisper woke me, and the hoarse voice of Cerdic
Bade me lie still and stir not, but feign death
For fear of it; telling me the fight was over
And lost, and that my life hung upon silence.
At first I knew not what he said, or where
I was lying—though it seemed to me for a while
I was stretched in the hall at home, and that old Bran
Tugged at a jingling chain, and I was racked
By a fierce pain in my side. But soon my senses
Fought back to clearness, and I knew that sound
Was the clink of mailed men, walking in their armour,
Who laughed, and swore in French. And when I winced
To blink my narrowed eyelids, I saw the light
Of lurid torches flaring, and lit by these
A great man with a fiery face, who sat
Unhelmed upon a mound of dead, and hungrily
Munched bread, sliced with his bloody dagger, and swilled
From a flagon of dark wine. Beneath his spurs
They had spread the proud Dragon of Wessex, daggled
With dirt and blood; and when he had filled his belly
He clapped his brother Odo on the shoulder
And the twain rolled off together . . .

                         Then I slept
For a while; and when next I woke it was daylight,
And the wives of the dead came to bear their bodies away,
Though the King's wife came not. Yet two good canons of [Waltham,
Old Osgod and Æthelric the Childmaster,
Who had followed the host, but fought not, being better

            Christians

Than the Bishop of Bayeux, sought for the King's body
Amid the mounds of slain—yet found it not
Till the lady Eadgyth Swansneck, who searched with them,
Marked on his mangled groin a mole that none
But she had known; and they covered his mauled limbs
And the marred kingly head, with a purple cloak,
And bore him to the shore and buried him
Beneath a cairn of stones. Thus ended Harold
Of England—and England with him. . . .

And what more can I tell—but that I lay
Athirst, and still as Christ upon his cross,
In feigned death all that day, and how, at eve,
When the field was emptied, leaning on old Cerdic,
I limped into the Weald; how, for a month,
We lurked in the woods of Wessex and woodwards' huts,
And crossed Cotswold by Fairford, and came at last
To Evesham, plodding through snow, and I was healed
Of my jagged lance-wound? But these were but the start
Of the woes that fell upon me; for my mother,
Who might have loved me better, feared to house me
By my own hearth; and my kinsman, Abbot Ælfwine,
Disowned me for a traitor—though he and Wulstan
Bishop of Worcester had treacherously ridden
On the morrow of Hastings fight to Berkhampstead
And truckled to the Norman, and for this
I scorned them ever after, though some have called
Wulstan a saint. Therefore (though none but he
Knew I had fought at Hastings) I hid myself
For prudence in Cerdic's hovel, ever hopeful
That the storm would blow over. But soon the Normans,
That smooth-faced seed of Sodom, with their greedy
Womanish cruelties, lapped up all the shires;
And soon the Bishop and Abbots were contending
With the king's sheriff, Urse d'Abitot, who should snatch
The choicest lands our Saxon thanes had held

Since Alfred ruled—and mine were reft, with the rest,
To swell the roll of Urse, save only my house
And a few lean fields beside it, that were left,
As the King's alms, to my mother, who had claimed them
As her morning-gift with which she was endowed
On the morrow of her marriage.

                  So I went landless
And dispossessed, being neither churl nor thane,
But a wanderer in the waste—and the very woods
Where I had hawked and hunted for meat were closed
By Urse's foresters, so that we should have starven
But that my monkish brother, who had become
Prior of the Abbey of Evesham, in grudging charity
Granted me lease of the lands my father had given
His Abbey on the morn the Comet shone,
To hold them at his pleasure and for the payment
Of some three pound a year—which are hard to come by
In these bare days! Here, since my mother died,
And the old hall fell to ruin for lack of money
To mend it, and my two sisters married, I have dwelt
In bitter idleness at the little watermill
(That is no longer mine) by the Whitsun Brook
And the pools where I fished for perch when I was a lad;
Though I have no heart to angle now, but live
Listless, and ever dreaming of that sweet time
That wilted when the Comet came, and was lost
For ever when King Harold fell at Hastings.

      Cold heart and bloody hand
      Now rule fair England.

X

FAREWELL TO ARMS

In the mid-watches of night Ruthe spake to me
Reproachfully: "See, you have smudged another page
Of your island-annals red; and I foresee
No respite from this cruel heritage
Of bloody deeds that tragic Man calls Glory,
Quaffing the dreadful cup to quell his fears
Or lull his conscience. Yet must all your story
Be written in the ink of blood and tears?

Then said I: "Mistress, though your plaint be guided
By Reason, you reck not how Man's nature is riven
Twixt that same Reason and Instinct; thus divided
Between the opposing sways of hell and heaven;
How, in his blood, cell with invasive cell
Struggles to keep its territory whole,
And guard within that fleshly citadel
The seed of Self that flowers in Man's soul;

How, thus, each nascent brood, by instinct tied
To hold Self's heritage holy, must maintain
The pattern breed has given, and the pride
Of its discrete integrity—nay, is fain
To court destruction rather than forsake
Its tribal virtues, fearing neither strife
Nor peril should another dare to shake
The freedom it loves dearer than its life;

How tribes that saw this nearing doom and feared
To lose their oneness, wan for lack of strength,
Clung to their kindlier neighbours and cohered
Like globules of bright quicksilver—and at length

Out of such fusion rose new nations, bound
By blood and tongue and custom to defend
All that they held in common and the ground
Their common forbears tilled. So, in the end,

An ampler Self was born; and in the roll
Of heroes those are held in honour most
Who gave their lives to save their nation's soul
And, losing all else, counted nothing lost.
Nor is such faith the special heritage
Of Man, but grounded in the marrow and pith
Of humbler creatures that know not the gage
Of glory, yet will die to fend their kith

Against aggression. See with what valiant might
The nesting stickleback defies the rival
That fans his favoured waters, and will fight
Till one be vanquished, reckless of survival!
See how the fiery robin-redbreast stakes
His chosen territories, and sounds the clarion
Of shrill defiance to challenge him who breaks
His marches or disputes his gauzy carrion!

See how the sexless droves of emmets band
Themselves in black-mailed legions; and honey-bees
Cluster them round their queenship to withstand
The death-moth's fingers on the sill; yet these
Feeble and small-brained folk will yield their stings,
And with their stings their lives, that they may see
Their threshold undefiled by alien wings!
There is no Ruthe in Nature, nor will be.

And Man, imperfect Man, as her prime heir,
Bears that red birthmark yet—nor had he risen
So high, nor fallen so low, did he not wear
Stamped on his brow the brand of Nature's prison;

Yet, since its hue affrights you, I will set
A song of rivers—Severn, with her mild daughters
Avon and Teme—and you shall thus forget
The noise of War in the running of sweet waters.

XI

SONGS OF THE THREE RIVERS

(1)

Severn is born of the sodden mosses
Where smooth Plynlimmon's dome is bowed
Under the rain the West Wind tosses
From tattered fleeces of sea-born cloud;
Where the sour-grass moors lie wet and wan,
And the mawn-pool's mirror is misted glass,
And the skirts of the sky's pavilion
Daggle the lint-white cotton-grass;
Where wild the curlew whinnies and cries
And whimbrels wheel in windy weather
And buzzards peck at the glazing eyes
Of sick lambs lost in the rain-lodged heather.
Only the carrion wings rejoice
Screaming above the smell of slaughter;
For the mountain's voice is but the voice
Of wind-stripped grasses and welling water:
Of water that whispers as it seeps
And water that tinkles as it drips
In a cup of stone before it creeps
To the moss where the meadow-pipit sips;
Of water that gurgles underground
To gush anew in the bubbling spring
Of brooks that run with the ripply sound
Of dimpling pebbles—and streams that sing
Such innocent strains as have their birth
In the joy of morning and maidenhood
And ambience of the April earth,
When the primrose blooms are pale, and the bud
Of the blackthorn breaketh snowy-cool.
Such songs they sing, so laughs their light
From glancing stickle to amber pool;
And their bubbled foam, it danceth white

From the waterfall as lambs that leap
In meadows on April evenings
When the fledgeling woods are stirred from sleep
And first the willow-warbler sings;
Till the wet wild moorlands fall behind
And the murmur of brooks and streams is blent
In the roar of a river that hath no mind
Of its mountain birth, but turbulent
As an untamed colt with foam-flecked shoulders
And fiery eyes and streaming mane,
Thunders over its bed of boulders
And falls in tumult to the plain.
So swollen Severn rolleth proud
Under the domed green hills of Wales
Dappled with flocks like shadows of cloud
In Summer; and all the Powys vales
Grow loud where the tumultuous floods
Of Vyrnwy, brimmed with Berwyn's snows,
Pour from their craggy solitudes
To stain her torrent. But Severn flows
With the graveness of a deepening stream,
Till her waters part—and high in air
The steeple vanes of Shrewsbury dream
Caught within her silver snare,
And her voice is stilled; for now she hath
Forgotten the madrigals that she sung
In the dalliance of her downward path
And the lilt of the valleys where she was young,
But hath put away such childish things
With the merriment of light-heart youth;
And the memory of her mountain springs
Is all forgotten—for now in sooth
She floweth mantled in sober state,
Laced with the fire of the rising sun,
And the turbid sully of Vyrnwy's spate—
Where the silver-sided salmon run

To their gravelly redds—doth not abate
The majesty of her tawny tide
Solemnly flowing towards the gate
Where the dark woods of Wenlock hide
Their brambled scarp, and Wrekin's dome
Shaggy with forest broodeth on
That crumbled city of Old Rome
Which dead men once called Uricon—
That white-walled City of the Woods
Whose stark, fire-blackened ruin guards
The mortal ashes of multitudes
Scattered amid their broken shards.
Yet the river recks not of the doom
Of the hapless folk who throve and died
And saw the white wild cherry-bloom
Lighten and rust on Severnside,
Who lived and loved and fell to dust
As the cherry-blow that whitens and wanes;
For her waters are timeless, and the lust
Of the salt stirs ever in her veins—
So the broom and the cherries of Wenlock Edge
Spend gold and snow for her in vain
As she roars through the cleft of Ironbridge
And veereth Southward to the plain
Where the blood-red rock of Bridgenorth frowns
On shoals of sand where the ravening Danes
Beached their dragons and burnt the towns
And lashed the land like Lammas rains
And spread afield like a Lammas flood,
Stripping the ripened cornlands bare.
Yet Severn recks not of fire or blood,
For she is timeless—nor tarryeth there,
But rolleth past on her seaward road
By villages that know not Time:
Alveley and Arley and Hampton Loade,
Whose gentle names together chime

Sweet as their Sunday church-bells ringing
For evensong in the month of June
When the lazy throstle mutes his singing
And the cuckoo flattens his April tune,
When the clang of their bells is wafted over
The moving water, to mingle and meet
In dim airs drenched with the honey of clover
And drowsy scents of meadowsweet . . .
But see! The river livens her pace
As she tugs at the ties of Arley ferry
And plunges headlong into the race
Of the Folly Rapids, and maketh merry,
And racing under the woods of Wyre
Like a two-year filly-foal recaptures
In one brief revel her youthful fire
And the ardour of youth and youth's fierce raptures;
Where Werewood broods on the water's brink
And leaf-shades dapple the delicate fallow
That steals from the shadow at eve to drink
From foam-fringed eddy and wave-lapped shallow.
But this fleeting zest is the last she will know
Of her morning joy—for the burden of years
And the load of care weigh heavily now
On the sobered water that laps the piers
Of Bewdley bridge, and the solemn stream
That ebbeth sullenly mile on mile
Without a voice, without a smile.
Yet rare and fugitive, hour by hour,
Fade on the moving mirror's face
The imaged beauty of Worcester tower
And Tewkesbury tower, and the stony lace
Of Gloucester's fretted parapet;
And the mournful stone of Berkeley's keep
Saddens her surface—but not yet
Shall dreaming Severn awake from sleep,

Not till the green vale opens wide
And the wrath of the bore rolls in from sea
And the stinging salt of the sudden tide
Mindeth her of her destiny.
Till, moving with more majestic gait,
She taketh seizin of the skies,
And robed in ever queenlier state
Spreadeth the firth in which she lies
With azure of the imaged vault
And clouds dove-grey and blinding white
And steely gleams of cool cobalt;
And the galaxies of indigo night
Spangle her raiment with cold fire
And burn within her broadened breast,
Till the hungry sea hath his desire
And she sinketh in his arms to rest.
Water to water . . . . Her life is o'er,
And the sea-born mists that fell to earth
On the mountain-tops are merged once more
In the bitter waves that gave them birth.

Yet, Mistress Ruthe, do not forget
How the seal of Liberty was set
On our rights when free men fought and died
For God's Crowning Mercy on Severnside.

(2)

Teme is Severn's wild, sweet daughter,
A wayward child; and her limpid water
Gushes and wells from the gentler rills
That trickle from the Kerry hills,
Where pale, cloud-tented sheepwalks lie
Meek beneath a rain-washed sky
In airs that are thin and crystal-clear
As spring-water, where the idle ear

[109]

Listening heareth little else
Than the rustle of harebells and heather-bells,
Or the boom of blundering bumble-bees
Drunken with honey culled from these,
Or the whisper of grasses, that is almost
Silence, or bleating of weak lambs, lost
In bracken too tall for them to spy
Their anxious dams—and so they cry
Desolately, but dare not move
For the hungry wings that hover above . . .

But virgin Teme knows naught of these
As she lapseth under her alder-trees
From pool to stickle and stickle to slide
Threading the thin-strung woods that hide
Her hesitant meanderings,
Where the pied water-ouzel sings,
Bobbing his breast on an island stone—
(Stir but a finger, and he is flown,
Whirring upstream from the shadow of harm
With a startled stutter of alarm
That is like two pebbles clashed together!)
Where, in the drowsier Summer weather,
Gleams for a moment and is gone
The burning blue of Halcyon;
And the redstart flits from a crannied wall,
Flashing above the waterfall
The rufous glow of a feebler fire;
And the light-hearted pipits spire
Tossing their bodies high in air
And twittering as they hover there.

So, with alternate gloom and shine,
Teme falls by Llanfairwaterdine
To Knucklas village and Knighton Vale,
Where the felled woods lie silver-pale

With floss of silken willow-weed;
And on her face the windblown seed
Lighteth softer than thistledown
To drift and skim, like mayflies blown
To their death in June—till a tiny waft
Of light air lifteth it aloft,
And the seed goes sailing on its way,
While sweet Teme floweth without stay
Between the wild flags' clustered swords,
Where gentle, wide-horned Herefords
Bend their white-muzzled heads to drink
From muddy pools on the trampled brink;
Or stand knee-deep in the cool stream
In an unimaginable dream
And slowly swing their tails, while flies
Settle on their uncurious eyes;
Till the roofs of a rising village strown
On a steep hillside, and a tower of stone,
Stand in her path and halt her flow,
And clear Teme feels the undertow
Of denser waters that have run
From the marly dales of Corve and Clun,
And the streams of the confluent rivers mingle
In a deep pool that laps the shingle
Where the twin sisters meet and twine
Under the bridge at Leintwardine
And the two waters flow as one . . .

So swollen Teme goes tumbling down
Over the rapids to Trippleton,
Then falls to peace in a shadowy slide
Where tall trees lean on either side,
And their drooping boughs are arched above
Water that hardly seems to move
Save for the drift of scum that floats
Dappled by foam and dense with motes

Of silt suspended in mid-stream.
Here, by the banks, the great trout dream
Daylong in sunless sanctuaries
Of root and snag—but when the skies
Grow cool, and the last loaded wain
Creaks home to Trippleton again,
Forth from their haunts they steal and lie
Heading upstream, with greedy eye
Waiting, a bare palm's depth beneath
The surface, for the drift of death
Or winged life that the current then
Washes within their hungry ken,
And, lifted on a quivering fin,
Suck the delicious morsel in
So gently that the water's skin
Is barely dimpled; but if their prey
Flutters or dips to flit away,
Then will they leap to snatch it, heaving
Their black backs arched in air, and leaving
On the broken water a ring that spreads
To rock the dabchicks in the reeds,
Or, borne in widening circles, fades
In the shallow tail of the pool, where shades
Of silvery umbers, ghostly-grey,
Sway on the gravelly ledge; for they
Hover not under the water's face,
But spring upright from their resting-place
To gulp their prey in the toothless gape
Of small, smooth lips—yet the grayling's shape
Outshines the stippled trout's in its mail
Of imbricate silver, for his broad tail
And fins are dipped in crimson dyes,
And when, forspent, on the bank he lies
He smelleth sweetly of mountain-thyme
Or cool cucumber. And in the prime

Of the mayfly-hatch, when Teme grows warm
And the limp-winged drakes are whirled like a storm
Of flurried snowflakes to spin and dip
In the brief, hapless fellowship
Of their nuptial flight, and, spent, go sailing
With draggled vanes—then trout and grayling
Forget their wariness and fall
With one accord to the carnival
Of June's fierce gluttony in the slaughter
Of gauzy myriads, and the water
Boils with the rises of great fish springing
Into the air, and swirling and flinging
Their silver bodies this way and that
In wanton greed—and the tiniest sprat
Of a fingerling may take his fill,
Till the mayfly-storm drifts by, and the still
Surface is turned again to glass,
Unflawed and lifeless as it was—
Mere mirror of the dusk that hears
Naught but the wimpling of the weirs
And murmur of the pebbled shallows.
Then zig-zag bats that swoop like swallows
Dart and flitter on web-winged fingers
Hawking the last mayfly that lingers
Unharmed in that fierce hecatomb
Of watery death. And when night's gloom
Falls deeper on the starlit dubs,
The otter whistles her frolicsome cubs
To cease their gambolling and tear
The eels she has dragged to the dripping weir
In her pointed teeth. But when day breaks,
A wild, aerial music wakes
The valley, in the curlew's calling
And cat-like cries of lapwings falling
Like tumbler-pigeons from the sky,
And the clear trilling of the shy

[113]

Hovering sandpipers that trip
With delicate feet on an island strip
Of sand, or the dipper's wren-like notes.
Sometimes through morning mist there floats
The shrilling of vigilant greenshanks,
Where, beneath grass-tussocked banks,
Grey wagtails, with their yellow breast
And gorget of black velvet, nest
In a cleft of clay, and flutter near
With a soft brilliance that hath no peer
In the English air . . . So Teme runs on
From Leintwardine to Burrington,
Stealing with a soberer pace
Past Downton Rocks to Bringewood Chase:
And here she floweth without sound;
For Bringewood Chase is holy ground,
Where *Comus* and his sisterhood
Of laughing dryads ruled the wood,
And wove about the enchanted vale
Their silvan magic—that was frail
As morning gossamer, yet fraught
With such strange potency, it caught
The mind of *Milton* in its net;
And leafy Bringewood liveth yet
With Vallombrosa's leaves, for ever
Sacred in song . . .
                          So the hushed river
Hurrieth, as her waters sweep
Under Ludlow's storied keep,
Where the castle's crumbling walls look down
Upon the many-chimneyed town,
And the sweet-tempered Ludlow chimes
Waver through wreathing smoke that climbs
From the draughty vale—and still they seem
Rapt in the other-worldly dream

That thralled them in the haunted wood
Of *Comus*—and this raptured mood
Dwells with those waters as they glide
Through tranquil meadowlands and wide
Stubbles, where seagulls, fluttering low,
Whiten the furrow behind the plough
And hover above the ploughman's head,
Watching the burnished mould-board spread
Its furrow-slice, and lighting there
To raven their choice inland fare
Of wireworms in the cloven turf
As greedily as they comb the surf
Of their native surge . . . So Abdon Burf
Falleth behind, and Titterstone Clee
Looms on the left—and Teme runs free
Through the spreading vale to Saltmoor Well
And the elms of Ashford Carbonell,
To drown the last of her panic fear
In the deep green of Worcestershire;
Where her marl-reddened currents fret
Cliffs of red sand, and hopyards set
With intricate trellises of twine
In quaint cat's-cradles, and the bine,
With eager tendrils spiring, weaves
Its clerestory of translucent leaves
Vaulting the alleys with their slight
Radiance of cool green light.
Here the gnarled cider-orchard breaks
Its shell-pink buds; here Autumn shakes
The ripe wind-fallen fruit to lie
Hid in lush grass—and when men pry,
Raking the windfalls into heaps,
A drowsy smell of pomace steeps
The valley. Yet Teme's chiefest pride
Is her miracle of Eastertide

When the white cherry-blow is whirled
In drifts upon a dazzled world,
And billowy blossom, tossed on high,
Beggars the brightness of the sky
With an innocence beyond belief
On this aged earth—yet fugitive
As the radiance of April's moon
Whitening the ghostly boughs—and soon
The mirror of Teme hath naught to show
But the lesser light of hawthorn-blow;
And ivory-plumed elder throws
Its image on a stream that flows
Deep-sunken through the tawny clay
Of the cold plain, and ebbs away
Sullenly, with the sluggard pace
Of age—till Severn's arms embrace
Her tired daughter, and tenderly
Carry her, sleeping, to the sea.

Yet, Sister Ruthe, remember well
How the first blow for freedom fell
Upon the powers of privilege
Where Teme joins Severn at Powick Bridge!

(3)

Avon springs from the mints and cresses
Of a gentle pastureland that lies
Midmost in Mercia's green recesses
Beneath mild-tempered midland skies;
Little she knows of the fierce birth
Of Severn her mother or sister Teme,
For her waters well from a kindlier earth,
And her youth is quiet as a dream

[116]

Unbroken by any stormy splendour
Of moor or mountain, or the loud
Tumult of torrents. Gay and tender,
She moveth idly as a cloud
In Summer, or a careless child
On a spring morning gathering posies
Of wet marsh-marigolds, and wild
Forgetmenots, and faint primroses,
And yellow-varnished celandine,
And rushes pithed as white as milk,
And sallies flossed with smoky silk,
And lilac ladies-smocks, and all
The moisture-loving flowers that twine
In April's dewy coronal;
For innocent are Avon's ways,
And meditative is her mien
As through the minty marsh she strays
In a shallow vale that runs between
Low hills of rolling grassland, pied
With gorse and spinneys of oak and ash
Where the horsemen halt at the covert-side
Till twenty dappled couples crash
In a burst of music, and the wail
Of the hunting-horn's sweet quavers
Wakens the leafless woods, and wavers
Over her water to the pale
Chequer of forty-acre fields
That the quick-set bullfinch shields
With triple thorn . . . So, like a skein
Of scarlet threading the green weft,
The bright hunt straggles over plain
And hillock, and Avon's vale is left
Empty—as when, on this same field
Of Naseby, Cromwell's Roundheads broke
Rash Rupert's cavalry—and they reeled
And scattered on the wold like smoke

And vanished . . .
            But Avon floweth still,
Gathering to her nascent stream
Clear tributary waters: *Leam*
And *Swift;* and many a nameless rill
Steals through the rushy watermeads
To filter through her fringing reeds
Unseen. And many a water-mill,
Fed by the borrowed race, returns
The flow the slatted mill-wheel churns
In a bright cataract that re-fills
Her dwindled trickle. And lifted high
On the smooth skyline of the hills,
Sails of gaunt windmills sweep the sky
With cumbrous lattice, languidly
Turning the low-geared pinion wheel
That rolls the gritstone, till the meal
Dusts the miller's shoulders white
As a mealy cockchafer or bee
That in high summer you may see
With pallid clover-pollen dight . . .

So Avon girdles in her sleep
The gabled roofs of Warwick town
Where the King-maker's castle-keep
Shadows her face, and floweth down
Into the unmysterious glades
Of Arden's oaks, no longer haunted
By dappled fallow—yet the shades
Of the sweet meinie that enchanted
This leafy wildwood, in the Spring
Of Shakespeare's youthful fancy, still
Brood on the twilight lanes and bring
Their magic with them, when the trill

Of May's last nightingale awakes
Infinite yearnings, and the fall
Of his dwindling cadenza shakes
The heart with hushed delight—and all
Arden lies breathless, listening
For the light step of Rosalind
And Amiens' song . . . Yet still the spring
Of a nimble squirrel that in the thinned
Woodland leaps from tree to tree
Trailing his feathery brush, is free
To traverse all the ancient girth
Of Arden without touching earth;
Still the glade's bracken-fronds unfold
Their croziers of mealy gold;
Still Arden's bluebells fan the verges
With silvan fragrance, and wood-spurges
With triple cups of golden green
Betray the woodland's old demesne—
And the lost forest lives in these
Its lowlier denizens, that held
Their stations when the mightier trees
Sheltering their humble growth were felled
To keel the fleets that kept the seas
In the days of great Elizabeth,
And carried to Virginian leas
Those words that are the very breath
Of England . . . But Avon knoweth naught
Of any music but her own,
And nothing of the magic wrought
By him who sleeps beneath the stone
Of Stratford's airy spire, and yet
Makes our imaginations seem
As thoughts that flower in a dream
And wilt on waking, or are flown.
Yet, swan-sweet Avon, can you forget
How one whose meanest word was lit

[119]

By passionate perfection, stood
Mirrored in your translucent flood,
Or idly on your banks would sit
Trailing his fingers in the water?
O swan-sweet Avon, Severn's daughter,
Do you remember how he moved
Through the pied meadows that he loved,
And how he smiled to catch those sweet
Elusive images, as fleet
And fiery as the kingfisher's
Arrowy azure, in his verse?
And did you hear his rustic tongue
Savour each salty syllable
Shaped on his lips when he was young?
Saw you him ever when he leant,
Undazzled by the glancing looks
That flickered from your stream, intent
Upon the many-storied books
Of Plutarch, or the turgid flow
Of Holinshed's grim chronicle?
And did you see his dark eyes glow
When fierce imagination fell
To burn upon the prosy page,
Till the wide skies became a stage
And, in the light of that rich birth,
Heroes walked again on earth?
But Avon answers naught, for she
Was passing-old when he was young,
And still may flow when all he sung
Shall live but in man's memory
As a crabbed text in a dead tongue.

So Arden's wasted woodlands sink
Behind; and white on Avon's brink
The widening Vale of Evesham throws
Its benison of blossomed boughs.

So dazzling-bright the orchards lie,
It seems as though the April sky
Had fallen upon earth and strewn
Its cloudy billows there—and when
Night falls on Bredon, and the moon
Silvers the prodigal blossom, then
The orchards of the vale seem lost
In a soundless sea of mist that laps
The bases of the hills and wraps
Their sleeping knees—where like a ghost
The dome of Bredon glimmers pale,
Islanded in the misty Vale . . .
But when lascivious winds of May
Have ravished the light petal-cloud
And fruit swells on the leafy spray,
Then are the plum-trees' branches bowed
With tasselled clusters of cool green
That August's bounty, warms to gold
Or deepening orange—and some are seen
Drooping with purple and tawny-red,
So closely set no branch can hold
Its juicy burden, but will shed
Ripe fruit at the first finger-touch;
And the bruised flesh, fallen, spills
Its heavy-sugared juice and fills
The Vale with vinous fragrance. Such
Are the Summer languors Avon loves:
For when the weedy lock-gates close,
Her listless current barely moves
Under the drooping willow-boughs
Where the deep-bellied, sullen chub,
Gaping through the scum and froth
That eddies in a sunless dub,
Sucks in the velvet of a moth

[121]

Faint-fluttering with sodden wings
In hapless circles—or hungrily
Heaving his slimy body, springs
To gulp it in mid-air, and sends
A ripple to the beds of reed
Where pike with olive-mottled flanks
Bask on the mud of shelving banks,
So drowsily, they will not heed
The shadowy roach that swim in shoals,
Or spectral perch with tiger-stripes
Lurking in their deep water-holes;
But when October's rigour tips
The elms with pallid leprosy,
And the first gales of Autumn shiver
The rustling reedbeds, then the river
Wakes from her lethargy: and you see
Slow Avon crisped with waves and rippled
With wind—and clouds of babbling stares
Wheel from their granaries in the stippled
Stubbles to roost in reedy cover.

And now the dome of Bredon wears
Its richest liveries—for over
Her falling flanks the tall elms stand
Robed in bright gold; and over all
The orchards spreads the yellow pall
Of Autumn; and the meadowland
Of Avon seems to hold its breath
In the mute majesty of death:
Till ice, with brittle crystal, edges
The shallows, and the frozen sedges
Grow stiff with rime. So Avon sweeps
Unsmiling through more sullen deeps
In a null nescience flowing down
By Nafford Mill and Eckington
To the wide, flood-whitened fields that lie

Beneath the tower of Tewkesbury:
A weary river that hath run
Her course—sunk in oblivion
So death-like that she hardly hears
The hollow thunder of the weirs
That draw her listless to her rest
In mother Severn's ancient breast.

Yet, Sister Ruthe, remember too
That day when freedom flamed anew
To perish in the darkened hour
When Montfort fell by Evesham Tower.

XII

*The Scene is the Infirmary in the Monastery of Our Lady of
Worcester, a capacious chamber, with a high-roof of rough-hewn
timber, dimly lit by slender lancets. In its darkest corner, on a narrow
pallet-bed, lies the mummy-like form of Brother John de Mathon, an
old man clothed in the habit of a Benedictine monk. He is so ancient,
indeed, as to seem hardly human. The wrinkled scalp that defines the
shape of his skull is the colour of dirty leather; his orbits are so
cavernous that the blind eyes are invisible, lost in their depths; and the
only parts of his anatomy that betray any sign of life are his hands,
disproportionately large compared with the stick-like wrists, whose
taloned fingers pluck with a restless automatism at the grimy coverlet
which has been thrown over him. By his side, on the stone-flagged floor,
a florid young man, robed in a similar habit, sits cross-legged, with a
parchment on his knees, a pen in his hand, and an ink-horn within
easy reach. He looks alternately bored and faintly amused as he bends
over the malodorous pallet to catch the words that issue from Brother
John's toothless mouth. Occasionally he scratches a perfunctory note
on the parchment; but for the most part he is content (or constrained)
to listen to a rambling tale that has little of interest for him, as the
old man speaks in a thin, toneless voice:*

Art thou still there, my son, and canst thou hear me?
It were well to press my hand lightly now and again,
For thus I may know that my scanty breath is not wasted,
And, should I fall asleep, thy touch will awaken me
And pluck my mind from dreaming. What did I say?
*The days of our years are three score years and ten:
And if, by reason of strength, they be fourscore years,
Then is their strength but sorrow.*

                      I was born
In the first year of Richard Lion-Heart,
When the Welsh kings rode to Worcester to make peace

With John Sansterre his brother; and of my boyhood
I have naught to tell—albeit therein my memory
Burns with the brightness of a lamp new-lit,
Discovering trivial things as doth the shaft
Of a mote-laden sunbeam. Little I recked
Of the realm's turmoil, or the march and counter-march
Of turbulent barons; for mine own earth was bounded
By the enfolding hills, and was no larger
Than the sweet-smelling cowslip-balls we made
In the meadows of Malvern Chase.

                I was but eighteen
When I trudged my way to Worcester, and first donned
The habit of our order, that I have worn
For well-nigh seventy years; and Prior Simon,
Marking my true, sweet voice, gave me more favour
Than a raw lad merited; and when I had learnt
My notes and conned the canticles, chose me to lead
The singing on high festivals. Many came
To hear me sing, and I, being callow, was puffed
With the glory I owed to God, who had endowed me
With this pretty talent. Ay, and I well remember
(But for Christ's sake set not this down!) how one bold wench,
Who was wife to a brewer in Silver Street, by the Shambles,
Heard Mass whensoever I sang; and as the procession
Trailed by where she knelt on the stones, and I passed so near
(For so had she placed herself) that I all but brushed
Her hair, which was mouselike in hue and sweetly-scented
As musk or clover in Summer—then did she peek at me
Through her crossed fingers, smiling, and blinked one eye!
At which I—as any might guess—blushed red to the crown
Of my tonsure, but, none the less, when those high notes came
In which I excelled, and I saw she still gazed my way,
Her face calm and pale in the distance, then did I carol
(God pardon me!) like any cock-chaffinch, perched
On an apple-tree's topmost bough, that fluffs his breast
To bursting with the might of his brazen challenge!

Yet, albeit I was a young fellow then and well-favoured,
I think there was more lust of pride than of concupiscence
In my error; and though, indeed, I made no confession
Till fifty years later, one day when I thought I was dying,
Yet doth the memory of her glance and the musky spice
Of her hair abide—though she, fond soul, is dust,
And I am a man no longer. Beyond doubt,
There is little true sanctity untried by temptation,
As Augustine knew to his cost. My sin was Pride;
And Time hath humbled me—as thou shouldst perceive,
Hearing the thin, cracked pipe of one who has ravished
The ears of kings . . .

                Kings, do I say? There were two
For whom I sang. The first was John the Landless;
And never, some say, was king more unkingly than he
In his treacheries; though I, being cloister-reared
And unworldly, saw not this blackness of heart, but was dazzled
By the mere shine of kingship, glorying in the flattery
Of a prince who favoured our house, and often abode here
With his lackey, Walter the Bishop (the same who stood
By his side at Runnymede) for the high festivals
Of our church, and ever delighted in the sweet music
We made—but even more in our Severn salmon
And lamperns and royal sturgeon washed down with the wines
Of Gascony and Touraine, when he made of Lent
A season of prodigal banquets. John was a man
Of ruddy and open countenance, well-fattened, and easy
Of laughter for them that pleased him; yet, were he crossed
In the meanest trifle, then would his Angevin blood
Blacken his face with wrath till the veins in his temples
Were swollen to bursting, and his small body was shaken
With such a tempest that he would writhe on the ground,
Rolling his eyes, and catch up sticks and straws
To chew them like a madman. Such, I have heard,
Were his ravings at Runnymede, when the magnates bound him
By dooms he had no intent to suffer; though we, being swayed

By his kingly graces and the words of our Bishop,
Walter de Gray, held this poor king ill-used,
And deemed the Barons' charter less an instrument
Of liberty for the common folk than a change
From the rule of one man, who had loved us well, to the power
Of a many who loved but themselves. For, mark you, my son,
There was naught in their vaunted charter that had not been
                                                    granted
Long since by King Henry the First, and more concern
For their own rights than for those of Holy Church,
As Pope Innocent surely knew when he laid his ban
On those barons and their shrewd counsellor, Stephen Langton,
Making the king's cause ours. So we of Worcester
Stood by our lawful liege, and reckoned his enemies
Accursed—the more so when Geoffrey de Mandeville
Called on King Philip of France to send his Dauphin
To conquer England and filch John's kingship from him:
For, know you this: when I was a lad we still called
One man a Norman and another English;
But now those Normans who had dispossessed
Our Saxon forbears boasted their Englishness,
And hated the foreigner fiercely as they themselves
Had once been hated; and when the Frenchman set foot
On the shore of Essex and marched his knights toward London,
Then was all England one, save for those few
Who, by duress, had bound the king at Runnymede
And sworn to oust him . . .
                            It was then that the cruelty
Of the king's heart first showed itself, as he fell
On the rebels of the North. Never have I known
Such a passionate fury as burned in his body and drove him
This way and that through the length of England, snapping
Like a mad cur at all that crossed his path,
Whether they were friend or foe, and never sleeping
Two nights in the same bed. Yet those who condemn him
Remember not that the king was hard beset

E*

As a hunted wolf; and if his fangs were reddened
With innocent blood, his hunters' hands were no cleaner;
Nor that the Holy Father himself had frowned
On their lawlessness. It was intemperate haste
That drove him to his doom; for, as he strained
Northward to harry Lincoln, with less wisdom
Than King Canute tempting the mighty malice
Of the untameable tides, his baggage-train
Sank in the quicksands of the Wash, and was lost;
And the king himself, struggling so far as Swineshead
To dry the draggled remnant, there fell sick
Of a mortal flux. There is a story told
How that he died of a surfeit of peaches swilled
With fresh-made cider—and I, of my own eyes,
Know him a glutton, having seen him bloated
With meat at the Bishop's board; yet that which slew him
Was but the flame of hatred, that burnt out
Like a fierce bonfire, consuming his tortured body
As they bore him to Lincoln, ever panting and groaning,
On a litter of horsecloth stiffened with woven withies
From the fen; and there, on the third day after, he died,
Duly shriven (as should be told) by the Abbot of Croxton,
And when they asked him where he would lie, he bethought him
Of our church of St. Mary at Worcester, saying: "*I commend
My body and soul to God, and to Saint Wulstan.*"
So here we buried him, even as Merlin foretold,
With the bones of Wulstan on one hand, and on the other
The relics of Oswald; that, when the trumpet sounds
And the graves give up their dead, he might take his place
In the bright company of Heaven—though some
Still call him Nature's enemy, and maintain
That not even their saintly sponsorship shall save
His perjured soul. Yet never will I believe
That any burn in hell who have died in grace
As he did. And, whatsoever havoc he wrought
In his evil life, his death brought England peace,

As is graven on his tomb: *Hoc in sarcophago*
Sepelitur regis imago, qui moriens multum
Sedavit in orbe tumultum—which is lame Latin
And middling rhyme, but, in the essence, true.
So may God rest his spirit, I say, who gave
His realm rest by his dying . . .

                       The second king
Before whom I sang (and never sang I more sweetly
Than on that day) was Henry, his son; a child
But nine years old, whom a splendid company
Of barons, earls, bishops and mitred abbots
Carried to Worcester for the dedication
Of the new cathedral church. And of this I will tell thee
A tale—though whether or no thou shouldst set it down
I am doubtful, seeing that it brings little credit
To our new bishop Silvester, once our prior.
Yet the story hath this moral: that impatience
May sink to sacrilege . . .

                     Know you, then, we had fashioned
A new shrine for Saint Wulstan, since the old
Had been stripped of all its richness to provide
The fine we were mulcted for our forced submission
To the French Dauphin. Never was a saint's shrine
More gloriously wrought. But when we came
To set Saint Wulstan's body therein, we found
The mason had mismeasured, the saint's stature
Being greater than ordinary. Then Bishop Silvester,
Vexed by our hesitations, and determined
To have done with the business, stripped off his robes
And with his own ringed fingers hacked and hauled
Saint Wulstan's body asunder, cramming his bones
Into the coffin, ay, and even boasted
Of his own ruthlessness, calling the sacred relics
Naught but dry bones. That was the sixth of June,
As I remember well, and six weeks later
All but two days, he died; and afterward,

[129]

On the festival of Saint Andrew, a whirling wind
Cast down two towers on either side the apse
Of the minster. From which signs let no man doubt
But that saints in deathless glory still are swayed
By mortal spites and passions . . .

        Once again
My ill-shepherded thoughts have erred; it would be pleasant
To let them stray thus browsing on the sweeter
Pastures of memory; and much could I tell
Of Silvester's successor, William de Blois,
Whom Gualo, the Pope's legate, thrust upon us;
For this man was a rare builder, and up-raised
The soaring arches of a new sanctuary
Above Our Lady's altar; and, being warned
Doubtless by poor Silvester's doom, disposed
The buried bones his masons marred in a pit
Beneath the new-built charnery, where mine
Shall rest when God so wills it. But of him
I will speak no more; for now my chronicle
Takes sterner shape, being shadowed by the presences
Of three huge men, who rise above the press
Of pettier persons as the craggy peaks
Of Ararat towered over the drowned wastes
Of Noah's deluge: first, Walter de Cantelupe,
My lord of Worcester; next Robert Grosseteste,
Bishop of Lincoln; last, and greater than either,
Earl Simon, called de Montfort, the noblest man
England has ever known—which is the stranger
In that this knightly paragon was born
In Normandy, and lived the greater part
Of his stormy days in Gascony. See, already
I have overshot my mark! Hear then, my son,
How that fair child whose kingly presence honoured
Our dedication, grew to belie the promise
Of innocent boyhood. Hapless is the realm,
Men say, in which a child is king: and never

[130]

Was saying more grimly proved than in the fruit
Of this enhavocked reign; for, from the day
When he was chrismed, his sapling strength was twisted
By the ambitions of ruthless men who schemed
But for themselves; and by their flatteries
Nourished a weak-willed tyrant, as unstable
As a wind-tossed aspen flurried this way and that
By every changeful gust—whereby our country
Became once more the prey of foreigners
Who battened on her bones. It was an evil day—
Though little we guessed—when John, his father, drowning
In surges of rebellion, clutched at the rock
Of Rome, and made the honour of England part
Of Peter's patrimony. For now the claws
Of the Roman dragon gripped our Church's throat,
And, throttling, squeezed forth the last gouts of blood
From her blanched carcase—not only in exactions
Of treasure to feed sinews of temporal might
In lands we knew not (first a tenth part of all
We had, then, appetite growing with gluttony,
One fifth) but also in the greedy gullocking
Of vacant benefices, from bishoprics
To simple chaplaincies that we had reckoned
Our natural right, till every cure was filled
With predatory aliens and pluralists
Who never set foot on English earth and spoke not
One word of English. And King Henry's court
Was little better, being crammed with sycophants
Of Anjou and Poitiers—the hungry crew
That, in the time of the Confessor, tempted
The Conqueror to Hastings. And when the King
Wedded the Princess Eleanor, to these
Was added a locust-swarm of Provençals
Who stripped all that was left, and soon, inflaming
The king's mind with vain schemes of foreign conquest
That fell to nothing, pitted his light wits

Against more practised players, till his crown
Seemed but a pawn upon the chequer-board
Of shrewd dynastic gamesters, and Church and Laity,
Being thrust at length into each other's arms,
Were joined as never before. Then was a murmur
Of protest, loud though late, wrung from the lips
Of England. Robert Grosseteste, Bishop of Lincoln,
Was our first champion, an old man steeped
In ancient wisdoms; and our own Bishop, Walter,
His friend and my loved master, stood beside him
With Simon, Earl of Leicester, when they brought
The King to Oxford—even as his father before him
Was haled to Runnymede. I, as Walter's chaplain,
Rode with him over Cotswold. There was the weakness
Of the King made plain; for when he saw the powers
Of Church and Baronage in arms, he cried:
"Am I your prisoner?" Whereon Roger Bigod
(For so I heard him) answered: "Nay, my Lord King;
For all we ask is that your Poitevins
And the alien placemen who have dispossessed
Both folk and faith of freedom, shall be banished
For the realm's honour and welfare. And we demand
That you and your son the Prince shall solemnly swear
To lay no burdens on us but with the leave
Of counsellors we shall choose." Then did King Henry,
Powerless to do aught else, submit himself,
Swearing as he was bidden; and by that Parliament
Of Oxford, clerk and layman, rich and poor,
Obtained protection, under the firm hand
Of Simon and his fellows. It was as if
We had waked from nightmare dreams into the peace
Of a clear dawn—though they that watched more shrewdly
Saw the sky streaked with presage of the tempest
That followed after . . .

                I have little to tell
Of the wars that wracked us then; for my own knowledge

Is naught but hearsay, save that the King forswore
That oath, in his father's fashion, soaking the land
With innocent blood, and that the jealous Pope
Released him of his promise to maintain
The charter sealed at Oxford. It is a tale
Of manifold treacheries. But the last page
Of this chronicle was writ beneath my own eyes
Downcast with shame and dim with tears. For, know you,
After the battle at Lewes, when Earl Simon
Had caged the elder hawk and thrid his leash
Through the young falcon's jesses, then that envy
Which has been freedom's bane in all her story
Gnawed at Earl Simon's powers. There is enchantment
In the very air kings breathe, as if the height
Of their station turned men dizzy, and the smiles
Of captive royalty were more dazzling
Than the light of reason—so that those who fret
At their peers' dominion are fain to grovel
Before a faithless throne. Thus, one by one,
Earl Simon's friends forsook him: Gloucester and Norfolk
And Bohun and Mortimer and Roger Bigod
Who had been freedom's spokesman—all forsook him;
And though Earl Simon held the King, Prince Edward,
Laughing at his fond leniency, slipped
His leash and fled to Wigmore, gathering
The Mortimers to his side. So, when Earl Simon
Turned toward faithful London, then he found
All Severn held from Shrewsbury to the sea,
With every bridge down-broken, and every boat
Scuttled or beached on the far bank, and half
The force he counted on, under young Simon,
Divided from him. Thus was he caged no less
Than his kingly captive; and in the extremity
Of need, called on Llewelyn of Wales for aid,
Erring therein—since no true Englishman
Who had seen our Marches harried by the Welsh

[133]

Could stomach such alliance.

                          Nine wasteful days
Earl Simon lay at Hereford, waiting for news,
That came not, of his son. But young Prince Edward,
Being swifter and more forthright in strategy
And warned by a certain woman, who, with the guile
Of Rahab, lurked in Kenilworth, broke from Worcester,
Fell on young Simon unawares and worsted him
Ere he could join his father. But of this
The Earl knew naught; and, on the second day
Of August, marching from Hereford, crossed Severn
At Kempsey, where my master, Bishop Cantelupe,
Lodged him within our manor. There I saw him,
And marked how cares had aged him, though his mien
Was calm and noble as ever, and his eye
Bright as a boy's beneath his grizzled brow.
There as we sate that evening, I heard him speak
With my lord, Bishop Walter, of how he planned
To mould a better England, when the legionary
Factions that rent her had been exorcised,
Saying: "There is none other land nor folk
Worthier of peace than ours, nor yet more temperate
In the uses of their freedom, be they but left
To its unvexed enjoyment. Such a firm peace,
Under such guidance, it is my intent,
By God's good grace, to give them." Then he spoke
Of his counsel for the morrow: how he would march
By Avonside to Evesham, where his friend,
Henry the Abbot, would house him till he could join
Young Simon at Kenilworth, and they together
Circle the Prince with greater force and scatter
The embers of rebellion. Then Bishop Walter
Bade me march with Earl Simon, being himself
Too feeble for such adventure—though I, in truth,
Was older than he.

                      That night we tramped fifteen miles,

And came footsore to Evesham as the dawn
Broke over Cotswold; and I, beside the king
Who told me he remembered how once I had sung
Before him, but I, though flattered, disbelieved him)
Heard the monks' Mass, and broke my fast. But Simon
Would neither eat nor pray with us, but climbed
To the tower's top to meditate alone,
Brooding upon the kingdoms of this earth
As Christ in his temptation; and fairer kingdom
No mortal eye could see than that ripened vale
Caught in the loops of Avon. It was noon
Ere he rejoined us; and even as his foot
Touched earth, there came a message: that the woods
To northward were alive with marching men
And bright with banners. One whose sight was keener
Than ours, his barber, Nicholas, clomb the tower
To see those banners blazoned with the bearings
Of Simon the Younger—and then he cried again
That this was true, but that the men who bore them
Were none of ours, but our sworn enemies.
And now, as they drew nearer, we could see
That those who led them wore the blood-red cross
The barons of the King had borne at Lewes,
And that the advancing host outnumbered ours
By three to one. Then would a feebler heart
Have quailed, but Simon's quailed not; for he smiled,
Saying: "By the arm of Saint James, they come on bravely,
But it was I who taught them this order! Let us commend
Our souls to God, for surely our bodies are theirs."
Then the monks thronged about us, urging Simon
To flee while there was time; and he himself
Begged his son, Henry, and Hugh Despenser, to ride
Over the bridge behind us; but already
The horsemen of Mortimer had swum the river
And barred their crossing. And when they told him this:
"Come then," he said, "and let us die like men,

For if we have fasted here we shall breakfast in Heaven!"
Then called he me by name, and did enjoin me
Not to adventure my brittle bones in battle
But to seek sanctuary. And I, in sorrow,
Turned from him, slowly climbing to the parapet
Of the great bell-tower; and from that vantage-point
Saw, though I was no soldier, the hopelessness
Of our case; for we were snared in the deep loops
Of the river, that embraced us on every side
Save one, where the road to Worcester ran between
The scarps of Crawcombe and the impassable ditch
Of Avon—one narrow sleeve of watermeadow.
And, as I stood there gazing, the sky darkened
To raven blackness, and a baleful blight
Settled upon the scene, as on that day
When Christ was crucified, and the temple veil
Was rent asunder. So, of that awful slaughter
(For battle none may call it) I saw little
But a tumult of living waves, tossed back and forth
From the bases of the hills to that bloody river
Choked with the carrion of the fugitive Welsh
Drowned in their thousands, whom William de Beauchamp's
                                                    me
From his castle of Elmley clubbed with pikes and staves,
So that those few who floundered to the bank
Were drowned no less. But of the tempest's heart
Where Simon, like a strong tower, rose above
The cowering king, with his two-handed sword
Sweeping a deadly circle, I saw naught,
And only heard thereafter how he had fallen
Crying 'Dieu merci', while the royal craven
Uncovered by his falling, whined and whimpered:
'I am Henry of Windsor, your king—for God's sake strike
I am too old to fight'—though, in very truth   [not
He was younger than Earl Simon. And at the hour
When Montfort fell, the western sky grew dark,

[136]

o that we could not see to chant our vespers
n the abbey quire—as though the sun itself
Disdained to show so foul a deed; but fouler
Was yet to come, when the Prince's butchers dragged
His naked corpse to Evesham, and Maltravers—
Cursed be his memory!—lopped off limbs and head,
And with a grosser obscenity mutilated
Those venerable loins, making a laughing-stock
Of the grisly members, as do the Saracens
Who know no better; but this man was called Christian.
And the young prince, now King, sent that grey head
To Mortimer's wolfish mother Maud, at Wigmore,
As a warning to the Welsh. Such was the end
Of Montfort, the strong mountain of our freedoms
And fortress of our hopes . . .

                     So, sorrowfully,
tottered home to Worcester, broken in spirit
And stricken in years, to end my dwindling days
n the service of God and Our Lady, and humble prayers
For the rest of that great soul; for never again
Did I leave this cloister, and never more will leave it
Till they carry my light bones to the charnery,
And I pray that it be soon—for, even in the telling,
This tale hath mortally wearied me. Give me a sip
Of water, my son, and leave my side . . . For now
fain would sleep.

XIII

We were the fools that trudged away
From ridge and furrow of chalk and clay,
From scythe and mattock and plough and cart
To follow King Richard Lionheart:

The plodding, patient English foot
That got no wage but drink and loot
And the glory promised to them that fell
Fighting against the infidel.

We knew hunger and we knew sweat
And the scorpion desert's blinding heat;
But never once did we know dread—
We were too slow-witted, the Frenchmen said.

And never did our uncurious eyes
Widen with wonder or surprise;
For whatever they saw in foreign parts
We still had England in our hearts.

We bawled our snatch and cracked our joke
In the reek of Etna's brimstone smoke,
And coughed in clouds of sand that hid
The feet of sphinx and pyramid;

Yet ever mid alien sand and stone
Nursed a green vision of our own,
And through the hot mirage of Nile
Saw the cool watermeadow smile.

We groused and bickered and swore and wenched
And roared our bawdy songs, and drenched
Our fiery throats with Cyprus wine
And the sun-warmed fruits of Palestine;

Yet each would willingly have given
His days on earth and hopes of heaven
To plunge his cracked mouth in a pail
Of Worcester perry or Stratford ale,

And thrown their peach and fig to rot
With the sun-freckled apricot
If but his teeth might crunch the fresh
Cool crispness of a pippin's flesh;

And each would gladly have cast aside
The dusky, amorous, almond-eyed
Women of Asia, once to quench
His want in the arms of an English wench!

But they shipped us North and matched our skin
With the Damascene blades of Saladin;
So we sacked Acre and trudged on
Through sleet and snow to Ascalon,

And hunted the Saracen like a fox
From cover to cover in Hebron's rocks
Till we'd shut the heathen seed of Shem
In the blood-red walls of Jerusalem;

Where we held them girdled with steel and fire
And took an oath we would not tire
Till we set the Cross we had sworn to bear
On the brink of the Holy Sepulchre.

But while we laid that siege, the sun
Clomb to the Lion's flaming zone,
And the parched soil was cracked and cleft
Till not a blade of green was left;

And the meat we butchered, blown with flies,
Grew quick with maggots beneath our eyes;
And the drinking-pools where our water stood
Curdled and stank and turned to mud;

And the air we gaped was like the breath
Of a jackal's throat that smells of death;
For a secret murrain that had no cure
Rotted the flesh of great and poor;

And many with madness in their eyes
Stared gibbering at the white-hot skies
Where foul birds, circling overhead,
Shadowed the living and the dead,

So high they seemed no bigger than flies—
But or ever men reached their agonies
The air was thrashed by the flutterings
Of a hundred hungry noisome wings.

And the secret murrain that none could stay
Wasted and wore our strength away,
Till the Lion Heart, that had beat so bold,
Suddenly faltered and then grew cold;

And he sailed and left us to pine away
Within sight of sad Gethsemane:
Not even Christ in those darkest hours
Knew passion more desolate than ours!

While they that had lured us forth rode home
Shriven and blessed by all Christendom,
To boast of the sacrifice they made
When they bore the Cross in Christ's crusade;

And their bones lie snug in the hallowed earth
Of the villages that gave us birth,
Covered by carven effigies
With their mailed legs crossed beneath the knees;

While ours, that earned no meaner fame,
Are lost in graves without a name,
Or bleached on the unhallowed sand
Of a waste miscalled the Holy Land:

The plodding, patient English folk
That never wavered and never broke,
And knew not why they fought and fell
In the deserts of the Infidel;

That had no crown but a crown of thorn
And perished unshriven and forlorn,
And gained no glory and won no wage
But the toil of a fruitless pilgrimage.

*The Scene—though one would hardly recognize it after the inter
vening centuries—is the slope of Bredon Hill, a few hundred feet belo.
the ramparts of the Iron Age Herdsmen's camp, and not far fro.
the site of the garrulous Centurion's villa. All traces of this ha.
long since disappeared beneath thorns and brambles, which, undisturbe
by superstitious hands, have formed an impenetrable thicket. T.
plain, too, has changed. It is noticeably less densely wooded; and wher
the forest of scrub-oak once stretched unbroken, a number of clearing
can now be seen, each occupied by a village in which humble building
of daub and wattle are clustered about a church and tower and mano.
and surrounded by the cultivated land of the 'common field,' divide
into elongated strips by linchet-ridges. Although there are no hedge
rows and few elms, the landscape has lost much of its ancient wildness
and a great part of it is now deforested. On the northern horizon th
choir and nave of the Abbey of Pershore rise above the roofs of th.
little town which has grown about it, and a tall tower, as yet uncom
pleted, shows that this foundation has not yet reached the full pitc
of its pride. At the point where the Centurion and his visitor halte.
for a while to observe the view, there now stands the dwelling of Ho.
the Shepherd, a free labourer on the roll of the Abbot of Pershore. H.
home is little more than a hut consisting of a framework of rough
hewn timber filled in with mud, with a single door and two unglaze.
windows. There is no chimney: the smoke of the fire which serves fo
heating and cooking escapes as best it can from a hole in the thatch
The room's only furniture is a trestle-bed, a long narrow table maa.
of one plank of oak, and two settles of the same wood. It is a mil.
May evening, the still air is drenched with the heavy odour of hawthorn
blossom whose whiteness powders the flank of Bredon like a snowstorm
and the birds are in full song. A lazy smoke rises through the hol.
in the thatch from the fire on which Hob's supper is seething, an.
mingles a faint reek of woodsmoke with the breath of the may. Th.
owner of the house sits on a wooden settle before his door and idl.
contemplates the wide landscape which stretches beyond Severn to th.
serrated ridge of the Malverns. Hob is a lanky old man, with a mo.*

white hair, an unkempt beard, and craggy features, of a certain
rugged nobility. He is dressed in a coarse woollen tunic, and his long
legs are strapped with thongs of leather. The blue eyes which brood
on the distance become suddenly aware of a solitary figure toiling up
the slope of the hill towards him. It is that of a spare man, as lanky
as himself, tonsured, and clothed in a torn cassock which is tucked
about his loins with a girdle of rope. Over his shoulder he carries a
long staff, with a bundle slung from it; but in spite of his shambling
gait, he is evidently a man of unusual strength; for he makes nothing
of the steep pitch and climbs it without slackening his pace. As he
draws near, his ill-shaven face lights up, and he waves his free hand to
Hob. It is a grim, sad face, but marked by a curious innocence and
simplicity and an air of refinement hardly in keeping with his personal
uncouthness. Hob returns his salute and rises to meet him.

THE CLERK:

Good evening to you, friend. Can you spare a traveller
shelter from storm and harbourage for the night?
Black clouds are massed on Malvern, and the tempest
Will soon be on us.

HOB:

I have no great liking for strangers. From your habit
I see you are clerkly. You should rather have rapped
At the rich Abbey of Pershore than thrust your company
On poor folk who know you not.

THE CLERK:

When I was a lad
Hearts were warmer in Worcestershire. Am I so aged
That you know me not, Hob of the Hill?

HOB:

My sight is dimmed,
And my heart grown cold with sorrows. You have my name,
But your face is strange to me.

THE CLERK:

Cast your thought backward
To an evening such as this thirty years ago

[143]

And one who halted here on his road from Malvern
To his father's at Wychwood on Cotswold. Do you not min
A lanky lad whom people called Long Will?

HOB:

What? Bist thee William Langland? That is a name
Known to the ears of many; but little I thought
To see you again in these parts, though I should have know
[yo
By your lambering gait and your gown. Ay, your face is no
[change
But I reckoned you had turned Londoner for good and all
And forsook old friends in Worcestershire. Come, sit you dow
Ease those long shanks and tell me how you have fared;
And then we will share a snack of boiled bacon and drink
A pint of perry together. That's the best I can offer;
But you're welcome to all I have. What brings you here
In these changeful times?

THE CLERK:

Alas, I am trudging back
To my prison-house in London, the land of strangers,
With empty belly and purse. But why I am here
Is a different matter. When April came, and I saw
The sally-buds puffed with silk in the water meadows
By Fleet and Tyburn, the sap began to stir
In my limbs and irked my feet, that are corned by the cobble
Of stone-paved streets, to tread on green grass again;
And my head was ravished in sleep by taunting visions
Of Temeside cherry-blow, and white clouds sailing
Over dappled Malvern, and primrose-banks
And nodding daffodils and the smell of the may,
Till I could abide it no longer; and so, one morning
When Spring blew through the city, I stuffed my pack
And kissed my dear wife Kitty and little Calotte,
And strode out over Chiltern, blithe as a bee
Winging to clover verges. And when I had trudged

[144]

our days on end, with a gay and humble heart
nd my muddled brain washed crystal by clean air
nd sweet verse chiming in time to my step, and I saw
rom Cotswold's brow those hills I loved as a boy,
hen fell I down on my knees and gave Heaven thanks
hat God still bides in Worcestershire. Yet this paradise
ures but the breath of Spring; and when the daffodil
ung his gold head, and the cherry-blow was dashed
nd hawthorn rusted on Malvern—then I knew
hat this miracle was over, with one more Spring
otched on my dwindling tally, and turned my face
ike Adam, from the angel-guarded gates,
ome to my dusty livelihood.

HOB:
What make you there, Will?

THE CLERK:
ly bare living, by murmuring of *Placebos*
nd *Domine diriges* and the Seven Psalms
or the good of my lean purse and better men's souls.
ometimes I toil at copying of crabbed texts
a Paul's Walk for fat lawyers, that like leeches
uck blood from quarrelsome fools; but oftenest
stray the idle streets, telling the rosary
)f beaded words that I have strung together,
ear after year and bead on bead, to fashion
ly vision of Piers Plowman—which is but the vision
)f poor Long Will. Often folk gape to see me
o muttering on my way, and in the stews
)f Tyburn raddled Flanders bawds will set
heir curs to snap my ankles, and rock to see
ly draggled hems in tatters. Often I lean
y tavern-doors to catch the blasphemies
)f sots and gluttons. Often my cheek is spattered
Vith mud thrown from the horses' hooves of lords

Riding to Westminster. Often I mingle
With chaffering crowds on Garlic-hythe, and routs
Of holiday prentices making cudgel-play
Or roaring to the cock-fight—yet all these folk,
Gentle or simple, fair or foul, are meat
For my imaginings, and find their place
In the stringing of my rosary, though many
Defy my cunning. Sometimes, when I have lain
Starven with cold in my garret of Cornhill,
A brave line sparks the night with lettering
Of fire, and I must rouse my wife and light
A rush to set it down by—but, like as not,
By dawn the gleam has faded, and the faggots
That flared so bright have fallen to grey tinder.
Yet still my rosary lengthens, and by long fingering
I think the beads grow smooth. 'Tis a strange life
We poets live; for half the things we dream
Slip back into the darkness whence they flickered
Like marsh-lights from the swamp of sleep to lure
Our minds in muddy flounderings. I had been happier
If I had not been learned, and had kept sheep
On Bredon Hill like you, Hob. I have grown old,
And wearier than my years warrant: a gnarled thorn,
Niggard of blossom now . . .

HOB:

Yet your Spring's burgeons
Bloomed not in vain. Piers' coulter has driven deep,
And the wordy seed you scattered, borne on the breath
Of common men and blown from mouth to mouth,
Hath fallen in fertile furrows, and sprouted valiant
As winter wheat in a mild season. Rightly
You dub yourself a thorn: your spines have pricked
A mort of bloated bubbles, and made folk laugh
Who had little stomach for laughter—or much else
In these unhappy days.

[146]

THE CLERK:
            Enough, enough
Of Piers and him who made him! Tell me, friend,
How you have fared these many years, and your wife
And your three lads? You see my memory
Is not so flimsy, though by now I reckon
They have children of their own.

HOB:
            All gone, all gone . . .
A careworn man am I, who pines alone
Like an old stag in the thickets. It was the Death,
The Black Death, that widowed and bereft me
Of wife and child.

THE CLERK:
            That was the deadliest frost
That ever nipped green England. Well do I know it;
For I was lodged in Cornhill when the Pestilence
First broke on London—where the dead lay drifted
Like Autumn leaves in Wychwood, and Winter's snow
Fell on them yet unburied: street and alley,
Charnel and graveyard, clogged with Christian carrion,
Till Bishop Ralph, out of Paul's patrimony,
Bought No Man's Land in Spittle Croft, and dug
Plague-pits to hold the nameless. Fifty thousand
Had perished by Pentecost. Yet I moved among
The mounds of dead unscathed,—having made strict vows
To Blessed Saint Petronel—ay, and carried many
On my bent back to heave them in the pits,
With my mouth and nostrils muffled in singed rags
To stem the stench of death. In those dread months
I saw strange sights, and listened to stranger words;
For, mark you, Bishop Ralph, seeing how multitudes
Went straight to hell unshriven, gave power to clerks
Of lesser orders to hear the last confessions

Of folk in dread of death—and I, who hearkened,
Reeled back in horror from the brimstone pits
Of black iniquity that yawned in souls
Of innocent-seeming men. Yet ever my mind,
Being given to tale-making, strained at the shackles
Of secrecy; and, but that my lips were locked,
I could have writ such tales as young Dan Chaucer,
With his new-fangled measures, never dreamed of;
Such loves, hates, lusts, torments and vanities
As would have made all Christendom hang on my lips
And plead for more.

                 There is another story
I might have made had I been younger, telling
Of how the Death began: how, in mid-Asia,
The hordes of Tartary besieged a city
Called Caffa, and, as they lay encamped about it,
Sudden the Pestilence smote them—how, in revenge
For what they deemed a hostile magic, they loaded
Their catapults with corpses, and hurled their dead
Into the leagured town; how certain merchants
Of Genoa, fleeing from that terror, carried
The seeds to Italy, and how thence it crept
By Avenon, through Gascony, to Bordeaux,
And so by ship to Melcombe in the shire
Of Dorset. That would have made a tale to freeze
The blood of generations, and stamped my fame
So deep, King Richard might have granted me
The boons he gave Dan Chaucer and his Philippa:
A pitcher of wine a day, ten pounds of pension,
And the Petty Customs of Wine in the Port of London!
But that will never be. You see how fond
Ambition's dreams have made me: the very pestilence
Brings grist to my mind's millstones . . .

                 Forgive me, friend
I had not guessed the Death had dealt so foully
With you in Worcestershire.

HOB:

Raise but your eyes
And scan the fields; the half our fathers won
By the patient plough has fallen back to grass,
A waste of riotous weeds: pass through our villages
And mark the sagging thatch, the mess of nettle
And bramble tangling hearths where homely gleeds
Once burned! Go to the mills of Avon and see
The broken sluices, the still wheels shagged with moss,
The rumbling gritstones moveless, the very rats
Grown gaunt for lack of grain. See how the tower
Of Pershore bites the sky like a broken tooth
As witness of our want. There is no dwelling
Nigh Bredon Hill but mourns the ruthless reaping
Of that black harvest and its aftermath
Of misery. We have neither will nor strength
To mould our sorry world anew. All England
Goes mourning to the grave of all her hopes
And hears no passing bell—for they that tolled
Lie mouldering with the rest; and there's no remedy
That men can see. The kite has built her nest
In the Tree of Life and caws for carrion,
While lords in London drown her hungry scritches
With drunken song—and you—you sniff the may
To mask the taint of death.

THE CLERK:

You humble me.
Tell me your tale; I'll make a song of it
To prick uneasy consciences.

HOB:

Songs? Songs?
Throats that are clemmed with hunger have no spittle
For aught but *Dies Irae!* Yet will I tell you
How this fair-seeming roseland, on which May smiles
So soft, within is cankered.

You know well

How in old time, we villeins of each manor
Paid our lords' dues in labour—so many days
At plough, haysel and harvest—and, in return,
Held our own strips of field, and shared the commonage
In the waste; and none complained—we were merry folk,
With ale a penny a gallon and hogs in plenty
Routing the woods for acorns. Then some lords
Impatient of our slow husbandry, made bargains
To pay our toil in silver. Such was the poison
First marred our peace; for hired men, over-spending
The pence they earned, light-headed with false freedom,
Forsook their forbears' settled ways and left
Their plots to fallow; and much good land lay waste
While they that should have tilled it went their ways
As labourers, bound neither to lord nor land
But to their new-filled purses, faring wastefully
In prodigal seasons, and in years of want
Sullen and starved . . .

               Then came the winnowing
Of the Black Murrain: when not one man in three
Was spared to drive a plough. The dwindled tilth
Shrank yet more piteously. That year's harvest stood
Unreaped and sprouting on the stalk. Loose cattle,
Straying unherded, trampled through fields of grain
Rotted untimely and unground, while Famine
Grinned at our door, and money earned or saved
By those who had boasted freedom (having lost
The land that made them free) was not enough
To buy bread for their brats. And, mark you, their lords
Were in no better case, seeing that the King
Still swinged them with fierce taxes to arm and feed
His fighting-men in France—and not one farthing
Dropped in their coffers save they sold their corn!
But when they called for reapers, the landless folk
Laughed in their faces: "What? You would pay us twopence
For a day's harvesting, when our children starve

nd corn is scarce and rye-bread costs us treble
Of what we gave before the Pestilence?
Nay, sixpence is our hire; and if you grudge it,
Then let your harvest rot!"
                                        Then all the gentry
Huddled together, and rode forth to London,
Cozening Parliament to frame a Statute
That bound all labourers to take the wage
They had won in days of plenty, and their masters
To pay no more—a penny a day for haymaking,
Threepence, at most, for reaping—and if they bowed not
To this decree, then should the lords pay forfeit
And labourers, bond or free, be haled to justice
And cast in prison. Yet still the harvest lay
Ingarnered; for land-bound folk were few, and landless
Had naught to lose, while they that were clapped in jail
Could swing no sickle. So the Hunger grew,
While houses fell to rubble, and the fallows
Lay foul with dock and thistle, and clogged ditches
Turned land in good heart sour. Then our taskmasters,
Still vexed by the King's taxes, grew ever more greedy
Of petty tolls and penalties: each man must render
A fine when his daughter wedded; all must carry
The corn they grew to their lord's mill, and pay
A monstrous fee for grinding; none could oppose
Oppression—since no land-bound serf might plead
Against his lord in the King's courts, or leave
The land that failed to feed him. Thus, desperate men
Banded themselves together and took flight,
Straying from town to town and shire to shire
In search of labour where none knew their names
Nor whence they came—so half England was harried
By homeless, lawless men, who dwelt like wolves
In the woods, and preyed on simple villages
To filch a livelihood; and our empty fields
Became a wilderness . . .

[151]

THE CLERK:
Yet you bode here on Bredon?

HOB:
I was too old and sad for such adventuring,
And had no land to bind me; yet my roots
Are so deep-set that, if they had been wrenched
From this dear soil that bred me, I should have pined
And perished.

THE CLERK:
　　　　　Tell me, then: what is the cure
For all these ills?

HOB:
　　　　　There is no sovereign remedy
That I can tell, nor counsel save the cold comfort
That old wives give to a young girl in labour:
"You must be worse before you are better!" And yet
I feel the first pangs of a great travail begin
To shake me. Mark how yon storm shadows the Chase
From Malvern foot to Ripple, and how the wind
That runs before it tosses the hawthorn-blow
And turns the hornbeam white with terror! Thus
Restless, the storm-wind wafts through England now—
Though whence it comes and whither it will carry us
I know not. But this I know: there is no secret
Cranny or nook it has not pierced; no bush
Nor humble bent but feels it. First it bore
But a vague whispering, such as those measured words
Minted by Piers your Plowman, that kindle the mind
And smoulder there unquenched, like a red ember
Kindling unquiet heat. But of late we have heard
Words homelier than yours, pointed with rhymes
That stamp them on the memory, which are made
By one called 'Jack the Miller'—such as these:

'*John the Miller hath ground small, small, small.*
The King's son of heaven shall pay for all.

[152]

Be ware or ye be wo;
Know your friend from your foe.
Have enough, and say "Ho!"
And do well and better and flee sin
And seek peace and hold therein
And so bid John Trueman and all his fellows.'

THE CLERK:

These are lame verses, with neither sense nor measure.
Jack Miller is no poet.

HOB:

For the measure,
I have but little knowledge; but the sense
Is plain to common folk. There is another
Word that has passed through all the countryside,
Whispered from mouth to mouth:

John Schep, some time Saint Mary's priest of York, and now of
Colchester, greeteth well John Nameless and John Miller and
John Carter, and biddeth them that they beware of guile in the
borough and stand together in God's name, and biddeth Piers
Plowman go to his work, and chastise well Hob the Robber, and
take with you John Trueman, and no mo; and look you sharp to
one-head and no mo.'

THE CLERK:

He has borrowed my Piers Plowman without leave.
The rest is windy raving; I can see
No meaning in it.

HOB:

Then you are duller-witted
Than ever I thought. I will tell you its meaning:
That the withers of common folk, who till for others
The soil that is their birthright, are galled to the bone
By the bonds that fetter them; and that some few
Who boast more wits than the many have asked this question:
'Since we are one in Christ, and in his Kingdom
There are neither bond nor free, but Adam's heritage

Is rightly shared by all his breed, how comes it
That most men fare afoot, perished with hunger,
While others ride full-fed and spend the substance
Won by their brethren's toil in waste and gluttony?
Answer us that!"

THE CLERK:
This has been fully answered
By Master John Wycliffe of Oxford, in the treatise
De Dominio Civili. All things, he says,
Belong to God, and are held of him directly;
Yet what men hold is only truly held
If they be righteous. The tenure of the wicked
Is unsubstantial; and what they seem to hold
Is never theirs in truth—seeing that the righteous
Already, in virtue of their righteousness,
Are seized of all God's heritage. Wherefore
It is idle for the righteous to dispute
Possession of what the wicked seem but to hold,
And have no seizin in. Further: if righteous men
Serve wicked lords and masters, for all that wickedness
They owe no less obedience; since it is written:
Render unto Cæsar the things that are Cæsar's
And unto God the things that are God's.

HOB:
That is no answer
To stop mouths clemmed with famine, but a mere juggling
With words and twisting of scripture that sounds strange
On the lips of one whose tongue was once as sharp
As a crab-apple and rough as a perry-pear
That would rasp the roof from your mouth!

THE CLERK:
Both brew good liquor . . .
Yet you are right: when I was young I was teart
As Tewkesbury cider; but marriage melloweth man,
And the sweets of cities are as raisins or honey

Dropped in the cask; so, when the froth of youth
Hath bubbled from the bung-hole, the liquor softens
To a cheerful smoothness—though, mark you, with age
It may grow ropey and turn again to vinegar
That hath no virtue but to pickle neats'-tongues
And sets men's teeth on edge.

HOB:
              A rougher answer
Will yet be given, and sooner than you guess,
By men who deal in deeds, and having known
Hunger in freedom, deem it preferable
To plenty in slavery. *The wind bloweth
Whither it listeth;* and this wind bloweth strong
And shrewd out of the East, where Jack the Miller
And his bitter kith have sworn to stand together
To see the new wrongs righted, and give men back
The ancient liberties wrested at Runnymede
From John Sansterre. And when that wind has gathered
And the storm breaks, the towers of privilege
Will crash before it as the walls of Jericho
Fell when God's people shouted. They shall no more
Withstand it than fond Canute could quell the tide,
Or we two, perched on Bredon, stay those ranks
Of heaped cloud charging on us. (Hark! Already
Low thunder rumbles in the Vale, and lightning
Rips their black bellies! We had best take shelter
Before we are caught.) But mark you this, Long Will!
Though this storm sweep all England, and in its wake
Tall oaks and elms lie toppled, torn from their roots
Or lopped of rotten timber, lowlier growths
And nearer to the soil, as we and ours,
Shall lose no leaf; and when the tempest passeth,
Stand glistering with raindrops in the May sun
And watch the coloured span of God's bow arching
Blue Cotswold . . .
        Come, then. Hasten! The first drops fall.

[155]

XV

John Ball was moulded from the clays
Of the cold vale of Ouse,
Blunt of speech and bold of gaze
Great of bone and thews,
And through his bitter blood there ran
The gall of a lonely, landless man.

He dwelt in plenty among the priests
In Saint Mary's Abbey of York,
But had no stomach for their feasts
Nor patience for their talk
Of heaven, when pestilence and dearth
Painted hell on English earth,

Where he saw the ermined gentry ride
Warm-clad as they had lain,
While folk that furnished them their pride
Trudged cold through wind and rain—
And their very dogs were better fed
Than the brats of the poor who whined for bread;

Where logs that warmed fur-slippered feet
Were hewn by frozen hands,
And the wealth they spent on wine and meat
Was wrung from stolen lands
By landless folk whose sires had won
Those very fields from barren stone,

But were now serfs, bounden to the soil
And galled beneath the yoke
Of the few who battened on their toil
Till body and soul were broke,
And their starved carcases at last
Into the nameless charnels cast,

While orphans gleaned the hungry lands
In ragged multitudes,
And fugitives in lawless bands
Like wolves lay in the woods,
Prowling forth at night to prey
On folk no better fed than they.

So from Ball's anguished heart there broke
At length a gathering tide
Of long-pent anger, and he spoke
His bitter mind, and cried:
"When Adam delved and Eve span,
Who was then the gentleman?

"For we are all God's sons by birth,
And save for mortal sin
Each one inheriteth God's earth
And all that is therein;
And if, in this, we flout God's will,
What wonder that the world goes ill?"

Then (for this doctrine touched their greeds)
The monks arose in wrath;
They stripped John Ball of his clerkly weeds
And drove him from the North,
Bounden to silence by the strict
Ban of their Bishop's interdict.

So he kicked the clods of his native clay
From his shoes and sought the South;
And they reckoned themselves well-rid that they
Had stopped this blabbing mouth
That dared to speak forth without fear
The truths they hated most to hear.

Southward he wandered without haste
To the agued Essex fen,
Lurking in hovels of the waste
With landless, hopeless men
Whose thoughts, for utter want, had grown
Darker and bitterer than his own;

And though no bishop would let him preach
In temples made with hands,
Men flocked to hear the forthright speech
That a plain folk understands
Better than mumbled Latin read
By priests who give them stones for bread;

For his rede was no fine-tempered sword,
But a bludgeon of tough oak
That hammered-in each uncouth word
Till those down-trodden folk,
Dumb with toil and blind with pain,
Blinked their bleared eyes and saw again;

Till hapless men in hundreds heard
The words John Ball had said,
Till from the fens the ferment stirred
Like brewsters' barm in bread,
And spreading forth from East to West
Leavened the hearts of the oppressed

And the hapless hundreds all agreed
As one man to maintain
The bare rights gained at Runnymede
And take their own again,
That freedom of their native earth
Be given to men of English birth;

[158]

Till, when the young king's officers
Sent his tax-gatherers forth
For gold to feed their foreign wars,
All Essex rose in wrath
And beat them from the shire, and sent
Word to their brother-men in Kent;

And starved serfs gathered everywhere
As the shire of Kent awoke,
And Canterbury and Rochester
Roared to heaven in smoke
While half the harvest's garnered stores
Lay spilt upon the threshing-floors;

And starven Kent, with pike and flail,
Swept through the Medway plains,
To break the walls of Maidstone jail
Where John Ball lay in chains,
And set him free and bore him on
To the barred gates of London town,

Where, on the bank of Thames, the rout
Surged like a foamy sea:
They burnt the palace of Lambeth out
And sacked the Marshalsea,
Calling on them that kept the gate
To give up London to its fate.

Then did the folk of London cower,
Seeing they were bestead;
For the King was shut within the Tower,
And the Queen, his mother, fled,
And the merchants had no spunk to fight
Against a cause they knew was right;

F*

So Alderman Sybele, who stood alone
And was scared for his own skin,
Sent the great drawbridge rattling down
To let the rabble in:
And the gutters bubbled with a flood
Of broached wine frothed with human blood.

For dazed men knew not what they did
And cared not whom they slew,
And nothing recked so they be rid
Of the stony-hearted crew
That had docked them of their dwindled wage
And robbed them of their heritage.

So, with no lust but to destroy,
Fierce Kent surged through the street
To burn the Palace of Savoy
And the Flemings of the Fleet,
While, from the North, the turbid spate
Of Essex thundered through Aldgate;

Till London was a shambles lit
With flame and drenched in gore,
And blood and fire in fury beat
On the bastions of the Tower,
Where the King, with his craven court,
Huddled in fear, but could do naught.

Then young King Richard rose and spoke:
"How should a king disown
These rude, benighted countryfolk
Who are subjects of his crown?
Rather will I ride forth to find
What maggot rots my people's mind.

"And if I deem their wrongs well-found,
Then will I do them right;
For so I swore when I was crowned,
And must fulfil the plight
I pledged them as their lawful king
To give them justice in everything."

So the King, by Aldersgate, rode out
To Smithfield Square; and when
They saw this noble child, that rout
Of simple, hapless men
Forgot their bitter wrongs, and cried:
"The King, the King is on our side!"

And Walter Tyler, who was their chief,
Set forth their just demands;
And the young king promised them relief
From tax, and that the lands
And forests should be theirs once more,
And lords no longer grind the poor.

But while he spoke this soothing word
And granted them their due,
The Mayor of London stripped his sword
And ran Wat Tyler through;
And when they saw their leader dead,
The crowd, bewildered, broke and fled;

And his aldermen called out the wards
To smite them in the rear,
And the men of London drenched their swords
In such a massacre
As the shambles of Smithfield had never seen
And never will know again, I ween;

And through all England the butchers rode
From Suffolk to Somerset
Wherever a feeble ember glowed
Of the gleed John Ball had lit;
And summer fields, from York to Kent,
Smoked with the blood of the innocent.

They caught John Ball in Coventry
And dragged him South in shame,
They broke his neck on the gallows-tree
And quartered his lean frame;
And they brought his carcase to London, and set
His head on the bridge-house parapet;

It grinned there, shrivelling day by day,
That mouth of speech bereft,
Till weather had sloughed the lips away
And naught but bone was left,
And careless folk who passed the gate
Thought no more of John Ball's fate.

And now the guard-house gate is gone
And razed the parapet;
But that mouth still asks the question
That none dares answer yet:
When Adam delved and Eve span,
Who was then the gentleman?

XVI

Interlude

Behold a more tempestuous age
Than England ever yet hath known:
See the embattled Roses rage
In tumult round a redeless throne:
See all her braggart chivalry
Driven from Gascony and Maine
Headlong to the narrow sea,
Dragging in their dishevelled train
The louts that laughed to burn the Maid,
Yet faltered when the shining lance
Of bold Dunois and Guesclin's blade
Flashed and smote them out of France:
Whose rustic wits could understand
No cleaner trades than rape and plunder;
Who fell upon their native land
And tore her living limbs asunder,
Who sold their mercenary might
To them that bid the most, and bled
Till the Red Rose was blanched white
And the White Rose blotched with red!
See the fierce falcons from the harsh
Eyries of Mortimer soar to fling
Their terror from the Powys March
To Verulam, where the hapless King
In predatory talons caught
Is rapt and caged and set at naught!

Yet while that changeful battle swayed
The bells of Alban's minster rang
For Vespers, and the barley-blade
From Verulam's buried ruins sprang
Enriched with death anew to yield
Life from the trampled battlefield.

See how the angry queen bereft
Rallies her broken host and falls
On York and Neville in Ludford cleft
And holds them locked in Ludlow's walls,
And the fierce Red Roses whirl away
The White Rose and the Ragged Staff
Like vapours blown at break of day
From Temeside, or wind-winnowed chaff
That is flurried from a threshing-floor:
Till Teme is sullied with the stain
Of death, as when dense waters pour
From Corvedale red with Lammas rain!

Yet even in that bitter hour
When York was broken and betrayed,
The masons perched on Ludlow Tower
Plied their patient craft, and laid
Course upon course the quarried stones
That made that miracle of grace
To bear the mellow chime whose tones
Waver above the market-place.

But see: the Ragged Staff returning
Ravages the midland plain:
See Northampton sacked and burning
And the crazed King caught again!
See the resurgent White Rose wilt
At Wakefield, where the rebel blood
Of stubborn York himself is spilt—

While March, last hawk of that fierce brood,
Wings to the West and whets the sword
That shall avenge his father's loss
On Pembroke's levies, where the ford
Straddles the Lugg at Mortimer's Cross!

Yet even as the fallen hopes
Of Lancaster lay drowning there,
The woodman's axe on Lingen's slopes
Rang through the February air,
And in the frosty folds that lie
On Lingen's sheepwalks, shepherds kept
Their starlit vigil, till the sky
Grew dim with dawn, and turned and slept
In peace, with neither ruth nor cares
For a quarrel that was none of theirs.

Once more on Verulam see the wrath
Of the Red Rose flame—as Neville reels
Driven in terror to the North
With Lancaster upon his heels,
Nor stays his rout nor stands his ground
Till the royal roses are laid low
By York's usurper, newly crowned,
At Towton in the crimson snow;
Till Neville's bitter brother slew
Percy at Hedgeley Moor, and caged
That fierce Queen, Margaret of Anjou!
So, for a while, the fires that raged
Through England's length and breadth are spent
In a smoulder of sullen discontent.

Yet even as the arrowy hail
Mingled with snow on helm and shield,
The plowmen of the Towton Vale
Led their patient teams afield;

[165]

And shepherds on the heathery moor
Of Hexham heard the plaintive bleat
Of yeanling lambs above the roar
Of battle raging at their feet,
Carried the orphans in their arms
To the warm ingles of their farms,
And laid them by the smoking peat.

See how the germ of vengeance breaks
From bloody seed at Hexham sown,
When Neville's treachery unmakes
The king he made, and on the throne
Plants the weak fool he first forswore!
See, nourished by the dynast's hand,
The Rose of Lancaster once more
Flaunt above a sullen land—
Till York, supplanted and betrayed,
Rides from the North to claim his right
And the Kingmaker is unmade
On Easter Eve in Barnet fight,
While his vanquisher pursues the rout
Of Barnet to the Severn Sea,
And stamps the last red embers out
In the bloody meadow at Tewkesbury!

Yet, while the sun of Lancaster
Blood-red in Severn's bosom sets,
The fishermen from Tewkesbury weir
Launch their boats and stake their nets
In channels where allice and salmon run
To seek their gravelly spawning-redd,
And little recked who lost or won
The battle so their mouths were fed;

And graziers from the wattled folds
Of Cotswold carried bales of fleece
To stow them in the greedy holds
Of Flanders gaping at the quays,
And rode back to their windy wold
On horse-packs stuffed with Flemish gold.

So, for long time, a bloodless truce
Broods on an exhausted realm—
Till dying York in death lets loose
His crippled brother, to overwhelm
Kinsman and foe in one red flood
Of indiscriminate slaughter, wading
To climb the throne knee-deep in blood;
Till the White Rose with the Red Rose fading
Fell together on Bosworth field,
Where the cold craft of Richmond brought
The savage Crouchback to his knees,
And in his brain's shrewd smithy wrought
The double emblem that annealed
Those two tempestuous flowers in one,
And with a kindlier wisdom sealed
His merciful dominion
In the long Tudor peace.

Yet while those barbarous warriors died
At Bosworth for a tawdry gage,
The patient printer Caxton plied
His craft, and from the virgin page
The magic of immortal words
Shone with a beauty to outlast
The scars their transitory swords
Graved on the tablets of the past;
And while ambitious dynasts broke
Their thews to prop a transient throne,
The spirit of the common folk

Flowered in imperishable stone—
When men whose names will ne'er be known,
The rude, anonymous builders, raised
Their village belfries to the skies
That God might be the better praised;
And master-glaziers' jewelled dyes
Shot the gloomy Norman vault
With shafts of sapphire and cobalt,
And from their silvery clerestories
Shed floods of radiance and fires
Of ruby on the shadowy quires;
And while the ruthless baronage
Flew at one another's throats,
The folk who paid the builders' wage
Gathered within their manor-moats
The meed of husbandry that heaped
Their granaries with the spoils of peace,
And shepherded their flocks and reaped
The harvest of the golden fleece;
And when the flames of that fierce age
With Bohun and Mortimer were spent,
These plain folk claimed the heritage
Of honourable toil, content
To see a soberer England rise
From the charred ruins of the old,
And welcome, with undazzled eyes,
The dawning of an Age of Gold.

XVII

On the second day of the month of May
When the cuckoo cried in the woods of Leigh,
The *Matthew* shipped her trade and slipped
Her mooring-cable from Bristol Quay.

Bristol-made and Bristol-manned,
With a crew as tough as any afloat,
She sailed that day in search of land,
And her captain's name was John Cabote:

A salty, swarthy Venetian,
Born of that race of roving men
That know the seas from Matapan
To the whirlpool of the Lofoden,

From the hungry fangs of Finisterre
And the sun-white sands of the Azores
To the banks of dripping fog that blear
The crags that girdle Iceland's shores.

Yet they who watched the *Matthew* drift
Baremasted on the falling tide
That ebbed through Avon's oozy cleft,
And hailed us from the waterside

To speed our parting, little guessed
(And we, her crew, no more than they)
The hazards of the lonely quest
That lured John Cabote on his way:

How, cold as was his outward eye,
There ever burned within his brain
A vision of new lands that lie
Westward of the Spanish main,

[169]

And a lust for landfalls stranger still
Than fiery Hecla's girdling ice:
For he saw the island of Brazille
And far Cipango's Isles of Spice,

Where, in a palace paved with gold
The Great Khan wields his awful sway
On slavish multitudes untold
In the seven Cities of Cathay.

Over Avon's oozy bed
We drifted seaward mile on mile
Till we cleared the bluffs of Portishead
And weathered Lundy Isle;

And hoisted sail at the tide's turn
Where the last known headlands one by one
With the loom of Lundy fell astern,
And we laid our course on the sinking sun

That set with never a sail in sight
Nor ever a single landward gleam
As the *Matthew* bore on through the night
With the lodestar dipped on her starboard beam.

Through empty leagues, with never a speck
Of sail, a week we ran close-hauled,
And a short sea spewed the after-deck
With icy sheets of emerald,

Till, where a haze of shredded spray
Whitened the fringes of Cape Clear,
The brisk North Easter died away
And the cold wind began to veer;

And for a second week, the wrath
Of a warm gale in the tropics bred
Drove us reeling to the North
With the drunken lodestar full ahead.

[170]

The hot wind in the halyards screamed
The wild wind stripped the shrouds,
The reefed sails split because of it
And were blown away like clouds;

It carried the foremast by the board
And cracked the mainsail-boom:
We could do naught but thank the Lord
At least we had sea-room.

Too dazed were we to care or ask
How soon our end might be,
As the *Matthew*, like a broken cask,
Plunged in the pits of sea,

Or like a spar of driftwood clung
To the wave's glassy cheek,
And climbed, and for a moment hung
Poised on the combing peak,

Straddled with bow and stern in air,
Enough to break her back:
And as the *Matthew* shuddered there,
We heard the keelson crack;

We looked to see the whole hull riven
And her timbers fly apart,
And vowed our sinful souls to heaven
With fear in every heart;

Till, strange as was the miracle
Christ wrought in Galilee,
The gale that so misused us fell,
And with it fell the sea

To a creaming swell as gentle grown
As a mother that rocks her babe;
And we checked our course anew, by stone
And needle and astrolabe.

[171]

Into the empty West we had sailed,
Three hundred leagues almost,
When the soft breeze from the South'ard failed,
And I smelt the breath of frost;

An icy Arctic current set
Upon our starboard bow,
Till the limp sails with fog were wet
And sprent with flurried snow.

The breath of yet-unfallen snows
Stiffened our clammy hair;
It crept into our mouths and froze
Our breath upon the air.

Blindly through fog the *Matthew* lurched
Till Cabote's cabin-boy
Sebastian, in the crow's nest perched,
Shouted 'Land ahoy!'

Then all the crew with one accord
Ran to the bows and blessed
Sweet Mary, Mother of our Lord,
Who loves poor seamen best;

But as I peered and arched my hand
To shade my straining eyes,
I knew this landfall was no land
But isles of floating ice.

Like the risen ghosts of mountains vast
In deeps of ocean drowned,
Their white-robed shapes came drifting past
Without a sigh or sound:

Without a sigh, without a sound
That ears of man could hear,
Those silent spectres gathered round
Like mutes about a bier;

And the seeping vapours that they shed
From icy flank and peak
Fell like the fingers of the dead
Upon each bloodless cheek.

Shrouded in snow and cered in veils
Of mist they loomed above:
They stole the wind from our slack sails
So that we could not move;

And the foolish whispered words we spoke
To bate our mortal dread
Backward in mocking echoes broke
And bellowed overhead.

So, clamped within that cruel vice,
We floated as the snow-light fell,
And waited for the grinding ice
To crunch us like a filbert-shell.

Huddled on the glazing deck,
We brooded on our hopeless plight,
And heard the riven icebergs crack
Like thunder round us in the night,

Till the dim snow-light paled again,
And a huge phantom of the sun
Rose wanly from the watery plain,
And lo!—the ice was gone!

A warm waft filled the frozen sails
And shed their crusted rime,
As the *Matthew* dipped her bows and crept
Into a kindlier clime.

Two hundred leagues and more we sailed
On the same westward course,
Till, through a haze of surf, we hailed
The sight of unknown shores,

Where the tall shape of a lonely cape
Shadowed a woody strand;
And the Master christened the cape, St. John's,
And the shores the New Found Land.

So we broached a keg of Gascony
To drink John Cabote's health,
Who had brought us safe through the icy seas
To lands of untold wealth

Where our eyes, he told, might soon behold
Those fabled Cities of Cathay
Where common streets were paved with gold
And flowers bloomed alway;

Where fruits hung down from blossomed trees
And bright wings flashed through groves of spice,
And sea-worn men might take their ease
In airs of paradise.

Such were the vain delights we planned
And such the empty hopes we nursed,
And guessed not that our New Found Land
Was desert and accurst:

For naught was there but a wilderness
Of barren rock, and trackless wood
Where no sound broke the silences
Of a deathlike solitude

But the boom of rollers on the beach
And the scream of seabirds overhead;
That awful silence muted speech
And crushed our hearts with dread.

Yet, though we spake not, every man
Saw panic written plain
In his comrades' eyes, and turned and ran
Back to the boats again.

Three weeks the *Matthew* southward bore,
Hugging that haunted coast;
Yet none that landed ever saw
So much as a man's ghost,

Nor any footprint but his own,
Nor any work of human hands
But a netting-needle of carved bone
Cast on the wave-ribbed sands;

Nor any curl of smoke by day
Nor glint of fire by night:
And our greedy visions thinned away
Like phantoms, out of sight.

Thus in our hearts a hatred grew
For this homeless faring without end
And a longing for the ways we knew,
For wife and child and friend.

So we begged our captain John Cabote
To cease his fruitless quest,
And he gybed and put the ship about
And set the course due East.

The elder bloomed on Clifton Down
And the cuckoo was flown from the woods of Leigh
When we saw the roofs of Bristol Town
And stepped ashore on Bristol Quay,

Where merchant folk that thronged the port
Stood agape on every hand
To see what booty we had brought
Back from the New Found Land.

But their curious faces fell, to know
That booty we had none,
And that all the treasure we could show
Was a netting-needle of bone;

And that all the marvels we could bring
Their eager ears was nothing more
Than a tale of bootless voyaging
And of a barren shore.

And now the *Matthew* of Bristol plies
A trade of greater gain,
For she carries the rich merchandise
Of Gascony and Spain;

But though Cabote his pension got
And we had but our wage,
Yet would I fain put forth again
On such a pilgrimage:

For oft, as in my bunk I dream,
Rocked within hail of friendlier land,
I hear the homeless seabirds scream
Above that haunted strand,

And I smell the mould of the forest sod
That never human eyes nor feet
Save ours alone have seen or trod,
And find it strangely sweet;

And my nights are lit by the wild gleam
Of the passion that beguiles
The hearts of islanders to dream
Of undiscovered isles,

Of chasms that no lead can sound
And deserts never crossed,
And the search for what no man hath found
And the finding of the lost;

And in those dreams I grope my way
North-westward through the grinding ice
To the Seven Cities of Cathay
And the fabled Isles of Spice.

XVIII

Once more the Scene is Worcestershire. To the skylark's eye the
e of the land on which Hob of the Hill and Will Langland looked
wn does not seem greatly changed in a hundred and forty years. In
foreground the tower of Pershore Abbey, then unfinished, has now
ached its full height, and the extent of the monastic buildings betokens
dignity of a rich and powerful community—already doomed, did
y but know it, to untimely dispersal. The wild region of Malvern
ase remains much as it was, and the area of tilth in the valleys of
vern and Avon does not appear larger than it was before the Black
eath, although the landscape has grown generally paler through the
inning of trees for fuel. Only North of Avon the great Mercian
odlands remain: the forests of Arden and Feckenham stretching
a dark band from East to West and merging, in the neighbourhood
Bewdley, into the dense oakwood of Wyre, which here embraces and
erflows the course of Severn to peter out on the less hospitable flanks
the Clees. Through the midst of this forest the Dowles Brook lapses
ietly over its ledges of sandstone to join Severn; and, roughly parallel
th its meanderings, through a shallow valley choked with brushwood,
sled-scored track penetrates the lonely recesses of aboriginal oak.

It is an early morning in middle June, with the cuckoo abroad, and
ough the oaks have broken into leaf, their foliage has not yet darkened
the opacity which, in late Summer, fills the forest with gloom.
et Wyrewood lies strangely silent. No sound can be heard but the
urmur of the brook, the sudden screeches of jays and magpies, or the
ugh of the stock-eagle. Over the track, already invaded by springing
acken, there slowly advances a horseman, on a shaggy pony, leading
packhorse, laden with two ill-balanced saddle-bags. The rider is a
urdy, black-bearded young man in maroon trunk-hose and doublet.
e wears a velvet cap of the same colour furnished with a silver medal
Saint Christopher, whose protection he might well feel the need of
such an outlandish spot—the more so in that he rides unarmed. At
e end of several miles of collar-work the track opens into a clearing

occupied by two thatched hovels protected by a stone wall on which the
flayed hides of deer are stretched out to dry in the sun. Outside this
wall, within a circle of black ash, the mound of a charcoal-burner
smoulders, emitting from its summit a thin spiral of milk-blue smoke.

At the sight of these signs of habitation, the rider, Hugh Baker,
son of James Baker, the famous shipwright of Southampton, cautiously
pulls up, and the led horse immediately lowers his head to crop the
grass that springs between the bronze croziers of unfolding bracken,
then tosses it abruptly, startled by his master's shout, in response to
which an uncouth figure stalks out of the nearer hut. It is that of a
gigantic man, clothed from neck to foot in leather. The parts of his
face left uncovered by his shaggy blond beard, are blackened by charcoal-
dust which intensifies the whiteness of his eye-balls and teeth and gives
his craggy face a ferocious aspect. In his enormous left hand he grasps
a long-bow, to whose string he has fitted an arrow. He is Adam
Woodward, servant of Sir William Compton, lately appointed Rider
and Verderer of the royal forest of Wyre. From the shelter of his
stone wall he challenges the intruder.

ADAM:

Who bist thee, stranger—and what makest thou
In the king's woodland without leave or warrant?

HUGH:

I am called Hugh Baker, shipwright of Southampton,
And travel in the king's service by the leave
Of your master, Sir William Compton, to make a tally
Of the wood's standing timber. For my warrant:
It is here . . . But for Christ's sake first unstring that arrow

ADAM:

I cannot read.

HUGH:

          See, then, the sheriff's signet
Stamped on the seal.

ADAM:

          What would you of me?

[178]

HUGH:

Your counsel,

nd what charity you can spare—against just payment—
r a stomach that is empty these fifteen hours.

ADAM:

ere is no hostelry. Better you had filled it
the inn at Bewdley.

HUGH:

So had I, but that I came
the bridge-house after nightfall and found it barred,
or would they loose the bolt.

ADAM:

Came you thither from Worcester?

HUGH:

y, and so told them.

ADAM:

Then there is little wonder
he folk misliked you: there is disaccord
wixt Bewdley and Worcester over the water-traffic
f Severn—though had you passed the bridge I doubt
ou would have gotten bed or victual; for the Council
ides now in Bewdley, and the town's beset
Vith greedy gizzards like a carrion
estered by wood-ants. Within another month
he Lady Mary cometh to dwell at Tickenhill,
nd swarms of bustling tradesmen flock to fettle
he palace for her court: there has not been
o foul a press in Bewdley since Prince Arthur
er brother's corpse lay there upon the way
o burial in Worcester! Hobble your horses:
they should range in the woods no eye could track them
ave mine. Then, if you will, you shall eat with me
mess of venison, and slake your gullet,

[179]

So it be not too mimping, with a swill
Of the teart liquor that we forest-folk
Crush from choke-pear and crab-apple.

                HUGH:

                        Were it verjuice
My throat would relish it. I give you thanks,
Woodward.

                ADAM:

             You owe me none. I give no welcome
To meddlesome trespass save a goose-winged shaft;
But you, who come in peace and with right warranty,
I reckon as my guest till you have stepped
Beyond the forest's liberties. Come, sit you down
Till the pot seethe.

                HUGH:

                    I have told you my name.
But yours I do not now.

                ADAM:

                 I am called Adam,
Woodward of Wyre.

                HUGH:

             You have dwelt long in this forest?

                ADAM:

I was born and bred in it, like my father before me
And his again. My grandfather was servant
To the Mortimers of Wigmore who once held
This chase. He fell at Tewkesbury . . .

                HUGH:

                    You dwell alone?

                ADAM:

Alone? Alone? How should my days be lonely
Amid the living multitude of creatures
That bear me company? There is no tree

all Werewood but knows me for his neighbour
nd one that loves him! I have fleeter friends:
art, hind, hare, wolf and boar, the five wild beasts
f venery, and a mort of humbler folk
aat list my step but fear not: the russet squirrel
ho chitters on the bough and fearless fills
is garner at my threshold; fitchet, weasel
nd spitfire catamount—and those shy rievers
aat slink by night: vixen and brindled brock,
nd the sleek-skinned otter-bitch that dives to snatch
ae great lax swimming in her golden livery
f Michaelmas to find my Lenten fare.
ll these are my familiars; yet I do reckon
love the tall trees best: they are no runagates,
nd quiet best befits this wilderness.

HUGH:

uiet? Knew I no livelier company
should go mumping-mad. My tongue would shrink
or want of wagging, and my ear-drums thicken
ll I grew adder-deaf.

ADAM:
Friend, you are wrong.

HUGH:

hat? Can these dumb stocks mark your word or make
rticulate answer?

ADAM:
Ay, and with many voices,
o you but hearken and the ear be tuned
o catch their tone and cadence. Every tree
as its own speech in season: the showery abele
hat sighs when all are hushed and the weak air
irreth no other leaf; the timid whitebeam
hat whispers faint alarm when the wind blenches
er ravelled tresses; why, even the stiff holly,

That broodeth mute and sullen in her thickets
Till mightier boughs be bared, breaketh her silence
In brittle chatter when November strips
All other leaves but hers. That is the season
When, in their nakedness, the great oaks stand
Girt with such godlike majesty that a heathen
Who knew not Christ might sink upon his knees
And worship them.

HUGH:

This is idolatry!
Surely your mind must have been mazed by solitude
To breed such wicked blasphemies.

ADAM:

Behappen
It is sounder than you reckon. I do but tell
The wild thoughts it has harboured in that season
Of deathlike stillness when the starlight falls
On a world cered in snow, and even the brooks
Ice-muted cease their babbling. There is no silence
Holier than this, or stranger. Yet I confess
I love my woodland best when all its voices
Are raised in riot: as when Lammas gales
Roar through the huddled treetops, and torn boughs
Leaf-burdened crash into the shuddering brake
With shrieks of rending anguish—and there is war
In heaven, as when the winged archangels battled
With the dark hosts of Lucifer and swept
His fiends into the pit. Then my brave oaks
Unbent proclaim their majesty, defying
The demons of the air. Oft have I leaned
With my ear pressed against them, striving to share
That fierce aerial tumult—yet not a tremor
Shaketh their steadfast boles! No progeny
Of earth is nobler or mightier than these—
No, nor yet wiser.

[182]

HUGH:
Wiser? That is too much
or a plain man to stomach! Would you maintain
hat these familiars partake the natures
nd passions of mankind?

ADAM:
Did you but know them
s I, you would not doubt it. For their natures:
hese are as manifold in variety
s their hues, shapes and statures. Some are frail—
Witness the frightened aspen that for ever
hivers with needless fear, and is so cold
t heart she will not burn—while some are gay
nd light of utter innocence, like the birch
hat laughs when the wind fondles her, yet is bold
o loose her shift of satin and stand poised
n slim and silvery nakedness, like a maid
Upon the river's brink. Others are gracious
s the honey-dripping and bee-haunted lime
Whose tender leaves my gentle fallows nip
With lips of velvet. Some, though seeming fair,
re jealous—as the shallow-rooted beech,
Whose greed, for all her graces, will not brook
Consort or rival—so that no blade of green
Can thrive beneath her, and the very oak
ines in her company. Some are treacherous—
Witness the elm, whose brittle branches fall
o build a coffin for the fool who trusts
His life to her false shelter. Some are crabbed
nd stony-hearted—as the grudgeful yew
hat dwells apart, black-visaged and withdrawn
Like a Welshman of the marches, and hath no joy
but in her length of days. Others are spiteful—
s is the poison-dripping ash that sheds
Death on the sward beneath her. There are many

[183]

G

Lesser and lowlier trees with neither malice
Nor virtue in their natures: the rugged alder
That sways her ravelled rootlets in our brooks
And smoulders into charcoal; the tough hornbeam,
That like a candle flares, yet is so stubborn
She dints the axe—and all the pliable tribe
Of water-loving withies whose silver buds,
Breaking in floss of palest primrose, kindle
The first cold fires of Spring. Yet, of all these,
I love the oak most dearly . . .

HUGH:
Your wise oaks!

ADAM:
How should he not be wise who hath outlived
Mankind's allotted span before he sets
A single acorn, and is not meet for timber
Ere he hath doubled it? There are oaks in Wyre
That had weathered their first winters when the Roman
Set foot in Britain, and had but reached their prime
When Harold fell at Hastings, yet still stand
Hale to the root.

HUGH:
I am too staid to follow
Such lightfoot fancies; yet I do confess
They are lordly trees: as pretty a standel of timber
As I have seen this twelvemonth. In the South
We have no such forests now. The Wealden woods
Have fed the smelters' furnaces and slaked
Their charcoal-mounds with sap. Our slips lie empty
For lack of sizeable timber-trees to build
The hulls this realm needs most. I think your oaks
Might end their days more nobly than by drowsing
To death in this dim cloister. Lay me that giant,
And from his fallen carcase the adze will fashion
Garboard, strakes, ribs and knees for such a ship

[184]

s never took salt water! From yonder elm
awyers will shear planking to case her decks
nd carve both keel and kelson. Cross-grained knots
haped by the turner's chisel-edge shall furnish
ead-eyes and pulley-blocks; your stubborn hornbeam
ield tree-nails that shall marry oak to elm
o the twain be one flesh; your springy ash
ind yards and cross-trees. From the pliable poplar
oopers will hammer water-butts and kegs
or gunpowder—whereof the fieriest
 mixed with alder-charcoal. Thus your staid forest
Vrought by man's artifice shall sweep the seas
1 a more splendid shape and prouder guise,
)ight with new dread and beauty!

ADAM:
I have never
eheld the sea, nor any vessel nobler
han the great drags and trowes that float our cordwood
)own Severn to Gloucester.

HUGH:
You would not count such craft
reat were you seaward-bred, or had you but seen
he huge bark *Princess Mary*, that my father,
ames Baker, built at Hampton. Six hundred tons
)f portage, manned by seven hundred souls:
)f mould so clean beneath, of sail so swift,
bove so sweet-proportioned—castles, coins
nd fights so cunningly disposed for majesty
nd terror of the enemy—yet withal
o weatherly and maniable! Ah, had you watched her
pon the day she thundered from the slips
nd floated on the water like a swan
mid a flight of mallard—then had you granted
he empire of the Hampton shipwrights' artifice

Above all others. Yet the *Princess Mary*
Seems but a shallop to me, whose eyes have seen
The *Henry Grace à Dieu*, that seamen lovingly
Call the *Great Harry*, lately launched at Erith,
Whose portage is a thousand, and her crew
Double the *Princess Mary's*, manning five tiers
Of brazen ordnance—cannons, demi-cannons,
Culverins, sakers and falcons, to say naught
Of her iron slings, fowlers and hail-shot pieces
And murderous hand-guns. There is no battle-ship—
Be she galleasse of Portugal or galleon
Of Spain or Venice—that can quench the fire
Of this formidable paragon. Yet now we plan
To build a greater.

ADAM:

           I cannot understand
Why we, a comfortable folk, should court
The perils of unquiet waves, or seek
Dominion of the seas that God hath set
To guard our natural liberties.

HUGH:

               There speaks
The landsman! Know you not that the fickle waters
Which fend us can prove traitor, giving passage
To jealous foreigners? So first came the Danes;
So came the Normans—and, now we are at odds
With our King's false uncousinly cousin France,
Our watery moat is narrowed, and the arm
Of enmity grows longer. But for the eyes
Our prowling fleet has given us, we should lie
Helplessly blinded by the mists that cloak
The Dover strait in Summer. This is a lesson
You land-bound folk have ever been loth to learn
And, once learnt, soon forgotten—though your forbears

[186]

knew better than yourselves, as when the Fifth Harry,
Of Monmouth, from the yards of Portsmouth launched
His three great dromonds: the first *Grace à Dieu*
The *Trinity* and the *Holy Ghost*, to guard
His passage to Picardy; and when Henry Tudor
(The huckster, as the witless called him) built
Four mightier yet—the *Sweepstake*, *Mary Fortune*
Sovereign and *Regent;* ships that in their prime,
Sailed without any peer, yet now have lost
Their admiralty.

ADAM:

Why so?

HUGH:

These were but round-ships,
Cumbersome and slow-paced, that had neither power
To hold the water nor sail close by the wind:
Their upper decks o'erburdened by the weight
Of their iron ordnance—and so ill-found
That one smart squall in a high sea could catch them
Unbalanced, and founder them. Since then, a Frenchman,
One Master Descharges, of Brest in Brittany,
Has dropped his cannon to the cargo-decks
That lie above the orlop, thrusting their muzzles
Through apertures called portes—bating thereby
That perilous lack of ballast and augmenting
His tale of ordnance fourfold. Thus, the *Great Harry*
Casts from her teeming belly such a weight
Of deadly metal as would stave and sink
The *Regent* in one broadside, and if by chance
She were outnumbered, show such nimble heels
No foe could catch her—for this kingly ship
Is limber as a greyhound. It is strange
That an instrument of war so terrible
Should be so beautiful. When first I saw her
Towed on the flood-tide of the Thames from Erith

[187]

To Barking Creek (for there my father had sent me
To spy upon her) I judged her lines uncomely
Beside our race-built Hampton craft—and once
She all but grounded on the shelving silt
Eastward of Roding river. That was jealousy
Feeding false hope: she was not yet rigged or sparred
With the tall masts of tapered spruce-wood felled
In the forests of the Hansa; and I told
My father she was but a monstrous drone,
Paunchy and sluggard. But when next I saw her
Put forth from Dover, carrying the King's Grace
To parley with his royal cousin Francis
Twixt Guynes and Arde in Flanders, then, suddenly,
My heart leapt to my mouth, like a young lad's
When first he sees his love, of sheer delight
In her perfection: for this huge hulk steered
Light as a pinnace and made our *Princess Mary*
Seem but a slut beside her. Never was ship
More gloriously apparelled; for all her sails
Were damasked cloth-of-gold. Upon the cagework
Of her high castles flew four royal standards,
Each flagstaff tipped with a gold fleur-de-lys,
And from her four mast-heads the golden tongues
Of flame-like pennants flickered. From the quarters
Of her main deck hung four white banners bearing
The red cross of St. George, that drooped athwart
A tier of heater-shields or targets charged
With the same blood-red ensign, alternate
With France's silver lilies and the rose
Of Tudor, and a gold portcullis blazoned
Upon a field of green; while on her forecastle,
Carven beneath a lion figure-head,
She bore the arms of France and England, quartered
And crowned within the Garter, and supported
By the Lion and the Dragon. These things I saw
But at a venture; for my eyes were fixed

pon the crowded main-deck, where King Harry,
uddy and stalwart, towered above the press
f halberdiers and courtiers, clad in gold
dged with pied ermine: I had never guessed
e was so lofty, but that the snow-white plume
/hich bound his bonnet over-topped the tallest
  double hand's-breadth. Smiling, he gave the word
o sound the trumpets and to hoist the sails,
nd the *Great Harry*, like a tower of gold,
ore on her course to Calais, leaving me
ocked in the wash of her tremendous wake
nd dazzled by her glory. When she had faded
eyond my envious sight, I could have wept
or pride—not envy—that such a miracle
hould have been wrought in England . . . I rode home
/ildered and shaken, yet the more determined
o drain my utmost wits and match this beauty
efore I perished. Five years have I bowed
bove my draughtsman's board, bemused and haunted
y that rich vision: five years have I laboured
eeking that vision's shape; and now, at last,
1y plans are finished: all I need is timber
'o give them substance. Let us be done with talk!
ind me oak, ash and elm—and in a twelvemonth
'our moveless forest shall be winged with sail
nd float till fire or water give it burial
eneath the waves. Come then, for I am burning
'o make my choice!

XIX

Interlude

A SONG OF THE LONG GALLERY. HAMPTON COURT: A.D. 1587

Rosy-pale the Palace lies
Mute beneath the moon:
It is the season of the rose
And a night of June;

Honey-sweet the jasmine's breath
Mingles with the musk
Of néw-mówn hay
In the midsummer dusk;

Milky down the winding walk
Steals the mist of Thames—
You can hear the petals fall
From the bent rose-stems;

Softly through the alleyed yew
A moth's wings move:
It is the season of the rose
And the hour of love—

When woven out of moon and mist,
In silver and white,
The ghosts of the Long Gallery
Dance by candle-light.

The maids of the Long Gallery
Are dust these many years,
And none that listens now may hear
Their laughter or tears;

The twang of lutes and virginals
Or the rustle of their shoon
As their feet brush the flooring
With swéet-rúsh strewn;

The dry swish of taffetas
And whispering mousseline
As their skirts sweep the daïs
Of the great, cold Queen.

Stiff in her jewelled robe she sits,
Austere and pale,
While Perrico, the little dog,
Peeps from her farthingale;

A ruff of cambric picarded
Props her pointed chin;
A stomacher of seed-pearls girds
Her proud heart in;

Her cheeks are drawn parchment
Blotched with crimson dyes,
And in that raddled mask there burn
Her hot Tudor eyes;

While, shrewd behind their smoulder,
The cool Tudor brain
Sifts and winnows word and look
And gives them shape again.

Hopes, ambitions, treacheries,
Envies, loves, lusts,
Shame and honour—all she sees,
Yet none she trusts.

Soft-tongued ambassadors
Tempt her with their wiles
And strive to pry her secrets out:
The cold Queen smiles.

Captains and counsellors
Cluster round her throne:
The Queen's eyes see them all,
Her heart needs none:

G*

Wise Burleigh and Walsingham
Wait on her command,
While Raleigh grips the sudden sword
Hilted in his hand,

While Leicester plies his flatteries
To keep the favourite's place,
And Sidney leans to catch the light
From Stella's starry face

As through their mazy galliards
In silver and white
The limber maids-of-honour dance
Deep into the night;

And the cold Queen's lonely heart
Is troubled as they dance
By many a sweet, unspoken thought
And shy, secret glance;

Her heart is warmed and troubled—
But all that she sees
Is the face of Robin Devereux
Crouched by her knees:

That young face and the other
Of parchment and of bone:
An old raddled woman
Sitting on a throne . . .

Down the darkening gallery
Fades the phantom rout:
The moon sinks in the river-mists,
The candles burn out;

The river-mist thickens,
It droops upon the lawn;
Slowly over Richmond Hill
Creeps a grey dawn.

> Gaunt and grim the palace lies
> Mere brick and stone:
> The ghosts of the Long Gallery—
> All, all are gone.

XX

DEUS FLAVIT ET DISSIPATI SUNT   A.D. 1588

Thus to begin: In the third week of July,
And the one-and-thirtieth year of the Queen's reign,
We saw the *Golden Hind* pinnace scudding up-channel,
With a strong tide making and a following wind
From the South West, into Plymouth. And Fleming, her
Stumping uphill to the Hoe in his sodden seaboots,   [captain,
Told Lord High Admiral Howard how, South of the Lizard,
He had sighted ten great galleons of Andalusia
Quartering the empty waves like a cry of hounds
That are strayed or shed from the pack, and go feathering
For scent at the covert-side. And this, indeed,
Was their case—for the Duke of Medina-Sidonia
Had mistook his tryst and lagged fifty miles astern
In the stormy loom of the Scillies; so here was a prize
To be snapped up with little ado if but we might pounce
On this portion before they were whipped together, though we
Were ill-placed for the spring, our English fleet being crowded
To leeward within the Sound and held there enleashed
By the freshening gale.

                              Yet no sooner had Fleming told
His tale than the happy news, like storm-water, ran
From the Hoe, where our captains were gathered, down every
                                                            street
To the Barbican and the Cattewater: the bells of St. Andrew's
Clashing forth: "They are come . . . They are come!" and a
                                                      hundred beacons
Casting their flames down-wind like the swaling-fires
Of Spring from headland to headland and hill to hill—
Till this wildfire swept all England, and farming folk
That watched for the morrow's weather saw the dark land
Lit like a star-pricked firmament.

                              But we in Plymouth
Had more instant work on hand; for had we been trapped

[194]

n that leeward haven, we knew we should fare no better
Than the Spaniards, a year before, when Sir Francis Drake
With *Elizabeth Bonaventure*, *Rainbow* and *Lion*,
Ran into the gullet of Cadiz, raked by the guns
Of Matagorda, and left that roadstead cluttered
With sixty ships, sunk, grounded, or set adrift
With fire in their bellies. So, all that night, we toiled
By torch and cresset, cramming our ships with shot
And warping them out with hawser-work, one by one,
Until, by dawn, there were fifty-four of them clear
Of the land, strung out abreast of the Eddystone
And tacking into a wind which began to weaken
As rain fell steadily—so that the waves that ran
In a long swell out of Biscay grew smooth and sullen,
Flattened by the grey drizzle. So there we lay
Heaving, mist-blinded, with lowered sails, and waited
For what should next befall us, hearkening
To the cries of the wild mews and knowing naught
Of where the foe might be . . .

                    But, as night neared,
A fishing-smack that had stolen from the Sound
With plashing sweeps, gave hail; and her skipper, hoisted
On board the *Ark Royal*, blinking in the light
Of her cuddy's lantern, stammered a halting tale
Of how certain fisherfolk that watched on the Dodman,
(Which like the blunt snout of a basking whale
Juts forth from Mevagissey) had suddenly spied
Through an opening in the mist, a spectacle
Of innumerable majesty: Spain's embattled might
Hove-to four leagues off-shore, in a half-moon
Seven mile from tip to tip. How many there were
They could but roughly reckon, for the haze
Thickened and thinned so swiftly, and by times
Their substance seemed but phantoms; yet one man swore
To a hundred and thirty sail, and of these no less
Than forty ships of battle, and half a hundred

[195]

Armed galleons of the Gold Fleet, with a swarm
Of fly-boats, pinnaces, and such nimbler craft,
Which, like torn fleeces of a thundercloud,
Trailed from the main fleet's denser heart to guard
The rearward hulks and transports. And at one moment,
When shafted sunlight pierced the rack and smote
Upon their vanguard, one huge ship had broken
Her banner at the main—an oriflamme
Whose gold burned through the mist; and they that heard
Guessed her Sidonia's ship, the great *St. Martin*,
And her banner the standard that the Pope of Rome
Had blessed, bearing the images of Christ Crucified
And his Mother, the Holy Virgin.

> Yet all that day
We could do nothing, being at the pleasure
Of a moveless air, but lay with sodden sails
Listlessly flapping, and whistled for a breeze
To waft us seaward of the Spaniard's rear;
And all that night enshrouded in dense mist,
Unseen and blind as we, the Armada crept
Past us upon the tide.

> It was still dark
When the dank air freshened somewhat, and the wind
Veered to the North of Westward, dissipating
The watery haze that hid them, so that by dawn
No shred of cloud was left between the blues
Of sky and sea. Then, through the crystalline
Of rain-washed air, at last we saw that vision
Of dread and of desire: the Spanish fleet
In order of battle standing up the sleeve
With the wind on their port quarter. Slowly they moved
(Or so it seemed) as though the very wind
Grew tired with carrying them, and the sea groaned
Under their wallowing bulk. Four galeasses
Of Naples, with sweep of flashing oar-blades, cleft
The unfurrowed deep before them; next there came

idonia's main battle-fleet: weathermost,
'en galleons of Portugal, their greatest
'he vast *Grangrina*, eleven hundred tons;
starboard of these, ten of the Indian Guard
With four ships of New Spain—and, in between,
Sidonia's own flagship, the *St. Martin;*
Next, four fleet pinnaces, that like snapping curs
Roved in and out, busily shepherding
The sluggard flock of hulks and victuallers
That floundered in the midst, and behind these
Four squadrons of their rearguard battle, ships
Of Biscay, Guipuscoa, the Levant
And swarthy Andalusia: twenty galleons
Of vast lading and armament; and a fifth,
Lighter of burthen, moving in a cloud
Of agile pinnaces where, last of all,
Two watchful galeasses closed the rear,
Looking to windward.

> When the Spaniards saw us
Heeled over on the port tack and sweeping down
Fast on their rear, Sidonia gave orders
To haul in sheets and beat towards the land,
With a cunning of double purpose; first to waylay
The remnant of our force, which, one by one,
Still straggled out of Plymouth, and next to weather
Our main fleet—neither guessing how nimble-heeled
And maniable were we, nor yet how slovenly
Were his own lumbering hulks. So, as they beat
To windward of the Cornish coast, we swept
Athwart their rearguard's starboard quarter, raking
The Levantiska of Leyva as we passed,
With a hot broadside of cannon-shot. Then we gybed
And closed upon their windward flank, where none
But that grim sea-dog Recalde, who, not long since,
Crossed wits and blades with Drake in Lisbon River,
Defied us, boldly bringing into action

The *Santa Ana* and the great *Grangrina*
Of Biscay; for they that followed fell away
In a piteous huddle, but these twain stood up to us
Till the *Santa Ana's* forestay was cut through
And two roundshot lodged in her mainmast; when Sidonia
Bore up beside her, right into the wind,
While Valdes, with the squadron of Andalusia,
Formed up behind him. So Lord Howard bade
The battle to be broken, albeit the day
Had scarce begun. But this he reckoned shrewdly:
That the Spaniards now had beat too far to leeward
To trouble Plymouth; that, in those pregnant hours,
Forty fresh sail had swelled our complement
To five-score fighting-ships—not thirty less
Than theirs—and that no craft in all the Armada
(Save for the great *Grangrina*, the *Santa Ana*,
The *Raggazona*, and the admiral ship
Of Andalusia) was of greater portage
Than our *White Bear* and *Triumph;* nay, even more,
That none of theirs could match our best in swiftness
Or weight of deadly metal—to say naught
Of seamanship, while, in the narrow seas,
Where that grim lion Parma waited, crouching
To spring upon our shores, a second fleet
Under Lord Henry Seymour stood to bar
The straits. Therefore we let Sidonia fly
Up-channel, dragging on his windward flank
The wounded *Santa Ana*, through the smoke
Of burnt-out beacons smouldering on the cliffs
Of the South Hams, and we hung upon his heels
Like an ambling wolf-pack that has tasted blood
And gotten the measure of its prey, but waits
Until the victim tires before it falls
To ravening. And, in mid-afternoon,
It seemed that hour had come: for suddenly
Their galleon *San Salvador*, of the squadron

[198]

Of Guipuscoa, blew up—her fighting-decks
Flying into the air and her shattered poop
Blown clear; but, as we closed on her, the Spaniards
Went in their galeasses, and we drew off.
Next, by the Start, Pedro de Valdes' flagship
Our Lady of the Rosary fell foul
Of two Biscayans. The first broke her foreyard,
The next her bowsprit—and when Valdes boldly
Put up his tiller to come into the wind,
The mainmast snapped close by the board and crashed
Athwart her bulwarks, draping her with torn sails
And cordage; so once again we closed, until
The *San Cristóbal* and the *San Francisco*
Covered her, and a Naples galeasse
Took her in tow—yet cravenly forsook her
When a pert London coaster, the *John and Margaret*
Of a bare two hundred tons, challenged their escort;
And we laughed to see so huge a victim falling
Into such puny hands.

                  But now, since wind
And sea were rising, the Lord Admiral
Bade the whole fleet heave-to, and called a council
On board the *Ark* to plan the strategy
Of the morrow's battle; and there it was determined
That our Vice Admiral, Drake, should lead the van,
His lantern on the poop of the *Revenge*
Guiding our course, with hope to overhaul
Sidonia and bring his fleet to action
West of the Needles, thereby heading him
From off Southampton. So, at midnight, we sailed
With a stiff Westerly breeze and a short sea
That made the spark on the *Revenge's* poop
Dance like a graveyard corpselight dizzily
Amid the sober stars; till, of a sudden,
That drunken light went out like a snuffed candle
And left us guideless; so we slackened sail

And hove-to, baffled, blinded, and perplexed,
While the Lord Admiral, in the *Ark Royal*,
With the *Mary Rose* and the *White Bear*, held on
The selfsame course, and the main fleet lay scattered
To rearward in the waste of troubled water
That foams above the Skerries; and when daylight
Broke over Berry Head, these three bold ships
Found themselves uncompanioned, without the topsail
Of a friend in sight, and the Armada's rearguard
A culverin-shot ahead—so that the Spaniards,
Had they been abler seamen, could have borne up
And utterly destroyed them. But of this
They failed: their jealous captains being busied
With licking of their wounds and bickering
One with another, so this pregnant hour
Was wasted, and by noon our nightbound stragglers
Drew up to the *Ark Royal*—save for the squadron
Of Drake, who (if his tale were true) had chased
Five great ships of the Hansa which, in the dark,
He had mistook for Spaniards; but Martin Frobisher
In his blunt Yorkshire tongue flatly maintained
This was a lie, and that naught but pirate greed,
O'er-mastering Drake's scant honour, had tempted him
To slip us in the dark and search the rear
For Valdes' galleon that, hulled and mastless,
Lagged there adrift. Yet Drake stuck to his tale,
Admitting, howbeit, that on the windward reach
Home from that fruitless chase he had fallen in
With *Our Lady of the Rosary*, and thought fit
To send her into Dartmouth with a prize-crew
Aboard her. And now, seeing both words and looks
Grow heated and hands fly to hilts, Lord Howard
Bound these two fiery captains to keep peace
Between themselves, and their malice for the Spaniards.
So Drake, being well-contented with his prize,
Laughing, consented, and the other grudgingly

ated his jealousy, while we bore on
astward before a weakening wind that died
t nightfall—yet not before Sidonia
Had shed a second ship, the *San Salvador*,
Which, maimed and burning, he turned loose to drift
thwart our course; and Hawkins, in the *Victory*
owed her charred hulk to Weymouth . . .

                                        All that night
The two fleets lay becalmed beneath the moon
ust out of gunshot: the warm air so still,
We could hear the Spaniards' voices, and the boom
Of a weary groundswell pounding on the stones
Of the Chesil Beach. At dawn the dead wind quickened
o a brisk North-easter, giving Sidonia
The weather-gauge; whereat he tacked about
o bear upon us, but Howard turned aside
On a long board to the North-West, thereby hoping
o fetch to East between them and the land
And steal the weather from them; and the Spaniards
Now showed their seamanship, sailing on the same tack
o cheat us; so Howard went about and beat
Close-hauled to Eastward, with the *Victory*,
Nonpareil and nine others close astern.
et these held on their board too long and left
Their admiral at the mercy of Recalde,
Who now came bowling down, with sixteen sail
n line abreast, abaft the *Nonpareil*—
All but their greatest ship, the *Raggazona*,
The mighty Levantisca—that held straight on
o cut off the *Ark Royal*.

                              And now Lord Howard
Lay in great jeopardy—for the *Ark Royal's* portage
Was but two-thirds the Spaniards', and her crew
But half; and had the *Raggazona* grappled
And thrown aboard her pikemen, he had been lost
And the fight ended. Yet, though he could not weather

The Levantisca, Howard's ship was handier
And, with her rapid firing, so confused
The Spaniard that he faltered—and the *Ark*
Stood off unscathed.

              But now a greater peril
Threatened our fleet; for in that windless night
Our left wing, led by Frobisher, had been caught
In the Portland Race and carried far inshore
To windward of the Armada; and Sidonia,
Seeing the *Triumph*, with five armed merchantmen
Of London, helpless on the leeward shore,
Thrust his oared galeasses into the wind
To make an end of them, while he, in haste,
Pursued our broken vanguard—yet was so blinded
By lust of easy conquest and the reek
Of our rapid gunfire that he failed to spy
Drake's wing of fifty fast sail weathering
Recalde's rearward squadron, and coming up
Upon them through the smoke—the wind having backed
To South-South-West. Thus, while Recalde turned
And fled to join Sidonia, Lord Howard,
Freed from that instant menace, sailed inshore
With the *Elizabeth Jonas*, *Leicester*, *Victory*,
Dreadnought and *Swallow*, to succour Frobisher,
And as Sidonia ran towards Portland Bill
To intercept, Howard bore up, until
He had the wind upon his starboard quarter
And the *St. Martin*'s fo'c'sle straight ahead.
Three times he crossed Sidonia's bows, and thrice
Landed a thumping broadside, then, returning,
Gave her the other; and now, as he swept on
Toward Frobisher, Drake followed in his rear
With a fierce weight of metal that pierced her hull—
That ripped the holy standard from her main
And left her making water fast and groaning
With half a hundred dead and sixty more

Bloodily wounded—while the galeasses
Whose teeth were in the *Triumph* dropped their prey
And fled in terror. Thus ended the fourth day
Of that running battle, and the first encounter
Of the main fleets, which, but for our sore lack
Of shot and powder, and the crippling wind,
Might well have ended all . . .
                                    That day we swam
Like wildfowl on a glassy mere becalmed
While the friendly Portsmouth folk replenished us
With bread and shot and powder, and Lord Howard
Re-formed us in four squadrons: on the larboard
Frobisher in his war-scarred *Triumph;* next
John Hawkins in the *Victory;* and to starboard
Lord Thomas Howard in the *Golden Lion*
And Drake in the *Revenge.*
                                    Now on the morrow
(being St. James's Day) two Spanish ships
The *Santa Ana*, that had been winged off Plymouth,
And the *San Luis*, limping fell astern;
And a cloud of petty English craft, like ants
Ravening a beetle's carcase, swarmed about them
And would have boarded—but that four galeasses
Like proudly-swerving peregrines swept between
And scattered them. Then Howard, in the *Ark*
And his cousin in the *Lion* towed their two ships
Into the tussle with longboats, and shot away
The lantern of one galeasse and the beakhead
Of her sister, while a third drifted away
With the crippled *Santa Ana*, heavily listing,
And might have fallen to us but that our launches
Were so peppered by the Spanish musketry
They could not tow us further; and as we stood
To hoist them all aboard, the wind arose
Once more out of the South, casting Lord Howard
To leeward of Sidonia, who now bore down

In the *St. Martin* with the fourth galeasse
And, having got the weather, so fiercely mangled
Both *Lion* and *Ark Royal* that they were fain
To fall away inshore, while Frobisher
Took up the fight—but paid dear for his daring;
For, as the wind veered West, Recalde ran
Twixt him and Howard, and with a chance shot splintered
His rudder; and though eleven launches strove
To tow the *Triumph* out of range, it seemed
She (and the *Ark* no less!) was lost—until,
In the article of doom her shipwrights botched
The broken rudder, and at the same moment
The fickle wind backed South—and Frobisher
Cast off the launches and so slipped away
On a long reach to Westward . . .

                        But already
The Spaniards had found cause to rue their rashness:
For Drake and Hawkins, profiting by that shift
Of wind that saved the *Triumph*, stole about
Their larboard wing, and with the *Nonpareil*,
Revenge and *Mary Rose*, drove their *St. Matthew*,
The weathermost of Sidonia's squadron, crashing
Into their huddled rearguard, crowding them
To leeward on the sandback of the Owers,
Where they had grounded—but that, in the fury
Of that hot fight we had burnt up all our powder
And emptied our shot-lockers. Thus, when they lay
Confused, we could not press them, and the promise
Of victory slipped from us as they cleared
The shoals and fled on Eastward up the sleeve—
Not without scathe: for, by this day, the rumour
Of the running battle had crept along the coast;
And many spirited gentlemen that were fain
For heart-love of their country to adventure
Their skins upon salt water, hired themselves
At their own charge boats, shallops, skiffs and hoys,

nd sallied forth in haste, like jolly ploughmen
o a bout of cudgel-play or London prentices
hat go roaring to the bear-pit: yet the quarrey
hey baited was no sullen bruin, chained
nd spiritless, but a horned fighting-bull
f Andalusia, that these picadors
nd pert banderilleros boldly pestered
/ith pricks and lances—running in and out
f the stately Spanish fleet like dabchicks darting
mid a game of swans. But, though we laughed
o see their reckless daring, yet were we troubled
y their impudent seamanship, that often placed
hemselves and us in peril. But no counsel
ould quell their gallant mischief; and, as both fleets
:ood up the channel wafted by the wind
hat in the dog-days blows from the South-West
/e soon outsailed them . . .

So, by evening
f the seventh day, we had cleared Dungeness
o see the chalk-white cliffs of Dover dyed
y a red sunset, and the friendly topsails
f Seymour fleck the straits. Whereat Sidonia
eered towards France, hoping thereby to gain
he forty Flemish flyboats he had begged
f Parma, that, so strengthened, he might cover
he Spaniards' crossing; but not one sail came forth
rom Dunkirk or Ostend: so, being counselled
hat if he ventured further the fierce tide
light carry him beyond the straits, he cast
nchor in Calais roads—with Howard's fleet
culverin-shot to windward, full astern,
nd, on the lee, the sunken sandbanks stretching
rom Sandettie and Outer Ruytingen
o the Wandelaar—a treacherous berth for such
s knew those soundings ill. Hither, at nightfall,
enton and Seymour, with six-and-thirty sail

Thirsting for battle, beat up from England, bearing
Meat and munitions, and the heartening news
That in the port of Dover they had made ready
A fleet of fireships that, loosed upon the tide
And sent down in the dead of night, might smoke
Or burn the foxy Spaniard from his holt
Ere Parma's pikemen mustered—but since no moment
Was to be lost (for the tide turned at midnight)
Lord Howard called for ships out of the fleet
So to be cast away. Then Drake, free-handed,
Offered the *Thomas*, and John Young the *Bear*,
A bark of seven-score tons; and other captains
Made up the tale to eight, which, being besmeared
With wildfire, pitch and resin, their bellies crammed
With brimstone, and every piece of ordnance charged
With cannon-balls and chain-shot, Young himself
Led them into the wind, with the tide racing
At full—nor loosed his tiller ere their decks
Were lit from stem to stern, and hot flames licked
The longboats lashed beside them. Thus they swept
Unhelmed into the black heart of the fleet
Of Spain, with cannon thundering and roundshot
Hurling on every hand; and when the Spaniards
Woke to this fiery peril they were cast
Into utter panic, reckoning it the work
Of the devil or Drake his offspring, in confusion
Hastening this way and that, incontinently
Hacking their anchor-cables and running foul
Each of his helpless neighbour—and, in a wrack
Of splintered spars and ragged cordage, swept
Out of the roads of Calais, through the straits,
Into the wild North Sea—while Howard's fireships
Burnt themselves out to leeward, and denser darkness
Fell on the deep . . .

                Now, as the great *St. Martin*
Lay tangled in that tide-borne rout, Sidonia

gnalled the scattered galleons to re-form
bout him—but none obeyed save the *San Marcos*
nd a handful more. Thus, when the break of dawn
Vhitened the shoalings, this mean force appeared
ead to the wind, and all the rest astraggle
ix mile astern, off Gravelines. Then Lord Howard
e-formed our line: himself, in the *Ark Royal*,
Iidmost; to port, Seymour and Frobisher;
o starboard, Drake and Hawkins—but, as they swooped,
ive squadrons all abreast, his watch espied
pain's last unwounded galeasse, *San Lorenzo*,
Iragged Eastward, rudderless, under the guns
)f the castle of Calais; so, close-hauled, he drew
)ut of the line to take her, while the rest
wung smart to starboard, hoping thus to run
etween Sidonia and Dunkirk and throw
Iis left wing on his centre, driving both
Jpon the Flemish sandbanks. But Sidonia,
Ilbeit a lame seaman, had no lack
)f manhood, and stood firm till the *Revenge*
ame within musket-shot, shattering his forecastle
Vith her bow-guns, then luffed, poured in her broadside,
Ind so bore on into the very midst
)f the huddled rearguard beating up to aid him;
Vhile Hawkins, Winter, Seymour and Frobisher,
wept past the great *San Martin* one by one,
ounding her with their cannon till she heaved
Vith yards and rigging torn, and hull shot through
y one great ball of fifty pounds that holed
Ier bowels upon the waterline. Yet still
he fought them off undaunted; and the squadrons
)f Lisbon, Guipuscoa, and Andalusia
Iathered about her in a huge half-moon
'hat slowly beat to the North Westward, striving
Jot to o'ershoot Dunkirk, where Parma's force
.ay fretting (as they reckoned) to embark

For the assault on England; and so stoutly
Did they persist that, ere the sun had soared
Half way towards the zenith, fifty ships
Had gained their battle-stations—with Recalde
In the *San Juan* keeping the weather flank,
Sidonia in the centre, and, to leeward,
Oquendo and Leyva in the Levantiscas
And Guipuscoans. Thus, while Hawkins held
Sidonia's mainguard, where the great *St. Martin*,
Shaken, but dauntless, thundered through the smoke
Of her own sullen broadsides, Seymour's squadron
Harried the wing to windward, and sheared off
Two ships, the *San Felipe* and *San Matteo*,
Which, though Recalde strove to cover them,
Lay so shot-riddled they could neither hold
Water nor wind, and, helpless, fell astern
Crippling two more—*Our Lady of Begona*
And the *San Juan of Sicily;* and these four
With yards and ropes entangled drifted down
Under the fire of Winter, in the *Vanguard*,
Whose nimble squadron charged in and went about
Like dancers in a galliard. Twice the *Matteo*
Shook herself free and turned on them; twice more
They closed upon her, firing their culverins
Point-blank at musket-range—but the *San Juan*
Had no fight left in her, being so shattered
That through her gaping portholes one could see
Her decks awash with blood. Nor could Sidonia
Come to her aid, being even more bitterly
Beset, with Drake and Hawkins placed athwart
Both bows and stern, and hanging on his flanks
Like grim bear-baiting mastiffs in the pit
At Southwark, while the wind, suddenly veering
Into the West, brought up three more great ships,
The *Ark*, the *Bonaventure*, and the *White Bear*,
Which, having sacked their crippled galeasse

[208]

pon the beach at Calais, now bore down
ke monstrous phantoms towering through the reek
f battle—which having seen, Drake put about,
eaving the great *St. Martin* to their charge,
nd while the *San Matteo*, and *San Felipe*
'ith the *San Marcos*, drifted to their doom
n the deadly Zealand sandbanks, the *Revenge*,
ike to a cunning sheepdog, singled out
he stragglers of their left wing, one by one,
nd shed them on the shoalings: fifteen ships
ut of Sidonia's fifty—the bold remnant,
utpaced, outsailed, outnumbered and outgunned
y four to one, and, in God's grace, delivered
nto our hands by such a miracle
s we had prayed for! Yet, in the article
f victory, that same wind that had so blessed us
natched from our mortal hands the means to strike
he death-blow—for suddenly a black squall leapt
rom the South-West and beat upon the sails
f both embattled fleets, heeling them over;
nd every captain cried: "All hands aloft!
eef topsails, or we founder!" And we who served
he reeking culverins cast away our tinder
o be sodden by the rain, and clomb the shrouds
o shorten sail, as our ships held to the wind;
nd from the lofty stations where we swayed
ike wind-tossed rooks, through sheets of icy rain
nd stinging spindrift, our bleared eyes beheld
sight most strange and terrible; all that was left
f that proud Armada, the pomp and boast of Spain,
cudding like windlestraws upon the foam
f the Zealand banks—a mightier hand than ours
Having compassed their destruction.

                           Yet, even as we watched
'hose doomed ships driven to their end, the wind
'eered to full South, and, as they gybed, it spewed them

[209]

Out of the very throat of death to seaward,
Nor could we overhaul them or come to grips
Again that day: for now they had sea-room,
And we no press of sail to clip their heels
As they fled before us. Nor had we any comfort
But that their spite was foiled, and that no Spaniard
Could now set foot on England. Of the rest
I can but speak by hearsay—for we were set
To guard the straits again and keep a watch
On Parma at Dunkirk. But I have heard
That, on the morrow, an even mightier gale
Rose from the West and drove them on the coasts
Of Norway; that there the foulest pestilence
Raged in their sweltering down-battened holds
And stinking cockpits, where the wounded lay
Festering above the dead, and that the lack
Of water and food so weakened them that few
Had strength to man the ropes. Therefore Sidonia
Decreed the Northern course to Spain, and led them
Through the fierce Pentland Firth, rounding Cape Wrath
And slinking through the Hebrides, where some
Were cast upon those iron coasts and gutted
Of life and treasure, while others staggering
Westward of Ireland, and falling on the fangs
Of Connemara, sank in sight of land;
And the sorry remnant of starved, sullen men,
In their maimed galleons, brought their anguish home
To Lisbon and to Vigo and the Groyne
And Port St. Mary, where Sidonia
Sulked in his orange-groves until he died,
A broken, ageing man . . .

                    As for the memory
Of this great mercy: men may read the medal
That the Queen stamped, saying—*He blew with His wind
And they were scattered:* and doubtless it is just
To give to God the glory—yet I do reckon
That we, her seamen, had some small part in it.

XXI

Interlude

AN ENGLISH GARLAND

Musing Meleáger once
In Gádara a garland made
Of herbs and blossoms that the suns
Of envious Time shall never fade:
Gifts of the Galilean meads
And Hermon's lonely hill, where slain
Adonis in the springtime bleeds,
With drifts of fierce anemones
Staining anew the Syrian plain.
Thus I, with neither grace nor powers
To match that orient music, twine
A chaplet lowlier than his:
A coronal of English flowers
The more beloved that they are mine.

Pluck first those eager Celandines
Whose gay, new-minted metal shines
In February hedgerows where
Hooded Lords and Ladies peer
From out their pallid wimples. Next
Gather me catkins of wind-vext
Hazel, and, ere the petal-snow
Be shed, a sprig of thorny sloe,
Scentless though it be. To these
Marry me frail Anemones
Ruffled in the copse when March
Crimsons the tassels of the Larch
And the first venturous Primrose frees
Her frozen heart. Now search the leys
For mealy Cowslip-bells that fill
Poor pastures, where the Daffodil

[211]

Dances, with perfumes headier yet
Than wafts of the White Violet
That shyly droops her head within
Grass-tussocks newly-fledged; and when
In glimmering pools the Bluebells lie
(But pluck not these, because they die
So soon) and turbulent Hawthorn floods
The air with spices—from the woods
Bear me one branch of living snow
From the Wild Cherry's bridal-show;
And see you tarry not—for now
The warm earth's bounties spring so fast,
They are no sooner seen than past
Their prime: so haste, before June suck
May's moisture from the marsh, to pluck
The valiant King-cup's globes of gold,
And in her sappy leaves enfold
Flags and Forgetmenots, and heads
Of plumy Meadowsweet that sheds
High Summer's drowsiest incense
Over the musky hayfield. Thence
Skirt me the standing wheat to glean
Black-pollen'd Poppies, and, between,
Cornflowers, whose royal azures dim
The Speedwell's bright eyes till they seem
Lustreless as the cooler blues
Of Alkanet. Next I bid you choose
From the dank ditch Hemp-Agrimony
And pungent Horse-Mint; from the sunny
Verges, where Broom-pods in the heat
Of noonday snap, bring honey-sweet
Claws of White Clover—nor despise
The Scarlet Pimpernel whose eyes,
Widened in sunlight, blink in shade,
With silvery Mulleins arrayed
In silk sleek as a leveret's ear,

And spendthrift Ragwort-stems that wear
Their gold like harlots; dock and sorrel
Decked in their panicles of coral,
And brittle Teazle-heads that slake
Their drought with dewdrops. Now forsake
The trampled verge's needy sward
To gather Foxglove spires that guard
Rampant hedgerows flaunting high
Their ivory trophies of July:
Where hemlocks, and the greeny-white
Elder-flowers conspire at night
With feathery kexes to imprison
Moonlight ere the moon be risen
And starshine when the stars have set
In Summer's timeless twilight; yet
I pray you let not evening end
In these enchantments ere you bend
One trailer of the Briar down—
And see her buds be not o'erblown,
Lest the faint-flushed petals fall
From the arching spray, and all
Her attar waste. Here, too, untwine
The rosy fingers of Woodbine
That, though her waxen trumpets breathe
Ravishment, will crush to death
The Hazel-rods round which they climb.
Next, from bare downlands, gather Thyme,
And, from their beechen hangers, green
Flowers of pallid Helleborine,
And, stippled on the high sheep-walk,
Orchises that love the chalk;
While from granite moors aglow
With the imperial lava-flow
Of August's Tyrian, you shall bring
Bunches of purple Heath and Ling
And Harebells, dim as dusk, that seem

[213]

To dance when no wind stirreth them:
Yet cull not these till you have found
By peaty pools on marish ground
Nodding above the emerald moss
Grass of Parnassus and the floss
Of milk-white Cotton-grass, where, bent
To pick them, you may catch the scent
Of Buck-bean and Bog Asphodels,
Or stoop to pick the violet bells
Of frosted Butterwort; and descending
Toward the plain at the day's ending
See meadows mantled in a mist
Of the Sheep-bit's amethyst,
Or lawns with lilac Saffron strewn
To cup September dews. Too soon,
Alas! my hedgerows tarnish now;
The sap sinks, and the fires burn low;
Yet growths that in the sober green
Of Summer dressed were hardly seen,
Now, tinged by Autumn's icy breath,
Flame in the article of death
So fiercely we forget almost
To mourn the blossoms that are lost;
And, though their earlier wealth be spent,
Stand laden with such increment
Of splendour that beholding eyes
Are dazzled. So, before their dyes
Be faded, and their mortal gold
Blacken in the common mould,
From hanging boughs I pray you reach
One bright fan of the flagrant Beech,
And from the Cherry's funeral-pyre
That sets the smouldering woods on fire
A brighter guerdon. Gather too
The crimson cuplets of the Yew
Brimmed with sweet mucilage; and bring

Translucent Nightshade-drops that cling
Like Bryony's to the naked bine,
Shaming the Spindle-tree's carmine
As doth the fruited Rose eclipse
The Hawthorn with her flaming hips.
Next, from the tangled thicket, tear
Reluctant Bramble-shoots that bear
Clusters of dew-bright berries, dark
As a young gipsy's eyes; and mark
How now the moon-pale Elder shows
Berries jettier than the Sloe's;
And last, from Winter's sodden weeds
Pluck Gladwins and the poison-seeds
Of Cuckoo-pints, whose fires will glow
When leafless woods are laid with snow,
And through their blackened boughs the sun
Fades like an ember. . . . I have done!

O Meleáger, wistful ghost
Roaming amid the ashen flowers
Of Acheron, couldst thou ever boast
A garland goodlier than ours?

H

XXII

THE TALE OF THE FAINT-HEARTED PILGRIM

PLYMOUTH HOE: A.D. 162(

I, Robert Cushman, wool-comber of Canterbury
And lately of Leyden, in Holland, having been seized
With an infirmity of body that I fear
Will carry me to my burial, and afflicted
With manifold reproaches and revilements
Wholly unmerited, at the cruel hands
Of most unloving brethren, do now rehearse
The truth of what befell. Of how our Church
Came first to Amsterdam, being driven forth
From our own dear country by the persecutions
Of prelates and their clergy; of how there
A further schism reft us; of how we settled
In the sweet city of Leyden, and abode there
Ten years in peace and piety, having won
The right to worship God in our own way
Unhindered by contentions, though oppressed
By toil and poverty—of all these matters
I will not tell, but rather how one evening
In Winter, when the Leyden waterways
Were locked in ice, and the bare lindens shivered
Beside them, pinched and naked as ourselves,
John Robinson, our pastor, summoned all
To the house we had bought in Cloch Staech, by the belfr
Of St. Peter's church, wherein we had our meetings,
There, after prayers and fastings, to debate
The adventure of Virginia that had warmed
Our shrinking souls a twelvemonth with the promise
Of comfort and of freedom. For, though the Dutch
Kindly entreated us, and gave our people
Full praise for industry, sobriety,
And godly living, yet were we ever irked

By certain discontents: how that our poorer folk
Lived scantlier than in England; how the rich
Had ate up all their means, and could no more
Succour their needy brethren; how it seemed
A grievous thing that we must bend our necks
To the yoke of foreign regiment, and so lose
Our speech and name of English; how, alas,
Our ghostly husbandry was vain, the seed
Being scattered on a stony soil and falling
To waste, in that our neighbours were so steeped
In carnal sin and fain to desecrate
God's Sabbath, that our children, for the lack
Of proper tutelage, ran the risk to catch
These foul contagions; how of our brotherhood
Many grew aged, and, if they went not soon,
Must lay their bones in Babylon, and the Church
Fail of their wisdom; last, how the ten-year truce
Twixt the States General and the tyrannies
Of Spain was near to end—and, with that day,
The broken dykes of Holland would let in
A welter of bloody warfare, or, at best,
A popish persecution.

                    Now, to these things,
The major part consented; yet some that prized
Their bodies above their souls were loth to leave
The scant fleshpots of Leyden, and afraid
Of the sea's casualties—not for themselves
(As they protested) but for the weaker vessels,
Their wives and children. "For what else," they cried,
"Waits us in the Virginias but want,
Famine, and nakedness, with the dubious change
Of diet, air and water—and what neighbours
But heathen savages that shall devour
Our living flesh in collops?" Or again:
"How shall our dwindled means support the cost
Of this portentous voyage, and provide

[217]

Our needs when landed? Is it not ill enough
That we came to Holland, a near-by country, rich
In gold and civility?" But others said,
(And these the weightier) that no worthy deed
Nor honourable action ever was done
But with great hindrance; and these carking fears
Might never come to pass, or, being met,
Prove antic scarecrows flapping in the mist
Of ignorance, by their affrighted eyes
Magnified beyond measure, as are mites
Seen through a burning-glass. For those fierce cannibals
They feared: Were they so deaf they could not hear
The muttered throbbing of the angry drums
And clank of deadly weapons that foretold
War pestilence and famine in the streets
Of Holland—and were the Spanish soldiery
Kinder than savages?
                              So they that feared
Were silent, and we fell to the debate
Of whither we should go. Now some were earnest
For voyaging to Guiana, where, they said,
Spring smiled for ever on wide valleys blest
With a perpetual greenness, bringing forth
Nature's abundant fruits without the labour
Or art of Man—and, in that radiant clime,
The poor would soon grow rich, having no need
For costly raiment or the kindling
Of hearths in Winter; nor had the jealous Spaniards
Planted yet in Guiana, having all
The colonies they could keep. But others said:
Such lands, uncleansed by cold, were pestified
By manifold diseases and impediments
Noisome to English bodies, as a tilth
Whose clods no frost hath powdered, yields a crop
Throttled by tare and bindweed. For the Spaniards:
These would but wait till we grew fat to filch

Our gains and so displant us, as they did
With the poor French in Florida, and we
Too feeble to resist. Then they that pressed
The project of Guiana murmured, complaining
That were we landed in the settled parts
Of the Virginias we were like to suffer
No lesser whips and scorpions for the cause
Of our religion than we had known in England—
And maybe greater. So it was resolved
By the larger number that we should acknowledge
The general governance of Virginia,
Yet settle by ourselves, and sue the King,
By godly friends at court, to grant us freedom
Of worship and belief—unto which end
We framed a Declaration of our Faith,
Showing in what slight measure we dissented
From that established; and it was agreed
That Master Brewster and I set forth to London,
There to spy out the land and seek the favour
Of Sir Edwin Sandys, the chief and treasurer
Of the Virginia Company, whom Brewster
Counted his friend, having held the Manor of Scrooby
From his father, the Archbishop, and kept him company
In the embassy of Holland. I deem it just
That the lot fell on Brewster, a grave elder
Of weighty means and learning; but why their voices
Were cast for me I know not; for I had small
Pretence save humble probity. Yet I do think
This choice occasioned envy, some preferring
Young Master Winslow, who was the better bred;
A gentleman of Worcestershire, whose father
Boiled salt at Droitwich, and was familiar
With Sir Edwin's brother, Samuel Sandys, that dwelt
Nearby at Ambresley . . . But of this no more—
Save that, had he been chosen, I had been spared
A grievous cross to carry, and the sharp thorns

Of cruel crimination.
               So we two sailed
To London, and Sir Edwin Sandys received us
As a loving brother, promising to bring
Our suit to the King's ears—which, when he heard
His Grace approved our purpose, yea, and called it
A good and honest motion, shrewdly asking
What profits we attended. And when Sir Edwin
Told him we would be fishermen, he cried:
"So God have my soul, this is an honest trade!
Such was the Apostles' calling." And instantly
It seemed the wind blew fair; but the King's mind
Spun like a flighty weathercock, and he said:
"Let them advise with the Bishop of Canterbury
And the Bishop of London"—which was an ill turn,
For no prelate could abide us. So we determined
To leave that prickly path and to draw back
Upon our former course, begging a patent
Of the Virginia Company, which, by the care
Of our loving friend, was granted at their court
Sitting in his house by Aldersgate. Thus were we freed
To settle in Virginia, and this progress
Momently dazzled us, so that we saw not
The darkness of our venture. But when we begged
The Company for craft to make the voyage,
They put us off, saying they had neither ships
Nor yet the means to furnish them, having been brough
To the brink of failing by the ill-success
Of earlier ventures and their servants' greed.
So turned we to the Dutch, craving the use
Of warships that might bear us to the port
They had named New Amsterdam, or a rough passage
In the fur-traders' barks. But the States General
Would have none of us, and, in this pass, we saw
Our project blighted, and the lively hopes
We had engendered blacken in the bud.

For, mark you well, we were but humble folk
Of poor condition that had only scratched
A bare living; and that the wealthier sort
(Though none was rich) had fret away their substance
In charity—so who could find provision
To float so vast a venture?

                In such a strait
Perplexed and daunted, there came to us at Leyden
A merchant, Master Weston, who, having heard
Our charter had been sealed, enheartened us
Not to be downcast, neither to lament
Our want of ships and money—for that himself,
And others that were his friends, would find us both,
Adventuring their fortunes and our slight means
In a common stock. And cheerfully he bade us
Think no more of Virginia, and have no truck
With the stingy Dutch—for that a new Plantation
Was planned, without the bounds and governance
Of the Virginias, to be called New England,
And thither we should go. So we took heart,
Subscribing the Articles that Master Weston
And his friends set before us, putting off
Our properties in Leyden; and though some few
Still hankering for Virginia, withheld
Their monies and themselves, we heaped together
Twelve hundred pounds, the Adventurers promising
Six thousand more. Thus, once again, they sent me
To England with Master Carver, there to make
Provision for the voyage—he in Hampton
To seek a proper ship, and I in London
To keep the common purse. There Master Weston
Came to me, with a face long as a fiddle,
Saying the Adventurers had grown ill-content
With our agreed conditions, and would draw back
Were they not more advantaged, two small things
Sticking in their throats: the first that, at the end

Of seven years, the dwellings we had built
Were not accounted common property
In which they had their several shares; the second
That, by these articles, they had no surety
That men would sweat but for themselves, neglecting
The general good. Therefore they now demanded
Their part, proportionate, in all we builded
And, of each labouring week, two days allotted
To serve the common wealth. And when I asked
What they would do if we refused, he said:
"Then all is likely to be dashed, for none
Will stake a single farthing—though myself,
Having pledged my promise for five hundred pounds,
Will stick to it—albeit it were a pity
That such a goodly project should be sunk
By cavilling at trifles when the voyage
Is under way, and, if we sail not soon,
The season will be lost." Then was I put
In a sad quandary, being so far removed
From the counsels of my brethren and invested
With such a heavy trust. But now, since time
And season pressed, and since their claims appeared
Not without rightness, oh, most unhappily
And rashly, I gave way—though not before
I had acquainted both my fellow-agents,
Carver and Martin, who, alike, consented
Unto the changed conditions, and conjured me
To doubt no more. Therefore I wrote to Leyden
Telling what I had done, in confidence
Of their approval, and moreover told them
How swiftly all matured, good Master Carver
Having hired a ship, the *Mayflower*, fit to carry
All to America, while I had treated
With a Pilot of repute, one Master Reynolds,
To lift them out of Holland in the *Speedwell*
That had been bought in Leyden, and that the rest

Might wait our joyful meeting. But there came back
From Leyden a stern missive of reproach
And accusation: that I had overstept
The bounds of my commission and had acted
With levity and negligence—not as the man
Of wisdom they had thought me, but the gudgeon
Of couzeners that with a specious bait
Had tricked my silly wits! Then, then indeed
My stomach rose in anger! Negligence?
Negligence? Negligence? Was I then negligent
Who, dazed with cyphering, had lain awake
Night after night, while antic figures skipt
Like inky mountebanks through my fuddled brain
Taunting my will to take them? I, who had clamped
The belt about my belly to compress
The fretful void of hunger, lest a penny
That I could save be spent? I, who had trudged
These London streets until their cobbles corned
My aching feet to serve them? Negligent,
I, who had neither thought nor spoke nor dreamed
These many months of aught but what could further
This darling enterprise? Why, if they deemed me
So faint a fool, had they not sent one better
Instructed and more zealous? Negligence?
Enough, enough! Even as I speak my head
Weakens and whirls! Yet stay—for now my breath
Heaves less tempestuous, and the headlong blood
Answers the curb of reason. Let me be calm . . .
I tell you, sirs, I am a simple man,
A wool-comber of Canterbury, and I wrought
According to my conscience. If I erred,
Theirs was the fault that sent me—and so I told them
Answering their cruel charge. Further, I said
That since they had so miscalled me I would lief
Be quit of the whole business, keeping nothing
But the poor clothes on my back. But no reply,

[223]

Came to my comfort ere the *Speedwell* dropt
Her anchor at Southampton.

                    On the morrow
Our Ruling Elder, Master Brewster, haled me
Before the assembled church, there to be judged
Like a bawd in a white sheet or malefactor
Clapt in the stocks for pelting; and when I rose
In that hushed gathering I saw men nod
And nudge and shoot their lips, and seemed to hear
Malicious whispers: *Cushman . . . This is Cushman . . .*
See this vile serpent Cushman that hath sold
Our bodies into servitude! Robert Cushman:
This is the man! But when, at last, I spake,
My voice dried in my throat, so that they craned
With leering looks to hear my plea, and smirked
To see me so discomfited. At which
My lips moved soundless, and all I would have urged
In my defence fled from my mind, while tears
Dripped down my cheeks. Then silently I turned,
Gazing at Master Carver and Master Martin
Who had been my partners; but neither of them spoke,
And the cock crew not . . .

                    And though I was assoiled
Of criminous intent or wilful error,
Yet, ever afterwards, I was the butt
Of pointing fingers and wry looks that told
Of scorn, not charity. And when, at length,
We were put forth from Hampton, contrary winds
Having hindered us a week, then I was lodged
In the lesser ship, under the regiment
Of a tormentor: that same Master Martin
Who lately had forsook me. Of this man
I will speak as little as I may, for fear
My tongue should master me; but of the ship
And her false captain, Reynolds, I must tell
The truth, and fear not. Know, then, that the *Speedwell*

[224]

Was bought in Leyden, and the Hollanders—
For lust of gain, and in the certitude
Our folk knew not the sea—had overmasted
Her hull so grievously that, ere she made
Southampton, she was leaking. And Master Reynolds
(Or so he said) durst not put out to sea
In such a sieve till she was searched and mended,
At a sore charge to our scanty purses. Next,
When we put forth under a press of sail,
He said the leak was worsened, and took us in
To Dartmouth for new scrutinies that showed
The Hampton shipwrights had as little honour
As they of Holland—for in the bilge was found
A piece of planking that a man could shift
With his fingers, and salt water pouring in
As through a mole-hole. So, once more, we trimmed
The vessel, and to meet the reckoning sold
Of butter four score firkins, ill to spare
On such a lengthy voyage, and, having lost
Of the favourable season ten more days,
Put forth in hope. But when she met the waves
That Westward of the Scilly Islands swell
Out of the main Atlantic, this poor ship
Sprang yet another leak; and the sea flowed
Into her hold so fiercely that the captain
Feared she would founder straight. Little cared I
(But for my luckless brethren) whether she sank
Or swam! So foully had the heaving sea
Misused my stomach, and the cunning spite
Of Master Martin racked my bruiséd mind
With brags and insults, that when the captain cried
For hands to man the pumps I could not raise
My quivering limbs, but like a carcase lay
Lifting and falling as the *Speedwell* groaned
And shuddered as in anguish, and the bilge
Soused my insensible body. Gladly then

Had I given up the ghost, freely committing
That body to the deep, and to my Maker
A trustful soul that in humility
Looked for the Resurrection. There, beside me,
Lay Master William King; and oft we wondered
Which of us twain should first be thrown to feed
The fishes; yet, so wondering, sank at last
Into a profound nescience that was nearer
To death than sleep. But when, at last, I woke,
And Master Martin rudely summoned me
To mount the ladder to the deck, I saw
The *Mayflower* close beside us, and the roofs
Of a grey city rising from the verge
Of quiet waters, that the seamen said
Was Plymouth. And though I fell upon my knees
To thank God for the miracle that had brought us
Out of those ravening waves, yet did I shudder
To think of setting forth once more. But that
Was not to be; for Reynolds, who I know
Had no liking for the venture and his promise
To bide with us a year, now flatly swore
He would never take the *Speedwell*, were she trimmed
A hundred times! Therefore it was determined
(And I too faint to question) that such of us
As had the courage should be put aboard
The *Mayflower* and continue on the voyage.
But I, alas! had none—my sufferings
Having utterly undone me—and was carried
To land upon the Barbican, where I lay
Nine days light-headed; for when my eyes were shut
The bed still heaved beneath me as though swayed
By the storm's groundswell. Thither, on the tenth,
Came Master King, who told me that the *Mayflower*
Had weighed and put to sea, and led me forth,
Leaning upon his arm, with painful steps
To climb the Hoe. As fair a sight it was

As Moses from the Mount of Pisgah saw
Gazing on Palestine: beneath our feet
The close-packed roofs of Plymouth; before our eyes
The firth, within its greening girdle, flecked
With tawny wings of fishing-craft that skimmed
The crinkled waves like seamews—and far, far,
Dipped in the watery horizon, a tower
Of lonely canvas, alabaster-white
In the seaward sun's pure radiance; a ship
Transfigured, yet so far away she seemed
Moveless and visionary. But I knew
This was indeed the *Mayflower*, and that she moved
With crowded sail to Westward on the course
Of the Virginias—yea, and that all my heart
And hopes had gone aboard her, with the friends
I had loved and served so faithfully, yet was I cast
Away like a worn clout, and so abandoned
To miserable emptiness . . . Forgive me,
Sirs, I can speak no more.

XXIII

Interlude

What were you carrying, Pilgrims, Pilgrims?
What did you carry beyond the sea?
 We carried the Book, we carried the Sword,
 A steadfast heart in the fear of the Lord,
 And a living faith in His plighted word
 That all men should be free.

What were your memories, Pilgrims, Pilgrims?
What of the dreams you bore away?
 We carried the songs our fathers sung
 By the hearths of home when they were young,
 And the comely words of the mother-tongue
 In which they learnt to pray.

What did you find there, Pilgrims, Pilgrims?
What did you find beyond the waves?
 A stubborn land and a barren shore,
 Hunger and want and sickness sore:
 All these we found and gladly bore
 Rather than be slaves.

How did you fare there, Pilgrims, Pilgrims?
What did you build in that stubborn land?
 We felled the forest and tilled the sod
 Of a continent no man had trod
 And we stablished there, in the Grace of God,
 The rights whereby we stand.

What are you bringing us, Pilgrims, Pilgrims?
Bringing us back in this bitter day?
The selfsame things we carried away:
The Book, the Sword,
The fear of the Lord,
And the boons our fathers dearly bought:
Freedom of Worship, Speech and Thought,
Freedom from Want, Freedom from Fear,
The Liberties we hold most dear,
And who shall say us Nay?

XXIV

The plain tale of Bill Shelton, taverner,
At the sign of the Talbot (which most men call 'the Dog')
In the city of Worcester, where I was born and bred
And still, thank God, continue—having endured
More changeful fortunes in these ten short years
Than most men in their lives—though, now they are past,
I would not change my lot for any other's,
Nor yet regret them. Well do I remember
How first the word of War came to my ears
By the mouth of young Sam Butler, whom I had known
As a boy at Bartonbridge, and now abode
At Strensham, where his father leased a farm
Of Sir William Russell. Sam was a strong-set fellow,
High-coloured, with a head of sorrel hair,
And a tart tongue that lapped my sack more gladly
Than his dad's buttermilk, yet so fanciful
I never knew whether he spoke in jest
Or earnest. And Sam winked at me and said:
"Well, William, so 'tis war." And I, mistrusting
His vein, laughed in his face, till he, more gravely,
Told how the festering dissidence that had grown
'Twixt King and Commons, now had reached a head,
And with a wilful lancet-thrust the King
Had pricked it, leaving Windsor to set up
His flag at Nottingham, whence he had called
On all men of goodwill to arm themselves
And prove their lealty, and on all the sheriffs
To muster their militias. But when I swore
I was glad we dwelt in Worcester, where no harm
Could come to us, Sam Butler laughed again
And slapped me on the back and went his way,
Leaving me in a ferment. For strange it is

[230]

That this very syllable of War has power
To whip the pulses and inflame the thoughts
Of ordinary folk, who have no liking
For violence, yet will run a hundred yards
To watch a dogfight or a drunken bout
Of fisticuffs, yea, and take sides. Thus I,
Who cared nothing for the Parliament, and little
For the King's Majesty, found myself stirred
To sudden excitation, and ran indoors
Breathless to tell my good wife, Kate, who stood
A-scouring of the pewter, and, when she saw me
Red-faced and bivering, bade me souse my head
Under the pump to cool it, saying that this
Was but another of Sam's fooleries,
And I an oaf to credit him. But, for once,
Hers was the greater folly, as we knew
Within a week when ten troops of dragoons
Rode clanking through the Sidbury Gate, and some
Were billeted upon us: Sir John Byron,
Their colonel, and his lieutenant usurping
Our very bed. And in Kate's buttery
They locked some hundredweight of silver brought
From the colleges at Oxford. Many have said
That the King's cavalry were a vile crew
Of profligate pillagers; but most that came
To Worcester with Sir John were simple lads,
Small farmers' sons and country gentlemen
Of the lesser quality, who brought the Talbot
Good custom—yea, and paid their reckonings
In ready money, nor ever laid a hand
On wife or maid unwilling; though some few
Were roaring blades bred in the insolence
Of foreign wars, whose braggart manners changed
When once they found I had learnt to use my fists
In the boxing-booth of Pitchcroft at the fair
Of Barnabas. So, a full month, we lived

[231]

Right prosperous and merry, till word came
That Lord Essex, with some twenty thousand men,
Was marching upon Worcester. That same night
We woke to hear the rattle of musketry
And a battering on the Sidbury Gate, a stonesthrow
From where we slept: whereat I leapt from bed
And clutched my sword, determined to defend
My native city; but Kate snatched at the tail
Of my shirt and hauled me back, miscalling me
A fool to make or meddle in a business
That was none of ours—and since I knew no sword
(Once it was drawn) was sharper than Kate's tongue,
I got me back to bed and lay there, strained
To listen, while the musket-shots and the hammerings
On Sidbury Gate died down, and the great bell
We call Hautclere in the cathedral rang
At the first hour for Matins. All that night
I slept no wink; but early on the morrow
Heard how a body of Roundhead cavalry
Under Nathaniel Fiennes, thrusting in front
Of Essex's main force, had hoped to find
The gate unguarded, but, their courage failing
In the event, had faltered and ridden on
By Pixham Ford or Clevelode to the West
Of Severn, where now they sate astride the road
To Shrewsbury, waiting for the rest to close
On Worcester from the East. And next we heard,
By messengers from Bewdley, that Prince Rupert
Was pressing South to succour Sir John Byron
And pluck him forth ere he was ground to meal
Between two millstones. But we little knew,
When Byron's trumpet called his men to horse,
That Rupert was already come and bivouacked
By Powick in the Wickfield. Here as he lay
Beneath a thorn, and his horse grazed beside him
Knee-haltered, suddenly there rose a cry:

[232]

"The enemy is upon us!"—Fiennes's troop
Having crossed in double file the narrow bridge
That spans the Teme at Powick, and straggled through
A narrower lane that skirts the Chequers Inn
To spread abroad in Wickfield. Instantly
Prince Rupert and his brother Maurice leapt
Into their saddles—and a short space behind
Came Wilmot, Digby, and Sir Lewis Dives,
Launched on a charge; and these five cavaliers
Tore like a thunderbolt into the midst
Of those bewildered Roundheads, while the rest
Of Rupert's horsemen, swiftly following,
Fell on the scattered van and hurled them back
On their advancing comrades, crowding all
Into the sunken track that, to this day,
Is known as Cut-throat Lane. Ay, many throats
Were slit in this encounter, but even more
Bodies and limbs down-trampled in the mellay
Of plunging horses that crashed through the hedge
On either hand to crush them. And the remnant
That reached the bridge to Powick, fled flock-meal
Till they were safe in Pershore! Such was the first
Battle of Worcester: a rousing victory
For the King's cause, and, to my simple mind,
A husk blown from the threshing-floor to show
How moved the wind. For surely now, I thought,
We might sleep in our own comfortable bed
Until the war was over; but Kate, more prone
To see things darkly, said they must be worse
Ere they were better—and God in heaven knows
She was right for once: no sooner had Rupert gone
With Byron and his precious plate to Shrewsbury,
Than out we went again—our bed being filled
By a renegade cousin of Sir Samuel Sandys
Wounded at Powick; and next day at noon
Essex's army, of twenty thousand men,

[233]

Poured in through Sidbury Gate and overflowed
Our streets and dwellings, like the locust-plague
That ate up Egypt; and these Parliament men
Were not as Byron's lads, who spoke our tongue
And knew our ways, but an unbridled host
Of Cambridge and East Anglia, that reckoned
Worcester a conquered Canaan, and its people
Idolatrous Amalekites to be harried
And smitten, hip and thigh. There was not a house
In the city left unpillaged, not a man
Of worth not held to ransom, not a church
Unrobbed or undefiled; and when these brutes
That labelled themselves godly men had rifled
The taverns of the city, and reeled forth
O'erflown with drunken arrogance, they broke down
The doors of the cathedral, where they turned
The nave into a camp, lighted by fires
Fed from the organ-casing; and they made
The choir and aisles their privies, and the cloisters
A stable for their horses, with a midden
Heaped in the garth—while some, that deemed themselve
Most righteous, fell upon our monuments
And sacred images, hacking off the noses
Of prelate and of saint, and shattering
The painted windows, till the polluted aisles
Were paved with splintered glass. And the dragoons
Of Essex, in their orange scarves, put on
The canons' vestments, prancing on College Green
In blasphemous buffoonery, and mocked
Service and sacrament. It has been said
That Oliver did these injuries; but I know,
Having seen with my own eyes, that they were wrought
By the rabble of Lord Essex. From that day
I have hated every Roundhead—and Kate, my wife,
Was bitterer than I. For three hard months
They battened on our substance, till defeat

At Edgehill made them fearful, so Lord Essex
Abandoned Worcester to the King, and left us
To lick our sores in peace. Peace, did I say?
Ay, there is peace in death—and Worcester now
Was but a fly-blown carcase, or an oak
Blasted by lightning, that, when Spring returns,
Puts forth a feeble show of wonted leaf
Though hollow at the heart. So, when that tempest
Had rolled away from Worcester, she was left
A hungry, sullen city, on every hand
Compassed by neighbouring tumult, and within
So rent by civil faction that none dared
Speak his mind openly—nor could one venture
Beyond the gates for fear of roving bands
Of either party, that now profited
By the storm's aftermath to make a prey
Of hapless travellers. Now no provision
Of wine or victuals reached us: for the roads
Were mired by trampling horsemen and the wheels
Of heavy guns and limbers, and every bridge
Was cracked or broken down. Therefore my wife,
Wise in her generation, did conjure me
To bide indoors and keep my blabbing mouth
Tight-padlocked—which was irksome for a man
Companionable by nature, and no less
For the purpose of his trade! Thus we abode,
Shut in the Talbot, while the bloody tides
Swung to and fro about us; and though it seemed
The royal cause went ill, no rebel force
Dared touch us for a twelvemonth, till, at last,
They sent Sir William Waller—him they called
The Night-owl—with three thousand horse and foot
To take the city; and his trumpeter
Rode to the Sidbury Gate, and sounded there
His summons to surrender. But William Sandys
Gave back a scornful answer, telling him:

[235]

"This was not Hereford." Whereat the Gloucester Blues
Charged on the Friary Gate, but were thrown back,
While Waller's cannon loosed their fire on Sidbury,
Nor could we answer them—for Will Berkeley's house,
Without the gate, covered their batteries—
Till, in the night, we sallied forth and razed
That hindrance to the ground; and all our women,
My wife among them, with mattock, spade and shovel,
Levelled our field of fire, uprooting hedges
Fences and mounds to give the gunners ease.
And Waller, hearing that Prince Maurice came
From Oxford to relieve us, slunk away
With his tail between his legs—for, as he said,
He had no luck in Worcestershire—and left us
Unfallen, if not unscathed. In the fourth year
Of this lamentable war our plight grew graver,
Dudley and Hartlebury and Madresfield
Having fallen to the Roundheads, one by one,
Like over-ripened choke-pears, and at last,
No loyal garrison in all Worcestershire
Save ours surviving, Fairfax, who then beset
The City of Oxford, sent forth Colonel Whalley
To make an end of us. Two woeful months,
All but one day, we were besieged and bore
The weight of Whalley's cannon that cast their shot
Whither they would, till every second house
In Sidbury was riddled like a colander,
And many fired. Little do I remember
What happened day by day. There is a measure
In human torment when the mind grows void
Of feeling and is numbed, and, though the body
Goes through the actions of a living man,
The heart is mortified—when pain and hunger
Nay, even death itself, seem incidents
That have no power to move us. But this I know:
That, on the day Prince Maurice sent us word

Oxford was fallen, and we could no longer
Hope to resist, and when our gates, so boldly
Defended, were thrown open to the enemy,
We hardly knew the import, but stood dazed
And staring on the street as they marched in.
And this I know: that those who stood beside me,
My neighbours and familiars, seemed shrunken
To gaunt anatomies; and I, not guessing
How I was withered too, looked at my wife
And found her an old woman. Then a wave
Of pity overcame me, and fierce anger
Against the crass stupidity of the passions
That had set us by the ears—so that I cared
Neither for King nor Parliament, but only
That we might go about our ways in peace
And die in our own bed. But when I spoke
My mind, my wife's eyes quickened, and she chid me
For a despicable chicken-hearted recreant,
Saying that while the King was yet alive
We were bounden to stand by him and to serve
His cause, no matter what the cost. So I,
Rather than vex her (for I loved this woman
Most dearly) did consent, and locked my grudge
Within my breast. Three miserable winters
The war dragged on, while we grew spare and wan
With waiting, till the Scots betrayed the King
To Cromwell, and his bloody-handed crew
Condemned their hapless prisoner to suffer
A traitor's death. At this a dreadful shudder
Shook the whole body of England; for even they
Who had borne arms against him never had looked
For such a monstrous ending. My poor Kate
Wept for a week, inconsolate, and I
Who had seen him in his glory, could not but feel
Compassion for this little man—no bigger
He looked, than a child's puppet—yet withal

So rich in majesty, who had been dragged
To the shambles by such butchers. Yet, for myself,
I must own I was less shaken—this sacrifice
Foreshadowing the end, that blessed day
When men with God's name on their lips would cease
From the slaughter of their brethren. But my wife
Rated me through her tears: "True, they have slain
Our King, but not his Kingship; that lives on
In Charles, his son." Whereat I held my peace
And let her have her say, knowing, alas!
How bloodshed breedeth bloodshed without end,
And nothing but exhaustion can abort
This foul fecundity—till, at length, we heard
That the Prince was landed in the North and marching
Hot foot on London, with an avenging host
Of eighteen thousand Scots; and, as he came,
The great Lords of the North and loyal gentry
Of Wales and Westmorland and Lancashire
Flocked to his banners. So speedily they moved
We could not count their progress, hearing one day
He was at Kendal, the next at Lancaster,
And in a week at Warrington, where we reckoned
He would turn aside to Shrewsbury, but instead
He held straight on for Worcester, confident
Of our proven loyalty. That joyful eve
The bells clanged ceaselessly, and bonfires lit
The venerable cathedral that had lain
Cold as a tomb and sightless since the Roundheads
Shattered the painted glass—but now it seemed
To be warmed to life once more; and on the morrow,
When I saw the King go there to pray, I thought him
More manly than his father, and little less
Majestic in his mien; a swarthy fellow
Who laughed like any other when he was pleased,
And had a jest for all, and a bold eye
To make a maiden blush—which common manhood,

In one that was so great, kindled my loyalty
Anew—though I confess it burned less briskly
Than my poor wife's, who would have given her soul
To please him. What is this strange emanation
Of royalty, that beclouds the sight and dizzies
The brain like liquor? Who was this lanky lad
Black-browed and dusky-visaged, that I should risk
My skin to honour him? Yet it is true
I liked him well enough—but for the Scots,
Now camped on Pitchcroft, I had neither liking
Nor reverence: for sorrier soldiery
I never saw—the very lees and leavings
Of an impoverished land, as ill-equipped
In spirit as in raiment, more uncouth
Than the Welsh drovers whose bedraggled ewes
Limp into Hereford! For body-armour
They had naught but buff-coats, and for weapons, durk,
Cleaver, half-pike and cutlass; as for their horses:
They had no more sinew in their spavined hocks
Than would drag them to the knacker's. So, when I thought
Of the well-fettled steeds and tough cuirasses
Of Cromwell's redcoat Ironsides, my heart fell,
Boding disaster—though I little guessed
How, at that very moment, Oliver,
Having spurred southward on a parallel road,
Had ridden into Evesham, where, reinforced
By Lambert and Fleetwood, he lay between the King
And London. Thus the chequerboard was set
For the Second Battle of Worcester, and the last
Of this insensate strife, whereof the issue
Was never in doubt: for they outnumbered us
By two to one, of these the greater part
Toughened by war and tempered by the will
Of a famous captain—while the wayworn Scots
And levies of the North were far from home,
Ill-armed, ill-horsed, ill-nourished, and worse-fed,

With little spunk for fighting in the face
Of insufferable numbers, and consumed
By intestine jealousies. Only the King,
Serene and sunlike, smiled above the gloom
Of his faint-hearted followers, whether deluded
By flatterers or in deliberate despite
Of dooms foreseen, I know not; but he moved
Gaily among them, sedulous to compose
Their differences, and with a glancing wit
Rallying the doubtful. Ere the battle broke,
On the Second of September, he clomb the tower
Of the cathedral, where we saw him strut—
A manikin, no bigger than a fly
That specks the ceiling—with his optic-glass
Propped on the parapet. But what he saw
(And we saw not) had daunted stouter heart
Than his: the city caught in a snare of steel,
Made visible where glinting metal flashed
Through summer's heavy leafage or between
The stooks of ripened cornfields. On the hills
To eastward, from the verge of Perry Wood
To Severnside, the regiments of Fairfax
And Cromwell in a drooping crescent closed
The roads to Bath and Evesham. Beyond Severn,
Where Keith held Powick and Piscotty's foot
The hams above Teme's confluence, he espied
Fleetwood, with Deane and Lambert, who had straddled
The broken bridge at Upton, and, advancing
Northward by night, now menaced the main line
Of his defences: the deep-sunken channel
By which Teme, slinking through the marly meads,
Empties herself in Severn. Thus it appeared
That Cromwell's purpose was a double drive
Along both banks of Severn: and thereby
He courted mischief—for, if either thrust
Faltered, the King could hurry his reserves

Across the bridge at Worcester, and press home
The immediate mastery, while the Roundheads wasted
Inestimable hours in crossing Severn
Six miles downstream over the broken bridge
At Upton. But this Cromwell, who had learnt
War in the school of failure, was no dunce;
And on the morn of battle—which was the Third
Day of September, and the sun more fierce
Than midsummer—he threw a bridge of boats
Over the deeps of Severn, a pistol-shot
Above the mouth of Teme; and Fleetwood cast
Another over Teme, thereby contriving
To cancel our advantage; and, at the signal
That both were passable, then, East and West
The double thrust began. First Fleetwood launched
A hot assault on Powick, driving back
Keith's outposts from the church, while Lambert crossed
The second bridge to fall upon Piscotty,
And, East of Severn, Cromwell's culverins
Opened upon the earthwork of Fort Royal
That guards the Sidbury Gate, foreshadowing
An attempt upon the city. But though Keith
Gave ground awhile, and fierce Piscotty's highlanders
Momently wavered, yet they held their lines
Unbroken, and fought back so valiantly
That Fleetwood first, then Lambert, each was fain
To give them best, and sullenly withdrew
To whence they came. Then was the mystery
Of Cromwell's battle-craft made plain: for now,
Seeing his generals on the westward bank
Repulsed, he gathered to him three brigades
Of his own invincible Ironsides, and led them
Over the creaking bridge of boats, impetuous
As a hedge-skimming sparrow-hawk, and his van
Smote on Piscotty's flank, right shoulder forward,
Scattering the highlanders, and by this rout

Uncovering Keith, whom, caught upon two sides,
Deane overpowered and drove him out of Powick
Fighting from bank to bank, over the bridge
Into that very Wickfield where Prince Rupert
First thrashed Nathaniel Fiennes! When the King saw
How ill Keith fared, he fervently besought
Leslie, on Pitchcroft, to throw the Scottish horse
Into the wavering battle; but Leslie said:
That, "well as they might look, they would not fight";
Whereon this royal youth, with greater gallantry
And more resource than had been credited,
Burst forth from Sidbury Gate into the teeth
Of the roundhead cannon, hoping thus to breach
Their eastern lines now weakened by the lack
Of Cromwell's Ironsides. As he rode out,
With a recklessness not Rupert's self had equalled,
The Duke of Hamilton swerved left, and carried
The guns in Perry Wood, while the young King
Charged in the van full on their centre, driving
Lord Fairfax from the crest. Then, then indeed,
Had Leslie's cavalry been worth their keep,
Or shown one spark of loyalty to follow
Their King, the battle had been won, and Britain
Vowed to a different destiny! But none
Budged from his tent; and as the doubtful fight
Swayed on the hill-top, Cromwell's Ironsides
Came thundering back from Powick and rode through
The faltering ranks of foot, which, taking heart
From this mighty reinforcement, now surged back
Over the bloody crest and then swept down
Upon Fort Royal, irresistible
As the foam-capped bore of Severn that in a wall
Of angry water, when the moon is full,
Roars from the brimming estuary to be spent
On Diglis Weir. So that resistless tide
Of men engulphed Fort Royal; and as the flow

Of Severn is heaped upon itself and whirled
Backward, so now the very pith and flower
Of the King's army, in a direful rout,
Poured through the conduit of the Sidbury Gate
Into the city's heart—and where of late
The Lion of Scotland had flaunted on the fort
Fluttered the rebel blue, while from the scarp
The parliament gunners turned the captured cannon
To blast a way before. Yet, even now,
The King fought on, fearlessly rallying
A handful of his bravest—and had been taken
At the Commandery door, but that Will Bagnall,
A simple waggoner, lugged his plunging team
Betwixt him and the rebels, while he slipped
Within the gate to safety, and, once again,
Rallied the fugitives to turn and face
His enemies. Yet no sooner had he gathered
A faithful few about him, than he heard
A clatter of galloping hooves, and turned to see
The winnowed remnant of his cavalry
Whirling like chaff down Lich Street in full flight
From Fleetwood's men and Lambert's, that had carried
The Severn Bridge. Then, then, alas, he knew
The battle lost—and only then bethought him
Of his own safety, though whither he should flee
'Twas hard to tell: the Foregate being blocked
With stones, and Bridge Gate, Friar's Gate and Sidbury
Held by the Roundheads! But one loyal soul
(Whose name, for his skin's sake, I will not utter,
Though you may guess it) led him roundabout
Back of the Cornmarket to St. Martin's Gate
And a green lane running northward. From that hour
This man hath heard no word of him, though it is said
He is safe in France; but of our city's fate
Much may be told: for now we knew the difference
Between a city ceded and one sacked.

All day, till it was dark, the roundheads hewed
Their way through teeming streets and wet their blades
In the bodies of the innocent, and by nightfall
Sidbury was strewn with powder-blackened dead
Lying in swathes like beanstraw, and the gutters
Smelt like a shambles smoking with warm blood.
A body of braggart redcoats took the Talbot
For their Lord General's quarters, whither he came
At midnight, and there slept, if such a man
Could close his eyelids after such a deed
As was the sack of Worcester! Now that night
We did not see him, for neither Kate nor I
Could bear to look upon him; but next morning
They told us he was hungered, and commanded
That we should give him meat—whereon my wife
Swore we had not a morsel; but they brandished
Their swords so threateningly that I, to save her
From worse, consented, saying that all we had
Was a stale crust and a tankard of small beer,
Which I set upon a platter and bore upstairs
To the Lord General's chamber. Thrice I knocked,
But had no answer; then, with shrunken courage,
Entered, and saw there were but two men within:
The one, a clerk or secretary, sate
With a paper on his knees, and in his hand
A quill, intently listening. The other
Stood with his back to me: a thickset man
Of middling height, in a buff doublet, girt
With a scabbard-belt—and when he stirred, his sword
Clanked on the floorboards. And this man, I guessed,
Was the Lord General Cromwell—but neither he
Nor the clerk heeded me as I stood waiting
And the platter dithered in my hands. At last
He spoke, in a harsh voice: "What hast thou written?"
And the penman, softly: *"Great fruit of the success . . ."*
"Ay, that was it: *"Great fruit of the success . . .*

Of the success . . . Now dip thy pen again:
The dimensions of this Mercy are above
My thoughts. . . . *My thoughts.* . . . *It is, for all I know,*
A crowning Mercy. Lord God Almighty, frame
Our hearts to real thankfulness for this
Which is alone his doing!" Then he paused
While the pen creaked, and pausing, looked on me
Who stood abashed and quaking. But I doubt
He saw me; for his melancholy eyes,
Deep-sunken in the blotched and furrowed face
Of an ailing, ageing, weary man, stared forth
As blank as lightless windows—nor could I guess
What dark impenetrable brooding filled
The sombre brain behind them. But those eyes,
And that face, so sad in victory, are stamped
Upon my vision yet; and still I see
That craggy frame, whose shape might have been hewn
From a block of Malvern granite, stand before me,
Not as a ruthless conqueror, but a man
Of sorrows. And this also I perceived,
That the presence of this commoner breathed forth
A majesty so awful and a power
So palpable that the King, for all his valour,
Seemed only pitiful, and the princely graces
That had won my heart, mere gauds and ornaments
Beside this homespun greatness. Suddenly
Cromwell's eyes fastened on me, and his face
Flushed as he clutched his sword-hilt: "Who art thou?
Who gave thee leave to enter?" Then, seeing me
Unarmed and stammering, he shot back the sword
Into the scabbard and laughed aloud. And now
His voice seemed kindly, and the saddened eyes
Good-humoured. "What?" said he. "Hast brought me
Then art thou welcome! This is the first bread [breakfast?
I ever broke in this malignant city!
Who knows if it be poisoned?" But when I said

I could swear there was no harm in it, he frowned,
Bidding me not to swear after the manner
Of the ungodly; but this reproof, I reckon,
Was not unfriendly meant, for then he smiled
And took the platter, bidding me be gone
And strive to mend my speech. But when my wife
Waylaid me on the stair and badgered me
To tell her all, and I, poor fool, affirmed
That this monster (as she called him) was a gentleman
Humane and kindly, then she rated me
For a giddling weathercock, saying she rued
The day that we were wed, and from that hour
Never forgave me. Yet I still maintain—
And none shall shake me—that the Lord Protector
Was an honest man, who, having set his hand
To the plough, scorned to turn back, but drove his furro
Straight to the end foreseen, and that the harvest
Of our present peace would never have been garnered
But for the coulter of this ruthless ploughman:
For he that sows in tears, the Psalmist saith
Shall reap in joy, and doubtless come again
Bringing his sheaves with him. . . .

XXV

Twice in the fires of sacrifice
Consumed has London lain:
Twice has London burned, and twice
Has London lived again.

First there came the lustral flame
That in a woeful day
Was sent to cleanse the pestilence
And burn her sins away;

When through her crumbling tinder
Winged by the frenzied East
The fire that none could hinder
Ran like a ravening beast.

From East to West the wildfire swept,
It flew from street to street;
It carried Temple Bar and leapt
The Tyburn and the Fleet;

Then, wheeling back in the wind's teeth,
It licked the city's walls
And kindled with its panting breath
The roof of old St. Paul's,

Whose fragments flown from white-hot stone
Like plunging round-shot fell,
While molten lead from overhead
Flowed fast down Ludgate Hill,

And shepherds from the lonely height
Of Hampstead gazing down
Saw heaving in a lake of light
The heart of London town,

And heard, like distant thunder,
Roofs, towers and temples crash,
As London's heart sank under
A shroud of smoking ash.

Yet on that charred and cindery shard
Of ash and calcined stone
There rose a London lovelier
Than ever man had known,

Of towers and spires and pinnacles
Whiter than cloud or foam:
And over all the church of Paul
Upreared its kingly dome.

From chambered spire and steeple
Each with a different voice
Her belfries called her people
To mourn or to rejoice;

Their chime and change and clanging peals
The risen city crowned,
And wove above her roaring wheels
Their fabric of sweet sound

Their voices sang of shine and gloom,
Of triumph and of rue;
Men heard them boom o'er Nelson's tomb
And peal for Waterloo.

But in the end there came a day
With darker boding filled,
When the wings of hate were at her gate
And London's bells were stilled;

When from Penzance to John o'Groats
The bells no longer swung—
For a seal was set upon their throats
And clamped each iron tongue;

ORDEAL BY FIRE, A.D. 1666–1940

When on the chimeless chantries,
On steeple dome and spire,
The Prussian's dread fire-raisers shed
A night-long rain of fire

That kindled rafters overhead
And cleft the graves below,
Thrusting the unremembered dead
Into the furnace-glow;

When soaring sparks whirled through the dark,
And towering billows tossed
Their crimson foam where Paul's grey dome
Rose like a deathless ghost.

Night after night in droning flight
We heard the raiders come;
Our steeples crashed about our feet
But still their bells were dumb;

And still we wait, for soon or late
Those bells will speak once more,
And the belfries reel with such a peal
As never was rung before,

To give these folk who never broke
The guerdon of their pain:
That the peace they earned when London burned
Has come to her again;

And on the soil they loved so well,
Their gay and dauntless eyes
Shall see from out that blackened shell
A phœnix city rise.

Twice in the fires of sacrifice
Consumed has London lain:
Twice has London burned—and twice
Shall London rise again!

XXVI

Interlude

THE ISLE OF VOICES

Ours is an isle of voices whose mild air
And gentle skies are sweetened everywhere
With a winged music that by day and night
Instils an essence of supreme delight
Or secret rapture on the listening ear,
Where is no season of the changing year
But hath its meed of song. Often in days
Of midmost Winter when the miry ways
Crinkle with cat-ice and the ebon thorn
Is sheathed in crystal shall a cloudy morn
Ring with the rapid notes the redbreast throws
To skies o'erburdened with unfallen snows,
When over frosty furrow and sere steep
One hears the whirring flocks of fieldfares sweep
With harsh, exultant clamour as they glean
Their beggarly harvest: often have I seen
The missel-thrush his stormy challenge cast
Full in the teeth of Winter's foulest blast,
While brindled dunnocks humbly chirp and stir
In starveling bushes of grey lavender;
While in the crannied wood-pile the wren flirts
His tail and frees his song in fiery spurts,
And the tiny goldcrest, like a flittermouse,
Cheeps in the swarthy cedar's topmost boughs.
And when at midnight the cold catalyst
Of arctic air has cleared the enshrouding mist
To star-shot crystal, and the earth revealed
Lies wan and desolate as a lunar field,
Out of that spectral stillness, beyond view,
Ripples the mellow quavering halloo

Of snow-soft owls that from the luminous dark
Answer the mating vixen's peevish bark.
Oft when grim days of February gird
The chastened brooks with iron have I heard
The chuckle of garrulous rooks that prize and peer
Within their ragged homes of yester-year,
Or lighting on the wind-swayed trivets test
The strength of twigs to bear the new year's nest;
Oft over seaward crags, where thrift and thyme
Are mingled, watched the pairing ravens climb
In widening circles, while the curlew pours
That liquid laughter which shall wake the moors
When snows are gone—and heard the whimbrel shrill
O'er saltings where dun estuaries spill
Their tidal fringe. Yet these disjointed cries
Are but the prelude of the pæans that rise
When the South West unseals the frozen springs,
And every bush is quick with whimperings
And flutings, as each tiny instrument
Strives to perfect the theme that shall be blent
In April's airy counterpoint. How sweet
The morn when the first chiff-chaff doth repeat
His tenuous distich that is pure and frail
As blackthorn petals that a whiff of hail
Or sleet can tarnish! How far richer then
The limpid cadence of the willow-wren,
And those clear torrents of excited song
The spiring whitethroat sheds! How blithe and strong
Waxes the blackbird's whistle as he weaves
His leisurely melismas—though he leaves
The spendthrift phrase unfinished in despite
Of laboured artifice! With what rich delight,
Ere the first gleam of orient amber breaks,
The throstle's jubilant reveille wakes
A multitudinous chorus to proclaim
Unclouded hope, sheer bliss without a name

Or reason—save that it is doubly sweet
To live and love in April, and to greet
The first-created miracle of light
As it were unfamiliar. There's no night
In April now but wafts upon their way
New clouds of witnesses—no dawn of day
But brings its new diversity of notes
To swell this ambient music from the throats
Of new-come singers, while from overhead
The sunlit carolings of the lark are shed
Like glancing raindrops, silvered as they fall.
Now from bare orchards bursts the clarion call
Of the bold chaffinch, where the firetail flits
With anxious chirpings; now the ox-eye whets
His rasping scissors, and the reedy plaint
Of the yellow-hammer wheezes far and faint;
Now, in shy coverts, where translucent leaves
Half hide her nestling, the green linnet weaves
Her heart-subduing tissue of soft trills
And inward murmurs; now on windy hills
The curlew whinnies wild, and tawny springs
Feed the fierce torrents where the ouzel sings
His wren-like snatch; now over upland vales
In wide-winged majesty the buzzard sails—
So high, his feeble melancholy call
Scarce reaches earth; now pewits swoop or fall
Harrying the air with frenzied catlike cry
Far from the nests where their pied fledgelings lie;
Now on the brambly waste, when eve is still
The blackcap and the garden-warbler thrill
The brake with flutings that the prentice ear
Deems the first nightingale's—but when we hear
That mastersong of May, without a peer,
In the swift lapsing of the lover's moon
We smile to think the blackcap's artless tune
Could ever have bewitched us, and remain

Rapt in mute ravishment as that golden strain
Rises and falls . . . and rises once again.
And oft we wonder how the sounds that shower
From that small syrinx can transcend the power
Of the mightiest music-makers to express,
In one brief burst of song, despair, distress,
Exultant joy, serenest happiness,
Hope, triumph, dread, inconsolable woe,
And pity such as none but angels know—
Till, with one exquisite note, more finely drawn,
The lingering cadenza fades on dawn
Or moonless dusk, and in our ears bereft
Of that ineffable beauty naught is left
But the craking of shy landrails as they cower
Couched in the dewy grass and hour on hour
Utter their rasping plaint—until the skies
Of May are mellowed by the cuckoo's cries
Gladdening the mists of morning as he floats
From elm to elm—and in these wayward notes,
So richly confident, we seem to hear
The authentic theme of Summer, though the ear
Grows weary of his clamours before June
Has cracked his voice—when, in the heat of noon,
Only the croonings of the ringdove lull
The leafy woods, and hedgerows that were full
Of song are silent as their singers lie
Mute in the tired contentment of July:
For now their greedy fledgelings are all flown,
And who should sing of love that sings alone?
These are the deeps of silence; never more
Returns the tenderness we knew before
The wild rose shed its petals: now we hear
Naught but harsh notes of petulance and fear
Or angry chattering as the magpies break
Their cover, and the jay's excited shriek
Startles the stillness, while from orchards bowed

Beneath their luscious burden rings the loud
Wild laughter of the yaffle, when between
Dark boughs he flashes in a streak of green
More brilliant than the hues of any bird
Save halcyon's azure. Now no more are heard
The swallow's twitterings as her fledgeling leaves
Her cup of dabbled clay beneath the eaves;
For the first brood is sunward flown, and they
That linger grow more venturous, day by day
Fettling weak wings for their prodigious flight
To the far South, as in the dwindling light
Of August evenings, when thin clouds of gnats
Dance in the dusk, they vie with flickering bats
To hawk this gauzy carrion—while on high
Shrill storms of swifts whirl through the darkened sky
Circling their dizzy steeple till no gleam
Of day is left, and, faint as in a dream,
We hear the nightlong clouds of waders pass
To their warm sands and saltings. Now, alas,
Dawn brings no murmurs of content nor songs
Of hope—but hurried wing-beats as the throngs
Of frightened linnets, scurrying overhead,
Whirr to the silken-seeded thistle-bed,
With greenfinch, twite, and amoret to dispute
Its plumy granaries; now from the scarlet fruit
Of yews and rowans, stealthy throstles gulp
Mouthfuls of sapid nectar and sweet pulp,
And from the berried elder blackbirds cull
Vinous ambrosia till their craws are full;
Now, on the new-turned tilth, wide-ranging flocks
Of daws and starlings feed, and patient rooks
Explore each furrow with deliberate care
And awkward gait—yet, when the cooling air
Of eve with risen vapours rings the sun
These hordes of silent foragers rise as one:
Slowly the rooks flap homeward, while the stares

In myriads gather, till the sky appears
Black with their cloudy cohorts as they sink
To their foul roosts upon the river's brink
Amid the shivering reeds and withy-beds,
Where from their hidden multitude there spreads
A babble of wild water . . . Long before
September lawns are spangled with the hoar
Of silvery cobweb where the spider spins
His weft of dewy gossamer, begins
The secret flight of singers that by day
Have long been silent, but now steal away
Borne on invisible wafts of air that glide
For ever Southward, like a soundless tide
That ebbs in darkness—till of those bright strains
That thrilled the prime of April, none remains
But the first-come, last-lingering chiff-chaff's call,
Fitful and feeble now—and with the fall
Of the first yellowing leaf, he, too, is fled.
Yet sometimes, in the opulent drowsihead
Of Luke's or Martin's Summer, comes a day
Of golden stillness, when the woods that lay
Bemused in deep autumnal slumber wake
To hear a flood of sudden music break
From out their tangled thickets—and it seems
That Spring has come again, and Winter's dreams
Are surely ended. Never rings more clear
The redbreast's voice than when the dying year
Chastens his ardour. Never did throstle sing
Louder in the green lustihood of Spring
Than when the glory of the stricken leaf
Lightens the glooms of Winter! Brief, too brief
Are these enchanted moments: soon dun floods
Shall drown the valleys, and November woods
Stripped of their mortal raiment naked stand:
Yet, even when December's leprous hand
Blanches our garden walks, the robin flits

I*

With bright eyes peering at the frozen spits
Of tawny mould turned from the gardener's spade,
And, like a gay familiar, unafraid,
Perches on his bent shoulders as he breaks
The crumbling clod, and, fluttering downward, takes
His morsel. But, at last, a season comes
When birds and men alike must keep their homes;
When, in still night, the flying snowflakes sift
Upon the dying year her funeral shift;
When, from our breath-bleared windows, we espy
A silent earth beneath a songless sky—
And of the vanished singers naught may know
But their starry signets printed on soft snow.

XXVII

DIASPORA

Salute we now the first adventurers
Of those storm-clouded or unsullied seas
That in their jewelled ambience enclasp
This many-coloured island: yet remember
How these were ever bred in cognisance
Of the sea's neighbourhood: there is no brook
Of midmost Mercia but can taste the brine
Of Trent or Severn, when the tidal floods
Of bore and eagre meet their lapsing flow
Of mountain-waters—no lark-haunted down
Nor upland arable but the sea-mew's wings
Whiten the ploughman's furrow, no native blood
Unstirred by those salt savours that beguiled
Celt, Saxon, Dane and Norman to forsake
Their homely garths and fields, and to explore
Mysterious oceans! So John Cabote sailed
From Bristol in the *Matthew;* so the *Mayflower*
Westward to barren Massachusetts bore
The zealots of a sterner creed; so Drake,
Half poet and half pirate, wholly brave,
Girdled the watery globe, and ballasted
With spice and silver, brought the *Golden Hind,*
By the Horn's perilous seaways and the Cape
Of Storms, safe home to Plymouth; so Chancellor,
In the *Edward Bonaventure*, braved the fangs
Of the fabled North-east Passage to Cathay,
And thwarted of that icy enterprise,
Over frore steppe and snowy tundra trudged
To Muscovy's drear heart, there to unveil
An empery undreamed of; so Ralph Fitch
In the *Tiger,* out of London, disembarked
At Tripolis in Lebanon, and bewitched

By the lure of beckoning distances, fared on
To fierce Aleppo, where the caravans
Of Babylon were gathered, and from thence,
Launched on the huge Euphrates, drifted down
To Bussorah, whose burning gulf divides
Desert Arabia from the ochreous isle
Of Hormuz—yet, provoked by discontent
Of such tame voyaging, must set forth anew
To Bantam, where the slant-eyed Javanese
Crawled to their hideous gods; so Frobisher,
Probing the deadly icepack on the coasts
Of arctic Labrador, furled his frozen sails
In Hudson's Bay, and with squat Eskimos
Trafficked his English wares for the sleek pelts
Of fox and sable; so a hundred more
Anonymous voyagers followed in their wake
Down the far vistas of a widening world—
Not of a settled purpose, nor in lust
Of treasure, like the Spaniard, but constrained
By mysterious compulsions to seek out
Strange climes and customs. Thus, when the dead ha
Of grudgeful Spain, loosened at Gravelines,
Relaxed its grip, then did the energy
Pent in this plodding island breed burst forth
Strong as a snow-fed torrent in the prime
Of lusty Spring, and, by that generous flood
Nursed and refreshed, a new-born nation rose
Sudden to its full stature. Never before
Was such a blossoming: heart hand and brain
Nerved by such ardour that the very skies
Seemed to be lifted and earth's bounds dissolved,
As, from imagination's loftiest peaks,
Their eyes, undazzled, saw a world in fee
To their bright daring, and in seas unknown
Their natural birthright. Now, from cove and creek,
These venturous islanders put forth, their holds

Crammed with the product of a nation rich
In handicraft and husbandry, for gold,
Silver and fragrant spices and soft silks,
Bartering their homespun fleeces from the looms
Of Cotswold—till there was no landfall left
In the known world but saw their topsails float
Like clouds on the horizon as they stole
Shoreward to anchor, no dusky race but knew
The uncouth accents of their island speech
And their bluff island ways. From the storm-vexed
Antilles to the tideless seas that lave
Old Tyre and Sidon, from the Golden Horn
To ageless Egypt, from the Baltic ice
To sweltering Madagascar and the flats
Of Mozambique, from the Arabian gulf
To jealous Goa and the coralline sands
Of the palm-fringed Moluccas forth they fared,
Wafted on tireless sails—and where they went,
Shrewd merchants followed after, stablishing
Marts for their musky trade, and from excess
Of unimaginable wealth, sent home
Fleets of fantastic lading and rich wares
That made this thrifty isle the cynosure
Of envious nations and chief counting-house
Of the old world, luring ambitious youth
To stranger voyaging. Many there were
Cut loose the ties that held them and forsook
Their motherland, transported by the zest
Of obstinate endeavour to subdue
The spite of stubborn nature and remould
Their chosen wilderness—yet gave their dreams
Familiar forms and substance, in the void
Shaping another England; and when their strength
Faltered, their progeny took up the task
Left by their fathers' fingers, to maintain
Their heritage of custom, faith and speech

Inviolate. But of all the alien lands
Wooed by these daring wanderers there was one
Most consonant with their nature, and most kind—
For all its rigours—to a blood that craved
The salt Atlantic air. It was a land
Hard on the coulter, where reluctant soil
Yielded a niggard harvest, and the fruits
Of earth were few; it was a treacherous land
Of tangled forests and swift waters, haunted
By fierce elusive enemies; a land
Vast and impenetrable, whose farthest bounds
No human strength could compass; a mute land
Of silences more terrible than sound;
A land of harsh extremes—of durable snow
Alternate with insufferable heat;
Of calms and hurricanes; of drought and flood;
Yet here these English settled, and here throve,
Their senses quickened with adversity,
Their sinew steeled by hazard, and their hopes
Buoyed by unfading visions of a bourn
Infinite in promise, ever beckoning
Yet ever unfulfilled; and, of their loins,
Within one toilful century, was begotten
A nation of a million souls, diverse
In creed and polity, yet one in race,
Custom and speech—their ancient blood refreshed
By the strange soil's infusions, yet the same
In virtue and defect. Thus, from the bounds
Of French Acadia, where St. Lawrence pours
His lake-fed torrents; from the woods of Maine
And Massachusetts to the palisades
Of Hudson and New Jersey; from the creeks
Of Maryland, where the great Delaware
Flows full from Pennsylvania, to the swamps
Of old Virginia and the coastal sands
Of southmost Carolina—there this breed

Gathered their strength, forgetful of the seas
That drew their fathers forth, their landward eyes
For ever brooding on the wealth that lay
Westward beyond the ranges, challenging
Their stalwart thews and spirits to forestall
The subtler Frenchmen who from North and South
Bade fair to fill their marches in the plains
Of Mississippi. Such was America:
Such were her sons . . . Toward our island too
In that same hour, stole an imperious shade
Cast by the Sun-King's glory. Little her wealth
Availed her, should the predatory power
Of rising France and fallen Spain be joined
In enmity—for now her pride of bloom
Seemed over and her branches overburdened
With rotten fruit; her ancient pieties
Relaxed in greed and luxury, her crown
Pledged in the dynast's pawnshop, while the fleets
Launched by the great Protector lay dispersed
Abandoned or unmanned. Yet, in those days
Of shame and peril, when that shadow stole
Across the plains of Flanders, menacing
Her narrow seas that were both livelihood
And safeguard, suddenly our land awoke;
Brushed from his throne the last of that light race
Whose perjuries had abased her, and sought out
Two saviours: first Dutch William, a dour man
Who loved her little and was less beloved
Save that he stood for liberty—the second,
War's matchless chieftain, Marlborough, mightiest
Of all her native warriors, whose cool mind,
Patient beyond belief, serene, humane,
Clear, swift, dispassionate, neither the guiles
Of labyrinthine Europe nor the malice
Of envious faction could confuse or turn
From his appointed task, that was to free

The coasts of Flanders from the dominance
Of overweening France, and this dear isle
From fierce aggressions. Four and twenty years
He waged unceasing war, time and again
Victorious, though frustrated by the doubt
Or sloth of timorous allies, yet returning
Patient as toilful Sisyphus to surmount
The pinnacles of hope—and, in the end
Gave back to the faint hearts that sent him forth
The peace they craved, the honour they had lost,
And with his palsied fingers turned a page
Bright with the glories of the Augustan Age.

XXVIII

From plough and cart, from byre and mart,
From hamlet, heath and town,
They pressed us out to swell the rout
And pull the French king down;
From jail and tavern, doss and ditch
We heard the fifers squeal:
Malbrouk s'en va-t-en guer-re
Mais quand reviendra-t-il?

In distant lands our clumsy hands
Took to the butcher's trade;
They learnt the use of flint and fuse
And smouldering grenade—
To keep the firelock's tinder dry
And whet the bayonet's steel:
Malbrouk s'en va-t-en guer-re
Mais quand reviendra-t-il?

We crossed the reedy Maas and freed
The marches of Brabant;
We laid our siege about Liége
And drove Boufflers to Ghent;
We loosed Venloo and Ruremond
From the invader's heel:
Malbrouk s'en va-t-en guer-re
Mais quand reviendra-t-il?

'Twas in the pride of cherry-tide
They turned us from the Rhine
By mountain roads that overflowed
With honey-coloured wine;
Through the soft vale where Neckar's stream
Turns many a water-wheel:
Malbrouk s'en va-t-en guer-re
Mais quand reviendra-t-il?

[263]

When fruit hung low on the August bough
And the corn was in the ear,
From Nevel's banks our red-coat ranks
Swept round on Tallard's rear
From Blenheim to the Danube's brink
In a ring of fire and steel:
Malbrouk s'en va-t-en guer-re
Mais quand reviendra-t-il?

When Flanders ways were mired in May
And the Whitsun fog lay white
For mile on mile along the Dyle,
Villeroi came out to fight;
Through the green rye to Ramillies
We made his whitecoats reel:
Malbrouk s'en va-t-en guer-re
Mais quand reviendra-t-il?

When earth grew dry in a hot July
The Frenchmen stole about
Our rearward guard at Oudenarde,
And turned to fight it out;
But we beat Vendôme and chased him home
To lick his wounds in Lille:
Malbrouk s'en va-t-en guer-re
Mais quand reviendra-t-il?

September rain had drenched the plain
When Marlborough met Villars
On the bitter day of Malplaquet
In the bloody wood of Sars—
When we drove the French from hedge to trench
And brought their king to heel:
Malbrouk s'en va-t-en guer-re
Mais quand reviendra-t-il?

[264]

But now this grudgeful land we trudge,
Forgotten as our dead;
And we that freed the world must needs
Cringe for a crust of bread
From folk who cheered us when they heard
The bells for Blenheim peal:
Malbrouk s'en va-t-en guer-re
Mais quand reviendra-t-il?

XXIX

Ille terrarum mihi praeter omnes
Angulus ridet . . .

The Scene, again, is Worcestershire: this time the extreme North
of the county, where the main watershed of middle England divides
the sources of streams flowing into Severn and the Atlantic Ocean from
those which feed the tributaries of Trent and are discharged into the
North Sea. This is a countryside very different from the vales of
Severn and Avon, which, when we last saw them, a hundred years ago,
consisted either of aboriginal oak-forest or hedgeless fields. Here one
might imagine oneself on the borders of Wales; for the landscape is
wild and tumbled and (as its politer inhabitants would call it) 'bosky':
a country of combe and coppice, sparsely cultivated, and cloven by deep
valleys through which flow the numerous brooks that are joined to form
the Stour. Though English agriculture has not yet been 'regulated' by
general enclosure, there are many hedged fields, of small size and
irregular shape, of the kind that characterize Herefordshire and
Shropshire to-day. Indeed, the little market town of Hales Owen,
which lies in the cup of the Stour valley, is actually attached to the
County of Salop. On a shelving slope half-way down the face of this
well-wooded escarpment, stands an undistinguished farmhouse, which,
during the seventeen years of its present occupancy, has become (according
to Dr. Johnson) 'the envy of the great and the admiration of the
skilful.' At this moment 'the great' are doing it the honour of a visit:
a distinguished company having just alighted from the horses which
have carried them over the rough road from Hagley, the seat of Sir
Thomas Lyttelton, past the graceful spire of Hales Owen church and
the nailmakers' tinkling anvils, to view Mr. Shenstone's walks and
inspect his improvements. A chaise, drawn by a tandem, and carrying
a plump, middle-aged man with a solemn face and large, sleepy eyes,
brings up the rear of the cavalcade. The leader of the party is George
Lyttelton: a tall, thin loose-limbed man of thirty-four. He is dressed,

[266]

with slovenly elegance, in a full wig, which frames his long, serious features, a purple riding-coat, tight breeches, and silver-buckled shoes: his attire a compromise between that of a courtier or clubman and that of a rustic squire, and a contrast, in any case, to that of Mr. Shenstone, whose ill-fitting grey coat and red waistcoat, unbuttoned and dusted with snuff, do not add to the grace of a figure already going to seed. Mr. Shenstone, moreover, 'wears his own hair', and has apparently paid little attention to it. The other visitors are a robust, jolly-looking fellow, with a rubicund face and lively eyes; a young sailor, a lad of sixteen, to whom he appears to be much attached; and a figure of far greater distinction, in a tie-wig: small headed, grey-eyed and thin-lipped, with a prominent aquiline nose. From a cage above the front door, a dishevelled blackbird surveys the scene without interest, while Mr. Lyttelton makes apologies and introductions in a mellifluous voice and measured phrases which largely mitigate his physical awkwardness.

LYTTELTON:

Dear Mr. Shenstone, I pray you will forgive
This sudden visitation; for my guests
Would have thought little of my entertainment
Had they not seen your Leasowes, and paid homage
To its creator. You know my sailor brother,
Tom Smith?
    (*The rubicund gentleman smiles and bows.*)
           His young companion's Alec Hood,
His servant in the *Romney*.
    (*The boy grins and bows awkwardly.*)

Mr. Pitt

You surely must remember? We had the privilege
Of coming here ten years ago—since when
The world has heard much more of him—*and* you, Sir.

SHENSTONE:

A name and face not easily forgotten.

LYTTELTON:

But wait! My chief surprise!

[267]

(*The plump gentleman has dismounted, with difficulty, from the*
tandem chaise, and strolls aimlessly towards them, pausing to
look at the view.)

Another servant
Of the Sacred Nine: my good friend Mr. Thomson.
Jamie, for heaven's sake wake up! Our host
Awaits your pleasure.

THOMSON:

(*With a start*) Sir I beg your pardon
And Mr. Shenstone's. I am quite bemused
With the languor of a prospect that would turn
A clod into a poet: a Parnassus
Whose very air breathes music. Mr. Shenstone,
I envy you your heritage.

CAPT. SMITH:

(*With a mischievous twinkle*) Do you reckon
It equals Hagley, Jamie?

THOMSON:

(*With a strong Scots accent*) Sir, comparisons
May sometimes illustrate, but never prove,
And seldom edify. (*He sighs.*) My indolent Muse,
Inspired by such environs, might have ventured
On more ambitious wings.

SHENSTONE:

Sir, she has soared
Beyond my sight already in your *Seasons*.
If she flew higher still, she would be lost
In heaven—and we the poorer. But your envy
Seems disingenuous in one who dwells
At Kew Foot Lane, within an hour of town,
Where wits are tempered by the Social Flame
And sharpened by the talk of Men of Taste,
While mine grow dull and rusty. If a man
Could eat his cake and have it, I would choose

[268]

our lot rather than mine, Sir; but, alas!
My fare's but bread and water, as becomes
My rural hermitage, and nothing varies
ts plainness but the occasional condescensions
Of cultivated neighbours, who convey
Their friends to view my walks. This happy day
Shall mark the lonely Shepherd's calendar
With a red letter, long to be remembered
n his tedious annals.

PITT:
I think you undervalue
Your blessings, Sir. Indeed, Nature has done
Everything for you.

SHENSTONE:
I dare to hope I, too,
Have done something for Nature. I shall be honoured
f you will judge the improvements I have made
n my *ferme ornée*. . . .

SMITH:
Glancing at his watch) Ay, ay, Sir: Let's weigh anchor,
Or we shall miss the tide and spoil our dinner.
Eight bells, upon my soul!

HOOD:
In a whisper) What is that bird, Sir?

SHENSTONE:
My blackbird: a poor fledgeling my man Tom
Found fluttering near the nest: a quill of spirit
And elegance, both masculine and musical.
But, like his modest master, he don't sing
To order or in company. A true poet!
Eh, Mr. Thomson?

THOMSON:
Then he's like to starve
For lack of patronage. Send him to London,
And he'll soon learn that lesson!

[269]

SHENSTONE:

               If Master Hood
Fancies a cage-bird, I have little doubt
My man could find another that would bring
His native woodnotes to an ear that knows
Only the roaring seas.

SMITH:

            What say you, Alec?

HOOD:

Thank you, Sir. But I'ld rather have a parrot
That swears in Spanish, like the bo'sun had
On board the *Romney*—or the blue mockaw
He got from Pernambuco.

SHENSTONE:

             Then, by your leave,
I will precede you, gentlemen. Mr. Pitt,
Doubtless you will perceive how I have wound
This walk, to cheat the eye, lest it foresee
The ground the foot must travel? At this alcove
It opens on an avenue composed
By smooth transitions to produce the effect
Of distancing.

PITT:

        How so, Sir?

SHENSTONE:

             You will observe
This end is planted wider, with black yews,
Then firs, then oaks and alders, by degrees
Passing through greens more fadey—till, at length,
Birch, almond-willow, and silver-osier close
A nebulous visto that appears to end
Remotely.

PITT:

(*Enthusiastically*) Most ingenious! You combine
The hues of Nature as Zuccarelli blends
His pigments!

[270]

SHENSTONE:
By the sad necessity
Of my *angusta res.* Had I the scope
Of Hagley's ampler acres, such devices
Of Art would not constrain me . . .

(*He pauses, the flow of his period disturbed by a burst of philistine
laughter from behind him.*)

Captain Smith,
May we not share your merriment?

SMITH:
(*Still chuckling*)　　　　　　　　Egad, Sir,
It was this young limb of Satan who suggested
That jealous folk might show your avenue
From the wrong end.

SHENSTONE:
I fear he is not the first
To have discerned my weaknesses and made them
The butt of malice.

(*With a significant glance at* LYTTELTON.)
Some have even shown
My walks in Winter, when ruffian Boreas
Denudes their Fauns and Dryads.

PITT:
(*With corrective courtesy*) Pray proceed.
I am all attention. Your Philosophy
Of Gardening enchants me.

SHENSTONE:
(*Encouraged by the compliment*) As a Poet
Rather than as a Painter, I regard
My landscape as an Epick, where the sublime
And pleasing are commingled, or succeed
With gradual alternation. Yet, in my faith,
There is one cardinal tenet: to respect
The forms of Nature. Every Artifice
That thwarts her is high treason; every trick

That makes discovery of Art an outrage.
Ars est celare artem. You observe
This shaven sward we traverse? Ten years since
It was a wilderness, thick with horrid thorns
And brambles. Now, the unimpeded eye
Has gained the liberty it loves to reach
That belt of noble beeches, where the axe
Has cleft a ruthless passage to disclose
The shine of water. In a windless air
You may hear the babbling of the rivulet
That falls to feed it. Once my lazy rill
Flowed mute; but I have coaxed it into song
With gifts of pebbles—and now it never stays
An artificial prattle that enchants
The ears of bashful Naiads. From this seat,
Sacred to silvan Pan, Imagination
Can watch their watery frolic.

SMITH:

(*Loudly*) May we know
What hour they bathe, Sir?

SHENSTONE:

(*Archly*) *Procul*, Captain Smith,
Este profani!

LYTTELTON:

(*With a smile*) Mr. Shenstone means
He wants no Peeping Toms. You, as a sailor,
Might ask with equal aptness: *Festo quid potius
Die Neptuni faciam?*

THOMSON:

(*His fat paunch shaken with chuckles*) Verra neat, George:
Prettily capped. (*To* SHENSTONE) There's only one ingredien
Mars this delightful landscape. Yonder cot
Should be made habitable or pulled down.
If it were mine I'ld raze it.

[272]

SHENSTONE:

Even more hurt than indignant) That, Mr. Thomson,
Is a Romantick Ruin, only built
Last Autumn! I have pointed it with care
To variegate the visto where it seemed
To want diversity. I have always held
That rural scenes are lifeless and imperfect
Lacking the mark of Man, and that the charms
Of a ruinated structure woo the mind
To pensive sadness.

THOMSON:
Think no more of it:
I'm a mere townsman with no claims to Taste
In Rural Elegance.

SHENSTONE:

Still rather hurt) Had I the advantages
Of my friend Lyttelton, I might have planned
A more ambitious edifice, and begged
Some arches from his Abbey; but my means
May not presume to vie with Stowe or Hagley.
My ruin fits my purse. (*To* LYTTELTON) Sir, it is whispered
You contemplate a Temple in your park?

LYTTELTON:
We think to build a Rotund, in the style
Of the Temple of Vesta. It's a dainty foible
Of Mr. Pitt's, to memorize our friendship
And family alliances. He himself
Has marked the chosen site—but you must see
The drawings, Mr. Shenstone.

PITT:
Yes, indeed.
We should be most gratified.

SHENSTONE:
And I most honoured.
But let's proceed . . . This gentle glade I call

[273]

The Lovers' Walk. My assignation-seats
And mottoes mark its nature, as do the urns
To faithful lovers. A certain Noble Lady
Considers it my masterpiece . . .

SMITH:

(*In an amused whisper*) Who's that, George?

LYTTELTON:

That black-maned gorgon Henrietta Luxborough
Bolingbroke's sister.

SMITH:

Is *she* his 'Delia'?

LYTTELTON:

No.

I've seen his Delia—and what a Delia!
I'll tell you later . . .

SHENSTONE:

For myself, I'ld choose
These more funereal shades, through which my brook
Steals voiceless under pendent tapestries
Of beech: a spot conducive to sweet sessions
Of meditative thought and soft regret.
I call it Virgil's Grove: and yonder urn
Of marble, in its alcove of dark yews,
Commemorates the Mantuan's lordly name.

HOOD:

(*In an awed whisper*) Sir, are his bones inside it?

SHENSTONE:

(*Disregarding the general laughter*) No, my young friend,
It is a cenotaph, planned to suggest
The melancholy aspects of mortality
Rather than its horrors. Here the mind may brood
On elegiac themes. The very paths
Are pledged to silence; for the strewn beech-mast
Muffles our footfalls. Here, when I am gone,
Another urn shall bear a humbler name

Than Maro's, and the sentimental eye
Grudge not the tribute of a casual tear:
I sometimes think my urns and obelisks
May well outlast my verses . . .

PITT:

Why, my friend,

Pursue this dreary subject? You and I
Are somewhat of an age—and neither of us
Need think of urns as yet.

SHENSTONE:

(*Shaking his head*)   Ah, Mr. Pitt,
Your fame may light the future, and your voice
Direct the destinies of nations: mine
Dies with my fading laurels . . .

SMITH:

(*Impatiently*) What's all this talk
Of death and burial? The man's a hypochondriack
Who'll never hear a shot fired, and will die
Of ripe old age, in bed. All that he needs
Is a blue pill once a week. He's much too fat—
And so is Jamie Thomson. What's the time, George?
I'm famished.

LYTTELTON:

So am I. I'll do my best
To rescue Billy from his tentacles—
But give me time: the fellow's most fastidious,
And prone to take offence.

Dear Mr. Shenstone,
I fear we have deranged you . . .

SHENSTONE:

On the contrary,

I find the converse of such company
As yours exhilarating. Had I but known
This honour was in store, my frugal board
Had been prepared to greet your guests.

[275]

LYTTELTON:

Alas!

We are bespoke at Hagley—so I fear
We must drag ourselves away from the delights
Of your exquisite Arcadia. Can you tell me
The hour, Tom?

SMITH:

(*Taking out his watch*) By my stomach it's past one.
Egad! It's nearly two, George! We must scamper.
Dinner's at three.

SHENSTONE:

(*Regretfully*) And I have hardly spoken
A word with Mr. Thomson!

THOMSON:

Let's not repine.
We have communed in the spirit, Sir. Moreover
I have seen your famous Leasowes—and the half
Had not been told me! When you come to town
We must forgather at Richmond: all our wits
Will flock to meet a master in the realm
Of Landscape as in Letters.

LYTTELTON:

(*Firmly*) By your leave then
We will retrace our steps.

(*The whole company follow their host, who has attached himself
to* THOMSON. LYTTELTON *and* PITT *walk arm in arm.*
CAPTAIN SMITH *and the* BOY *bring up the rear. After a series
of elaborate courtesies, the visitors depart—last of all* MR.
THOMSON, *who turns to wave his farewells from his seat in the
tandem. When* SHENSTONE *has watched them out of sight, he
enters the house. His face is flushed, and he is still too much
excited to consider the meal that awaits him. With an impatient
gesture he sweeps back the dirty tablecloth and sits down to write.
First a letter.*)

[276]

SHENSTONE:

(*Writing and speaking as he writes*).

To the Right Hon. Lady Luxborough.

Tis now somewhere about

September the Tenth, and I write from The Leasowes.

Madam, I believe I shall write very incoherently.

Mens turbidum laetatur. . . .

(*He stops, lays the sheet aside, and begins again: this time in verse.*)

Ev'n Pitt, whose fervent periods roll
Resistless thro' the kindling soul
    Of Senates, Councils, Kings,
Though form'd for Courts, vouchsafed to rove
Inglorious through the shepherd's grove . . .

(*For a long time he hesitates; then adds, with evident satisfaction:*)
And ope his bashful springs.

(*The reluctant blackbird has also suddenly burst into song* . . .)

XXX

Marlbrouk is gone and will not come again.
His laurels wither. There's a subtle bane
Mingled in victory's vintage, that betrays
All but the wisest, when their rearward gaze
Dwells with contentment on the dizzy slopes
Their toil has conquered—and delusive hopes
Bedazzle every eye that looks before,
Bidding the victor pause, and toil no more.
Oh, happy island! Never had our race
Reaped in such measure the rewards of peace
And sober industry; never had known
More ample freedoms or a kindlier throne;
Never, in all our story, since the flood,
Of the fierce Roses drowned our fields in blood,
Or Rupert's careless cavalry laid low
The standing corn upon the trampled plough,
Had simple folk so prospered, or the great
Feared less the storms of faction or the hate
Of envious neighbours! Now a paradise
Of ungrudged plenty this green island lies
Within her watery moat, whereon no sail
Threatens her peace. Now, in each fertile vale
Striped by the linchets of her village-fields,
Unravished earth a bounteous harvest yields:
Green grows the bearded wheat; her barley pale
Shall brim the vats with brown October ale
To dull the edge of Winter; high above
Her valleys, on the dappled downland, move
Flocks of innumerable fleece; where furze
And bramble shag the waste, her cottagers
Pasture their heath-fed cattle without heed
Or hindrance, and with wind-torn faggots feed

The crackling hearths, where February's flitch
Smokes in the chimney till 'tis black as pitch.
Now from her noisy belfries clang no more
The exultant peals or harsh alarms of war,
But mellower tones that measure with their chime
The tranquil flow of unregarded time,
Which, like a quiet river, carries all
From birth and love to death and burial;
Or, wavering on drowsy sabbath airs,
Summon plain folk to say their simple prayers,
Unvexed by doubt, in humble certitude
That life is bountiful and God is good:
That, even when doctrinal schism rends
His holy Church, His children may be friends:
That—though legitimists are prone to mix
A pinch of Popery in their politics—
The greater part stand firm for Church and State,
And martyrologies are out of date,
Since Priest and Presbyter alike may praise
And worship the same God in different ways;
For these are reasonable times, that need
The licence of a more elastic creed.
First, let's be tolerant, while the world's trade
Sticks to our hands, and markets can be had
Without contention. Let the foreign fool
Prate about Glory: give us Wheat and Wool.
Snug country-seats and comfortable farms
Outweigh the most resounding feat of arms.
Let us have ease with dignity—but pray note
That he who gives us both will get our vote:
And votes still count in England, though we're told
A rotten borough costs a mint of gold.
Yet what is gold to-day? A thing of naught,
When power and patronage can both be bought,
And twenty fortunes lost or won on nights
When play runs high at Newmarket or White's.

K

For tact, no less than charity, should abate
Our judgement on the foibles of the great:
Since Ministers who live in mortal sin
Can still make Bishops or prefer a Dean;
And why should dubious origins debase
The coinage of a pension or a place,
Or puritanic moralisms perplex
The generous instincts of the frailer sex?
Let us be strict—but never over-nice
In judging what is virtue and what's vice;
Our weaker vessels ever have been brittle,
And virtue's price has altered precious little
Since Mother Eve discovered—and deplored—
The fact that Virtue is its own reward!
Let's be abstemious—and seldom take
More than three bottles for the stomach's sake,
And with the pleasures of a casual bout
Forestall the pains and penalties of gout!
Let us be Men of Taste—and exorcize
The errors that bedimmed our forebears' eyes;
Remould their uncouth Gothic, and replace
Its wayward fancy with a formal grace;
Unbuild the ancestral fortalice that bore
A six-week siege in Cromwell's rebel war,
And on Plantagenet foundations raise
An edifice to suit more civil days,
Whose chaste façade and generous glazing show
Our taste for fighting left us long ago;
Indulge in ampler space and loftier height;
Let all within be graciousness and light;
Roll up the moth-worn tapestries, and line
The rough-cast walls with panels of smooth pine;
Fill up the yawning ingles grimed with smoke,
And change the massive board of British oak
Neath which your grandsire sank in Charles's reign
For choice mahogany from the Spanish Main;

And, where their Spartan mothers sate austere
Sewing their samplers in a high-backed chair,
Let your sophisticated ladies lie
On silken sophas—where they often sigh
To think how fondly poor Clarissa strove
Against the stratagems of unlawful love,
And hope some Lovelace yet may cross their path
While their good husbands cure the gout at Bath!
Let us be Men of Judgement, and maintain
The classic maxim of the Golden Mean!
Let us be learn'd—and since we have become
Presumptive heirs of Athens and of Rome,
Affect an Attic diction undefiled
By any strain of native woodnotes wild,
And, soundly whipped at Eton, learn by rote
Just so much Horace as a peer should quote!
In short, let all be comely—as beseems
The balanced mind that shrinks from rude extremes:
So let Life's reasonable tenour flow,
Too high for diffidence, for pride too low,
Unruffled by despair, unswoll'n by hope:
Smooth as a couplet penned by *Mr. Pope*.

An Age of Matter, you may say—and yet
It boasts some virtues Time will not forget.
What though venality and vice abound
In court and senate? England's heart is sound;
And through her ardent pulses runs apace
The vigour of a sane, full-blooded race:
A race by proven strength and prowess steeled
To hold its own and not an atom yield;
A race by industry and shrewdness grown
To wealth unmeasured, civilities unknown,
Which, in one sovereign city, has combined
God's greatest gifts of matter and of mind:

The widening world's pantechnicon and mart,
The hub of Commerce and the goal of Art:
London!—a murky microcosm, lit
By *Johnson's* common sense and *Garrick's* wit;
London, whose squalor *Hogarth's* pencil flayed,
Where *Wesley* preached and saintly *Whitefield* prayed,
Where *Purcell's* native tenderness was drowned
By *Handel's* torrents of majestic sound;
Where *Reynolds'* glowing canvasses portrayed
The masters of an Empire newly-made—
Faces of men not easily beguiled
(With something of the look of a spoilt child)
Whose confident lips and sanguine eyes protest
That, of all worlds, their own small world's the best,
And that the climax of Creation's plan
Is, beyond doubt, an English Gentleman,
Soothed by the present, pampered by the past,
In days—if he but knew!—too good to last.
Thus to a nation surfeited with wealth,
Comes Nature's reckoning—and it comes by stealth.

There is a moment in the Northern year
When the o'erburdened earth can hardly bear
The wealth of her own bounties; when the wheel
Of the slow-circling seasons seems to feel
A drag upon its felloe—as though the sun,
Impatient of long constancy, had grown
Aweary of earth's wandering and loth
To turn his jolly face on the frore South
When he might stay and with warm fingers brush
The velvet-winged vanessas that outblush
Full Summer's brightest bloom. How can one sing
Of this illusive hour, this mimic Spring
That, like a strayed lamb, frisks her innocence
On Autumn's drear and draughty threshold, whence

[282]

There steals by night a waft of icier airs?
And see—one bough in the dark woodland wears
Tinges of leprous pallor that forecast
The ravishment of all; and though at last
The sun smiles forth undaunted, yet we know
That glory is departed. It was so
With England in this tranquil age bedecked
With grace and opulence; but few men recked
That melancholy stigma, since it shone
Not in her native woods but in the lone
Forests of savage Pennsylvania
And Canada, four thousand miles away.

XXXI

Four thousand miles away . . . But first observe
This young colonial, George Washington;
Born in Virginia, of a sound yeoman stock
Uprooted from the lias of Northamptonshire
Twixt Banbury and Towcester; sparely bred
On his father's farm above the tidal creeks
Of the Rappahannock: a lanky, likeable lad,
Six-foot-three in his stockinged feet; of a countenance
Ruddy and cheerful, with a masterful eye,
Long arms and monstrous hands—says Lafayette:
"The biggest ever I saw." Small wonder the Governor,
That dour, shrewd Scot, Dinwiddie, fancied him
For a ticklish errand beyond the Alleghanies,
Where those damned Frenchmen, friendly Indians said,
Were trickling South from Canada to join hands
With their kinsmen in Louisiana. "Just go and see
What they're up to," Dinwiddie said, "and what can be dor
To scare them off the Ohio."

        Major George Washington
Rode West—the eyes of Virginians always looked West—
Over the rolling waves of foothills whitened
With dogwood-blossom and flushed with the Judas-bloor
Of April; over the great ribbed ranges shagged
With pine and hemlock; through break-neck ravines
Clogged with dense woods of hickory, oak and sassafras,
To a willowy vale where sluggish water seeped
Through squelching swamps to feed Monangahela
And Alleghenny, where their confluence swelled
The fierce Ohio. There he found the French
Housed snug as beavers within the charred stockade
Of Fort le Bœuf—but, having not their tongue,
Nor a liking for captivity, turned back

[284]

And told what he had seen, urging his chief
To hold that frontier firmly, and keep watch
Against further penetration.
                                        So, next Spring,
A force of forty tough Virginians, tanned
Swart as sun-dried tobacco, hacked a clearing
And laid Fort Trent's foundations; but the French,
A thousand strong, fell on them as they worked
And drove them to the East. Now, once again,
The name of Washington, like a meteor, burns
Momently on the horizon—to be quenched
In the blackness of defeat, when Fort Necessity
Capitulates, and its beaten garrison
Trails back into Virginia. This war—
For war it is, open or undeclared—
Demands more competent handling than the shifts
Of mere provincials. Therefore, let General Braddock,
A veteran (of the barrack-square) newly-landed
At Hampton Roads, instruct them in the elements
Of Military Art, and teach John Frenchman
The lesson he deserves! So Braddock marches
West from Potomac, with twelve hundred redcoats,
All spit and polish; crosses Monangahela
With colours flying and regimental bands
Blaring forth martial music, to deliver
A copy-book assault on Fort Duquesne,
Light-heartedly neglecting to secure
His flanks. Result: incredible confusion,
And a panic-stricken rout! George Washington,
Unwounded, has four shot-holes in his coat,
And of his three full companies of rangers
Not more than thirty left. As for poor Braddock:
"We shall know better how to deal with them
Next time," he gasps. There will be no 'next time'
For General Braddock . . . They buried him next day
At the halt they called Great Meadows. Over his bones

The transport of his beaten remnant rolled
Waggons and limbers to conceal his grave
From desecration; while the three Northern columns
His clerkly pen had launched marched on Niagara,
Crown Point and Nova Scotia—to be lost
In the drip of endless forests; and the French
Still hold their own.

                 Ten thousand miles away,
In Hindustan, the prospect looks no better.
Here, too, Dupleix is nibbling at the fringes
Of a nabob-ridden Empire more corrupt
Than Westminster itself; while, nearer home,
Dunkirk, still undismantled since the peace,
Threatens the narrow seas. Brest, Havre and Rochefort,
Crammed with flat-bottomed barges, only wait
For the signal of invasion to be broken
When de la Clue shall bring his Toulon fleet
To join Conflans at Brest. One is reminded
Of the 'Forty-five,' when gentlemen at White's
Laid wagers on the wind, and the Pretender
Lay fretting at Dunkirk; but then, at least,
Our coasts were stoutly guarded, and the veterans
Of Marlborough's wars still lived—while now the Govern-
Floating on seas of claret, idly drifts   [ment
Without a helm, lulled by the siren-songs
Of vanished glory, deaf to the only voice
That speaks unwelcome truth: "We have provoked
Before we can defend; we have neglected
The inevitable results of provocation;
In every quarter of the globe we are found
Inferior to the French, and forced to buy
Defence and courage, when it is our duty
To raise a strong militia!" But Pitt's words
Fell on besotted ears, until the storm
Breaks in a thunder-clap: Minorca lost—
And with it the whole trade of the Levant;

Ticonderoga and Oswego seized
By the French Canadians; Calcutta sacked
In scenes of unspeakable horror; at Versailles
Habsburg and Bourbon in devilish compact bound
To share the spoils of Europe and divide
The loot of decadent England! There is one man,
And one alone, of stature to surmount
This human tempest, equally detested
By Court and Council. "I am heart and hand
For Mr. Pitt," poor Newcastle protests.
"But Mr. Pitt won't come," the King maintains
With evident satisfaction. Mr. Pitt
Does come . . . in his own time, on his own terms;
"I know, my lord," he says, "that I can save
This country, and that nobody else can!"

(2)

He was forty-eight years old when he kissed hands,
Austere and arrogant, outwardly little changed
From the elegant figure who, thirteen years ago,
Vouchsafed to rove (as Mr. Shenstone put it)
Inglorious through his groves. Such men are born
To spiritual loneliness: in their brains
The flame of confident purpose burns too fiercely
For casual human intimacies to survive
Its heat. Yet when a universal danger
Blackens the sky, it shines forth like a beacon
To gladden all the land, and to enkindle
Faith, Hope, and Courage in the anxious hearts
Of unknown millions. Such a beacon flamed
In the King's Speech, revealing, without mercy
The damnable drift of unpreparedness
And bland futility that had abased
This most distressful realm—at every turn

K*

Confronted by the insolent aggressions
Of her ancient enemy. Then came a call to arms
And self-defence: the standing army strengthened
By fifteen new battalions; new formations
Of gunners and marines; a new militia
Thirty-two thousand strong, and two new regiments
Raised in the Highlands by Montgomery
And Fraser. The House gasped. It was but a breath
Since Butcher Cumberland had won Culloden,
And Lovat, Fraser's father, lost his head
On Tower Hill! Pitt brushed their doubts aside:
"I have sought for merit wherever it could be found;
I found it in the mountains of the North
And called it forth, from an intrepid race
Whose valour and hardihood well nigh overturned
The State twelve years ago. To-day their loyalty
Is no more questionable than the eagerness
Of our American brethren to maintain
Their vast and vulnerable frontier
Of fifteen hundred miles. I have one object,
Plain and unalterable: to fight the French
Wherever we may find them—in America,
Africa, India, Corsica, on the Rhine,
On every ocean of the globe—relying
Upon this House's wisdom to prefer
More vigorous efforts to a less effectual
And so more frugal warfare, my heart being fixed
First on the succour and the preservation
Of our American colonies. That is a debt
Of honour to our kinsmen."
                                        In this man
So vehement by nature, action followed
Fast on the heels of thought. "He will come in
As a conqueror," poor Newcastle complained.
Pitt came in like a whirlwind, fluttering
The dusty files and dossiers of Whitehall

Into a paper snowstorm; rapping out
Questions and orders in a *feu de joie:*
"The American establishment? Eight thousand?
Send them eight thousand more, backed by a fleet
To keep the St. Lawrence open and attack
First Louisburg, then Quebec! Loudoun reports
The colonial levies are unreliable?
This means they're badly handled. Let each province
Know how we value them. Beg them not to clog
The flow of men and money simply to salve
Their tender feelings. Tell them we are all subjects
Of the same Crown, and serve on equal terms
Against a common enemy! India?
There the mere distance baulks us: all we can do
Is help the Company to hold their stations
By tardy reinforcements. What of Mauritius?
A swift stroke on his bases there might cut
Dupleix's communications! The West Indies?
Bring up the island garrisons to full strength,
Beginning with Jamaica! Home Defence?
That rests on my Militia, seconded
By one strong squadron stationed at Spithead
To watch the French in Rochefort, and another
Shadowing the coast of Flanders. Hanover?
Send back His Majesty's Hessians: that will please
The Militiamen, and put them on their mettle;
Pay Prussia a fat subsidy, and bribe
The Danes into neutrality with a treaty
Of trade to their advantage!" Now the moment
Grows ripe for action: it grew even riper
For vengeance. How could comfortable placemen
Who had battened on corruption and intrigue
Abide this cleansing tempest? How could a King,
Bred in an air of flattery, tolerate
This exigent upstart commoner who perplexes
His wits with such long speeches? At one blow

Pitt, with his kinsman Temple, is dismissed—
And the Court breathes once more—but in the City
The stocks fall with a crash, and from the boroughs
It rains gold boxes. Even the most obtuse
Of monarchs now can read the nation's will,
Plain-writ on civic parchment. With reluctance
He summons Pitt.

                  Eleven weeks have passed,
Eleven precious weeks ineptly squandered
In idleness: the urgent expeditions
To Senegal and India countermanded;
The force that sailed for Canada still anchored
At Halifax, two months late—while at Calcutta
The Black Hole claims its hideous toll of thirst
And suffocation, and through the Carribean
The French sails pass unhindered. Worst of all,
The King of Prussia's beaten at Kolin
With crushing loss, and Hanover uncovered
By Cumberland's retreat. To this scene, darkened
By new threats of invasion—how that nightmare
Hag-rides our island's slumbers!—Pitt returns
With energies unabated, nay, refreshed
By forced inaction. First of all, America—
America always first! He reinforces
Holburne, delayed at Halifax, with drafts
Of Highlanders and Artillery; calls Boscawen
From his watchdog's duty at Brest to intercept
The French fleet, homeward-bound from the St. Lawrence
To cover the invaders—ten thousand strong,
And strung out from St. Valéry to Bordeaux.
Defence is not enough. Far better strike
A sudden blow at Lorient or Rochefort
And throw them off their balance. This demands
Strong naval escort. Admiral Anson pleads
A dearth of ships. "Why, then, you'll have to find them:
Otherwise I'll impeach you, Sir." Such language

To a senior officer! But Anson finds enough
To make a swoop on Rochefort. Sir John Mordaunt
Commands the raid: his Quartermaster General
A young officer of promise with red hair
And a receding chin—by name, James Wolfe;
And though the raiders fail to land in force,
The French are rattled, and the immediate menace
Of an invasion lifted . . . Meanwhile, at Halifax,
Loudoun does nothing but squabble with the colonies
Over their levies, building a few sham forts
And planting a few cabbages—while Montcalm
Attacks Ticonderoga. Admiral Holburne,
Finding the French have one more ship than he,
Sheers off from Louisburg—and when he sails,
On Pitt's implicit orders, to waylay them
Upon their homeward course, is blown to pieces
To windward of Cape Breton. So the year ends
In mere frustration. "I fear we do not stand,"
Pitt warns the Commons, "in the smile of Heaven.
May a degenerate nation take some profit
From these misfortunes: its present state is fitter
For meditation than discourse . . ."
                                        Suddenly
The picture changes. First, the King of Prussia
Shatters Soubise at Rossbach. Clive, at Plassy,
Regains Calcutta. Keppel takes Goree,
And Hobson Guadeloupe—all the West Indies
Falling like rotten mangoes, one by one!
Even in America the disgruntled colonists
Forget their grievances, swiftly retaking
Niagara, Ticonderoga, Fort Duquesne.
Boscawen, Marlborough's nephew, now redeems
The shame of Louisburg; then, sweeping Eastward,
Falls on the Toulon fleet in Lagos Bay
And cuts them off from Brest, while Rodney's cannon
Splinter the invasion-barges in the roads

Of Havre to matchwood, and the British infantry,
Unblooded since their stubborn squares were broken
At Fontenoy, on the field of Minden wither
The flower of France's cavalry. Such was this year
Of wonders! Now naught but unconquered Canada
And the immutable threat of a hostile Flanders
Envenomed Victory's cup.

(3)

It was after Rochefort
That, combing the welter of reputations wrecked
In that lamentable fiasco for any fragment
Of martial merit, Pitt had singled out
The name of Wolfe. Now, with that lively instinct
Which leavens his cool reason, he invites
This young officer to meet him. There is a tale
Told at third-hand, a generation later,
How Pitt was staggered by the gasconades
Of this fragile fire-eater; but even so
He must have liked him—for within a month
Wolfe sails for Halifax, under his personal orders
To take Quebec: a formidable task
For an ailing, nervous man of thirty-two,
Inferior in age and social standing
To his own Brigadiers, and handicapped
By an unfriendly staff! One friend he had:
The new admiral, Charles Saunders, a sound sailor,
Who groped his deft way through the changeable channel
Of the St. Lawrence—a stream more treacherous
Than its own Indians. It was sheer devilry,
Canadian pilots said, that any foreigner
Could have brought ships of the line so far upstream
Without a scratch. There, for three idle months,
James Wolfe lay gazing at Quebec, a citadel

By nature made impregnable: his ranks
Thinned by desertion and disease, himself
Coughing his lungs out in a hectic fever,
The butt of his subordinates, the scorn
Of his own baffled mind. Landings were made
And landed troops withdrawn with heavy casualties
From the fire of floating batteries and snipers
Hidden in the forest. Rations were running short.
The days, too, shortened: in the maple-woods
That bordered the St. Lawrence soon would flare
A crimson flag of warning—soon the ice
Would clamp his transports in its iron fetters,
Cutting off reinforcement or relief.
It was surely now or never . . . but Wolfe's sick mind,
Sapped by his wasting body, momently
Lost faith in its own powers;   and in an agony
Of doubt, and fear of imminent death, he begged
His jealous Brigadiers to frame a plan
That might bring Montcalm to action. It is strange
How often genius finds an inspiration
In violent disagreement. As Wolfe read
This laboured product of pedestrian minds,
His own caught fire—and instantly he saw,
By the fierce light of scorn made crystal-clear,
The master-plan, the inevitable design,
Which, under clouds of sickness, had been woven
Deep in his anxious thoughts—and, from that moment,
Doubt vanished. "I know well you cannot cure me,"
He told his surgeon, "but if you can patch me up
To do my duty for the next few days,
I shall be quite content." With a sad prescience
He makes his will (it is witnessed by Barré
And Bell, his aides-de-camp): a few small legacies
To friends and servants, and the pitiful residue
"To my dear mother." Then, a last dispatch
To Pitt in England. It is a sober document,

Void of the old *panache*, and gives no details
Of the new 'desperate plan.' Secrecy, secrecy . . .
That is its mainspring. Not even to his generals
Will he breathe a word of it; but on the morrow
The watchmen in the citadel are perplexed,
No less than they, to see the English ships
Moved upstream through the narrows, towing boats
And barges. Beyond doubt the Frenchmen judged it
A prelude to new landings north of the city,
Or an attempt to cut their waterline
With Montreal. Not till the very eve
Of battle were his jealous Brigadiers
Made privy to his secret. Junior officers
And rank and file knew nothing till they found themselve
Afloat . . .

             It was a cool September night,
Moonless and overcast. At half-past one
A lantern blinked from the main-topmast shrouds
Of Saunders' ship, the *Sutherland*. Then the boats
Cast off in absolute silence, and lay hidden
Between her and the shore. At half-past two
A second light appeared. The *Sutherland's* long-boat,
With Wolfe aboard her, swung into the stream
That washed the southern bank. It was a passage
Tranquil and soundless, with no plash of oars,
For a three-knot current and a following breeze
Assured their course. There is another story—
Such names breed legends—that, as the leading boat
Drifted downstream, a voice, no man knows whose,
Murmured Gray's Elegy; and, when it fell to silence,
Wolfe whispered: "I would rather have written that poem
Than take Quebec to-morrow." All we can say
For sure is this: that, when his brother-officers
Divided his belongings, there was found
A volume of Gray's Poems, much bethumbed
And underscored—one line prophetically:

The paths of Glory lead but to the Grave.
Perhaps he guessed . . . One thing at least is certain:
That, as they floated past, a British sloop,
Forewarned by two deserters of a French convoy
Likely to pass that night, levelled her guns
And would have opened fire and given the alarm
But that they rowed alongside, thus averting
Disaster by a hairsbreadth. A little later,
A French post on Point Sillery snapped out
Its challenge: *Qui va là?*
> *France!*
>> *A quel regiment?*

A la Reine! (It was a lucky guess!)
>> *Pourquoi*
Est-ce que vous ne parlez pas plus haut?
>> *Tais-toi*
Pour l'amour de Dieu! Nous serions entendus!
And the sentry let them pass . . .
>> At half-past four
They ran aground in Foulon Cove. The general
Himself leapt first ashore. There was less need
For silence now: the nervous batteries
Of the fort on *Pointe des Pères* were thundering
An aimless cannonade. Above the landing-place,
Mysterious in the grey of dawn, arose
Tremendous cliffs, shagged with dense undergrowth,
Through which one winding gully gave faint promise
Of a precarious foothold. Wolfe himself
Probed this forbidding track. "I doubt," he said,
"If we can possibly get up; but we must try."
And up they scrambled: first a forlorn hope
Of two dozen volunteers, and then two hundred
Light infantry. Luckily they found the crest
Fringed with a wood that gave the climbers cover
While they regained their breath, re-formed their ranks.
Another challenge from a sentry, answered

Again in muttered French, gave them a moment
To fix their bayonets. Then on they went
With a hoarse cheer which told their friends below
That the heights were firmly held. Within an hour
Five hundred men had scaled them; in another
A thousand more; and, as the ships dropped down
St. Lawrence one by one, the cove of Foulon
Was crammed with landing barges, hurriedly
Off-loading shot and cannon to be hauled
Over the wheel-churned beach, and then man-handled
Up the sheer precipices to the open plain
West of Quebec, while from the southern shore,
Under the covering fire of Saunders' guns,
Twelve hundred infantry were ferried over
From Goreham's Point to Foulon Cove. By sunrise
The whole force had been landed: six battalions
Of British regulars, and in reserve
Two more of Royal Americans: in all
Forty-eight hundred men . . . Too few, indeed,
To hold both front and flanks—so Wolfe was forced
To spin them out two-deep (a flagrant breach
Of martial usage!) trusting to atone
For lack of numbers by superior discipline
And accuracy of aim.

               These were his orders:
"Stand firm at all costs. Let the enemy
Do all the attacking. Not a single shot
To be fired until they come within forty paces:
Then let them have it!" It was pretty hard
To make no reply when snipers and skirmishers
Enfiladed the British line from a wood on their left:
Yet no shot was fired. When men in the front line fell,
The gaps were instantly filled from the second rank.
Wolfe himself was hit in the wrist: he merely smiled
And bound up the gash with a handkerchief—more concerned
As it seemed, for his brand-new uniform. (One is reminded

Of Nelson insisting on wearing his orders) Once more
He was wounded—this time in the groin—and limped away
To the point he had chosen, in front of the Twenty-eighth
And the Louisburg Grenadiers. It was ten o'clock
When Montcalm, on his great black stallion, splendidly
                                                        sheathed

In a shining cuirass of steel, gave his order: Advance!
And the French, with a shout, moved forward. Observers say
That Wolfe's face, as he saw them, glowed with a joy and [radiance
Beyond description. They made an imposing sight
The white uniforms of their line-regiments mingled
With the blue of the Royal Roussillon and iron-grey
Of the local levies. On they came, at a double;
Then slowed down—as though puzzled to see the British
                                                        standing

Stock-still, with shouldered arms. At three hundred paces
Some few Canadians nervously opened fire,
Then threw themselves down on the ground to reload, thus
                                                        upsetting

The general alignment; while others, with little stomach
For a frontal attack, slunk off to the flanks to fall in
With the skirmishers, leaving a ragged gap to be filled.
The well-trained whitecoats closed it; but now the attack
Had lost cohesion. A desultory crackle of musketry
Broke out from their foremost rank. Again and again
They halted and fired without orders, straggling on
A few score yards at a time—until they had come
Within forty paces . . . Then, from the British ranks,
Came a shattering double volley—so nicely timed
That the sounds of two thousand musket-shots merged in one
Tremendous detonation. Then two more volleys
At point-blank range . . . The Languedoc Regiment wavered:
They broke—as the Forty-Seventh went in with the bayonet,
The Highlanders with the claymore. Only the Blues
Of the Royal Roussillon stood up to that torrent of steel.
Then they, too, cracked and fled. It was only ten minutes

[297]

Since the British first opened fire . . . and the battle was won
But Wolfe fell, mortally wounded. They carried him throug
To the rear, where he lay with closed eyes, breathing heavily
With a musket-shot in the lung. When they told him the
                                                          Frenc
Were running, he gasped one order: "Tell Colonel Burton
To cut them off from the bridge over Charles's River."
Then he turned on his side and said: "Now I die content."
He was thirty-two years old . . . Let us not forget
How this ailing Englishman, with British arms
And British lives, once saved America
For the Americans . . .

(4)

                              The news of Quebec reached Londo
In mid-October. Within a month her belfries
Clanged for a great sea-victory that dispelled
The last threat of invasion—when Admiral Hawke
Stooped like a peregrine on the Breton coast;
When, in a nightlong hurricane that drowned
The din of battle, the engrappled fleets
Of France and England poured through the narrow throat
Of Quiberon, and stormy daylight saw
The French burnt-out or broken. Little wonder
The Bourbons longed for peace, and lesser Englishmen
Were eager to placate them! Pitt, like a rock,
Stood in appeasement's path, the more determined
To keep soft, mischievous hands from bartering
His hard-won conquests. "Some are for keeping Canada,"
He taunted them, "some Guadeloupe. Who will tell me
Which I shall be hanged for ceding? The West Indies
Nourish us with their produce? Ay, but America
Buys what we manufacture. I affirm
The importance of America—not merely

[298]

As a market of consumption and supply,
But as fountain of our fealty, nerve of our strength,
Nursery and basis of our naval power.
Some time ago I should have been content
To bring France to her knees: now I'll not rest
Till I've put her on her back! We are confronted
By a second enemy. These defeats have driven her
Into the arms of Spain, who brazenly
Supports her wounded sister, covers her trade,
Aids and abets her in the worst kind of war—
War undeclared. It is time this country realized
That France is Spain, Spain France: we are at odds
With the whole House of Bourbon—but remember:
For open war with Spain we are prepared,
And she is not. If, Sir, this House prefers
An untimely, a humiliating peace,
I will lay down the vast and dangerous load
That bows my shoulders: I will go on no longer.
But, being responsible, I will direct;
And for whatever I do not direct
I will not be responsible."
                                        His challenge
Fell on a hostile House. The pampered placemen
Were sick of his heroics and of a war
That touched their purses. Pitt was no easy bedfellow
For time-servers or sluggards. His very virtues
Stuck in the throats of meaner men. The Court—
His 'good old King' was dead—detested him
As an unbearable upstart, an embodiment
Of all they feared and hated most: Democracy.
Single, imperious, proud, enthusiastick,
Impetuous . . . Ay, and arrogant, too. His arrogance
Was unforgiveable. It had made enemies
Of his old friends and kinsmen. Grenville, Lyttelton—
The famous 'cousinhood' who, in the prime
Of his cometary magnificence had soared

[299]

Like a fiery tail behind him—were now shed
And sunk in jealous darkness, while his star
Blazed at the zenith. It was mortifying
For statesmen who had ruled the realm to brook
His fierce impatience: "Fewer words, my lord;
Your words have long lost weight with me!"—for officers
Nursed in routine's procedure to keep pace
With his swift decisions: "Impossible? Impossible?
I walk on impossibilities!" as he brandished
The crutch that eased his gout—for humbler men
Who questioned his least whim to bear the sting
Of withering irony, or the fire that flashed
From those commanding eyes. Now, when he threw
This haughty gage, coupling a war with Spain
And a personal ultimatum, in their faces,
They picked it up with glee, knowing full well
With what sweet persuasiveness the word of Peace
Flatters war-wearied ears. The King, no less,
Snatched at this heaven-sent chance to rid himself
Of this overbearing commoner . . . and Pitt fell,
Gloriously as Lucifer!

           They offered him—
Perhaps to salve his pride, perhaps to wound it—
The Governorship of Canada: odd employment
For one whose lightest words were gravely pondered
In the chanceries of all Europe! He declined it
With ironical humility. (Courtiers said
He bowed so low to the King that his bony nose
Could be seen between his breeches). Then they tempted [him
The incorruptible commoner, with the bait
Of a pension, and a peerage for his wife.
Surprisingly, he took it—he who had thrown
Such baubles to his comrades with the contempt
Their vanity deserved. It showed a strain
Of inexplicable weakness, and his enemies
Were quick to find his principles dishonoured

By such vain honours—his bewildered friends
To see their idol fallen. One suspects
That the bearing of that 'vast and dangerous load'
Had over-reached his powers, already sapped
By paroxysms of pain; that, when the tension
Was once relaxed, his weary mind and body
Demanded instant rest. So Mr. Pitt
And the Lady Chatham gracefully retire
To their country seat in Somerset.

(5)

Burton Pynsent

Was a sheer gift of fortune: the legacy
Of an obscure Somersetshire baronet
To the Saviour of his Country. No distraction
Could have been more opportune. It carried back
Pitt's mind to those rich days of youthful promise,
Far sweeter than fulfilment, when George Lyttelton
And he had planned their classical rotunda
In Hagley Park, and solemnly discussed
The Philosophy of Landscape at the Leasowes
With Mr. Shenstone. Burton Pynsent stood
On a high, semicircular plateau, looking North
Over the Sedgemoor flats, where Alfred's Athelny
Rose from a sea of land, to the dim firth
Of Severn and the cloudy hills of Wales:
A soft and somnolent prospect, more conducive
To dreams of past achievement than to action.
Yet, even here, the inveterate energy
That had shaped an Empire calls Pitt to remould
His miniature kingdom. He must needs demolish
His benefactor's mansion, and rebuild
The left wing for a library. Lady Chatham
Must have her bird-room; Capability Brown,

[301]

Shenstone's successor in the hierarchy
Of Landscape, plant new avenues and devise
New vistas—such as would fill poor Lyttelton
(His friend, alas, no longer) with despair.
Cypress and Cedar of Lebanon by the thousand
Must mark or shade his walks; deep-sunken roads,
Delved at incalculable cost, insure
A lordly privacy; stables and cowsheds,
Graced with Corinthian pilasters, house
Horses and herds of pedigree. The expense
Might beggar Crœsus—but what does money mean
To one who in the exigences of war
Has thought in millions? The Georgian Cincinnatus
Enjoys this pastoral holiday, engrossed
In a more luxurious rusticity
Than his rude exemplar, savouring the delights
Of haymaking and coursing in the midst
Of an adoring family, immersed
In Somerset's Lethe. . . .

(6)

Through those quiet airs
There runs a disquieting whisper: America—
His beloved America! Things are going wrong:
George Grenville grubbing up every root of commerce
And planting taxes. His latest imposition
Is a Stamp Tax, burdening every legal document
With a petty charge. The moment is ill-timed;
For America is touchy, and embarrassed
By an Indian revolt. George Grenville's officers
Are seized, and their stamps burnt. Next, the Assemblies
Of Massachusetts and New York submit
A reasoned protest to the Privy Council,
Which is duly pigeon-holed. Then a General Congress,

While acknowledging allegiance and submission
To the British Crown and Parliament, asserts,
With admirable propriety, its right
To levy its own taxes. In the meantime
American barristers refuse to plead
In cases that involve stamped instruments,
And American merchants solemnly engage
To buy no goods from England. At a glance
Pitt sees the fatal drift. Wincing with pain
And swathed in flannels, he drags himself to town
To urge the Act's repeal in a debate
On the King's Speech:
     "Sir, I cannot be silent
On a question that may mortally wound three millions
Of brave and virtuous subjects. In my opinion
This kingdom has no power to lay a tax
On men as much entitled as ourselves
To human rights and the particular privileges
Of Englishmen. These men are England's sons,
Not England's bastards! As subjects, they can claim
The common right of being represented
In Parliament. Not being represented,
They are not bound to pay a single farthing
Without consent. The Commons of America,
By their Assemblies, have enjoyed the right
Of granting their own money: they had been slaves
If they had not enjoyed it. But all taxes
Granted to the Crown are voluntary gifts:
We give what is our own; we cannot give
The property of others. If the House
Suffer this Stamp Act to remain in force,
France will gain more of us by our own colonies
Than if, by force of arms, she had been triumphant
In the late war."
    A querulous Grenville makes
The lamest of apologies, taking cover

Behind the Crown's prerogative, and recounting
His own innumerable generosities
To the ungrateful colonies. He deplores
America's obstinacy, and charges Pitt
With fostering sedition.

                 Instantly
Pitt's on his gouty feet again ("Order! Order!"
No member may speak twice in one debate.)
But, as he hesitates, St. Stephen's Chapel
Rings with another cry: "Go on! Go on!"
And he goes on . . . so hotly that he forgets
Even to address the Chair! "Gentlemen . . . Sir,
The House has heard me charged with giving birth
To sedition in America. I regret to hear
Liberty of speech imputed as a crime
In this tribunal. It is a liberty
I mean to exercise. Next we are told
That America is obstinate—nay, that America
Is almost in open rebellion. I rejoice
That America has resisted. I come not here
Armed at all points with precedents—the statute-book
Doubled down in dog's-ears—to defend the cause
Of Liberty! For the defence of Liberty
Upon a general principle, I stand firm,
And dare meet any man! The gentleman boasts
Of his bounties to America. Are not his bounties
Intended for the benefit of this kingdom?
(If he can't understand the difference
Between internal and external taxes,
I cannot help him.) He asks: "When were the colonies
Emancipated?" I desire to know
When they were slaves. Our profits by their commerce
Are two million pounds a year. This is the fund
That carried us to victory: this is the price
They have paid for our protection. Yet he boasts
He has brought a peppercorn to the exchequer

Against the loss of millions! Much has been said
About American strength. In a good cause,
On a sound bottom, I doubt not we could crush
America to atoms—but in this cause
Success is hazardous. If America fell,
She would fall like a strong man—she would embrace
The pillars of the state and, falling, wreck
The constitution. Is this your boasted peace:
To sheathe the sword of victory not in its scabbard
But in the bowels of your American brethren?
Will you quarrel with yourselves, when the whole House
Of Bourbon stands against you? It is true
That, in all things, the Americans have not acted
With prudence and temper. But they have been wronged;
They have been driven to madness by injustice.
Rather let prudence and temper be displayed
On our side first! It is my firm opinion
That this lamentable tax should be repealed
Totally, absolutely, and immediately."

Twice more, with dwindling bodily strength, he fought
The selfsame battle—and within a month
The Stamp Act is repealed. America,
More generous than her enemies, celebrates
Her victory without rancour. In the South
Charleston flares up in fireworks; at New York
An ox is roasted in the street, and banners
Bearing the legend "Pitt, George and Liberty!"
Carried in triumph.

(7)

                    Pitt would have been shocked
At his arbitrary precedence; but by now
He had shot his bolt: the cumulative strains

[305]

Of unremitting war had overtaxed
Even that titanic spirit; and though the King
Recalls him—since no lesser reputation
Can prop his selfish purpose—the Earl of Chatham
Is but a shadow cast by the setting sun
Of the Great Commoner's fame. That shadow soon
A darker cloud obscures. It is a changeling
Who dreams at Burton Pynsent: the falcon eyes
No longer bright; the brooding mind oppressed
By months of utter nescience; the ancient pride
Humbled by mountainous debts. And while his name
Shelters their mischiefs, Chatham's Ministry—
"That tesselated pavement," as Burke calls it,
"Of Patriots and Courtiers, treacherous Friends
And open Enemies."—undermine the fabric
Pitt's wisdom built. George Grenville and the King
Burn for revenge—and in the featherpate
Of Townshend find an instrument to bring
America to heel, with a sly series
Of irritating pin-pricks: customs-duties
To take the place of taxes; the forced billeting
Of British soldiers—and not only British
But Hanoverian. ("Why should a foreign garrison
Be needed, now that Canada is ours?
Why, above all, in Boston? Do they think
We should be intimidated?") Jeering crowds
Pester the innocent redcoats; shots are fired,
Civilians wounded. The Assembly of Massachusetts
Refuses to find billets for any garrison
Within the town: the British Government
Rakes up an obsolete statute that compels
The deportation of political prisoners
For trial in England. Townshend's custom-duties
Prove useless and are dropped—save only one,
A trivial duty on tea. This is retained
As a matter of principle. Americans, too,

[306]

Are interested in principles: so three cargoes
Of the East India Company's choice Bohea
Are soused in Boston harbour. As a penalty
The port is closed; the charter of Massachusetts
Suspended—and then remodelled in such a manner
As gives the Crown control. This is the end
Of bickering: now these obstinate colonials
Shall taste coercion . . .

                     As the ominous sky
Blackened above New England, that other cloud
Of nescience which had lowered on Chatham's mind
Suddenly lifted, and his eyes beheld
The gathering human tempest. Within a week
He is jolted up to London to consult
That wise American, Franklin. His liveried servants
And crested chariot are observed outside
The Doctor's lodgings in Craven Street. Franklin listens
To four hours of magnificent monologue. Each of these men,
So great in their several ways, is quick to see
The other's greatness: Chatham recognizes
The protest of the Continental Congress
As 'decent, manly, and properly expressed':
Franklin, with no less courtesy, affirms
Its intrinsic loyalty. Both are conciliatory;
Yet neither (and this is strange) appears to realize
That a wider breach than the Atlantic separates
America and England; so Chatham presents
A Provisional Act for the Immediate Settlement
Of the Troubles in America. Their lordships
Refuse it a first reading, and Sandwich suggests
That Franklin has had a hand in it. Chatham rises
In a blaze of anger:

                   "I am not much astonished
That men who scoff at Liberty should detest
Others who prize it. The conduct of this Government
Is one long tale of weakness, despotism,

Temerity, ignorance, negligence, futility,
Servility, incapacity and corruption!"
The flame burns out . . . Now, thickened by the smoke
Of that conflagration, the old cloud descends
On its exhausted embers. Two years must pass
Before that cloud be lifted: two tragic years
Of needless civil warfare. Lexington,
Bunker's Hill, Trenton and Ticonderoga—
These are the names that mark the decadence
Of British arms, the utter bankruptcy
Of British statecraft! When he wakes again,
He knows it is too late. He sees himself,
A frail and aged man, amid the ruins
Of the proud Empire he alone had built:
America, darling of his hopes, allied
With France, the inveterate enemy, from whose toils
His will had saved her. With prophetic words
And faltering voice he pleads for peace;

                                        "My lords,
If this struggle be not ended before France
Confirms this treaty, then England will be ended.
You talk of forces gathering to disperse
The rebels: I might as easily talk myself
Of driving them before me with this crutch!
If you conquer them—what then? You cannot make them
Respect you. You have said: "Lay down your arms!"
America returns the Spartan answer:
"Come, take!" You cannot take. We are the aggressors:
We have invaded them, even as the Great Armada
Invaded England. If I were an American,
As I am English, while a foreign troop
Was landed in my country, I would never
Lay down my arms! No . . . Never — never — *never!*"

Five times he crawled to Westminster to plead
For that lost cause of peace with the Americans,

Of war with France and Spain. When last he rose
Within the Painted Chamber, he stood propped
On either side, by William Pitt, his son,
And Mahon, his son-in-law: an antic shape
Swathed in black flannel; his great aquiline nose
And flashing eyes were all that could be seen
Beneath his bushy wig. He raised himself
Painfully to his feet. The whole House rose
In tribute to his majesty. Then he lifted
The hand from off his crutch, and spoke so feebly
As hardly to be heard:

                "I thank God," he said,
I have been enabled to come here this day
To perform my duty. I am old, infirm;
I have one foot—more than one foot—in the grave,
And have risen from my bed but to stand up
In the cause of my country. My lords, His Majesty
Succeeded to an Empire in extent
As great as in its reputation
Unsullied. Shall we sully that repute
By an ignominious surrender of our rights
And fairest provinces? Shall this great kingdom,
That has survived the Danish depredations,
The Scottish inroads, and the Norman conquest,
Fall prostrate now before the House of Bourbon?
Shall a people that only fifteen years ago
Was the terror of the world, now stoop so low
As to tell its ancient and inveterate enemy:
"Take all we have—but give us peace!"? I say
That any state is better than despair.
If we must fall, then let us fall like men."

He ceased—and with the last inaudible word
Sank backward, helplessly, into the arms
Of Mahon and William. A more terrible silence
Fell as they carried his insensate frame

Forth from that august chamber which had echoed
So often with the impassioned eloquence
Of that tremendous voice which never more
Would sway the will and steel the wavering faith
Of his beloved land. His living eyes
Saw not the loss of all his pride had won,
Nor that far prouder England that would rise
To greater glories builded by his son.

XXXII

Interlude

Over this moonstruck world the tidal flow
Of warring dynasties swirls to and fro,
While underneath the fury and the sound
Of tumult stirs a portent more profound
Than causes lost or won: a monstrous birth
Risen from Time's teeming womb to rack the earth
In throes more fateful than the rise or fall
Of envious empires—destined to enthrall
Victor no less than vanquished, and to bind
In equal servitude all humankind!

In Matthew Boulton's foundry at Soho,
Where sweltering puddlers tend the lava-flow
Of molten ores, and clanging hammers beat
On airs that faint and quaver with fierce heat,
The new-born monster stands: an uncouth mass
Of cold insensate metal—iron and brass
Shaped by the cunning of Man's eager brain
And shrewd inventive fingers to contain
The marriage of discordant elements,
Water and Fire, and from unthrottled vents
Unloose their mightier offspring: the supreme
Slave of Man's will, his new-tamed genie, Steam.

Master or slave? The question well might flout
Less confident minds! Its makers have no doubt
That, in one leap, the feet of patient Man
Have scaled a summit whence his eyes may scan
Realms of unbounded conquest fading far
Beyond imagination. A new star

[311]

Burns over England to proclaim the hour
Of a new dispensation. Power . . . Power!
The plunging piston sinks, and the vast beam
Tilts to its task as in the hiss of steam
The wheel turns on its axis. We behold
A calculable energy, controlled
To the last ounce of pressure. Motive force
Is measured with precision. (A draught horse
Exerts a strength—so Mr. Watt has reckoned—
Can raise five hundredweight in every second
Twelve inches from the ground; therefore we call
Our unit Horse-power.) Gone, for good and all,
Are those hard days when industry was bound
To seek the hills where water could be found
And turn machinery from the running leat!
That source of power's completely out of date,
Now there's no inch of England that need lack
The heartening vista of a chimney-stack
Whose pillared smoke or flame shall lead a band
Of trustful pilgrims to a promised land
Where energy no longer need be rated
In terms of toil. It has been calculated
That Mr. Watt's steam-engine supersedes
The bulk of manual labour: all it needs
Is fuel, lubrication, and an eye
To keep a watch when pressure runs too high
Or bearings stiffen. For the rest, it works
Untended; and your engine neither shirks
(Like indolent mankind) the weightier task,
Nor tires with toil. None but a fool could ask
What other crafts shall claim the idle hands
Steam-power displaces, when in countless lands,
Famished by warfare, naked multitudes
Stand yearning for the innumerable goods
Our frames and spindles furnish. There's no room
In this economy for the cottage loom

Where homespun fleece is woven on the fells
By rustic fingers. Now the factory-bells
With harsh, impatient clamour summon all—
Man, wife and child—to swell the carnival
Of dumb, inhuman labour that shall turn
Green fields into foul cities. All can earn
Some kind of pittance from the spilth of gold
That crams our bursting pockets. None's too old,
Too weak, too young: mere children in their teens
And shaky crones can tend our new machines.
The spinning-jenny and the patent mule
Make better scholars than the village school.
Since Man (the Scriptures tell) is born to toil
And trouble, it were sacrilege to spoil
Creation's plan. So surely God will bless
Child-labour. Incidentally, it costs less,
And spares our manufacturers the means
To build new factories—and still more machines!
There's no skilled craft plied by a human hand
But steel and steam can mimic and expand
A hundredfold. Our engines gape for food
To stoke their fires: here, also, God is good.
Was it not Providence that underspread
The living green of England with the dead
Bones of primeval forests, and compressed
Their ooze to coal? Was it mere chance that laced
Those buried coal-beds with the limey silt
Of vanished seas, and on their margins spilt
Grains of volcanic iron-ore to blend
In the red furnace? There shall be no end
To these God-given benefits until
The coal-seams dwindle. Then—go deeper still!
Engines shall sink new shafts, and engines lift
From sunken galleries the blear-eyed shift;
Engines shall pump the oozy bilge that seeps
Through fissured rock to swamp those sunless deeps

No glimpse of day has lighted since the time
When giant lizards foundered in black slime.
What matter that a free and forthright race
Toil sixteen hours a day at the coal-face
For fourteen pence? The modern troglodyte,
Damned, for our profit, to perpetual night,
Must learn that mills and factories overhead
Need engines—and those engines must be fed;
That life, in mill and factory, will be found
No sweeter than the miner's underground;
For unskilled labour's even more poorly paid,
And competition is the salt of trade.
How can we flood the world with English ware,
If ignorant factory-hands and miners dare
To calculate, to argue, or to think?
Time presses. Give the working-classes drink
To stive their empty stomachs. Gin will keep
Reason benumbed—and gin, thank God, is cheap!
We`ve other problems knocking at our door:
To house—and where to house—the Labouring Poor.
But these are easy; any hutch will do
For folk whose hours of leisure should be few—
(Just long enough to booze and breed and sleep,
Then limp back to the mill like foot-rot sheep)
And any building-site will suit us well
So long as they can hear the Factory Bell
Clang through their dreams. Build walls of noggin-brick—
(But take good care that these be not too thick,
For bricks cost money!) and to cure the lack
Of warmth in Winter, build them back to back:
Warped doors and broken windows will admit
Sufficient air at night to keep men fit
For labour on the morrow. Water-mains
Are needless luxuries, no less than drains:
So, in each noisome courtyard, sink a pump—
And if the cesspit leaks into the sump

[314]

Of surface water that their children drink,
So much the worse for them! We cannot think
Of everything. Enough that we can give
Wages to hungry millions. How they live
Or how they die is no concern of ours—
Provided they put in sufficient hours
To keep the fly-wheels spinning, and the flow
Of steam-power so profuse that we can show
In our shop-windows wares to tempt the eyes
Of needier nations: piece-work merchandise
From Manchester and Bolton; coals from Shields;
Woollens from Bradford; silks from Spitalfields;
Steel from our Sheffield forges to lay low
Primeval forests, and to arm the plough;
Cannon and coulter, mattock and grenade;
Brummagem pinchbeck for the trinket-trade—
The beads we cast for rosaries serve as well
For barter with the naked infidel,
And any glittering metal that we mix
Will make an idol—or a crucifix!
Thus, from our workshops, we supply the need
Of every culture, climate, race or creed—
Except, of course, our own: for everywhere
In Britain meat is scarce and bread grows dear.
But that's their fault. How can the common field,
That barely fed a backward hamlet, yield
Grist for our teeming cities? Times have changed:
Those heath-fed geese and cattle, that once ranged
The village waste, have been the basic source
Of rural idleness, and—what's far worse—
Of stiff-necked independence. The new State
Decrees that grazing-rights are out of date,
Nay, even immoral! Nothing will avail
But well-planned husbandry on a larger scale.
Therefore enclose the commons, and proclaim
The landlord's right to shoot or snare all game;

THE ISLAND

Pull down the squatter's hovels, and condemn
The idle cottager to work or clem!
Such is the Law of Nature. Large estates
May need less labour. But our factory-gates
Stand open. The unwanted overplus
Should lay the blame on Adam—not on us!

So, from the windy hills and quiet vales
Of this green isle, a sad procession trails
Like waters of the desert that are spent
In thirsty sands: uprooted, ill-content,
Hungry, bewildered—never more to hear
The lark at dawn, or sniff the morning air
Fragrant with meadow-sweet or mountain thyme,
Or honeyed wafts of hawthorn in the prime
Of June, when cuckoos call and landrails crake
Lost in lush mowing-grass; no more to slake
Midsummer's drought in limpid brooks that run
Ambered with peat and sparkle in the sun!
The sun shines rarely now, with sickly beams
Halo'd in soot and sulphur; the clear streams
Of Mersey, Aire and Irwell, now run thick
With ordure through straight culverts of slimed brick:
Waters of Babylon . . . but no willows lean
Beside those banks forlorn; no blade of green
Unwithered can survive the searing breath
Blown from the furnace, or the silt of death
Fallen from the mournful sky that with a pall
Of acrid dust and carbon smothers all.
No more through magic meadows shall the feet
Of children stray: their playground is the street,
And idleness breeds vice. A child of five
Can earn enough at least to keep alive.
No more shall aged men whose days of toil
Seemed ended pore on the sweet-smelling soil

[316]

Of homely garden-plots, or watch their seed
Break into leaf: wage-earners have no need
Of gardens when the tommy-shops supply
Far more stale produce than their wage can buy.
Seed-time and harvest? Each is but a name
In streets where every season smells the same,
And flowers are useless. You should know, my friend,
The rose has never paid a dividend.

So, in soft Midland vales, where surface coal
Lies thick, and on the shelving plains that roll
Seaward from Pennine sheepwalks, there arose
Prisons of hope abandoned: rows on rows
Of courts and houses, crowding street on street,
Whose cobbled causeways echoed with clog'd feet;
Cities whose only gods were steel and steam,
The nightmare terrors of a drunkard's dream,
By Greed begotten in the womb of Haste,
That, like slow cancers, gnawed into a waste
Of slag and cinder—cities that were doomed
To suffocate in denser smoke than plumed
The falling towers of Sodom when the rain
Of fire consumed the Cities of the Plain.
And where their phallic smokestacks fouled the sky
Burned those unholy fires that never die:
Fierce furnace-throats—not only fed with coals,
But with the agonies of bewildered souls
And aching limbs, damped with the tears and sweat
Of those who, even in sleep, could not forget
The bondage of the foundry, mine or mill,
And woke to hear the pitiless siren shrill
As monster Moloch from his iron throne
Howled for his toll of human blood and bone,
And skinflint Mammon, with a leery grin,
Rubbed his thin hands and checked the stragglers in:

[317]

Workers of England, mistress of the earth:
A merry England that has lost her mirth.

Ah, would that the Almighty had seen fit
To grant mankind the sense to match their wit!

XXXIII

ON WINDMILL DOWN   A.D. 1789

*The scene is open downland in South Hampshire. Neither the
nclosures, which have already alienated a good deal of common land
this county, nor Mr Watt's steam-engine have made much difference
the landscape of the pleasant countryside which lies between the chalk
the South Downs and the marls of the Forest of Bere. It is a morn-
g of late August in the year 1789, a day of blue and white, with a
arm breeze stirring the heads of cumulus cloud that drift in from sea.
n Windmill Hill a cricket match is in progress—the last of the
ason, and a large crowd of rustic folk, clad in smock-frocks or
berdines, encircles the field of play on which the local side are bringing
eir visitors' first innings to an untimely close. On the dry turf,
mediately behind the wickets, a middle-aged labourer, evidently
ippled with rheumatism, leans on a blackthorn stick and watches
ery ball that is bowled with an expert intentness. A younger man,
earing his hair in a pigtail and carrying a bundle of dunnage over his
oulder, comes panting up the slope and accosts him.*

SAILOR:

an you tell me the name of yon village, master?

LABOURER:

Surelye:

d ought to, for 'tis my native. Only to think
here be anyone don't know Hambledon! Mayhap you're a
[foreigner?

SAILOR:

foreigner? *Me?*

LABOURER:

Nay, 'tis only our Hampshire fashion
Of speaking of upalong folk. Bi'st come from the sea?

SAILOR:

y, landed last night from the frigate *Boreas*,
aptain Nelson, at Portsmouth. Now I'm homeward-bound

L*

On a No'therly course. The navy has no more use for me:
They're paying men off at Spithead a hundred a day
And laying-up ships by the score.

SAILOR:

LABOURER:

                    There can't be no call
For you chaps now we're all at peace.

SAILOR:

(*Indignantly*) Ay, that's what they said
Before the last war broke out—and they'll say it again
When the next war's ended. But what is a man to do
Who's been bred to the sea? Go sweat in a factory? Not me
Turn back to the land, like my dad? You can't learn a new trad
At my time of life. I'm an able-bodied seaman,
And good for naught else. You'll see a sight more like me
Set adrift before they've finished.

LABOURER:

            If you aim to go North
You'd ought to be making for Alton. How come you to stra
So far from the turnpike?

SAILOR:

        I'll tell thee straight: when I sighted
All you folk on the hills, I reckoned it must be a prize-figh
Or a fairing or some such frolic, and come about
On a reach to starboard. You South-country chaps
Must have brass to spare to waste good harvest weather
Watching men play ball like lads!

LABOURER:

            This bean't no child's-play.
Were you Hampshire-born you'ld know better nor talk so
                                            [foolish
I do 'low there's no schooling like cricket for making a ma
Stand up and sharpen his wits. Hast ever played?

[320]

SAILOR:

Not me! I come from Yorkshire. Up in the North
We reckon to work for a living. The only game
They learnt us at sea was long bowls with twenty-four pounders,
And we plays that one hot enough to give the Johnnies
A bellyful, I can tell thee!

LABOURER:

(*Not impressed*) Just look at that, now!
'Twere a beautiful ball. Didst mark how she turned in the air
And broke off the bent? That happens this time of the year,
After sokey nights, when the wicket be starked-up on top
And brick-hard underneath. I reckon old Mr Nyren
Must 'a counted on that when he chose the pitch and ardained
To put them in first. By the time the sun's full overhead
Twill play sweet and easy. Ay, he be foxy-headed,
Be old Mr Nyren! Many's the time I've a'see'd en
Traipse up to Broad Halfpenny at six o'clock of a marnin'
For to choose a pitch to his likin'!

SAILOR:

(*Indulgently*) Who's old Mr Nyren?

LABOURER:

Who's Mr Nyren?

SAILOR:

Was that him bowling?

LABOURER:

Nay, nay
That's Tom Brett—as steady a bowler as ever us had,
But he be getting past of it now. You'd ought to 'a see'd en
Twelve years agone, when Hambledon larruped All England
By a hundred and sixty-eight and an innings to spare.
That was bowling! Five wickets he took: the Duke of Darset,
Lumpy Stevens, Jack Wood, Stock White and Gamekeeper
[Miller—

[321]

And 'a caught out two more! There was nothing fancy about e
Just length and straightness. Tom Brett, mind, was never s
Not even in his pride, as Dave Harris.   [furiou

SAILOR:

And who was *he?*

LABOURER:

An Odiham chap, a potter by trade. At the start
He was apt to give tosses; but Nyren soon took'en in hand
And made him keep down. When once he had gotten the knac
He skittled 'em out like ninepins. Dave loosed the ball
From up here—right under the armpit—and liked to pitch
On rising ground. It used to come up like a cannon-shot,
With a nasty curl on it too, as would grind a chap's fingers
On the haft of the bat. 'Twas as good as a picture to see
Where Dave had scrazed 'em. I've heard Lord Frederick sa
Dave's bowling was one of the grandest things he'd a' seen
In his natural life.

SAILOR:

(*With affected interest*) Could he bat as well as he bowled?

LABOURER:

Nay, Dave were no batter. (*Severely*) You can't have everything
And Hambledon never wanted for runs in them days.
There was Aylward—another farmer from Farnham way:
Him that notched a hundred and sixty-seven not out
In the match I was telling you on—the Hambledon Club
Agen All England, five hundred pounds a side.
Arter that, Sir Horace, he tooked'en up into Sussex
And made'en his bailey; but Jim never done no good
When he played agen we. Mr Nyren knew all his faults
And foxed'en out in no time. Then there was Beldham,
William Beldham—Silver Billy us always called'en,
For his hair was so white as a wheatfield, come October.
Harry Hall, the gingerbread-maker, learnt'en the game:
Hall were no great player himself, but he made young Beldham

[322]

eep his left elbow up and hold his bat plumb-straight
the line of the ball when he swung. 'Twere a gallant sight
o see Silver Billy smack 'em all over the field,
nd never lift one. That lad, he danced on his toes
ike Jack Broughton, the boxer. And run! He could lance
[like a deer
o pick up the ball full-pelt, so neat as a swallow
ips gnats in the air! You'd ought to a'see'd'en cut
ff the point of the bat, with a crack like a pistol-shot,
he ball shaving daisies all way to the boundary,
nd shepherds a'lepping like lambs of an April evenin'
o save their old shins—not one of 'em could a'stopped it
owsomever he tried. But I 'low the best of all
Vas when him and Lord Frederick Beauclerk was in together:
ord Frederick had royal blood in'en, so 'twere said,
or his grammer were Nelly Gwynn, King Charles's fancy,
ut when Billy and him walked out to the pitch, side by side,
ou couldn't tell which were the farmer and which the gentleman,
he pair on 'em looked that majestic. And when they got set
ou'ld a'thought they was brothers born, the way they gloried
n basting the bowling between 'em. There wasn't a ball,
ong or short, high or low, but Lord Frederick went into it
Vrist and shoulder. And Billy the same. They looked something grander
han human mortals, them two—so light on their feet
As hobby-hawks skimmin' a hedge, or pewits a'runnin'
fore they do light on the down. I can see them now:
illy Beldham's silvery head and his lordship's white hat
hridding to and thro like shuttles: the crowd on their feet
ollerin' out: "Go hard ... go hard! Tich and turn, tich and turn!
ry another! One more!"—and the fielders runnin' like hares
n every side of the wicket. Ay, that was music!
fore now I've a'see'd Silver Billy notch ten runs
ff one snick past slip and an overthrow. Them was the days!
The Duke was a good'un too—as jolly a sportsman
As ever stripped for cricket—and so was Sir Horace:

[323]

He be gettin' upalong now, but you'll likely see him
This marnin'. Ay ... there he be! Look over your shoulder—
Short and black as a gipsy, a' swipin' off daisy-heads
With the tip of his cane.

SAILOR:
                    I reckon the company
You cricketers keep is too high for me! In the *Boreas*
The officers' cuddy was one thing, the fo'c's'le another:
We knew our place and kept it.

LABOURER:
                    I do know mine
So well as thee, lad. But that be the beauty of cricket:
A batsman's a batsman, be he a lord or a labourer,
And the flick of the ball, her do come as hard to white hand
As to horny ones. I do 'low 'tis the same as the graveyard,
Where one honest corpse be as good as the next, trick and tie
And after the stumps were drawn, it were just the same
Round a casty of beer at the *Bat and Ball*, when you told
What you'd ought to 'a done and didn't when you got out.
Talk? It used to run on by the hour; and then, maybe,
George Lear—Little George we called 'en—would strike up
                                                        [song
And John Small start scrapin' his fiddle. But that's not all:
There's no end to cricket: for when you be done with play,
The last ball bowled and the sheep drove back for to graze
On the lattermath, your mind do still smell so sweet
As an apple-loft in November; and Winter nights,
When the snow-blossom's fell and ice-candles hang from the
                                                        thack,
You can set by the fire, like a dog, with your eyes a'blink
And go over the Summer again—match by match, ball by ball,
Stroke by stroke. . . . (*He suddenly throws his hat in the air.*)
I'll be drattled! He's caught! That's the last man out;
And I'll wager your throat be adry same as mine. Come your
And we'll give 'em both a wet with a pint of fresh.   [ways,

[324]

The SAILOR accompanies him willingly. As they stroll towards the bough-house, which has been set up on the edge of the field, a smart yellow chariot comes lurching over the down like a ship on a choppy sea. The driver throws the reins to his groom and dismounts. JOHN SACKVILLE, Third Duke of DORSET, his Majesty's Ambassador at the court of Versailles, is a tall, dark man in the late forties, with the short arms which may so often be remarked in the anatomy of a great hitter. He is fashionably dressed in a full-skirted coat, knee-breeches, and a white beaver hat. As the players trip off the field he waves cheerily, greeting several of them by name. Then he sees SIR HORATIO MANN, still busy with the daisies, and advances rapidly towards him, with hand out-stretched.

DORSET:

Good morning, Horace. I half expected to see you.

MANN:

Jack Dorset? Well, I'll be damned! What are you doing here?
I thought you were still in Paris. To tell you the truth,
We were rather anxious.

DORSET:

I made up my mind that discretion
Was the better part of valour, and made myself scarce.
Things were getting too hot for my liking. The French have
gone mad.
'Twas like living in Bedlam, after they'd sacked the Bastille.

MANN:

The Bastille? What's that?

DORSET:

An old castle, half prison, half fortress,
In the middle of Paris. I happened to know the governor,
A pleasant old man named de Launay. The mob swept in,
Hauled him out and hacked off his head. The unfortunate Swiss
Were trampled and torn piecemeal—their *disjecta membra*
Thrown into the gutter like garbage.

[325]

MANN:

But how the devil
Did these fellows get arms?

DORSET:

They broke into the *Invalides*
And took all they wanted.

MANN:

But this is a regular revolt!

DORSET:

That's just what the poor King called it. My friend Liancour
Put it better. "No, sir," says he, "it's a Revolution."
And by God you'ld have thought so yourself if you'd seen tha
rabbl
From my Embassy window! They poured through the narrow
Like a river in flood—torn limbs and heads on pikes   [stree
Bobbing up and down like driftwood. All that night
You could hear Paris throb and hum like an angry beehive.
Sometimes, when the bells broke out, it rose to a roar
Of hoarse cries, with sabots pattering over the *pavé*
Like a cavalry charge. I never slept a damned wink.
Next morning 'twas still as death: they'd had their fling
And were sleeping it off, I suppose; but the cobbles were crimso
With blood and wine—you couldn't tell which—and the city
Smelt like a burnt-out shambles.

MANN:

What are they after?

DORSET:

I doubt if they know. Their obvious taste, at the moment,
Is blood—and the bluer the better. France has flared up
Of itself, like a damp-hot hayrick. Paris was bad enough;
But the country, I'm told, is far worse. All the way to Calais
My road was lit by the flames of burning *châteaux;*
And when I got to the coast, I found the quays crammed
With hundreds of fugitives, people like you and me,

Who'd run from their homes in wild panic—all scrambling
For a passage to England. Terror's an ugly thing.
Every man for himself! 'Twas a picture of human nature
Old Voltaire would have relished. For myself, I confess
It revolted my stomach.

MANN:
But had you any idea
That such troubles were brewing?

DORSET:
I wasn't precisely happy.
Day by day, as I drove to and fro between Versailles
And Paris, the contrast leapt to the eye: on one hand
The most brilliant court in Europe—a glittering surface
Stiffened by protocols that made poor old St. James's
Look dowdy—yet all as flimsy and artificial
As a piece of puff-pastry: nothing whatever beneath it
But empty frivolity. One felt that France was bankrupt
In body and spirit. And then, on the other side,
That grim city, *terre à terre*, if you will, but simmering
With frothy ideas like a brewer's vat. You could feel
The perpetual ferment. I used to stroll through the streets
(French noblemen never walk anywhere, but you know
I can't do without exercise)—and the coffee-houses
Of the *Palais Royal* were clamorous, night and day,
With excited talk—political orators
Jumping up on chairs and tables, haranguing the customers,
And a crowd, outside on the pavement, straining to listen
A gorge déployée. How any business gets done
In Paris is quite beyond me. And then, the deluge
Of printed pamphlets—more than a dozen a day!
The booksellers can't keep count of them. Stockdale's shop
Or Debrett's may seem crowded to you: they're the merest
deserts
Compared with Desein's. Every literate person in Paris
Reads and talks incessantly. Sometimes I used to go down

[327]

To the poorer quarters, in spite of the stench, to ease
My bewildered ears. They don't talk in the *Faubourg St. Antoin*
But they look at you—God, how they look at you—and the
Make you think of rats in a corner. You have the feeling [ey
That they're measuring you up and wondering what you'd
        look li]
With your clean clothes stripped from your back and your
        well-fed carca
Swung from a lantern-bracket. You know, my dear Horac
I've always liked the French—but there's 'summat about 'em
As Nyren would say, 'that froughts me', something cruel ar
Clear and brittle as ice, combined with a temper of tinder: [col
One spark, and they're all on fire! Their very humour
Is whetted so razor-keen that the edge draws blood
Before you've felt it. On my honour, it gave me the shive
To walk through those grudging streets, so utterly differe
From England, where every soul you meet by the way
Will touch his cap and give you good-day with a smile.
These people just stared. It took me a goodish time
To realize that they were starving—not merely hungry,
But starving, Horace! France has had two bad years
Of harvest; and then, to make matters worse, the crops
Were bought up by speculators. Fortunes were made
By a small group of greedy men, and the millions of peasan
Who'd tilled the soil left to starve. Their best arable
Is nibbled as close as a Winter sheepwalk. Of course
These poor devils flocked to the towns, because they imagine
'Twas there that the grain had gone—and found them as bai
As the countryside. Half of the mob that stormed the Bastil]
Was made up of homeless peasants: rag-draped skeletons
With straw tied round their bleeding feet.

MANN:
        I know very well
That you can't trust townsmen, Jack. But I don't understan
Country folk behaving like that. They've too much horse-sens

nd balance and natural decency. Only imagine
en like Lumpy or Small or the Walkers losing their heads
nd brandishing ours on pikestaves—or leading a mob
o storm Farnham Castle! If ever I found myself
n a nasty wicket, there's no-one I'ld sooner have
n my side than our Hambledon lads—and every man jack of
ve Nyren is peasant-born.   [them

DORSET:
In France, my dear Horace,
he peasantry don't play cricket—and as for the gentry,
heir tenants rarely set eyes on them: they're too busy
laying parlour-games at Versailles. The labourer's lot
 that of a mere beast of burden, bowed to the ground
y feudal dues and taxes that haven't been dreamt of
 England since Magna Carta. The money that paid
or their wars against us, the fabulous wealth that's squandered
On empty pomp at Versailles, has been drained drop by drop
rom a wasting countryside. Now they have nothing left—
Not even bread for their brats; and you can't draw blood
rom a stone.

MANN:
Then surely it's time for the Government
o wake up and do something about it?

DORSET:
I've told you already:
The country is bankrupt. What is their Government?
A weak, well-meaning King; a frivolous Queen,
Who happens to wear the breeches; a handful of ministers
Each jockeying his next-door neighbour to grab what he can
Of the crumbs of patronage—or so much as is left
By a gluttonous, decadent nobility
Battening like maggots on the living flesh
Of France.

MANN:
Have they no Parliament?

[329]

DORSET:

The King
Has summoned the Estates: they're now in session,
Like our long Parliament, at Versailles, and wrangling
Over their several rights. But that won't save
Their country from starvation. Nothing less
Than a miracle can save her.

MANN:

So much the better!
I'm no great hand at history, but I reckon
She's given us more trouble than all the rest
Of Europe put together!

DORSET:

Ay, there speaks
The true-blue Englishman! But there are others
Who might profit by her downfall. Nature, alas,
Abhors a vacuum; and, should France fall,
We might find ourselves with enemies as formidable
Uncomfortably near.

MANN:

I say: "Thank God
For the English Channel!"

DORSET:

There are deadlier things
Than arms can cross salt water. Revolutions
Are like the plague: they travel on the air
And sow their spores unseen. If this contagion
Of discontent and violence should take wing
Across your channel, you and I might find ourselves
Running from Knole and Linton like the poor devils
I saw at Calais.

MANN:

No, no. . . . I won't believe it.
England's too sound at heart and too well fed

'o stomach all these windy theories
'rothed-up by foreigners. God in heaven knows
Vhere their damned nonsense comes from.

DORSET:
                    I can tell you.

t comes from England.

MANN:
                    England?

DORSET:
                    The seed was sown
\t Runnymede; flowered in the Bill of Rights,
Vatered with blood by Oliver, and transplanted
'o Massachusetts—where we've lately tasted
ts bitter fruits at Yorktown. The 'liberation'—
\s the French call it—of America
'ires them to emulate it. Lafayette
s a popular hero.

MANN:
                    Surely you don't think . . .

DORSET:
 make no prophecies, Horace, but rely
On the known principles of inoculation:
Ve've had the small-pox once, and if we take it
\gain, the new infection may be mild
\nd not disfiguring. My Whig friends at Brooks's
Velcome this revolution. Charley Fox
s rapturously excited; and even Pitt,
n his dry way, condones it with a sort
Of shy benevolence. We must wait and see
Iow the cat jumps. For my part, I'm content
'o watch a game of cricket and thank God
England's still England. Nothing is more delicious
'han these last days of Summer, when the elms

[331]

Have just begun to turn. This blessed landscape,
So gentle and so moderate, always brings
A lump into my throat when I come home
From foreign service, and hear the friendly clack
Of leather on willow. . . .

MANN:

(*Anxiously surveying the field*) I shall have to leave you.
My chaps are coming out. We've a new bowler,
A garden-boy from Linton—devilish fast,
But Nyren says he throws. I wish you'ld watch him
And tell me what you think.

DORSET:

I'll keep an eye on him.

(SIR HORACE MANN *strips off his coat, sets his hat at a raki*[s]
angle, and walks determinedly to the centre of the field. The DUK[E]
waves his hand and smiles, throws back his coat-tails, and spraw[ls]
on the grass. The SAILOR *and his new friend return from t*[he]
bough-house. Farnham hops and barley-malt have done the[ir]
work, and both are 'concerned' in liquor. Even the discharge[d]
seaman's face has lost its morosity, and the other appears to [be]
glad of the support of his blackthorn stick. They are indeed s[o]
deeply engrossed in some private joke that he almost stumbl[es]
over the Duke's outstretched legs.)

LABOURER:

Beg pardon, Sir. . . . I should say Your Grace!

DORSET:

No matter. . . .
No matter. . . . Don't I know your face?

LABOURER:

You ought to, Sir,
Seeing as I bowled you out twice, near twenty year ago.

[332]

DORSET:

y God, you've a long memory!

LABOURER:

I shan't forget
'hat there match to my dying day, Sir.

DORSET:

What's your name?

LABOURER:

Iogsflesh, Your Grace.

DORSET:

Of course I remember you.
remember the match as well. It was up on Broad Halfpenny.
was off my game that day.

LABOURER:

Howsomever that be,
bowled Your Grace out twice.

DORSET:

You did indeed.
But that's an old story now. Tell me, what do you think
Of Sir Horace's new bowler?

LABOURER:

I think he do throw.

DORSET:

'm inclined to agree with you. He comes off the pitch
Devilish fast.

LABOURER:

Ay, Your Grace; but he bean't so fast as Dave Harris,
Nor nobody ever will be. Those were the days!

DORSET:

Yes, those were the days! No doubt of it. Good luck to you.

[333]

THE ISLAND

LABOURER:

The same to you, Sir.

(*He doffs his cap. He and the* SAILOR *move off uncertainly. A* *soon as they are out of earshot he seizes his companion by th* *arm and declares emphatically*):

Now that's what I call a gentleman!

XXXIV

Now, like spores launched on the mysterious flow
Of ocean-currents, the seeds of Revolution,
Ripened in Massachusetts, then dispersed
By civil war's rash winnowing, are upcast
On Europe's tidemarks; and in the fiercer soil
Of France, hotbed of hunger, germinate
With more prodigious zest—until her wastes
Are reddened like a fallow poppy-sown
In August. Now behold the fettered French
Shake loose their feudal chains, and stagger forth
Drunk with new freedom. Naught but blood can quench
Their orgiastic thirst; and by that draught
Purged and exalted, a gigantic shape
Looms through the smoke of carnage and the mirk
Of conflagration: France—the cynosure
Of all who toil in servitude; France, the bane
Of privilege, the incubus that mars
The sleep of Kings and Prelates.
                              On her marches
A vulture-flock of dynasts wait the hour
When famine shall prevail, and the wild ardour
Fade from her haggard eyes. First Brunswick fends
The cause of injured Royalty, his anger
Fed by the fury of the dispossessed,
Yet dares not strike alone, lest failure open
His frontiers to infection. Austria
And Russia pay lip-service. At Coblenz
French emigrants plead for a coalition
Of all monarchic Europe. Only Britain,
Safe in her salty moat, dares contemplate
The havoc with complacence—a weak France
Being somewhat to her liking! Why, indeed,

[335]

Should a free, full-grown folk, that has enjoyed
The fruits of Revolution, be concerned
With the teething-troubles of Democracy
Beyond the sea? Who but a hypocrite
Could ape dissatisfaction at the downfall
Of her Bourbon enemies? Who but a fool
Would plunge into a needless war, his wounds
Being still unhealed? Let the French have their fling
And bleed themselves to death; or, if they live,
Learn wisdom in exhaustion. They who fear
This feverish infection would be wise
To put their house in order. As for us:
Paris is worth a Mass; and, red or white,
France is a valued customer.

                        The French,
Sullen and sobered now, with wary eyes
Survey the gathering legions of reaction
Camped on their frontiers. This is a matter
Of pride no less than safety—and France is proud
For all her rags and vermin. Better grasp
The Sword of Damocles! Brissot demands
Disbandment of the horde of Royalists
Camped at Coblenz in Treves; Danton will show
How much France cares for kings! Two royal heads
Roll in the basket of the guillotine,
And the world shudders. Even England feels
That things have gone too fast and far—forgetting
Charles Stuart's blood-stained scaffold in Whitehall.
So vengeful Brunswick marches. . . . At Jemappes
And Valmy, the undisciplined rabble of France,
Ill-armed, ill-fed, yet desperately inspired
By the passion for survival, overwhelms
The Prussian Guard; then, dazzled by the glory
Of such an incredible victory, surges on
Through Flanders to the Scheldt, where Holland hails
The banners of Revolution. This is no longer

An army of defence, but a whole nation
Risen in arms, quixotically pledged
To liberate its neighbours and establish
The Rights of Man. Britain's benevolence
Is coloured with disquiet: this infant Demos
Has not merely cut his teeth, but seems disposed
To flesh them greedily. Our ancient grudge
Of every militant might that may command
The coast of Flanders—fount and origin
Of all her foreign wars—is reawakened;
And when France, flushed with confidence, proclaims
The Freedom of the Scheldt (thus challenging
London's preeminence) that long-smouldering grudge,
Fanned by new tales of terror, suddenly
Flares into righteous anger. These damned Jacobins
Have overstepped all bounds of decency,
And must be brought to heel—or British trade
Will surely suffer. Even the sacred rights
Of property are endangered. None need fear
A long-drawn war; for France, thank God, is starved
And bankrupt: her immediate success
A mere flash in the pan, or the last flicker
Of a guttering candle. So this war began.
It raged for twenty years, to change the shape
And mind of Europe and the world. . . .

                                        At first
Reaction prospers, and the ragged French
Are flurried out of Flanders: British gold,
Broadcast in lavish subsidies, providing
Mouthfuls of mercenary cannon-food
To choke the guns of Valmy. England's fleet
Tautens the noose that grips the throat of France—
Though English dead, victims of greed, may rot
In the French sugar-islands. Holland, tempted
By lust of booty, joins the vulture-flocks
Of Austria and Prussia to pick bare

The bones of France—till her accomplices,
Sniffing the taint of richer carrion, wing
Eastward to where the Russian eagle gloats
On a dismembered Poland. Thus the French,
Stricken and reeling, gain a moment's respite
To gauge the forces of a hateful world
Arrayed against them. Now no more they cry
"The Revolution is in danger!" Now
'Tis France, proud France herself, that is beset
And persecuted: her beloved soil,
Birthright of glorious generations, threatened
With alien dominance. Faction and Terror
Alike must be forsworn. The guillotine
Rusts with disuse; while France's crumbling fabric
Cemented by external pressure, sets
In a new, adamantine nationhood
Such as the Sun King's self had never seen
In his noonday radiance. Lazare Carnot
Shall organize the incoherent strength
Of twenty million Frenchmen. None may shirk
His civic duties: and all France becomes
One arsenal of deadly weapons forged,
Not for the hands of hirelings, but to arm
A militant nation. What mercenary might
Can stem this human torrent? Now it flows
Over reconquered Flanders; soon the dykes
Of Holland crack and crumble. The Duke of York,
Mangled at Hondschoete, falls back from Dunkirk
Leaving his guns behind him. At Wattignies
The Austrians are routed, and recoil
In panic to the Rhine, abandoning
Alsace and the Palatinate. In the South,
Last foothold of reaction, the massed cannon
Of an obscure Corsican captain, Bonaparte,
In awful unison blast the British fleet
Out of the roads of Toulon. A new name,

Written in blood and lit by flame, imbues
The chronicles of War. Such master-men,
Monstrous alike in their capacity
For good or evil, have ever ridden on tides
Of Revolution, the gigantic jetsam
Of human tempest, finding in the flux
Of molten nations malleable stuff
To give their dreams an iron shape, and weld
The weapons of ambition. Such a man
Was this visionary Corsican, in whose mind
Nations and men were but the instruments
Of a personal predominance, and continents
Mere fields of battle whereon his mastery
Of arms, unmatched since Marlborough's, might achieve
Conquests that made the fame of Macedon
Turn pale. Nerved by his will, impetuous France,
Flaunting the cap of Liberty, imposes
New tyrannies on Europe: he, in return,
Sates her with glory. First he overruns
The Lombard plain: Lodi and Rivoli
Proclaim its liberation; and Milan,
Freed from her Austrian servitude, accepts
New chains for old. A crop of small Republics
Spring up like mushrooms—but the loot of Italy
Flows steadily to France, and even the Pope
Disgorges gold for peace—while Bonaparte,
Bored in his palace at Mombello, sees
Mirages of new conquest. Asia waits
Her second Alexander, offering
More fabulous empire lightly to be snatched
From the decadent British. The Army of Italy,
Launched by this land-bred arrogance, takes the sea
And grounds on Egypt, where its legionaries
Sharpen their bayonets on the prostrate stones
Of a forgotten empire. Never was given
To Fate a pledge more reckless! As their fleet

Lies snugly hidden in the channeled roads
Of Aboukir, an English midshipman,
Tree'd on *Goliath*'s dizzy masthead, spies
That cluster of bare spars: sixteen great ships,
The navel-cord of Bonaparte's invasion,
Anchored at ease. A signal flutters forth:
"Enemy in sight!"—and with supreme contempt
Of shoal or sounding, five British seventy-fours,
Goliath, Orion, Theseus, Audacious, Zealous,
Together brave the island guns that guard
The anchorage to Westward, sweeping in
Betwixt them and the shore. Now Nelson's squadron,
With all sails set, streams from the blood-red West
To pound their seaward flank. Egyptian night,
Made awful by the guns' incessant thunder
And flames of burnt-out ships, obscures the issue
Of this tremendous conflict. Morning shows
Unequalled desolation, and the dreams
Of an Eastern Empire ended. Bonaparte,
Thwarted—but, in the manner of his kind,
Callous beyond belief and undismayed,—
Leaves the abandoned flower of France to rot
In the deadly dust of Acre, and sails home,
An unrepentant prodigal, to resume
The paths of destiny. . . .

                     That season smiles
On the conqueror's ambitions, though dismay
Beclouds the skies of France: in Italy
Her vassal-states are crumbling like sand-castles
Sapped by the tide returning from the East
To lash her Alpine frontier; Naples yields
To the patriots of Calabria, who prefer
A home-made brand of Liberty; Nelson sweeps
The Middle Sea, denying her the means
Of passage or offence; about her throat
An iron torque, forged by the coalition

Of England, Austria and Russia, chokes
Her breath to suffocation. 'Tis no time
For faint hearts or half-measures. France demands
A sterner discipline: better any tyranny
Than national extinction. Bonaparte,
First Consul now, grasps at the absolute power
For which he long has lusted; and the French,
Rejuvenate in spirit and re-armed,
Follow this heaven-sent saviour, overbrimming
The Piemontese Alps to decimate
The Austrians at Marengo—while Moreau
Carries the tattered flag of Revolution
To Hohenlinden, and romantic Russia,
Bedazzled by these glittering feats of arms,
Forsakes her allies.
                                    Only Britain stands
Seagirt and unsubdued upon the flank
Of the European fortress; only Britain
Flouts that imperious will. What is this blind,
Unreasoning insular folly that can persuade
A nation of sixteen millions to resist
A power four times more numerous? Pitt should know
How hopeless is her case. One master-weapon
Rests in the conqueror's armoury—for our isle
Lives but by sea-borne commerce. A blockade
Of continental Europe from the Baltic
To Portugal and the Sicilies shall obstruct
The flow that feeds her sinews till she starve
And squeal for mercy! But Bonaparte forgets
The lesson ill-learned in Egypt, and his weapon
Proves double-edged, when Nelson of the Nile
Bursts through the Cattegat, and at Elsinore
Shatters the Danish fleet, to make an end
Of this League of Armed Neutrality. Once again
Sea-power prevails; and the shrewd Corsican
Is fain to cut his losses and accept

[341]

An honourable truce. . . .
                        They call it Peace;
And two war-wearied nations celebrate
This triumph of illusion in an orgy
Of mutual flatteries. But neither Pitt
Nor Bonaparte relaxes; for the despot
Knows well his dreams of Empire must be vain
While England lives; and Pitt, who longs for peace,
Can see no end until those arrogant dreams
Are broken. This uneasy interlude
Of eighteen months finds each antagonist
Mustering his forces for the final round:
Pitt building ships, while Bonaparte rearms
His wasted levies and constrains his friends
To keep the ring. There is no more pretence
Of a mission of liberation; no more talk
Of the Rights of Man. Imperial France discards
The rags of her outworn democracy,
And stands forth unashamed, pranked in the spoils
Of her predatory aggressions to proclaim
Man's only Right is Might, and her prime purpose
Dominion of the earth. All that she asks
Of Britain is connivance: a free hand
In continental Europe—but, meanwhile,
What about Malta? This island has been ceded
By the Treaty of Amiens, but still remains
In the Knights' hands. The mood of England stiffens;
For Malta, worthless in a world at peace,
Becomes, in war, a crucial point, commanding
The road to Egypt and the East, the basis
Of Bonaparte's vain dream. Malta must stand—
Or all be lost. If this should mean renewal
Of war, so be it! A disunited England,
Startled and disillusioned, stands to arms.

Now, from the Forelands and the slopes that shelve

[342]

To meet Reculver's sandbanks; from the crest
Of Dover's moon-pale scarp and Beachy Head
To Portsdown; from Wight's crumbling undercliff
To Purbeck and the flinty fields that lour
On Portland's roaring chesils; from the pale downs
Of Dorset to the blood-red rocks that fringe
The tawny marls of Devon; from the Start
To the unyielding serpentine that sheathes
The Lizard's fangs in adamant, arise
From their forgotten ash the phoenix-fires
That once foretold the Armada: while far inland,
Moloch the monster feeds his sleepless hearths
To forge war's armament. Now quiet cities,
Drowsed in the deeps of peace, suddenly ring
With eager tocsins and the tramping feet
Of shopkeepers turned soldiers; now the greens
Where country-folk played cricket lie bemired
By marching hobnails, and village goodwives scare
Their disobedient brats with a new bugbear:
The Corsican ogre, Boney, who, 'tis said,
Gloats on the flesh of children. Now in mart,
Club, cloister, palace, hovel, the old fear
Shadows the minds of men; the ancient question
Dwells on their lips: "Folk say the French are coming.
When will they come?"—and the inveterate,
Unreasoning confidence answers: "Come when they will,
They will get more than they give us. Let them come!"

XXXV

CONVERSATION PIECE   A.D. 1804

*At this hour of the September afternoon, when the Manager M
Martindale's House-Dinner is still being served downstairs, the Car.
Room at White's appears gloomy and deserted. Its only occupant a
the moment is an elderly member in a military uniform that seem
hardly in keeping with his years or his figure, which is that of .
sedentary townsman. The candles have not yet been lit, and in th
yellowish autumnal light of the nearest window, he is perusing th
latest entries in the Betting-Book. The trivial character of most o
the wagers inscribed in it appears oddly incongruous with the stirrin
and perilous times through which the country is passing at this momen.
Mr A., for instance, has bet Mr B. that the Marquess of C. wi.
not propose to Miss D. Ten pounds have been wagered that Lor
Rockingham's filly will not finish in the St. Leger, and twenty tha
Mr Pitt will not outlive Mr Fox. On the surface it would appea
that the Tory Ruling Class, which the membership of White's mor
or less represents, is more deeply interested in domestic affairs tha
in the fate of England or the future of Europe. As the militar
gentleman closes the Betting-Book and returns it to its table, the doo
swings open to admit a remarkably handsome old man. From the cu
of his clothes (he wears breeches instead of the now fashionable panta
loons), his powdered hair (in a mode which has been discontinued as .
protest against Mr Pitt's powder-tax) and from his weather-beate
complexion, one might judge him a country gentleman only lately com
to town. As he turns away, apparently disappointed to find no pla
in progress, the first member advances rapidly and touches him o.
the shoulder.*

TOWN MEMBER:
I think you have forgotten me. We last met
At Croome, if you remember. I rode over
From Madresfield with Lygon. . . .

CONVERSATION PIECE, A.D. 1804

COUNTRY MEMBER:
                      Pray forgive me:
This fading light and your resplendent scarlet
Quite blinded me.

TOWN MEMBER:
                      You behold a corporal
In the St. James's Volunteers, commanded
By that old firebrand Colonel Sheridan.
We are all soldiers now, Sir: neither station
Nor age exempts us. The Prime Minister
Drills his own troop at Walmer, and instructs
Grey-bearded veterans in the elements
Of Modern Warfare. Poor old Charley Fox
Has turned a true-blue patriot, and commands
The volunteers at Chertsey; and all our ladies
Affect a military mode, arrayed
In jackets of green velvet and short skirts
That show their ankles. Their new Rifle Hats
Are most becoming: Boney's *vivandières*
Are quite eclipsed in smartness. But pray tell me
The news from Worcestershire.

COUNTRY MEMBER:
                      A shocking harvest,
And partridges damned scarce. Our last excitement
Was a visit from Lord Nelson, who came through
On his way from Wales to London in the company
Of old Hamilton and his Lady. Worcester went mad;
Took out his horses at the bridge, and dragged
His carriage to the Guildhall, where they gave him
The Freedom of the City. I must confess
I was disappointed.

TOWN MEMBER:
                      Why?

COUNTRY MEMBER:

     The Admiral
Is the merest wisp of a man; poor Hamilton
A doddering dotard, and her ladyship
A monstrous creature, mountainously fat,
With the manners of a fishwife. You can't imagine
A less romantic trio.

TOWN MEMBER:

     You should have seen her
When she was Charley Greville's mistress: then
Her form was almost sylphlike, and her face
Angelically lovely. In her 'Attitudes'
She was incomparable, and every movement
Ravished the heart like music. You make me glad
I have not seen her since. There is no spectacle
More melancholy than the decadence
Of a beauty that has moved us. That will live
For ever in Romney's pictures. But, to be serious,
How's your Militia shaping?

COUNTRY MEMBER:

     Well enough.
We have reached our quota. The Loyal Volunteers
Parade on Pitchcroft under my boy George
On Sundays, and our patriotic ladies
Meet once a week to gossip and embroider
Colours for ensigns. If our Worcester lads
Were armed and taught to shoot, they'ld take some
But brooms and mopsticks are a poor substitute [beating
For rifles, and all this martial ardour seems
To me a thought unreal. You, no doubt,
Stand at the heart of things, and can assess
Our problematic dangers. For myself,
I won't be scared. Whatever else he may be,
Boney's no fool; and if he planned invasion,

He wouldn't rant about it. I regard
These tales as a chimaera, purposely
Magnified by the Government to distract
Small minds from graver matters.

TOWN MEMBER:
What could be graver?

COUNTRY MEMBER:
Consols at fifty-seven, sir, rising prices,
And now this new confounded Income-Tax
Of a shilling in the pound!

TOWN MEMBER:
Well, my dear Sir,
I wish to God you were right. Unluckily,
The known facts are against you. I agree
That Bonaparte's no fool. This very circumstance
Confirms our fears. None but a fool would muster
So huge a force at such a vast expense
Unless he meant to use it.

COUNTRY MEMBER:
So you swallow
These old wives' tales?

TOWN MEMBER:
No: my beliefs are based
On grounds more solid. If Bonaparte's no fool,
No more is Pitt. Our two protagonists
Face one another, on either side the channel,
Like wary gamesters; but, with much good fortune,
Backed by more skill and daring, we have learnt
What cards the Frenchman holds. Our information
Is copious and precise: there's not a movement
Of troops or barges, not a casual word
Dropped from Napoleon's lips, but finds its way
Into our records to be docketed,

Conned, sifted, pondered and interpreted
By practised wits. This weight of evidence
Is overwhelming. You can take my word for it:
They will invade us.

              COUNTRY MEMBER:
       How the deuce do we manage
To find out all these secrets?

              TOWN MEMBER:
            You must remember,
No more than twenty miles of misty sea
Divides us from the French. In peace or war
This no-man's-land-or-water has been haunted
By smugglers of both nations. Should you desire
To visit France and see things for yourself,
I have no doubt our Sussex fishermen
Would see you safely landed.

              COUNTRY MEMBER:
            Landed, yes—
And then shot as a spy! Your invitation
Doesn't attract me.

              TOWN MEMBER:
            The danger is much less
Than you imagine. Thousands of French loyalists
Detest the Revolution—and even more
This Corsican upstart. Many who have sought
Sanctuary in England from the Terror, burn
To stake their principles against their necks
And overthrow him. Nor should you forget
That, by its very nature, Tyranny
Is always rotten at the core, consumed,
Even when it seems to thrive, by inward jealousies,
Envies, ambitions; that base men who have climbed
To mastery on the ruin of their rivals
Command no loyalty; that in a state

[348]

Where all men are deemed equal, discipline
Depends on force, and underneath the shows
Of unity 'tis each man for himself,
And the devil take the hindmost. Thus it is
That in the very midst of those who share
The Corsican's confidence, we have our friends
(Or he has enemies) who would not be loth
To profit by his downfall.

COUNTRY MEMBER:

I'll be damned
If I'ld have truck with traitors!

TOWN MEMBER:

Our trust is tempered
By the wisdom of the serpent. Their reports
Are checked and counterchecked by the intelligence
Of our own agents. You may be shocked to hear
That the best spies are Englishmen.

COUNTRY MEMBER:

Well, well,
'Tis a dirty business—though I'ld trust them sooner
Than any Frenchman! So Pitt really thinks
That Bonaparte's not bluffing?

TOWN MEMBER:

I can give you
Boney's *ipsissima verba*: "Caesar's fling
Was the merest child's-play; mine is an enterprise
Of Titans. They want to make me jump the ditch,"
Says he, "and we will jump it."

COUNTRY MEMBER:

The damned braggart!

TOWN MEMBER:

His words may seem flamboyant, but reports
Give substance to his boasts. Since early Spring
We have spied flotillas of flat-bottomed craft

[349]

Concealed in every inlet from Dunkirk
To Cherbourg. The remotest inland communes
Have furnished funds for these, their hopes inflamed
By an exhibition of the Bayeux tapestry
Sent round on tour, expressly to recall
The Norman Conquest. Now this scattered force
Is gathering at Boulogne: a huge armada
Of various design, yet all contrived
For the purpose of invasion. First there are *prames*,
Poor seaboats fitted with three keels and rigged
Like a corvette. Each *prame* is built to carry,
Besides her crew, a double company
Of infantry and twelve twenty-four-pounders.
Next, the *chaloupes*, of greater complement
But ordnance far less numerous—though they carry
A six-inch howitzer. These craft are rigged
Like brigantines, and draw, when fully laden
Less than six feet of water. Add to these
Their *Bâteaux Cannoniers*, three-masted wherries,
Lug-sailed, like Cornish fishing-smacks, equipped
With stables, stalls and sheds for the conveyance
Of cavalry. Lastly, a multitude
Of smaller lug-sailed pinnaces, each designed
To carry fifty men, a Prussian howitzer,
And an eight-inch mortar.

> COUNTRY MEMBER:
> How many of these ships
> Has Bonaparte assembled?

> TOWN MEMBER:
> They must number
> At least three thousand sail, their admiral
> Being Eustache Bruix.

> COUNTRY MEMBER:
> That name means nothing to me.

TOWN MEMBER:

Our sailors know it well. In the Rebellion
He served in the American frigate *Fox*
As a junior ensign. But the master-mind
Of the whole enterprise is Denis Decrès,
A veteran of the Nile, who in the *Diane*
Escaped us, and later, in the *Guillaume Tell*,
Fought, single-handed, the *Lion*, the *Foudroyant*
And the *Penelope*: a most gallant seaman
Of infinite resource. 'Tis he who has made
Napoleon's project feasible by the building
Of wharves, pontoons and causeways to assure
Smooth embarcation for three hundred transports—
This from Boulogne alone—on every tide.

COUNTRY MEMBER:

What forces will he venture?

TOWN MEMBER:

              We cannot fathom
The Corsican's deep mind. But this we know:
He has never been deterred from any sacrifice
Of blood when his ambitions were at stake.
This Army of England, as it's called, comprises
At least fifteen divisions, every man of them
A seasoned veteran, under the command
Of youthful marshals who have proved their metal:
Ney, Soult, Davoust and Victor. For six months
This formidable weapon has been forged
And tempered by manœuvres that reflect
The conditions of invasion—embarcations,
Landings and tactics of assault—each movement
Rehearsed in detail, and every man equipped
To the last button. A month ago they left
Their training quarters, and are now assembled
In coastal camps and billets, to await
Their sailing-orders.

COUNTRY MEMBER:
                When do you expect
Such orders to be given?

TOWN MEMBER:
                        If we knew that,
We should be happier. Early in July
We thought the hour had come—but Bonaparte,
Incalculable as ever, changed his plans
And left us guessing. But since this fateful Summer
Is drawing to a close, and no sane seaman
Dares risk the equinoctial gales, we reckon
It must be now or never. By God's grace
The Emperor (to give him his new title)
Is neither sane nor sailor. Yet every sign
Points to a swift decision. Only yesterday
A trusted agent sent us his report
On a great review, designed to celebrate
Napoleon's birthday. . . . No doubt you know
                                        [Boulogne?

COUNTRY MEMBER:
No Sir, I don't. In fact I'm proud to say
I've never set foot outside the King's dominions,
Nor don't intend to. England's good enough
For me!

TOWN MEMBER:
No doubt, no doubt. . . . And yet Boulogne
Has a charming situation. It stands high
On the right bank of the Liane, the ancient town
And citadel encircled by a line
Of thirteenth-century ramparts. Farther East,
On the cliff edge, you see a ruined watchtower
Called the *Tour d'Ordre*, which antiquaries attribute
To the Emperor Caligula. It was here
That the review was 'staged'—if I may use
The word that best befits a ceremony

So brazenly theatrical. Here Napoleon
Took the salute of eighty thousand men
From a tall throne, atop of which was placed
The chair of Dagobert.

> COUNTRY MEMBER:
>   And who the devil

Is Dagobert?

> TOWN MEMBER:
>   A great King of the Franks,

Last of the Merovingians.

> COUNTRY MEMBER:
>   I'm none the wiser;

But pray continue, Sir.

> TOWN MEMBER:
>   Before this throne,

Like consecrated elements outspread
On a high altar, stood du Guesclin's helmet,
Crammed with insignia of the *Légion d'Honneur*
Ready for distribution, and the shield
Of Bayard; behind, a lofty reredos
Of bullet-riddled banners from the fields
Of Arcola and Lodi and Marengo.
Then, as the Emperor rose above the ranks
Of his bodyguard of Mamelukes, the guns
Thundered in unison, and silver trumpets
Sounded a shrill fanfare. (Our correspondent
Notes, by the way, that while all eyes were fixed
On this resplendent vision, he could espy
Far sails of British frigates quartering
The sultry seal) Next, when the cheers and salvoes
And fanfares had died down, the Emperor
Administered an oath: "Commanders, Officers,
Citizens, Soldiers: swear, upon your honour,
To serve the Empire; to devote yourselves
To your Fatherland's integrity; to defend
Your Emperor and the laws of the Republic!"

COUNTRY MEMBER:

Republic? Emperor? That don't make sense.

TOWN MEMBER:

The French have their own logic. He went on:
"Swear to contest, by all means in accord
With Justice, Law and Reason, all attempts
To re-establish feudal rights! In short,
Swear to maintain, with your whole might, the principles
Of Liberty and Equality, the basis
Of all our institutions!" A deep rumble
Rolled through their ranks, as eighty thousand men
Muttered "We swear!" At this climactic moment
Of the solemn celebration, a flotilla,
More than a thousand strong, should have been entering
The roadstead of Boulogne. Unluckily,
Ironical Fate willed otherwise: a black squall
And clumsy seamanship alike conspiring
To throw them in confusion. A high wind
Roared through the Straits of Dover, scattering
The ill-found fleet of transports. Then the rain
Came down in bucketfuls. Napoleon,
Soaked to the skin, turned nasty, bickering
With Berthier, his new marshal, biting his nails
With irritation at the irreverent trick
The elements had played him. The parade
Dismissed in silence, and the drenched legionaries
Trudged back to billets.

COUNTRY MEMBER:

　　　　　　　　A very proper curtain
For such a farce!

TOWN MEMBER:

　　　　　　　I grant you, the French taste
For the theatrical is apt to offend
Our native modesty. Yet this performance,

Shorn of its false heroics, does suggest
That all their plans are laid, and any moment
May launch the invasion.

COUNTRY MEMBER:
     If a puff of wind
Could scatter their flotillas, how would they fare
With our frigates on their heels and the great guns
Of our battle-fleet before them? That would test
Their seamanship more shrewdly.

TOWN MEMBER:
     I admit
That Bonaparte's no sailor, and despises
The judgment of his admirals. He awaits
One of those tranquil intervals that follow
Gales which have forced our frigates to stand off
Or run for shelter. In such a breathing-space
He may seize his chance. He only needs to master
The channel for twelve hours—and don't forget
His transports are well-armed.

COUNTRY MEMBER:
     If Bill Cornwallis
Gets in among them, I'll wager all their guns
Will soon be on the bottom.

TOWN MEMBER:
     There's a factor
(I speak in confidence) which might upset
Your sanguine calculations. They have perfected
A secret weapon.

COUNTRY MEMBER:
     Ah, we're sick to death
Of these fantastic rumours of Balloons,
Bridges of Boats and Tunnels! Only simpletons
Credit such fairy-tales.

[355]

TOWN MEMBER:
                        So you've not heard
Of the warship that can travel under water?

COUNTRY MEMBER:
No . . . nor I don't believe it!

TOWN MEMBER:
                        None the less,
The thing exists. A young American
Named Fulton's the inventor. He submitted
His plans to Pitt a year ago, and claims
That his craft, the *Nautilus*, which he built at Havre,
Can move submerged, and so invisible,
For several hours. She carries a vast charge
Of powder sealed within a tapered cylinder
Called a torpedo, which can be attached
To her doomed prey with grapples, and exploded
By clockwork.

COUNTRY MEMBER:
                        Well, what did Pitt do about it?

TOWN MEMBER:
Referred it to the admirals. Old St. Vincent
Pooh-poohed the whole idea. Its use, he said,
Would do away with the whole British Navy,
On which depends our strength and our prestige,
Encouraging, in short, a mode of warfare
Which we, who now command the seas, don't want,
And which, if it succeeded, would deprive us
Of our predominance.

COUNTRY MEMBER:
                        What happened next?

TOWN MEMBER:
Why, Citizen Fulton offered it to Bonaparte
For forty thousand francs. . . .

COUNTRY MEMBER:
　　　　　The treacherous dog!

TOWN MEMBER:
And Bonaparte, with more imagination
And sense than Lord St. Vincent, jumped at it.
He has built a number of them, and declares
They may change the course of History. Imagine
A score of these infernal craft escorting
His army of invasion, and our great ships
Blown sky-high, one by one!

COUNTRY MEMBER:
　　　　　　　　　I'ld rather back
The judgment of St. Vincent than the fancies
Of a damned Frenchman, Sir!

TOWN MEMBER:
　　　　　　　　But if they land?

COUNTRY MEMBER:
Why then, by God, we'll fight them—on the beaches,
The Weald, the Downs, from every ditch and hedgerow
In Kent and Sussex! And if they come to London
We'll fight 'em street by street! You under-reckon
Our spirit, Sir. In fact, this kind of talk
Borders on treason. Admiral Cornwallis
Is a member of this club!

TOWN MEMBER:
　　　　　　　　Pray understand
I merely state the chances. If you should care
To venture on a wager, I'ld be ready
To back my own opinion.

COUNTRY MEMBER:
　　　　　I'm your man, Sir.
(He picks up the Betting-Book and mutters as he writes
in a shaky and somewhat unformed hand):

[357]

Lord C. betts Mr B. a hundred pound
That Bonaparte won't land on British soil
Before next Christmas Day. Does that content you?

TOWN MEMBER:
Completely. If you have not dined, perhaps
You will honour me with your company?

COUNTRY MEMBER:
Not I.
London's no place for me at such a time
As this. I'm going back to Worcestershire,
Where people don't talk nonsense, but behave
Like Englishmen. Good day, Sir. . . .
(He goes out in a fluster. The TOWN MEMBER *shrugs his shoulders, and methodically blots the entry in the Betting-Book.)*

XXXVI

A BALLAD OF THE *VICTORY*   OCTOBER 21ST, 1805

'Twas at daybreak on a sober-mantled morning of October
When our nimble frigate, *Sirius*, a'quartering the deep
Like a questing hound that feathers on the fringes of a cover,
In a haze of thickening weather saw the Frenchman's vanguard
One by one, in open order,   [creep
Past the guns of Matagorda,
Through the throat of Guadalete to the jaws of Cadiz Bay;
And she sped the news to *Mars*:
We can see their canvas shine
And the glitter of their spars:
There are twelve ships of the line
And a squadron of five frigates that have cleared the river bars,
And they're standing out to Westward. *Gone away.* . . .
                                    Gone away!

Then a livelier current raced through our pulses, for we guessed
That our stern and fruitless quest from the Straits to Martinique
And homeward from the main
Of Trinidad to Spain——
The long pursuit was over, and the foe no more to seek:
For we'd drawn him from his berth
Like a badger gone to earth;
We had flushed him from his cover and caught him face to face
Where no Admiral of mettle could refuse the gage of battle:
And aloft the signal fluttered: *General Chase!*

But whither they were bound lay more deep than wit could
                                    sound:
Were they heading to the West to join Ganteaume in Brest?
Could they dare to run the gauntlet of our fleet and seek
                                    Toulon?
Would they face us? Would they falter? None could tell. . . .

Then Lord Nelson took his station in the fairway of the
                                          Stra
Well to Westward of Gibraltar—as a wary huntsman waits
With an eye on either quarter; but no welcome signal shon
So all day we lay there heaving on the huge Atlantic swell
Till the breeze died with the daylight, and night fell.

But at dawn the South wind woke on a wide and empty sea,
And the frigate *Phoebe* spoke:
"They have put their remnant forth;
They are bearing to the North, and they number thirty-three
Then we knew the Straits were free; so we clapped on every sa
And stood out on the larboard tack with Spain upon the lee-
Till the South wind veered and failed, and a second night we l
Becalmed and sick with waiting, Sou' West of Cadiz Bay.
And now the frigate-captains came on board to tell their tal
How they'd watched five columns clear, with Alava in the van
How Villeneuve led their centre and Dumanoir the rear.
And the heart of every man was uplifted by their story:
Thirty-three to twenty-seven—and so much the greater glor
And on high the signal ran with new orders for the fleet:
"Clear your quarters. Set your steering-sails and royals, and
                                      shake ou
The reefs of all your topsails"! They were running—not a
                                      doubt!-
Forming line upon the larboard tack to shield the Cadiz bar,
To find refuge in retreat
If they knew that they were beat.
So they laid their heads to Nor'ard, and we followed from afa
Where on our leeward quarter shone the shoals of Trafalga

And the British fleet bore on in two columns line-ahead—
'Twas Nelson led the windward and Collingwood the lee—
And a sight more winged with beauty and majesty and drea
Eyes of man will never see
As in battle-order came all those ships of deathless name:

[360]

A BALLAD OF THE VICTORY, OCTOBER 21ST, 1805

llerophon, Defiance, Revenge and *Victory,*
gamemnon and *Leviathan, Colossus, Temeraire,*
jax, Neptune and *Achilles*—all were there!
or the wind had veered due West, and its waft now blew so light
hat our vast three-deckers, crowned with their towers of
dazzling white,
loved like stately clouds that sail on the far horizon's bound
Vithout stay, without sound,
a silence naught could break
ut the craking of their timbers and the ripple of the wake
s their fo'c's'les rose and fell on the green and glassy swell
hat swept them toward the shore,
ntil they seemed no more
nsensate monsters moving at the mercy of the wind,
ut sentient things endowed with the gifts of will and mind:
lind and will together vowed to one purpose stern and plain,
o sweep the French from off the seas and crush the might of
Spain.

et the will that urged them on drew from one man's mind alone,
.nd the master mind was Nelson's, that had brewed our
battle-plan:
low one column, line-ahead, should pierce the Frenchman's
van,
)oubling on his foremost ships, while the other held his rear
ocked in a deadly grip, ship to ship and man to man,
)n a larboard line of bearing—two blows to fall as one.
o the endless moments passed, as he bade the *Victory* steer
'or the gap that lay between the French flagship, *Bucentaure*
.nd the Spaniards' *Trinidada*, the mightiest afloat;
.nd our hearts leapt to our throats when we heard the sudden
roar
)f Collingwood's first broadside, as the *Royal Sovereign* smote
)n Alava's *Santa Ana*—and a cloud of curdled smoke
3lurred the leeward column's battle as it broke.

.   .   .   .   .

But as *Victory* bore down upon the gap, with *Temeraire*
Crowding close upon her quarter—not a cable-length to
spare-
Nelson hauled us out to larboard, and we felt her check an
swerv
Like a hunter when he shies at a fence for lack of nerve;
And we wondered what he meant, and whither we were makin
With our starboard sails still bent and our studding-sails
a'shaking
Till we guessed 'twas but a feint—to put their van in fear
Of doubling to give cover to their sorely troubled rear
And free the ships that Collingwood had ta'en;
But his purpose soon showed clear—for he gybed and swun
her ove
Hauled to starboard and turned in upon their centre once agai
With *Temeraire* and *Neptune* and *Britannia* in his train.
And as on we slowly crept—every moment losing way,
Since the wind was but a breath—our crowded decks were
By a hurricane of death: [swep
For they raked us, one by one, gun by gun, as we passed—
Twenty killed and thirty wounded, the mizzen-topmast gon
And the steering-wheel in splinters, was the price we had to pa
For a fight too warm to last!
But still *Victory* bore on;
And her bloodier counterstroke was not long to be delayed
As the French were now to learn—
For as we passed the stern
Of Villeneuve's flagship, *Bucentaure*, our fo'c's'le carronade
Crashed through her cabin windows, cleared her deck fron
stern to stem
With five hundred dead or mangled—and so much the worse
for them
While our double-shotted broadside, fifty cannon fired point
blank
Broached the bulwarks of her flank; and the vomit of her smoke
Blew back into our portholes in a suffocating cloud,

nd our quarterdeck was strewed with black dust and crumbled
wood
rom the crippled *Bucentaure*, which would trouble us no more.
o we left her with her dead. . . .

nd as *Victory* came hard round on two Frenchmen full
ahead,
'heir *Neptune* and the *Redoutable*, our captain cried: "My Lord,
Vhich of these shall we board?"
nd he answered: "Take your choice!"
ut new thunders drowned his voice
s the *Neptune* raked our fo'c's'le, sweeping guns and crews
away;
o we ran on board the *Redoutable*—and there those monsters
lay
Vith their yards and ropes entangled; but neither we nor they
ould hope to board the other—for our main-deck guns were
dead,
nd the boarding-party mangled by a rain from overhead
f langrage-shot and musketry, while they, no less, were stayed
y the *Temeraire's* full broadside and our starboard carronade
Vhich sprayed their deck with roundshot, while our lower
guns replied
ouring salvo after salvo through the Frenchman's gaping side.

nd it chanced, as we lay grappled in that desperate embrace,
'hat a marksman in their mizzen-top saw Nelson as he passed
Vith his stars and ribbons blazing; and he laid his gun in rest,
imed, and shot him through the shoulder; and he fell upon
his face.
And he murmured, as they raised him: "They have done for
me at last:
My backbone is shot through." And as he spoke, he drew
A kerchief o'er his features to hide them from the crew.
Thus they carried him unseen to the sultry cockpit strewed
With the dead and wounded lying in the reek of fire and blood;

And there they left him dying—for he would not have them sta
Till he knew the fight was won. So they let him have his wa
While the *Victory* fought on. . . .

.   .   .   .   .

And the battle of the van waxed more fierce as *Temeraire*
Past our starboard quarter ran, and her seamen leapt aboa
The thronged deck of the *Redoutable* and cleared it with th
         swor
And a ringing cheer went up as her ensign from the truck
Of the mainmast fluttered down—and the gallant Frenchm
But the *Temeraire* herself was scarce in better fettle; [struc
For the guns of the *Fougueux* had shot her through and throug
With a mort of deadly metal, and her decks were choked wi
         slai
But her gunners gave the *Fougueux* back as good as they had go
Returning shot for shot, while her daring crew had lashed
The rigging of the Frenchman to their for'ard anchor-chain,
When the mainyard of the *Redoutable* fell from the mast and
         crashe
Athwart their poop and smothered it in twenty tangled tor
Of spars and sails and cordage; yet still the foremost guns
Of the fighting *Temeraire* kept up a ceaseless cannonade
On the Spaniards' mighty flagship, the *Santisima Trinidad*.

Now our *Neptune* followed fast through the smoke and flam
         that poure
From the carcase of the *Bucentaure*, and raked her as she passe
Then she shot the *Trinidada's* main and mizzen by the board
Next her foremast cracked and fell—and the Spanish admir
         lowere
His flag, while on their quarter they waved an English Jack
As *Britannia* and *Leviathan* bore in to the attack;
And when these two had passed her by, the *Conqueror* took
         their plac
Hauling up to give the dying *Bucentaure* her *coup-de-grâce*

[364]

s the tricolor still flying from her topmast fluttered down,
nd the *Conqueror* reaped the glory that the *Victory* had sown.

ut by now we knew for sure that this bitter day was won:
or their centre had been broke, and their vanguard's counter-
         stroke
eld or parried. And South Westward the wan October sun,
hat like a red-hot cannon-ball sank through the battle-smoke,
howed the remnant of their sorry rear which Collingwood had
         shattered:
very ship—save only nine—of their splendid battle-line
ismasted, sunk or taken! Yet we felt it hardly mattered,
Vhen our Admiral lay dead with a bullet in his spine. . . .

nd as the sun went down, we heard no more the roll
Of sullen drumfire thundering from ships that spoke as one,
ut single shots which echoed like the mournful minute-gun
hat speeds a passing soul.
nd at last these too ceased firing, and a solemn silence fell
On the scattered fleets that rode above the dark and glassy
ifty giants of the line—each with her awful load   [swell:
Of carnage and of doom;
nd as the deepening gloom
Of that Autumn eve descended on the battle that was ended,
hose mighty phantoms veiled in their shrouds of tattered sail
eemed to stand about the *Victory* like mourners round a tomb.
nd though our hearts were sore for the hero that was gone,
Ve knew that never more could the fleets of France and Spain
hreaten our native shore or flout us on the main:
hat mid all deeds of fame in the chronicles of war
Jo name would brighter flame than the name of Trafalgar.

XXXVII

Saved is our Island! . . . The victorious fleet
Homeward in heavy-hearted triumph bears
Her saviour's body, while the mournful roll
Of muffled drums summons his soul to meet
Those rare immortal dead that were his peers;
Yet ten more bitter years
Shall pass before the havoc that has laid
To waste this generation shall be stayed.

For, foiled on the indomitable seas,
The Corsican thrusts landward, from Boulogne
Striking at Europe's heart where, one by one,
More tangible foes are worsted. Ulm decrees
The doom of Austria—and even Pitt's
Proud heart is broke at last when Austerlitz
Joins Russia to the rout. Now Jena deals
A blow as deadly, and French cannon-wheels
Thunder upon the cobbles of Berlin
As the Imperial Guard comes marching in;
Now the vain Russian, tamed by flatteries,
Forswears his plighted trust—and Europe lies
Palsied and cowed, fondling the upstart's throne,
Too sorely-spent to master
That torrent of disaster,
And England stands alone.

Alone. . . . And yet how often in the dust
Of universal conflict, when the bands
Of Law were loosed, has dying Freedom thrust
Her broken sword in these unwarlike hands!
How oft has England stood,
Grim as her native granite, brow bedewed

With blood and sweat, to fend the victim's part!
How oft has her great heart
Drawn from the wrongs of others a strong flood
Of resolution, veiled in a strange calm!
How often have the promptings of alarm
Bred not despair but courage in her blood,
That, when the cause of Liberty seemed lost,
Strove to regain it, counting not the cost!

What is this purblind folly that offends
The Teuton's laboured reasoning? What is it
That flouts the law of numbers, and transcends
The logic of the Gaul's dry-pointed wit?
A courage that begins where reason ends,
Drawn from those mystic sources where the dreams
Of poets have their birth:
Blind valour that beseems
A race impatient of the bonds of earth,
That recks not present suffering nor dearth,
But in imagined heavens seeks a prize
Unsought, unseen by more material eyes;
A breed of tongue-tied poets, who pursue
Unreasoning hopes in regions where the view
Of more far-sighted folk begins to fade:
Such must we ever be, for so we are made!

Thus, while the landlocked conflict Eastward sways,
And the doomed victor sows the seeds of hate
On Europe's ravaged soil, the broad sea-ways
Waft to our Isle the wealth of happier lands,
Fostering the strength of Britain while she stands,
Staunch and inviolate,
Against that day when arrogance overflown
Shall reap what it has sown.
Thus, screened by an impenetrable cloud
Of sail, that strength finds foothold where the loud

Atlantic beats upon the Iberian shore,
Where, from that hope forlorn, there springs once mo[re]
Promise of hope firm-founded—as the chain
Falls from the neck of Portugal and Spain,
And Europe, that seemed dying, breathes again!

Now Russia, wakened from her wintry trance,
Bestirs her monstrous limbs, as when the green
Banners of Spring o'er the sere steppes advance,
And in the teeth of France
A ruder challenge flings;
Now Bonaparte, still smarting from the stings
Of Talavera and Vittoria, turns
Eastward in wrath; now royal Moscow burns;
Now, wilting in the keen
Blast of the arctic tundras, the rank flower
Of his Grand Army withers, and the flood
Of icy Beresina drinks the blood
Of its poor, tattered remnant, straggling back,
Hungry and disillusioned, on the track
Of ruin, undisguised and undenied;
Now, one by one, the bulkheads that divide
The prison-cells of Europe crack and cave,
Falling to dust as the resistless wave
Of rightful retribution overflows
Their arrogant gaolers, dizzied by the blows
Of unforeseen defeat. Leipzig redeems
The routs of Ulm and Jena, while from Spain
Unloosed, the patient might of Britain streams
Through the rent bastions of the Pyrenees
To flood the Gascon plain;
While trembling Paris opens wide her gates
To let the victors in—and Europe waits
To see the tyrant beaten to his knees.

At last the narrow shores of Elba chain

One who had found the world too little room
For his ambitions: yet that brooding brain
Chafes at restraint, defiant of the doom
By Fate decreed, and breaking forth again,
Summons his scattered eagles to redeem
The glory they have lost—but France has paid
Too stern a price to prop the wanton dream
That squandered her rich youth
And manhood without ruth,
And sowed the fields of Europe with her dead;
And they that pinned their faith upon this last
Most desperate cast
Of the great gambler's greed had cause to rue
Their fruitless valour, when the battle-scarred
Columns of the invincible Old Guard
Broke on the British line at Waterloo,
And, callous to the end, their leader fled.

Now they that strove on land may take their wage
In lust or loot: for them the tragic stage
Is empty, and the proud protagonists
Departed. 'Twas for those who kept the sea
In patience, searching the Atlantic mists
Unthanked and half-forgotten, now to see
The play's ironical peripety!

XXXVIII

TALE OF THE NAVAL OFFICER   A.D. 1815

Nine days since Waterloo . . . but not one word
Of credible news had reached us where we lay
Tossed in a loose-linked cordon from Dunkirk
To Finisterre, though frightened fishing-craft
Brought rumours by the score of a great battle
Lost, won – – – who knows? – – – in Flanders. The
Superb,
Lame duck of Nelson's famous wild-goose-chase
To Trinidad, hovered off Quiberon Bay,
While *Myrmidon* watched Bordeaux and *Pactolus*
The Tête d'Arcachon. We, in *Bellerophon*—
'Old Bully Ruffian', as our sailors called her—
Cruised within sight of Rochefort, staggering
On the huge swell of Biscay. There, one evening,
The frigate *Slaney* spoke us with dispatches
And orders from *Superb*: "Napoleon,
Hammered at Quatre Bras, has slipped through Paris
And is heading for the coast. Keep a sharp eye
On all American shipping—in particular
The *Susquehannah*, Captain Caleb Cushing,
Of Philadelphia. The Emperor may embark
In one of the French frigates sheltering
To landward of Ile d'Aix. It is imperative
Not to let him escape." Within an hour
A second message followed: "It is known
That the *Epervier* is taking in
Powder and fresh provisions. The French Government
May ask for a safe-conduct—which, of course,
Will not be granted. Numerous civilians—
Query: the Emperor's suite?—have been observed
Landing on the Ile d'Aix." Then came a third:
"If Bonaparte puts out, *Bellerophon*

Must stop him at all costs: she and the *Slaney*
Will deal with the French frigates; then proceed
Directly to Torbay."

                    But not a sail
Stirred in the roads of Rochefort till, next day,
The schooner *Mouche*, wearing a flag of truce,
Came bobbing up alongside with a letter
From General Bertrand: "The Emperor
Has abdicated—not, be it understood,
Compelled by force of arms or by the will
Of the French nation, but solely actuated
By Motives of Humanity. Now he craves
Safe-conduct to America, as the due
Of an honourable foe, whose one desire
Is to withdraw into obscurity
And end his days in peace." That was the word:
Peace, from those perjured lips! But Bertrand got
His answer: No safe-conduct, and no terms
Save unconditional surrender. Thus
The *Mouche* returned to Rochefort, while we lay
With slip-buoys on our cables, and the yards
Of topsails and topgallants swayed to the mast,
Their canvas stopped with rope-yarns—as alert
As a greyhound on the leash; and all that night,
Our guardboats, with soft plash of muffled oars,
Rowed round their frigates; for the air was thick,
With rumours: first that Bonaparte was lodged
In the Grand' Place at Rochefort and acclaimed
By cheering crowds; next, that he had been stowed
In a huge wine-butt hidden in the ballast
Of a neutral brig, a Dane, being determined
To run the gauntlet—though, in truth our zeal
Was wasted, for the Corsican knew better
Than we that he was cornered; and that same night,
A row-barge, under flag of truce, put out
To warn us he would come on board *Bellerophon*

With the ebb-tide next morning. But the wind
At daybreak blew dead in; so we were forced
To send a barge for him.

               As four bells clanged
She swayed alongside, and with leisured steps
Mounting the leeward gangway, Bonaparte
Boarded us, in a silence only broken
By a feeble cheer which the *Epervier's* crew
Sent up to speed his parting. None who lived
That moment will forget it; for this man,
Whose vast malignant will had cursed our lives
For twenty years, seemed far less formidable
Than fancy painted him: a paunchy figure
In an olive-coloured greatcoat lined with scarlet
And a small cockaded tricorne, which he doffed
With a dramatic sweep as he saluted
Captain and quarterdeck, uncovering
A head of thinning dark-brown hair untouched
With grey. But when he spoke the bitterest words
That ever had passed his lips, that voice, whose tones
Had thundered in the ears of kings pronouncing
The doom of devastated nations, sounded
Mild and melodious: "I am come to throw myself
On the chivalrous protection of your Prince
And of your laws." Yet such was the assurance
Of speech and look, he made surrender seem
A condescension, and *Bellerophon*
No prison, but a prize; and though he winced
To hear himself styled 'General Bonaparte',
His confident bearing gave that scene the air
Of an admiral's inspection—his grey eyes
Keenly appraising the line of officers
Drawn up to greet him, with a smile for each,
And a patter of questions in such rapid French
That few could understand. So he passed on

[372]

To his allotted quarters, there to lounge
The livelong day in a strange lethargy,
Reading on his camp-bed—the green silk curtains
Drawn to denote his mood—or bickering
With his unhappy suite: dapper Las Cases,
His Chamberlain; Bertrand, his Chief of Staff,
Tall, slender, melancholy; the swarthy Lallemand,
Strong, thick, morose, abstracted—every one
Slave of his arrogant whims. And there he dozed
Like a sick lion, till, at five o'clock,
Food and a glass of claret loosed a flood
Of table-talk, such as a courteous host
Might use to charm his guests: shrewd questions veiled
In subtlest flatteries—the born quartermaster
Probing the causes of the French defeats
At sea; the skilled artilleryman discussing
Problems of gunnery, laced with compliments
On our sailors' cleanliness, and a special tribute
To the Marines: "Had I a hundred thousand
Men of this calibre, there's no enterprise
I would not venture." Sometimes came a spurt
Of humour, on the unconscionable bulk
Of the English breakfast; then a wry reflection:
"Since I must spend the remainder of my days
In England, I may as well get used to it!"
He laughs his gay Italian peasant laugh;
Then, suddenly, swift as a tropic sunset,
The bright mood fades; black thunderclouds descend
On his imperious brow—and once again
He is the sullen Titan, dispossessed
Of a world's dominion. By half-past seven
He has stalked off to bed. To brood? To sleep?
To dream? Who knows . . . ?

                So the *Bellerophon*
Weighed anchor and set sail, the Biscay swell

Lifting her larboard quarter, and old *Superb*
Envious of her rich burden, wallowing
Two cable-lengths astern. By the eighth day
We had sighted Ushant's crags of granite, ringed
With foam and wreathed in mist, the most forbidding
Of landfalls. Here, in the clammy dusk of dawn,
When drowsy seamen of the middle watch
Swabbed the salt-sodden deck, a midshipman
Spied a squat figure, muffled to the ears
In an olive-coloured greatcoat, staggering
Along the slippery planks, and armed him safely
To the poop-ladder. There this lonely man
Stood motionless till noon, a pocket-glass
Held to his eye, in passionate absorption
Scanning the coast of France, till Ushant sank
Beneath the horizon. 'Twas a sight to melt
A heart of stone, and no indelicate stranger
Intruded on that vigil. We are a race
Cloyed with soft sentiment. Why should we pity
This ruthless ruffian who had scrawled his name
In blood all over Europe? What did he care
For France, save as the willing instrument
Of his self-centred passion? What did he reck
Of France's sacrifice? Time and again—
At Acre, on the brink of Beresina—
He had cut his losses, and the greater loss
Of his devoted dupes, to save his skin:
I think he gazed on France, not as a lover
In desolate farewell, but as a gamester
Who sees his last, his most ambitious stake
Swept from the board—yet still cannot believe
That Fortune has disowned him. . . .

                                    And, for proof,
See him next morning, those rebellious dreams
Exorcized or forgotten, as *Bellerophon*

[374]

Steals round the snout of Berry Head to anchor
In Brixham Roads. Behold him now, attired
With scrupulous elegance: silver buckled shoes,
Silk stockings, buckskin breeches, a green tunic
With scarlet cape and cuffs: the full-dress uniform
Of a Chasseur of the Imperial Guard,
Slashed with the Legion's cordon, and ablaze
With orders of chivalry. This garb reflects
The spirit's buoyancy. He has never seen
England so near before; and now the loveliness
Of that green bay, backed by the girdling tors
Of Dartmoor, takes his breath: "I never knew
Your country was so beautiful: it reminds me
Of Porto Ferrajo in Elba." The mere strangeness
Of the new scene inspires him with a presage
Of undivined adventure. Fate has turned
A virgin page unsullied by the errors
Of the too turbulent past, on which—who knows?
New exploits of more temperate complexion
May yet be written! No inkling of despair
Shadows his thoughts. There is a code of honour
Among kings no less than thieves; so fallen kingship
Can count on generosity. Though the Emperor
May have forfeited his throne, no power on earth
Can rob the Man of grandeur. Only see
How these crowds of fisherfolk and townsmen, drawn
Over the surface of the crinkling sea
Like particles of iron to the magnet
Of royalty, flock out in rowboats crammed
With craning faces! The familiar
Incense of notoriety, by now
Breath of his life, sustains him as he struts
On the *Bellerophon's* quarterdeck, or poses
At her gangways and stern-windows, drinking in
Awe if not adulation. Let them take
Their fill of gazing at this spectacle

[375]

N

Unique in history! Now he singles out
A pretty, well-dressed woman, sweeping off
His hat with Latin gallantry, and laughing
To see her blush. It seems this wintry exile
May have charming compensations!

                    That same evening
The rainbow bubble bursts, pricked in mid-air.
Orders from London thus: *"Bellerophon*
Will sail forthwith to Plymouth and re-embark
Her captive in *Northumberland.* Captain Maitland
Will break the news to General Bonaparte"
In two words . . . Saint Helena. The stunned man
Confronts his doom in silence—then erupts
Like a live volcano in gusts of wounded pride,
Rage and self-pity. "Is this your English honour—
This, England's vaunted liberty? I come hither
As a guest, not as a prisoner, to invoke
The protection of her laws. All that I ask
Is air and water: in return she gives me
Sentence of death! Better had I been thrown
On the mercy of the Bourbons, or cooped up
In your Tower of London! This is a barbarity
Worse than the iron cage of Tamerlane;
But even that Mongol savage would have spared me
Gratuitous insults. Sir, you call me 'General':
Why not 'Archbishop?' Why not, at least, 'First Consul?'
Such was the title under which your King,
Who named me 'his brother', once accredited
Ambassadors to my court. But let that be . . .
It is enough that England, by this deed
Of rank duplicity, has smirched her flag
And forfeited her honour. History
Shall have the final word."

It is recorded
That he slept ill that night, waking to hear
The ship's bell clanging forth each hateful hour,
And, through the dark, the watchman's windblown cry:
"All's well!"—All's well with whom?—while the
Bellerophon
Bore Westward for the Start. The last scene closes
Off Cawsand, where *Northumberland* appears
To claim her prisoner. A Captain's Guard
Turns out, draws up in silence. (The quarterdeck
Looks like a scaffold!) Suddenly we hear
Three ruffles of drums: the muskets of the guard
Snap up to the 'Present!'—and here he comes
With firm, unhurried steps; his sallow face
Unshaven, haggard, overcast; his eyes
Sullen, expressionless. At the gangway-top
He halts and ceremoniously bows
Three times to the ship's company assembled
In the waist and on the fo'c'sle. Then he turns,
Clutches the gangway man-ropes, and goes down
To the barge that waits beneath. Above, the guard
Grounds arms, dismisses—and the play is done.

XXXIX

Ours is a many-coloured isle, whose face
Scored by the furrows of the plough betrays
The tincture of earth's ancient alchemies
In tones so various that unwonted eyes,
Wearied by tropic suns or arctic snow,
May scarce believe so small a plot can show
Such rare diversity. There is no heart
Exiled from England but must feel a start
Of pride and pleasure when her moon-pale clifts
Loom through the reek of channel-spray, or rifts
Of earth-born vapour; not a soul but yields
Its paean of thanksgiving when pale fields
Of flint-bloomed arable or smooth downlands show
The veiled effulgence of the chalk below;
Nor feels less rapture when the oaken shades
Of Wealden woodlands open on broad glades
Of meadow-land, where roofs of tile or thatch,
Mellowed by moss and lichen, warm to match
The amber glow of sunset, and the vanes
Of village steeples twinkle o'er the plains
Like too-precocious stars—or suddenly
The blossomed orchard boughs of Medway vie
With moonshine yet unrisen, as they throw
On twilit vales their coverlet of snow.
Yet move a space to Westward—and the land
Changes its hues, as though a bolder hand
Mingled the pigments. Here the shallow sand
Of hungry heaths defies the valiant plough
To tame a waste where no tall tree may grow
Save the black-visaged pine, whose greed disputes
Scant moisture with tenacious heather-roots
And tangles of tough brake—yet when July

Loosens their papery bloom, these deserts lie
Drowned in a spate of purple, and the stark
Trunks of those gloomy pine-trees shed their bark
To glow like blood-red pillars. Once again
Step Westward. Here the dry dun-coloured plain
Of Salisbury, crowned with hoary cromlechs, seems
Rapt in remote and other-worldly dreams
Beneath lark-haunted skies, while in her sleep,
Like shadows cast by cloud, slow-moving sheep
Dapple her face—yet, from those plains forlorn,
Five freshets of unfailing water—Bourne,
Nadder and Wylie, Ebble and Avon, spill
Their limpid moisture on the meads and fill
The tributary valleys with a light
So crystal-clear that unaccustomed sight
Blinks at their lucid richness, every hue
Brilliant as green blades seen through drops of dew.
Yet dwell not by these voiceless waters, lest
A nympholepsy seize you ere the crest
Of Egdon, famed in tragic story, frowns
On Dorset's sodden marls and those sheer downs
From whose scored flanks the shameless giant heaves
His antic phallus skyward—where the leaves
Of haunted woodlands whisper in your ears
Forgotten incantations, darkling fears,
Ageless forebodings: for there is no shire
Of England deeper foundered in the mire
Of earth-fast magic—so wise men beware
That gentle, innocent-seeming, milkmaid air,
And flee her witching accents as they pass
Westward to lowland Devon, whose lush grass,
Unseared by blenching frost, finds winter keep
For herds of silken kine that browse knee-deep,
Bright as the cloven chestnut when it spills,
Ruddy as fallen beech-leaves, or clear rills
Ambered with moorland peat; and ruddier yet

Gleams her rich tilth that, when the sun is set,
Gives back the glow that warmed it, and in days
Of midmost Winter, when her inland ways
Lie glazed with ice, or choked with vagrant snows
Down-drifted from her tors of granite, shows
A mimicry of April warmth, which frees
Untimely primrose-buds, and tempts the bees
To fruitless roving. Here unsullied seas
Shine with the azure of a halcyon's wings,
And from the sun-warmed cliff the furze-bush flings
A waft of almond-scented air that mingles
With saltier odours rising from her shingles,
Or whispering sands that pave some sheltered cove
With tawny gold. Yet some there be who love
More tenderly those Cornish capes, where Spring
First lights on England with the blossoming
Of naked blackthorn-twigs that gleam as white
As a gull's pinions. Here the seaward light
Is more subdued; for every rasping gale
That roars from mid-Atlantic sheds a veil
Of thin-spun gauze upon each craggy clift
Where creeping thyme, sea-campion and thrift
Weave their pale patterns in the headland turf,
And venturous rock-samphires drink the surf
That rimes their glaucous fingers; where the hues
Woven in that flowery carpet—tenderest blues
Of vernal squill and milkwort, amethyst
Of thyme and thrift, are mingled in a mist
So delicately shaded and so dimmed
By evanescent vapours, they seem limned
In pastel, not in pigment, and to share
An element that's neither earth nor air,
But born of drifting sea-reek as it laves
Those far Bellerian headlands, where huge waves
Break on the granite Longships in wild spray
That shrouds the Scillies, thirty miles away.

And some there be who love more dearly yet
The kindlier, homelier hues of Somerset,
Where Quantock's rufous fields and leafy chase
Rise from a sullied sea, whose changeful face,
Silken in calm or ruffled in unrest,
Wears the bloomed nacre of the ring-dove's breast;
Where, one wide arm dipped in the turbid waves,
Grey Mendip broods above her dripping caves
And subterraneous waters—while between
Those girdling hills outspread the levels green
Of Sedgemoor, laid on Severn's tidal silt,
Where angry blood in Britain last was spilt.
Yet, though the mine-dry wastes of Mendip hold
More ghosts than living souls, and lie a-cold
When the plain burgeons, earliest April fills
Her valleys with a dance of daffodils,
And her grim face never more lovely is
Than when her brows are wreathed in clematis
Whose awns of wintry silver fling their foam
On the stark thorns that cling to batch and combe;
And never doth a light more tender dwell
On English earth than when the passing-bell
Of Summer stills; when rime-white gossamer
Blanches the bent at dawn—yet the bland air
Of noontide, moisture-laden, seems to hold
Those turf-moors cradled in a weft of gold;
When the scarred walls of lime-washed farmsteads shine
Like ivory, mirrored in the peaty rhine;
When apples clustered on their orchard-trees
Gleam like rare fruits of the Hesperides,
Or dappling the lush lattermath in heaps
Of fallen gold, diffuse a warmth which steeps
Their garths in drunken fragrance. Slowly steals
The homeward herd to milking, and the wheels
Of distant farm-carts rumble—but no creak
Of rusty hinge or axle here may break

[381]

The slumberous stillness of a land that lies
Drowsed in fulfilment. . . . Now to ampler skies
And airier upland fields we take our flight,
Where over coloured Cotswold leaps the light,
And, like a wind-flawed sea, her bearded wheat
And barley bend their tasseled heads to meet
Wafts of a shrewder air, as cool and sweet
As mountain water. Once these naked wolds
Whitened with myriad flocks, and from their folds
Gave forth at shearing-tide a wealthier fleece
Than Jason from his fabled Chersonese
Oared home to Hellas. Now the ploughman pares
Their russet substance, and his armoured shares
Turn the sheep-nibbled sward to chequered fields
Of crumbling tilth, and stone-walled Cotswold yields
Less wealth if no less beauty. Miles on miles,
Far out of sight, her sunlit cornland smiles,
Splashed with fierce sainfoin and the cooler green
Of purpled trefoils, or the pallid sheen
Of beanfields that on windless nights pervade
With vagrant scents the roads the Roman made.
But deem not that this vacant upland fails
Of human fellowship—for the narrow vales
Deep-sunken in its rolling contours hide
Shy hamlets, whose remembrance is the pride
Of many a homesick heart; whose dimpling streams,
Colne, Evenlode and Windrush, lull the dreams
Of thirsty exiles with a song that seems
Sweetest on earth, as through the tremulous haze
Of fever, wandering minds recall the ways
Of Burford, Bibury, Lower Swell and Slaughter,
Stanton and Stanway, Bourton-on-the-Water,
Farmcote and Snowshill—blest epitomes
Of all remembered England; since in these
The inventive eagerness of man's device
Has joined with nature in the artifice

Of Court and Manor, cottage, church and farm,
All wrought with equal graces from the warm
Fine-textured oolite which is the heart
Of Cotswold—and each village makes a part
Of the sweet earth that mothered it, resumed
Into her quarried matrix, and illumed
By the same inward radiance. Nor alone
Doth Cotswold profit by this peerless stone;
For wheresoe'er Jurassic seas have spilt
Their shelly slimes, the hands of men have built
Dwellings and shrines of mellow ashlar hewed
From the same stuff, with various aptitude
Of art or handcraft. Ever to the North
That core of freestone stretches and gives forth
Its tawny riches: from the clover-leys
Of green Northampton to the Rutland clays;
From Leicester's foxy coverts, on the bleak
Grasslands that feed the springs of Soar and Wreak,
To Welland's clammy vale, where Stamford lours
In lonely splendour, and her steepled towers
Brood on the drearness of the Deeping Fen,
Black-soilèd and sodden—rising once again
Seaward of Market Rasen to enfold
The thirsty hamlets of the Lincoln wold,
Where, straddling Humber's sandbanks, it invades
The boulder-clays of Holdernesse, and fades
In iron-hearted Cleveland. It were vain
To hope for livelier hues in the sad plain
That skirts the Pennine sheepwalks, or to seek
Light in that sombre soil—save where the Peak
With pinnacles of dazzling limestone cards
The smoke of Sheffield, and in deep gorges guards
Pellucid Dove and Derwent. Rather turn
Westward anew, where blood-red sunsets burn
On wastes of blackened ling, or flawless snow
Sweeps from untrodden moors to swell the flow

Of more impetuous streams; where Wharfe and Swale
Roar through their dripping woods, where Wensleydale
Outspreads her wealthier pasturage, and Ure
Flows full past Jervaulx. There's no air more pure
Than the thin dome of crystal that enskies
Those Pennine fells with blue faint as the eyes
Of wan forget-me-nots. Even in Summer's heat,
Their shallow rain-fed puddles floored with peat,
And marshy plats where drifts of cotton-grass
Whiten the brink of many a black crevass,
Reflect a wintry gleam. Yet, where the crest
Of Ingleborough scowls upon the West,
Where cloud-capt Whernside bares his stony flank
Or the cold fells of Calder spread their rank
Acres of ashen sour-grass, that no sheep
Will graze, see how lime-laden waters seep
Fanwise in arrowy flushes of fresh green,
Tender beyond belief; and on the lean
Ledges of earth that flaw the naked lime
Spring creeping cushions of insurgent thyme
That streak their scarps with purple. But beneath
Spreads a wide prospect that no rival hath
In wealth or squalor—where the skyward smoke
Or settling fumes of mill and factory cloak
Mersey's drear mosses, and a phantom sun
Fades like a death-sick comet on the dun
Wastes of a God-forgotten earth, where man
Has murdered beauty, and set an iron ban
On all that's comely; where the heart of night
Throbs with a red apocalyptic light,
And day shows naught unsullied but fierce plumes
Of hissing steam. Yet from these savage glooms
Raise but an instant your dejected eyes,
And they shall view a virgin paradise,
A green immaculate Eden, undefiled
By fallen man's devices—where the wild

Valleys and fells of Cumberland condense
In compass small more beauties than the sense
Or mind may measure: stark magnificence
Of untamed mountain, thunderous cascades
And singing streams that thread the narrow glades
Of birch and oak with silver, or dispersed
In pastures where a living green is nursed
By their unbridled floods, serenely sink
To deathlike stillness on the shelving brink
Of meres that in clear crystal circumfuse
Their ambient mountains with the changeful hues
Of earth and sky, and in translucent deeps
Lock the drowned image of a world that sleeps
In timeless trance—till some faint waft bestirs
Their limpid water, and the surface blurs,
And all that mirrored wonder vanishes.
Such visions you may mark where the sharp screes
Of Wasdale plunge into the inky womb
Of her dark water, or profounder gloom
Leadens the waves of Crummock; yet I think
A tenderer beauty girds the grassy brink
Of gentle Rydal, through whose fringing reeds
The lapsing current of clear Rothay feeds
Green-islanded Winander, where dark woods
Shadow her shores. Yet all the fitful moods
Of these sweet-smelling lakelands have their birth
In moist Atlantic airs that cleanse both earth
And sky, within whose pure transparency,
By glancing showers freshened, crag and tree,
Fell, fold and cottage, tarn and torrent, wear
A heavenly radiance—only to compare
With that which sparkles from night-fallen snows,
Gleams through the dewdrop's crystal lens, or glows
In the soft rainbow's arc of splintered light,
Or frosty starshine on a cloudless night.
And where, from the black throat of Borrowdale,

Cold Derwent pours to chill the widening vale,
Some remnant of that magic light persists
To smile on Solway, shrouded in the mists
That ebb from Esk and Liddel, as she wends
Seaward through her sad firth—and England ends!

XL

RURAL RIDE   A.D. 1830

When Cobbett rode from Salisbury town
September dews bespread the down
With weft of silvery gossamer;
On Salisbury's sunlit spire the vane
Sparkled in the morning air.
He rode toward the open Plain,
A well-fed man without a care,
Whose lively, smiling face belies
The smoulder of pugnacious eyes;
Abundant health and conscious power
Race through his pulses as they beat
In rhythm with his horse's feet;
The radiant hopes of youth revive:
On such a day, in such an hour,
How sweet it is to be alive—
To leave the stifling street behind,
To climb the downland's shelving sides
And greet the morning with a mind
Unclouded!
            Mr Cobbett rides. . . .

He rode uphill with a loose rein—
The springy turf that clad the Plain
So soft, he seemed to ride on air;
And sweet and clear as April rain
Larks were singing everywhere.
Alas, for him the fluttering lark
Shed his crystal notes in vain;
For Mr Cobbett's brow grew dark
With anger, and his buoyant mood
Sank like a plummet, when he viewed
The hateful hill of Sarum, crowned

With barren scarps—that lifeless mound
Whose loathly name bespoke the worst
Of rotten boroughs: the accurst
Outmoded system that decreed
Wealth to an idle few, and need
To toiling millions; the dead hand
That throttled his beloved land
With ice-cold grip; the avatar
Of feudal greed and wasteful war;
The fount of paper money poured
To glut the insatiable horde
Of smug tax-eaters, lawyers, bankers
And city squires; the worm that cankers
The rose of England, overblown
With ostentation pomp and pride;
The *Thing* which bloats the swollen town
And starves the lank-ribbed countryside:
The *Thing* that fouls the fly-blown Wen
With a hatch of tinselled 'gentlemen'
Spawned in the midden-heap of war—
While those who held the shattered farms
Of Hougomont and Quatre Bras
Limp the roads and beg for alms!
And through his bitter blood there ran
The anger of an honest man
Who sees the rights he loves the most
Scorned or irrevocably lost.
So he drove the spur in his horse's flank
To leap the roadway's chalky bank
And leave that devilish sight behind
As he galloped into a freshening wind
That cleansed his brain of much besides
Its anger.

      Mr Cobbett rides . . .

[388]

He rode as lonely and as free
As a ship that sails an empty sea,
Blithe as the roving honey-bee
That on wind-lifted wings boomed over
The sunlit verges white with clover;
And through his spirit, as he went,
Stole a miraculous content,
As the healing calm of unconfined
Wind-swept spaces soothed his mind
With memories of a happier day
When, long since, as he rode that way
To Netheravon, unawares
He came upon a field of hares
And paused to watch their gentle play:
Half a hundred hares as one
Nibbling the blades of dewy grass
And frisking in the morning sun—
Till the wind shifted, and, alas,
They smelt as one the charnel breath
Of Man, and crouched as still as death
Each within his grassy form!
And Mr Cobbett's heart grew warm
With the remembered tenderness
Of that rare sight—till new distress
Poisoned its sweetness; for he saw
Another he could not forget,
A vision of vindictive law
That chilled his new-warmed heart with hate:
Two village lads at Winchester
Hanged for the taking of one hare.
Two hapless lads, whose only crimes
Were hunger and the hardihood
Bred of these disjointed times;
Who, maddened by the reckless mood
That heartens men without a hope,
Preferred the scaffold and the rope

To starving on the parish dole!
And harrowed by that piteous scene—
The victims, mute and woebegone,
The black cap and the scarlet gown—
Mr Cobbett's kindly soul
Sickened with profound despair
To think what England once had been,
When such poor folk, by right of birth,
Claimed an inalienable share
And tenure of their native earth;
When even the least enjoyed the yield
Of labour in the common field,
And kept his pig, and grazed his cow,
And gathered firewood on the waste
To warm his bones in Winter. Now
The hirelings of a heartless caste,
Owners of factories and mills,
Puffed with undigested pride,
And flushed by the tax-eater's greed,
Have stolen half the countryside
With their accursed Enclosure Bills;
While humble folk who've earned the meed
Of painful husbandry, despoiled
Of their scant share of paradise,
See high park-walls and palings rise
About the land where once they toiled.
Now the mantrap's iron teeth
Lurk in the woods and on the heath,
And never a rabbit or a hare
Sweetens the labourer's skimpy fare—
Though men with hunger-hollowed eyes
Hear the grain-fed pheasant's cries
Taunting their stomachs as they gaze
Disheartened on the dwindling blaze
That lights their cheerless chimney-sides,
And shiver.

Mr Cobbett rides . . .

He rode where the bare downlands sink
Like a falling wave to the green brink
Of Wylie, gentlest and most clear
Of the welling rivers of the Plain;
Where, tangled in the silvery skein
That nets their shining water-meads,
Neighbouring hamlets lie as near
As loosely-threaded necklace beads
Or daisy-heads in a daisy-chain:
Wyshford and Fisherton de la Mere,
Sherrington, Beyton, Codford, Wylie,
And Upton Lovell, nestling shyly
Under the fleece of the Great Ridge Wood,
Rapt in the blessed quietude
Of a child that sleeps and sleeping smiles:
Each village in itself complete
With Farmstead, Manor, Tower or Steeple—
(Five churches in as many miles!)—
A Vicarage and a winding street
Of cottages, where simple people
Had lived and loved and aged and died
Unwitting of the world outside
Their sanctuary. And as he rode
The heart of Mr Cobbett glowed
With joy to think that here at least
The Eden he had loved and lost
Still throve unseen. But when he crossed
The crumbling bridge and leaky hatch,
He saw the signet of the Beast
Stamped on every mouldering thatch
And rafter sagged with age; he saw
Dank bedrooms, gaping at the skies;
Broken windows, stuffed with straw;
Smokeless chimneys, empty sties;
Gardens, abandoned and unsown,

With squitch and bindweed overgrown;
Manor and manse with windows blear
And blank as are a dead man's eyes;
And in the midst a monstrous church,
Cold as an empty sepulchre.
In such a void 'twere vain to search
For hope—and yet that shrine was built
In the firm faith of happier days
By prosperous folk who thronged the choir
And filled the nave with songs of praise.
Whose was the blame? Who bore the guilt?
Perchance some wastrel of a Squire
Who scorns his forbears' settled ways
Of frugal husbandry to seek
More pungent pleasures in the reek
Of London, where the squandered rent
Wrung from neglected farms is spent
On sluts and panders, drink and dice:
Perchance some Priest, whose darling vice
Is indolence or avarice;
A smooth, plump, tithe-fed absentee
With four fat livings in his fee;
An unrepentant pluralist
Who thinks the pittance that he doles
To one starved curate amply pays
The plighted debt he owes to Christ
His Master, and the immortal souls
Of an abandoned flock that strays
In pastures waterless and drear:
Perhaps some tight-lipped Overseer
Who culls that sorry flock to feed
His friends the farmers' wolfish greed;
Who recks not if the labourer thrive
Or starve, so he be kept alive
To work. What matter that the wage
Of long-drawn toil fails to assuage

The pangs of emptiness, or fill
The stomachs of his hungry brats?
The Poor Box, and the Parish Rates,
Will bury them and foot the bill;
And, at the worst, the workhouse waits
To spare a pauper's nameless tomb!
Thus, as he rode, a deepening gloom
Shadowed Mr Cobbett's thought;
To see long centuries of toil
And patient virtue turned to naught;
To see these folk, who lately fought,
Not solely for their native soil
But others' freedoms, more enslaved
Then those whose liberties they saved;
To see them left to starve and die
Unfriended, by their cold firesides.
Were these the fruits of victory
And valour?

Mr Cobbett rides . . .

He rode by Wylie's banks to where
The comely town of Warminster
Simmered in the noonday heat—
The pavements and the spacious street
Between its white-stone houses loud
With the chatter of a lively crowd
Driven in for Market Day:
A crowd so debonair and gay
That Mr Corbett half forgot
The squalors of the labourer's lot,
Seeing this show of country riches:
For here were portly farmers, dressed
In their Sunday-go-to-meeting best
Of Wilton broadcloth coat and breeches;
Pretty daughters and thrifty wives
With buxom shapes and beaming faces

[393]

Swarming round the pedlars' pitches
Like honey-bees about their hives,
Cheapening ribbons threads and laces;
Grooms that showed a stallion's paces;
Buyers, fingering horses' legs
For windgalls; gipsies hawking pegs
And frails and flaskets wove from withies;
Farriers in their cave-like stithies,
Tinkling anvils, blowing bellows;
Wheelwrights whittling spokes and felloes
For gaily-painted gigs and floats;
Fat horses, nuzzling chaff and oats;
Butchers' shops, beyond belief
Hung with primest pork and beef;
Chandlers cluttered hugger-mugger
With chests of tea and loaves of sugar,
Kegs of vinegar, jars of spice,
Tubs of treacle and sacks of rice;
Drapers' shelves, heaped bale on bale
With Lyons silk and Suffolk kersey,
Woollens from the Taunton Vale,
Cottons from the mills of Mersey—
And from that bustling street there swells
A medley of provoking smells:
The pungent scent of horseflesh wet
With lathery foam or runnelled sweat;
Warm fumes of stable and of byre;
The reek of singeing hooves and fire;
The tang of pomace, balm of malt,
Uprising from the tavern's vault
To quicken thirst, and overhead,
The bakehouse smell of new-made bread,
That, clearer than the noonday chime
Wafted from St Denys' tower,
Told him it was dinner time.
So he hitched his horse by the tavern door,

And his thoughts forsook the hungry poor
To seek the joys he relished most:
A country inn, a smiling host,
A market-ordinary filled
With farmer-folk, a trencher piled
With juicy cuts from a smoking roast,
And a tankard topped with creamy foam;
For never was Cobbett more at home
Than in the jovial company
Of men who lived by husbandry:
Small squires and graziers, met together
To talk of prices, crops and weather,
To pass the steaming jorum round
And stuff their stomachs with good fare;
And he smiled to think how staunch and sound
At heart these Wessex yeomen were:
Wiltshire's very blood and bone,
Tough as leather, strong as stone,
Yet full of kindly cranks and quips,
And English to their fingertips.
But while they gorged, the whisper ran
That this prodigious trencherman
Who shared their feast none other was
Than Mr Cobbett . . . and the sweet
Incense of deference and applause
Brought Mr Cobbett to his feet
And launched him on a hot harangue.
He told how half their trouble sprang
From War's illusive wealth: those days
When wheat was five-pound-ten a quarter
And easy money flowed like water:
'Twas then that farmers first began
To scorn their fathers' thrifty ways
And ape the landed gentleman,
With hunters housed in every stable,
And port wine on the dinner table.

[395]

But then came days of Peace, that set
A swingeing burden on their backs:
Nine hundred million pounds of debt
And twenty million pounds of tax
Sucked from their blood to feed a crew
Of war-contractors, bankers, brewers,
And holders of fat sinecures,
Who battened on the nation's purse
Like maggots on a fly-struck ewe.
Next, paper money—the prime curse
Of palsied, spendthrift governments—
Downed their prices, raised their rents,
And drove the feckless to the shame
Of debt and bankruptcy, or worse—
Since many a farmer soon became
No more than a day-labourer
On land that once he called his own.
But what the remedy? There was none
Of worth that did not first abate
The crushing loads that Church and State
Thrust upon their aching backs.
Therefore: Away with Tithe and Tax!
Give every full-grown man his vote:
Rub all their rotten boroughs out,
And teach the tax-devouring swarm
Their lesson! In a word: Reform!
He ceased; and one and all agreed
They liked a man who never minced
His words—though some misliked his creed,
And many of the wealthier winced.
So Mr Cobbett left them there
To cool their tempers, as he rode
Northward, where Avon's waters flowed
Through meadows ambered by evening air
That ebbed from out the Pewsey Vale:
A land of milk and honey, pale

With shaven stubbles and the green
Of new-fledged aftermath between;
And, riding there, his heart was moved
By an unwilled, unreasoning bliss
To think that of all lands men loved
None was more loveable than this.
So, as the westering sun declined
And sank beneath the fiery hem
Of eve's new-risen clouds, his mind
Dreamed of a New Jerusalem
Builded on this dear soil, where none
Should profit by his kinsmen's dearth,
But without grudge or lust of gain
Partake the matchless benison
That God had given to English earth
In kindliness and brotherhood. . . .
Yet, as he muses thus, the Plain
Grows dim with dusk; that magic light
Fades from the shapes of field and wood,
Leaving him visionless—as night
Falls on the darkling solitude
Of an unfeatured land, and hides
Its promise. . . .

Mr Cobbett rides . . . .

XLI

I was a Ploughman. . . . Proud,
My trampling team behind,
I whistled as I ploughed
And strode into the wind;
Keen upland breezes tanned
My temples as I drove
My coulter through the land
My faultless furrow clove,
Till wrongs and hunger cramped
My brooding mind . . . and now,
In chains of iron clamped,
These barren waves we plough.

I was a Shepherd. . . . High
On the bare downland's breast
My gentle flock and I
Like clouds would stray or rest;
Often, at lambing-tide,
Late-homing folk would mark
How on the lone hillside,
My lantern's moving spark
Glimmered through flakes of snow,
Then seek their beds and sleep
Blessing my vigil. . . . Now
A stranger folds my sheep.

I (so my comrades tell)
Was naught but a bad penny:
A poaching ne'er-do-well
Who ne'er did ill to any;

A gay, high-tempered lad
Who fancied sport and liquor,
Not wholly good nor bad,
But that my wits were quicker.
I chanced my luck and failed—
'Twas my wits against theirs;
Squire's keepers had me jailed,
And here I lie. . . . Who cares?

Mine was a comely trade:
Few labouring men could match
The hedge my billhook laid,
The neatness of my thatch;
I smoothed the pikel's hafts
And shaped the ladder-stale;
Mine were the ancient crafts
Of sickle, scythe and flail—
Till men found cheaper means
To thresh their corn than me;
I wrecked the damned machines
That robbed us. . . . Here I be.

I was a soldier. . . . Few
Envied the trade I plied:
I fought at Waterloo
And lost a leg beside.
I joined the wreckers' gang:
'Twas better to be thrown
In Salisbury jail or hang
Than beg and starve alone.
Now to the utmost ends
Of earth I fare to die.
These felons are my friends:
Who asks for more? Not I!

No felons we—but folk
Of hardihood and worth;
Sound as our native oak;
Salt of the English earth;
From our strong loins shall spring,
For all these shameful gyves,
A race whose name shall ring
As long as freedom lives:
Anzac shall know their deeds
And flaming Sari Bair:
Wherever England bleeds
Our children will be there!

XLII

(1)

Thus England, rich in honour—in all else
Impoverished . . . Her old unhappy King
Mutters and weeps at Windsor; soon the Regent,
Sot, glutton, libertine, unlamented sinks
To an inglorious grave, and a buffoon—
The bluff, thick-witted sailor, William—makes
The throne a laughing-stock. Who shall succeed
This oafish brotherhood? Clarence and Cumberland—
Thank Heaven!—are childless; the well-meaning Kent,
Harried by exigent creditors, retired
To his wife's home at Amorbach. It seems
England will soon have done with Kings—and few
Bewail their loss; for never has the star
Of Kingship sunk so low. The word 'Republic',
Now muttered by innumerable lips,
Suggests a panacea. Suddenly,
The bankrupt Kents, flushed by their proud performance
Of a dynastic duty, beg their way
From Amorbach to London. An Heir-Presumptive
Is duly born at Kensington, and christened
Alexandrina Victoria: a new name,
Foreign in savour, yet destined to adorn
A reign unmatched in greatness, dignity,
And length of days.
                        Here in the Spartan air
Of that half-dismantled palace, unaware
Of her exalted destiny, unshaken
By the earth-quaking quarrels and intrigues
Which heave about the innocent epicentre
Of her calm, moveless life, the Princess Drina—

'Our little Mayflower', her father calls her—
Thrives on her native soil: a sturdy child,
High-spirited, not uncomely, fiercely guarded
By two possessive dragons: first, her mother—
Disliked, despised, but fretfully resolved
To profit by her daughter's station; next
Her governess, Fräulein Lehzen, paragon
Of middle-class propriety, yet steeped
In the strict observances and protocols
Of a petty German court. It is their duty
And privilege to shield the precious heiress
From the scandalous contagions that pollute
Her wicked uncles' lives. Princess Victoria—
('Drina' sounds too familiar now) must learn
The good old German virtues: Modesty,
Courage and Thrift, in implicit reproach
To British laxity, never forgetting,
When Queenship gives her wealth, the debt she owes
Her childhood's mentors. Her very dress is chosen
To emphasize a flawless innocence:
A white lace frock, a swansdown bonnet trimmed
With small white rosebuds. Was she so innocent
As they believed? There is a wary strain
Of Tudor shrewdness in our royal blood.
Did not those prominent blue eyes observe
The Stuart emerald flashing in the hair
Of Lady Conyngham, and the bastard brood
Of her FitzClarence cousins? Were there not hints
Of a liberty dear Lehzen would deplore
In the conduct of her mother with Captain Conroy,
Her Irish major-domo? Did she not grasp
The meaning of that shocking scene at Windsor
When Uncle William, flushed with wine, laid bare
The family feud, and brutally berated
Her dearest mother? In old age she mourned
A 'sad, unhappy childhood' . . . Childish memories

Are long, and royal memories even longer;
Yet she had cause for happiness in the love
Of her strictly-chosen playmates: her half-sister
The Princess Feodora, and her own namesake,
John Conroy's little daughter, in cloudless days
Refreshed by simple pleasures: breathless canters
On her 'sweet little Rosy'; dancing-lessons
From La Taglioni; (how she loved to dance!)
State balls at Windsor; as a special treat
The Opera; then, even more exciting,
Visits from her German cousins that like the breath
Of a Spring breeze dispelled the cloistral airs
Of frowsty femininity which stifled
Her life at Kensington: Ernst and Alexander
Of Wurtemburg—the very first young men
She had ever known! Small wonder this Miranda
Was ravished by their masculine graces! Next,
Ferdinand and Augustus, even taller
And more distinguished. Last in this crescendo
Of fascination, the Saxe-Coburg brothers
Ernest and Albert. Ernest, she admitted,
Was no Adonis; but his brother Albert,
Perfect in manly beauty, no less rare
In his native sweetness, made all others seem
Dull and ill-favoured. What a rich delight
To sit beside him on the sofa, turning
The pages of an album, or to listen
Enraptured while he plays! The three short weeks
Of this angelic visitation fled
Like a glimpse of Paradise. She was seventeen,
And he but three months younger . . .

                                    Meanwhile, at Windsor,
The King pursues his blundering way, or snores
Amid a yawning court. Within a year
The few small wits he ever boasted dwindle
To dotardry, and, as he lived, he dies—

[403]

With a platitude on his lips. In the soft hush
Of a June dawn, a post-chaise rattles up
To the palace-doors of Kensington, discharging
Two dusty figures: the Lord Chamberlain
And the Archbishop. A bedraggled Lehzen,
Smelling of sleep and caraway-seeds, protests
That the Princess is abed—and keeps them waiting
For a whole hour! Then, hurriedly descending
In slippers and dressing-gown, her hair undone,
Victoria receives them on their knees,
And learns that she is Queen . . .

(2)

What of our Island?
Perchance she broods or sleeps? Where are the great
Prophetic voices now? The hooves of War
Have trampled out those spiritual fires
That, kindled by the sparks of the Bastille,
Illumined a new earth with the false dawn
Of universal liberty: the torch
Of Byron spent in Greece; the white-hot flame
Of Shelley quenched untimely in the deeps
Of the Tyrrhenian; Wordsworth's beacon tamed
To the quiet shine of a domestic lamp
Amid his native hills. An age of Titans,
Elizabethan in its majesty,
Has flowered and faded. Yet the Spirit of Man
Like an impeded torrent ever seeks
New channels for its flood . . . nay, even gains.
Strength from obstruction. Now, at last, Reform
Has whirled away the rotten boroughs; now
An ampler franchise loosens the dumb lips
Of Industry: now Mr. Cobbett sits
In Parliament for Oldham: Manchester
Shall speak as loud as Sarum, and release

The rural labourer from the degradations
Of the old Poor Law. At a single stroke
Black slavery is abolished, and the dreams
Of Wilberforce fulfilled. This is the century
Of the Machine. If the hard-headed North
Has little use for poets, it has much
For thrifty mechanisms that shall whirl
Its thrumming spindles. Stephenson has given
Watt's Monster wheels: his locomotives race—
At fifteen miles an hour!—from Liverpool
To Manchester, with no more casualties
Than one wool-gathering Cabinet Minister
Dazed by their speed! Thus the steel network spreads
To our Island's most remote recesses, bringing
The seeds of ancient wisdom to young minds
Newly awakened. In rude laboratories
These humble seekers patiently pursue
Their proud and selfless task. Thus Humphry Davy,
Bred on an obscure Cornish farm, reveals
Flashes of intuition swift and wayward
As summer lightning; a Cumbrian weaver's lad,
John Dalton, born in poverty, propounds
The Atomic Theory, and Michael Faraday,
Reared in a village blacksmith's shop, displays
The falcon sweep of an imagination
Unmatched since Newton's, bending to his will
That force which Franklin, with his flying-kite,
Snatched from the lightning flash, and thus contriving
The rudimentary Dynamo—new source
Of powers invisible which shall change the fate
Of humankind. So Science, in rebirth,
Outsoars the poet's dream. But let none think
That Poetry is dead. Deep in the wolds
Of Lincolnshire young Alfred Tennyson,
Uncouth and swarthy, strides the wind-swept hills;
Hears, from afar, the solemn undertone

Of spent seas pounding on untrodden sands,
And mutters as he goes. The Pennine fells
Nurse the thin flame, precocious and foredoomed,
Of three strange sisters; and in London's grime
Charles Dickens kindles from the cinder-heap
Of a neglected youth a generous glow
Of kindliness and humour that shall warm
The hearts of generations. . . .

(3)

The young Queen
Sees nothing of these marvels, her blue eyes
Dazzled by sudden fortune—while her mentors
Meet, with dismay, an unexpected streak
Of adamant in their charge. Affairs of State,
Money, and Patronage are the sole concern
Of the Sovereign and her Ministers. Neither ties
Of blood nor debts of gratitude can impinge
On these prerogatives: even Uncle Leopold
Is snubbed for his advice! The child will queen it
In deed no less than name—discreetly guided
By Melbourne, fine (if somewhat faded) flower
Of the Regency's rank hotbed, who recaptures
Long-lost illusions in the fatherly care
Of this gay, impulsive creature. Innocence
And Charm, alas! are not enough: the realm
Desires more serious basis for its loyalty
Than Sentiment—and its unresponsive mood
Finds voice at Westminster, where a petition
Of thirteen hundred thousand signatures
Is rolled into the House. Democracy
Demands new measures of Reform, rehearsed
In the People's Charter. Ominous rioting
Breaks out in Birmingham: all the smoky North
Is in a ferment. Any stick will do

To beat old Melbourne with—and if the Queen
Gets in the way and shares the punishment,
So much the worse for her! An ugly scandal
Arms them anew. This bread-and-butter court
Is not so virtuous after all! The Queen
Is hissed—at Ascot! Something must be done
To stay the rot, or her worm-eaten throne
May crumble into powder. The shrewd wits
Of Uncle Leopold provide the remedy:
Marriage . . . These British are a romantic folk,
Prudish yet sentimental. All the world
Smiles on young lovers. Love's the talisman
That brings the unimaginable lives
Of Royalty to earth; the common touch
Of mere humanity which transforms a Queen
Into a woman. Let her subjects share
Raptures of lawful love, the anxious pride
Of a well-filled nursery!

                His homesick heart
Steeled by the call of duty, Albert of Coburg
Stalks to the altar. No unruly flame
Warms his dispassionate mind; but the young Queen
Has fire enough for both. It is a marriage
Of complementary natures: on one side
Ardent idolatry strong to assuage
The loneliness of Queenship: on the other
Much native kindliness and affection, mingled
With admiration. He will even bring
Some glimmerings of culture to enlighten
That dingy palace life, with its dull round
Of table-games and small-talk—for his brain
Is curious and acquisitive, his ear
Attuned to verse and music. Bach and Mendelssohn
Are given the *entrée;* Constitutional Law
Replaces gossip as a common theme
Of conversation. Then, a growing family—

[407]

o

Six children in ten years! affirms the legend
Of royal domesticity. Above all,
The Consort is a Man—in this the antidote
To a woman-ridden youth. Her nature craves
The stimulus of male company, first supplied
By poor old Melbourne. What wonder that she finds
More than enough in her dear Albert? Thus,
Strong in each other's comfort, they rebuild
The crumbling Georgian throne on sure foundations
Of unassailable virtue. Revolution
May rock the realms of Europe; civil strife,
Fruit of the Hungry Forties, may embitter
The life of Britain; ill-conducted war
In the Crimea bleed her; mutiny
Ravage her Eastern Empire: yet her crown
Abides, unchallenged and revered: the symbol
Of an innate stability, unchanged
Amid a changeful world. The impulsive princess,
Tamed by her Consort's wisdom, has become
A constitutional Monarch, the new pattern
Of British Royalty! Fashion's fools may scoff
At the unimaginative domesticity
Of Osborne and Balmoral. Character
Was the heart of this Queen's greatness. Character
Is what we ask of Kings.

(4)

Meantime our Island
In spiritual travail has brought forth
Portents of Power and Beauty. Let none doubt
Great spirits are abroad! Though Poetry
May slumber still—perchance may nevermore
Renew the ringing chorus of the dawn
Which hailed her second Spring—great novelists,

Rejecting formal fetters, and foregoing
The loftier exaltations, have perfected
A more demotic Art. These are the poets
Of the new age! They speak a common tongue
Which brings to myriads of ingenuous ears
And minds unlearn'd the ancient intimations
Of ecstasy and terror, which shall be
No more the mystery and perquisite
Of an instructed few, but the delight
Of an uncultured many. Let men laugh
Or weep their fill as DICKENS *wrings their hearts*
With humour and compassion; let them savour
The salt of pungent irony that seasons
The lucid prose of THACKERAY; *shiver with dread*
When the snow-laden North scourges the stones
Of WUTHERING HEIGHTS; *smile at the teacup storms*
Which rock the towers of BARCHESTER, *perpend*
The ethical doubts of MIDDLEMARCH, *and suffer*
The heart-pangs of JANE EYRE: *or, if they crave*
More formal measures, seek the nobler moods
Of IN MEMORIAM, *and from* SORDELLO'S *matrix*
Of uncouth granite quarry forth the gold
Of sterner truths! So shines the visible blossom
Of this Hellenistic Spring, while, deep in earth,
Through unseen rootlets wells the rising sap
Of the creative spirit. Other eyes,
In patient vigil, probe dim vistas lit
By DAVY'S *wayward gleams and the clear shine*
Of FARADAY *and* DALTON. *Electricity,*
The century's new toy, becomes an attribute
Of universal Matter. DALTON'S *atoms*
Are linked in molecules: CLARK MAXWELL *numbers*
These jostling particles, caught in the mesh
Of his mathematical hieroglyphs—nay, proves
That Light itself, first portent of creation,
Is a swift electromagnetic wave

Surging through seas of æther. DALTON'S *pupil*
JOULE, *the serene recluse, proclaims that Heat*
And Energy are interchangeable
And so conserved. Not only on these summits
Of physical abstraction do the seekers
Pursue their task. A lad of seventeen
In the Royal College of Science, WILLIAM PERKIN,
Shuffling the coal-tar molecules in his search
For a man-made quinine, shall synthesize
An aniline dye, faint-flushed and delicate
As mallow-flowers, and therefore call it 'mauve'.
Thus shall the unimaginable blossoms
Of the long-buried coal-swamps give us back
Their vanished scents and hues! Now tangible earth
Displays her palimpsest, etched by the claws
Of creeping glaciers, crumpled in convulsions
Of her vulcanic birth-pangs, yet embedding
Tokens of primal life. Geologists
May pore on these; but even earth's visible face
Hides marvels yet unknown. The new explorers
Sail not in search of treasure nor mere lust
Of hazardous adventure. They go forth
In the high name of Science, and their quest
Is Knowledge, nothing more. Thus LIVINGSTONE,
Lured by a deepening mystery, oversteps
The province of his labours, struggling on
Through the black night of Africa; thus FRANKLIN,
Piercing the North-West passage in the 'Erebus',
And caught in the cold Palæochristic Sea,
Shall perish; thus CHARLES DARWIN, *in the 'Beagle',*
Searching the Patagonian waste, perceives
In the clear pools of his reflective mind
Strange adumbrations of the unity
Pervading sentient life. MALTHUS *instils*
The catalyst that turns these cloudy shapes
To crystal—and the ORIGIN OF SPECIES

Shocks a too-credulous world; thus, in Soho,
At London's callous heart, that shaggy exile
KARL MARX, *of ponderous brow and glittering eye,*
Watches his children starve, and from the depths
Of a profound, embittered soul, indites
DAS KAPITAL. . . .

(5)

Why should our Island heed
Voices of sage or prophet? She is cloyed
With ease and liberty: the People's Charter
Granted, the Corn Laws gone. New railroads feed
The thews of industry; steam-powered paddles thrash
Her seas—and the Atlantic passage shrinks
To a mere fortnight; Wheatstone's telegraph
Flashes her will abroad; autonomous cities
Pave, cleanse and drain their quagmire streets, and build
Huge monuments of civic pride: new Schools,
Hospitals, Libraries. It is only fitting
The world should view our greatness and respect
Our culture. Thus, above the living elms
That spring from London's sooty soil, arises
A vault of glittering glass, fit to enshrine
The products of our genius, and proclaim
The confident dawn of a millennium
Of universal peace. Such was the dream
Of the ingenuous Albert. Fate appends
An acid commentary: within a twelvemonth
One War in the Crimea; three years later
Another in Italy. Birmingham and Sheffield
May profit by this carnage in the forging
Of arms, while Bradford clothes both combatants
In wool—or fustian. Parliament, unconcerned
With aught but its imperial greatness, rears
Palatial towers at Westminster that dwarf

[411]

The Abbey's airy vault, and a new voice
Booms o'er the roofs of London as Big Ben
First strikes the hour. Within another year
Albert the Good is dead . . .

                                   His widowed Queen,
Crushed and distraught, imperiously resenting
Death's outrage on her majesty, abandons
All shows of public state. London no more
Beholds her face: a loveless ghost, she haunts
The scenes of vanished happiness. When her Ministers
Duly entreat her counsel, she takes refuge
Behind her widow's weeds. But let not Palmerston
Nor any other dream he can dictate to her!
This lone recluse is yet their Queen—nay, more,
Heiress and instrument of the will and wisdom
Of her beloved Consort! Humbler subjects
Wonder why royal mourning should last longer
Than that of common folk—and even ask
Impatiently, how an invisible Queen
Can earn the sixty thousand pounds a year
Her people pay her. This hard-headed nation
Of shopkeepers wants value for its money,
And the bargain seems one-sided. The "poor Queen,
On her sad pinnacle of lonely grandeur",
Grows more and more unpopular, though she racks
Her conscientious brain from dawn to dusk
In mastering problems which, when Albert lived,
Had seemed so easy, now so hard. Meanwhile
Dread forces are unloosed. "Dear little Germany",
Child of pacific culture, has been gripped
In Bismarck's fist, and moulded to the shape
Of an aggressive monster. Denmark bows
To the new Teutonic Fury, Schleswig-Holstein
Snatched from her feeble hands. Then Austria,
Accomplice in her rape, is brought to heel
In seven weeks, at Königgrätz. One by one,

The lesser states of Germany, bedazzled
And awed by the new planet's magnitude,
Are swept into its orbit. Only France,
Impulsive, decadent France, now stands between
Prussia's iron-hearted Reich and the dominion
Of continental Europe. France's vanity,
Flushed by old tales of glory, leaps to meet
The Machiavellian challenge; and Sedan
Seals her abasement. Why should England care
For these remote convulsions? Is not France
The inveterate enemy? Are not these Germans
A friendly folk, linked with her by the bonds
Of interest, blood and culture? It is enough
That France, being humbled, can no longer threaten
Her guardian moat; that, in this blessed moment,
The sea-ways of the world are hers, the trade
Of the whole globe her perquisite. Thus begins
An age of unexampled energy
And wealth unmeasured. Mere prosperity
Mellows the fiercest passions; Time abates
The deepest woes. The Queen is doubly blest
In her Ministers—though the great Gladstone bores her
With his heavy-footed deference, delivering
Harangues more fitted to a public meeting
Then the royal presence; (Will he never learn
The Queen's a woman, and therefore to be won
By discreet gallantries?) but Lord Beaconsfield—
Though Albert found in him 'no element
Of the gentleman'—shows such an exquisite lightness
Of touch, such fine perceptions, such a wealth
Of human sympathy, that her prejudice
Soon yields to admiration. None but he
Has fully understood the depth and beauty
Of Albert's character; and if his letters,
Wreathed in rococo compliment, distil
The perfumes of the Orient, why not?

Is she not Empress? Does not the Koh-i-noor,
That peerless gem of old Golconda, pride
Of Aurungzebe and Nadir Shah, now blaze
In the Confessor's diadem, attesting
England's imperial destiny? Thus an age
Of mounting strength, more fabulous prosperity,
Rolls by, unvexed by threats of foreign war
Or civil conflict, till the Crown—no longer
The sport of jealous faction or the scapegoat
Of popular discontent, becomes a symbol
Of unity and greatness. Sixty years
Of dignity and decency have earned
A willing reverence, when the aged Queen
Puts by her weeds of mourning and drives forth
In state to Westminster amid the roar
Of many-throated London, moved by tears
Of gratitude, not sorrow. "From my heart,"
The message runs, "I thank my beloved people."
Beloved—and loving too. Benignant heavens
Smile on her Jubilee. Through the Summer night,
Red beacon-flames, leaping from hill to hill,
Roof her dear land with light. . . .

(6)

Was ever realm
So changed within a single reign? The clime
Of civility is Peace: beneath no skies
Gloomed by the dark uncertainties of war
Had common life so thriven, or the seed
Of abstract spiritual search attained
So swift a fruiting. Now no year but brings
Tales of new marvels, as more material minds,
Sifting the spoil-heaps of pure science, turn
Its theories to practice. Electricity
Becomes Steam's master: and Watt's Monster serves
The silken dynamo, whose transmuted power

[414]

Flows, swift and silent as the waves of light,
Through tentacles of copper—or conserved,
A captive genie, in frail cells of glass,
Freed by the contact of a switch, performs
Gigantic tasks. This is the force that speeds
The thunderous shuttles of the 'Underground'
Beneath the bones of Roman London; this
The spark that spans the sputtering arc, or whitens
Coiled incandescent filaments, transforming
Darkness to blinding daylight; this the source
Of those minute pulsations which transmit
Through mute æolian wires the authentic accents
And tones of living voices. Nor are these
Astounding miracles enough: for soon
The inductive impulse leaps from wire to wire
Through voids of æther. PREECE and HEAVISIDE
Exchange faint signals between Lavernock Point
And the Flat Holm—while that shrewd Latin realist
MARCONI, pledged to Science, but none the less
Greedy of Fame and Fortune, taking profit
From the vast lodes of payable ore unwon
In Maxwell's boundless Ophir, quick to seize
The salient hints of CROOKES and LODGE, contrives
More sensitive detectors—and from the cliffs
Of iron-bound Poldhu to Newfoundland
Launches those waves which shall engirdle earth
More swift than Ariel, on viewless wings
Carrying the words of man. Nor is man's frail,
Long-suffering flesh forgotten. Scotland claims
New mastery over Pain; for HENRY SIMPSON,
Treading in FARADAY'S footsteps, has compounded
Sweet fumes of chloroform, that shall assuage
The primal curse of Eve; while in the wards
Of his Glasgow hospital, where maimed men sickened
Like Winter flies, bathed in a charnel air
Foul with the stink of gangrene, JOSEPH LISTER,

[415]

O*

Irked by the tragic impotence of his conflict
With the dark angel, in one lightning flash
Of heaven-sent insight, suddenly remembers
Pasteur's description of those living spores
That turn sick wine to vinegar. Could there not be
Analogies between such fermentation
And the process of corruption? Patiently,
Unbaulked by sneering pedants, he prepares
Smears from the purulent debris, and perceives
Through the dim lens's crystal a minute,
Sinister, unimaginable world,
Teeming with lowliest lives—blind instruments
Of death and pestilence, whose invisible spores
Pervade earth air and water, and disperse
Their venom in man's blood. But how to master
This secret foe? Such the forbidding task
Of this unhonoured prophet, vainly preaching
To deaf or scornful ears—until at last,
Out of the chemist's armoury, he discovers
The weapon of his choice: Carbolic Acid,
The first, crude, Antiseptic, at whose touch
The microbe's myriads perish. Time has known
No greater victory . . .

Now, from the pitchy dregs
Of tar distilled, shimmers the radiant iris
Of Aniline. Now the madder-fields of France
Lie fallow; leaves of Indigo, unreaped,
No more are sodden, nor the Tyrian snail
Crushed for its murex; the bright carapace
Of the Mexican cochineal no longer tinges
The robes of cardinals, superbly dyed
With Azo-scarlets. Now the rose's attar,
Essence of orange-blossom, and the musk
Of the Tibetan deer shall be compounded
And blended in a test-tube. Now the twin sense
Of Taste, no less than Smell, perceives the savour

[416]

Of a synthetized Vanillin—while the lees
Of this molecular alchemy shall bring forth
Potent medicaments planned to extirpate
The microbes of disease, to dull the edge
Of Pain, and through the weary brain diffuse
The balm of Sleep.
                              Such are the dizzier flights
Of Man's poetic fancy. Humbler hands
Shall pen the prose of Science. Engineers,
In Sheffield's thunderous forges lend their minds
To the chemist's admonitions. HENRY BESSEMER,
Seething his molten ingots in a blast
Fed by their own impurities, contrives
Steel harder, yet more malleable; ROBERT HADFIELD
Blends that fierce flux with Manganese—and the Age
Of Iron yields its ancient dominance
To a new Age of Alloys. PARSONS' *turbines*
Rejuvenate Watt's Monster, harnessing
Low-pressure steam. Now, too, pedestrian man,
Freed from his leaden-footed plodding, skims
The roads on flashing wheels: town-deadened nostrils
Inhale sweet hedgerow gusts and limpid airs
Blown from far hills. Thus in man's heart is born
The accursed lust of Speed! Forces more sinister—
Did he but know it!—searching to contain
Vast energy in small compass, adumbrate
The Petrol-engine. BUTLER'S *motor-tricycle*
Appears—and vanishes; but the baleful seed
Is sown. Soon Daimler's mightier Juggernaut,
In clouds of dust and reek of burning oil,
Roars through the lanes of England; while above,
PILCHER *and* LILIENTHAL *on flimsy vanes*
Glide to their doom, yet in that watery death
Foreshadow the dread day when Wings and Power
Shall be united, and their native land
No more an Island. . . .

[417]

(7)

What should Victoria
Know of these miracles? She has outlived
The greatness of her era. One by one
The rough-hewn, bearded giants of that age
Go down to death before her. Though her hands
Still grasp the sceptre firmly, though her spirit,
Obstinately imperious, and fortified
By an Empire's veneration, still imposes
Its will upon her servants, she is old
And pitifully weary. Never more
Will she behold the billows of mimosa
Sweeping the slopes of Cimiez; even Balmoral
Seems all too distant now. Alone she sits
In her wheeled chair at Osborne, where the waves
Of the ruffled Solent sparkle through dark groves
Of arbutus and ilex long since planted
By her dear Albert. To this peaceful haven
Comes news of war in Africa. She doubts not
The justice of that quarrel: England's wars
Must needs be righteous—for is not she herself
England incarnate? Yet the bitterness
Of inexplicable failure, long frustration,
Lies heavily on a heart that has grown gentle
And vulnerable with age. Her faithful servants
Mark in her pendulous jowl and dimming eyes
A mortal decadence; even her memory
Loses its wonted clearness, and her mind
Gropes for plain words in vain. Thus, quietly
As a still Summer moonset, this proud soul
Sinks into painless nescience. Victoria,
Greatest of Queens, is dead. . . .

The minute-guns
Of her great ships salute her as *Alberta*

Steals between lines of grey Leviathans,
Bearing their mistress landward on her last,
Most royal progress, Mourning London waits
Her coming in mute gloom. Funereal silence
Broods on the streets, and even the humblest bear
Some token of bereavement. Do they mourn
Woman or Legend? Few of those who weep
Have seen her face or heard her voice; yet all
Know that for ever from this English earth
A glory is departed. They lament
The passing of an age, a way of life,
Climate of thought and feeling—so deep-rooted
In their familiar permanence, that the prospect
Of certain change affrights them with a presage
Of huge uncertainties. A dumb multitude
Stands with bowed heads as the sad cavalcade
Winds its slow length twixt crowded pavements hung
With dark festoons of laurel, house-fronts draped
With purple trappings. Not a whisper stirs
That tearful throng—nor any other sounds
But the crunch of rhythmic feet, the plaintive wail
Of the Dead Marches, swelling on the air,
Then fading, one by one. And now at last
Comes the gun-carriage: on its silken pall
The Crown, the Orb, the Sceptre—tragic symbols
Of mortal majesty. Behind her rode
Her son, the uncrowned King: at his right hand
A haughtier rider, with a withered arm
And proud, disdainful eyes: the Hohenzollern,
Emperor of Germany, superbly mounted
On a pale horse . . .

              In John's Apocalypse
It has been written that this rider's name
Is Death.

[419]

XLIII

Where the dead Stoneman's barrow crowns
   These lonely downs
We digged our trenches; and the wet
White chalk we shovelled from below,
It lay like drifts of trampled snow
   On parados and parapet;

Till spade and pick with rhythmic dint
   Neither struck flint
Nor cleft the yielding chalky soil,
But splintered shard and calcined bone,
Poor relics of that Age of Stone
   Whose ossuary was our spoil.

Home we trudged, singing in the rain
   That threshed the Plain;
But all the while, beneath our song,
I mused how many a year should pass
And still our trench-cuts scar the grass
   With stigmas of an ancient wrong;

Yet soon, I thought, the same green sod
   Those dead men trod
Will creep above our chalky stain,
And soften, as it clothes the face
Of trench and barrow, every trace
   Of violence to the patient Plain;

And curious folk who chance to stray
   The downland way
Will talk of both in casual tone,

[420]

Saying: "You see the toil they made;
The Age of Iron, pick and spade,
   Here jostles with the Age of Stone."

Yet either, from that happier race,
   By Heaven's grace,
Shall merit but a careless glance;
And they will leave us both alone:
Poor savages who wrought with stone,
Poor savages who fought in France.

XLIV

ELEGY IN WHITEHALL. NOVEMBER 11, 1920

Where the tall cenotaph like a shrouded ghost
Uprose, with rigid lips and downcast eyes
We stood in deathly silence, while the wail
Of plaintive bugles, sounding the Last Post,
Faded on wintry skies.
Two measured minutes borrowed from the tale
Of Time's unhurrying pulse-beats slowly shed:
And now it seems almost
That, roused by this rare stillness, England's dead
Hold converse with her mourners, and approve
With a wry smile their ritual of love.

But I, their living comrade, neither smile
Nor weep, too void of heart to spend a tear;
Slow through my mind a spectral column wends:
A million dead men, marching mile on mile—
So close, I seem to hear
The voices of those few that were my friends,
And some, scarce-known, that, ere their doomsday broke,
Bode with me for a while,
Who suddenly unlocked their hearts and spoke
Of little, piteous things that were their pride,
Then shyly laughed, and went their ways, and died.

Others I saw who long with me had shared
War's common torments and vicissitudes:
Thirst, hunger, mud, the unconscionable ache
Of leaden limbs forespent which no man dared
Move, lest the hostile woods
Crackle with fire, when, yearning for daybreak,
We lay, red eyelids gummed with dust and sleep,
As, hour by hour, we stared,
Tense fingers on the trigger, into deep
Impenetrable darkness—till there shone
One chink of dawn, and we went limping on.

ELEGY IN WHITEHALL, NOVEMBER 11, 1920

There was an age when feckless poets sought
Vicarious raptures in the clash of swords;
Nay, even in war's hideous features traced
A baleful splendour. Tell not us who fought
With Prussia's brutish hordes
That war breeds aught but butchery and waste!
Spare us your threadbare cant of chivalry:
War is no princely sport
But a fool's game in which Death loads the die:
So speak the truth for our dead comrades' sakes—
War maims and kills more heroes than it makes!

Whence flow the mystic sources that compel
Acceptance of such monstrous sufferings?
These were no heroes born, but simple folk
Who knew life's common joys and loved them well,
Yet yielded the sweet things
They cherished most to stifle in the smoke
And stench of death, to brave the thrashing sleet
Of lead, the hurtling shell,
The thrust of icy steel, the ominous beat
Of drumfire shaking earth and livid sky:
Why, holding life so dear, did these men die?

Ah, fruitless question! Let each mouldering heart
In that vile charnel housed, its secret bear!
Brave men boast not when they go forth to die,
Steeling rebellious nerves to play their part.
Yet some, there surely were,
Found exultation in mere mastery
Of their grim calling, their especial skill
In war's infernal art;
Schooled from their youth to suffer and to kill,
Who matched their wits with other men's, who plied
The same sad trade, and uncomplaining died.

Some were too young, alas, too young to hold
Aught but the moment's cares, so richly brimmed
With youth's bright ardours that death seemed no more
Than a vain scarecrow set to fright the old.
How should clear eyes undimmed
By dusty apprehensions look before?
Rather let life's enchanting tapestry
Its patterned weft unfold
As a fair landscape to the falcon's eye
Reveals each new swift miracle of light,
Till, of a sudden, all be lost in night.

Some, without will or reasoning of their own,
Swept to their doom like floating driftwood plucked
From copse and hedgerow by a Lammas flood,
Or fragments on a city pavement strown
Through swirling culverts sucked:
Mute myriads, who cared not nor understood,
But like beasts herded in a stockyard-pen
Followed their leaders down
The blood-slimed ramp and fought as other men,
Yet in mere human friendship found the seeds
Of matchless courage and immortal deeds.

Others there were in conflict found release
From spiritual torment or the fret
Of thwarted aspiration: the dull round
And grey monotonies of laborious peace;
Some who would fain forget
Domestic misery, and rejoicing found
Oblivion in war's numb anodyne;
Some hardier than these
Whose wanton natures craved a headier wine,
Who, drunk with their own frenzied daring, flew
Full at the throat of death—and paid their due.

But those there were, fashioned of finer clay,
Knew war's vile worst, yet, counting well the cost,
Took up the unwelcome gage with open eyes,
Deeming far more staked in this hateful fray
Than empire gained or lost:
Nay, Freedom's self, and those high sanctities—
Truth, Mercy, Justice, that divide mankind
From apes and beasts of prey
And fiends in human shape that slay the mind,
Stamp out the flame of Reason, and befoul
The springs of Beauty that make sweet the soul.

Some for the comfort of strict conscience wrought
A visionary England all their own:
Green hills and vales transfigured by the dreams
Of childhood. 'Twas for her dear sake they fought
And bled on fields unknown,
Wearing the patient spirit that beseems
A people slow to wrath—yet, in that cause,
With sterner courage fraught
Than the dumb slaves that wage a tyrant's wars.
Gladly they fell—and we, who live, complain
Not that they died but that they died in vain.

In vain? Ah, let no bitterness disprise
Their shining valour, nor with doubt becloud
Their vision of the peace they dreamed they won
For us, the heirs of sovereign sacrifice. . . .
But see. . . . The impatient crowd
Stirs: its brief rite of reverence is done.
Hark! The shrill silver of reveille shakes
The stillness of grey skies,
And with a mightier shudder, London wakes!
In her huge heart the quickening pulses swell
Their rhythmic beat. Dear dead, we wish you well.

XLV

FANTASTIC SYMPHONY.   A.D. 1918–1939

(1)

Allegro moderato

Clio, if e'er my name with thine were linked,
(And haply all the Muses aren't extinct)
Abate my natural virulence, lest all
I tell of this mad age be writ in gall;
Melt thou mine iron mood—for though I think
That gall and iron mingled make good ink,
That righteous ire should have no truck with ruth,
And satire's vain unless 'tis barbed with truth,
'Twere well to temper the corrosive rage
That spills its venom on this candid page!

Now, in the gilded chambers of Versailles,
Another Congress of Vienna hails,
Mid bickering and discord without cease,
Another prospect of Perpetual Peace,
While still the jungle echoes with the snores
And snarls of satiated carnivores,
And greedy lambkins thrust their muzzles in,
Bleating for scraps from each dead lion's skin.
An edifying scene . . . But let's be just:
Though lordlier beasts let go but what they must,
And meaner creatures clung to what they could,
Self is the natural curse of Nationhood;
And elemental passions, ill suppressed,
May rage within the most high-purposed breast.
Thus the Big Four in patient council sit,
Rebuilding jig-saw Europe bit by bit;

[426]

And what a Europe!—trembling with Hysteria,
Hatred and Fear, from Ushant to Siberia!
Russia's ablaze: the famished and the slain
Litter her steppes—and yet the starved Ukraine
Finds dregs of strength to fly at Poland's throat
And clutch Galicia; Serb and Rouman gloat
And scramble on the pitiful remains
Of Austria, rotting on Danubian plains,
And neither dearth nor death have power to lessen
The lusts of Czech and Pole alike for Teschen,
While the frore sky of Lithuania rings
With rabid cries and thresh of vulture wings
Claiming new carrion, as in slow debate
Her arbiters determine Europe's fate.
Let those who now blame their arbitrament
(Being rich in wisdom after the event)
Know that the peace they fashioned mirrored then
The common sense of most well-meaning men.
Austria must suffer: she unleashed the war;
The landlocked Poles must have their corridor,
France her lost provinces; Italy re-enter
The Tyrol and Trieste Irredenta;
The Czechs and Jugo-Slavs assert their right
To separate existence—while the plight
Of prostrate Turkey yields a whacking piece
Of Lesser Asia to a Greater Greece;
Roumania must recover the green shaws
Of Transylvania from the Magyar's claws;
Minorities accept with resignation
The shibboleth of Self-determination;
Or, if determination spells a fight,
Bow to the verdict of a plebiscite;
Reason must rule the world—and if they squirm,
The hand that pays the piper can be firm.
And Germany? Heaven forfend that we should show
The tigerish greed of Foch and Clemenceau!

[427]

'Live and let live!' is the mild-mannered law
Of this too-happy breed, that never saw
Their fields and cities trampled underfoot—
Twice in one lifetime!—by the Prussian boot,
That ne'er beheld the pickelhaube's shape
Foreshadowing torture, butchery and rape,
That never watched their homes go up in flames,
Bowed to an alien will, nor knew the shames
Of impotent surrender and defeat!
So tell the French that vengeance is not sweet
To us—who've never learnt (or so it seems)
To judge men by their deeds, not by their dreams.
Some Germans may have misbehaved—but then,
Think of Mozart and Bach and Beethoven,
Goethe and Heine—Heine, it is true,
Hated the Prussian beast as much as you—
Still, that's the real Germany: a nation
Misled into this monstrous divagation
By wicked rulers—though it may be wiser,
On ripe reflection, not to hang the Kaiser,
Or run the risk of being sold a pup
If Holland should refuse to give him up.
So, let's behave like sportsmen and befriend
The beaten side: 'twere churlish to offend
A backward race that has no Public Schools
To teach them cricket and the Queensberry Rules.
And let not hate, vindictiveness, or greed
Poison their minds: abate their desperate need
And lend them money—there can be no harm
In that, they're too exhausted to re-arm
Within *our* time—and if they should prefer
Cannons to butter, that's their own affair:
Russia's a wolfish neighbour; France, at least,
Fears not the cloud that reddens in the East,
But, swoln with reparations, now has grown
Well-armed, and strong enough to hold her own;

[428]

And if again the Germans threaten war,
Why, what on earth's the League of Nations for?

Thus, at Versailles, each conscientious shaper
Of Peace propounds his brave new world—on paper:
The Tiger, pledged to make the Boche disgorge
His gains; the subtler wisdom of Lloyd-George
Sweetening with Celtic honey the black bile
Of Clemenceau, eager to reconcile
French fears with safety, and Orlando's claims
With Italy's just earnings. Let their names
Be not dishonoured. Give these three their due;
Perhaps they builded better than we knew.
Yet every compromise sweet reason planned
Drooped at the touch of Wilson's icy hand:
Wilson, who from his shell-proof pulpit sheds
Prim-lipped reproof on the astonished Heads
Of unregenerate Europe—those who bore
Through four long years the burden of a war
Which, he explained, *he* was too proud to fight!—
Teaching that Right was godlier than Might,
Justice than Force, in platitudinous sermons
More properly directed at the Germans,
Or planned to win the uncritical applause
Of Women's Clubs, or Princeton sophomores.
A Daniel come to Judgement once again?
Say rather: Daniel in the Lions' Den:
A major prophet in a minor key
Bewailing Europe's immorality,
Sent from on high to scourge the ignorance
Of darkest England, Italy, and France.
Let them repent and raise their earthbound eyes
To more ideal regions: otherwise,
Though slow to wrath and chary to condemn,
America must wash her hands of them.
(Alas, in twelve short months, with humour grim,

That thankless country washed her hands of him!)
Why did he fail—this innocent abroad?
Was he too slight to bear the Titan's load
Of a distracted globe? He was a creature
Of contradictions: in his secret nature
A student, of the strict New England school,
Painfully anxious not to seem a fool
In such sharp company, yet resolved to prove
A Man of Iron; one that few could love,
Yet none could scorn; magnanimous, serene
In higher things: in trifles small and mean;
Calm as a judge, impulsive as a woman;
Kindly but cold; humane, yet not quite human;
Naïve, but suspicious; bitter in complaint;
Thin-skinned, but hard; half-bigot and half-saint;
A man who failed through being what he was,
Not what he meant or felt. . . . But now, alas,
Spilt in the gutter, trampled underfoot,
Lies half deliberation's hard-won fruit.
What's to be done? A reasonable man
Will cut his loss and pick up what he can,
Though from that remnant rise no lasting Peace,
But an uneasy, endless Armistice:
A Europe sick with fear and racked with fever;
A palsied League of Nations at Geneva,
Shorn of real powers of Sanction or Defence,
The laughing-stock of brazen prepotence;
A sullen Germany; a nervous France,
Driven by fear to reckless arrogance;
An Italy convinced she has been cheated;
An England weary of the overheated
Frenzies of war, now sluggishly content
To drowse, and damn the fretful continent
Whose feuds dragged forth her dearest sons to die.
The dogs of war are sleeping. . . .

                                        Let them lie!

(2)

Alla tarantella

Haul down the flags and let the laurels fade:
The warrior's day is done, the last parade
Dismissed; and now the heroes' homing feet
Trudge the unfriendly stones of 'Civvy Street'
In hopeful search for all life has to give in
An England fit for paladins to live in;
And find, instead, an England that's forgotten
Their faces, names and deeds: an England rotten
With cynic selfishness and heartless greed,
That scorns their valour and decries their need,
Where the New Rich, stuffed with war's loot, deplore
The thriftless ways of the Perpetual Poor:
A disillusioned land that's lost its soul;
A fretful changeling—— England on the dole,
Blind with class-hatred, jealousy and doubt,
Where heroes, as it seems, are odd-men-out
And military virtue's on the shelf.
Till the next war, 'tis each man for himself:
So scramble with the rest, take what you can,
Tear down the ancient civilties of man
And build a brave new world for Caliban!
The old, men say, is too far gone to mend;
So let's deride the past and make an end
Of all it prized, seeking but that which serves
To stifle thought, or drug war-jangled nerves.
Culture's betrayed us; Decency's a bore;
And what did Beauty do to win the war?
Duty and Discipline? We've had enough—
And some to spare!—of that old-fashioned stuff.
Let us be gay and ruthless: war has taught
One lesson—one alone—that life is short:
So let long-thwarted instincts have their due;
Kill Time—for Time will certainly kill you:

Let Lust and Liquor numb the uneasy fret
Of memory, and help us to forget
The horrors of the hell through which we've passed
And blue our blood-won earnings while they last!
Let garish light and pandemoniac noise
Blind our unhappy eyes, and drown the voice
Of Reason, lest some qualm of conscience chill
Our minds and bid our twitching limbs be still.
Dance then, like victims frenzied by the bite
Of black tarantulas, void of sense or sight—
Not to the sentimental violins
Your fathers loved, but to the devilish dins
Of thudding tom-toms and the wailful tones
Dripped from the mouths of sickly saxophones,
To music—save the mark!—spawned in the damp
Mephitic airs of a malodorous swamp,
Dredged up by Tin Pan Alley from the ooze
To vamp its Charlestons, Bunny-hugs and Blues;
Pray that the barbarous beat may never stop;
Dance till you're dizzy, dance until you drop;
Dance without joy: let your blank features wear
A mask of bitter boredom and despair!
Gone are the days when lightsome feet expressed
The buoyancy of Youth: for now the best
Of Youth has perished; now indecorous Age
Sweats like a satyr on the night-club stage:
When lusty partners are in short supply,
There's little that a lengthy purse can't buy,
And raddled hags renew their girlhood's glow
In the cold arms of the hired gigolo.
Vain to misprise their rapture, or his pay:
Money's the only thing that counts today,
And in the flush of war's foolhardihood
Money has flowed like water—or like blood.
Though millions still are homeless, the West End
Teems with a Gadarene herd with gold to spend

On tasteless luxury and ignoble pleasure:
An ignorant rabble that can only measure
Value by cost, exulting to revere
The champagne standards of the profiteer.
And who can blame them—when the ruling caste,
Once arbiters of manners and of taste,
Shares the same sty and gluttonously digs
For the same scraps: when Dukes turn guinea-pigs,
When high-born ladies lend historic names
And smirking faces to attest the claims
Of cheap cosmetics, and with harlots vie
To catch the seedy gossip-writer's eye;
When gangs of feather-pated mountebanks,
The Bright Young People, play their dull old pranks
When, in that social no-man's-land which merges
The Half-world with the World on Mayfair's verges,
The lion-huntress tames her chequered crew:
Political climber, gilded parvenu,
Monarch in exile, self-made businessman,
Princeling and mummer, priest and courtesan,
Painter or poet of the moment's vogue,
Professional wit and well-connected rogue,
With naught in common save that all are 'smart'
And none, except their hostess, has a heart?
What can earth offer to abate the need
Of bankrupt souls but Pleasure, Change and Speed?
Pleasure, however base, to fill the void
Of desperate boredom; Speed to be enjoyed,
Not as the means to Pleasure, but its end;
Change, as occasion and excuse to spend
Money on Speed and Pleasure, and pursue
The old indulgence in surroundings new?
Thus, like a locust-swarm on pillage bent,
The idle British range the Continent,
Battening on low exchanges: the Blue Trains
Packed with a greedy rabble that profanes

Traditions, taste and manners, yet demands
Respect and deference—till the southern sands
Of modest France and Italy are strewed
With grotesque samples of the British nude,
And the crammed Lido earns at last (Heaven save it!)
The epithet '*affreux*' which Musset gave it,
While British morals make Italians blench,
And shock the scruples of the tolerant French.
Is this the sane, phlegmatic race that freed
A decadent Europe: this barbaric breed
Of vulgar drones and spineless epicenes
Whose frivolous sensuality demeans
The dignities of man, and, dead to shame,
Makes the Satyricon itself seem tame,
Dimming the orgies of Imperial Rome?
Or do all decent Britons stay at home?
The stricken oak, long ere its branches drop,
Starts dying slowly downward—from the top.
So spreads the rot down England's social scale:
A 'noble' shipping-magnate's clapped in jail;
A night-club queen, protected by the police
Gets off her daughters with a peer apiece;
'Ex-public-schoolmen', frenzied with cocaine,
Grab jewels through a shattered window-pane;
No virtuous man dares venture after dark
For dread of blackmail in St James's Park;
While stranger vices flaunt in many a den
Of dim Soho, and ordinary men
Who hurry forth from Oxford dare not halt
Or gaze—for fear of being turned to salt.
"Yet surely," you may say, "what you deplore
Is but the jetsam of the storms of war?
Your tempest-writhen oak may strew the ground
With rotten boughs even when its heart is sound:
What of the sane, the sober Middle Class,
Backbone of British probity?" Alas!

Here, too, that subtle poison finds its way:
Clapham, like Mayfair, lives but for the day:
Province and suburb itch to emulate
The modes and morals of the idler 'great',
Mimic their speech, adopt their fashions stale,
And ape their vices on a lowlier scale,
Till the same stigmas their dim lives besmirch:
The crowded dance-hall, the deserted church,
The empty cradle and the vacant mind.
Small wonder that their starved emotions find
Vicarious Romance to fill the void
In visionary heavens of celluloid,
Where all life's 'glamorous' all passion 'stark',
And every slut's a Helen . . . in the dark;
Envy the lot of any lip-sticked miss
Who simpers from the pages of the press,
And trace with eagerness to its dull source
Each tortuous 'Society Divorce'
Or 'Scandal in High Places'. "Ah, but then,
You quite forget our British working-men,
The horny hands that make the world go round:
All else may rot, but surely these are sound?"
Ay, sound enough at heart: a patient folk,
Slow-paced, slow-witted (save to see a joke
Or scent a wrong) who little ask of life
But elementary dues: a home, a wife,
Children, the right to work and earn the meed
Of honest toil sufficient to their need,
To speak their minds, and go their sober ways
In peace, unvexed by scorn, unmoved by praise;
A tolerant folk, with no ambitious itch
To share the senseless pleasures of the rich:
Such is their nature—but when life denies
These just demands, what wonder that their eyes
Grow hard and grim, what wonder, when they see
Wealth flaunting in the midst of misery,

Prodigal plenty mixed with helpless dearth
And sloth more prosperous than plodding worth,
They choose the easier path, and join the dance
Of those who live by subsidy or chance?
"Something for nothing!" is the common cry:
"My neighbour loafs and thrives, why should not I?
"Something for nothing! So let's take our toll
Of *panem et circenses*—dogs and dole—
And sink our pittance in the Football Pool!"
For now, alas, the lusts of Mammon rule
Our very pastimes: Mammon wakes the loud
Tumultuous howl of the dog-racing crowd
That sees the favourite beaten; Mammon fees
The football crooks and boos the referees
Who spoil his bets; Mammon, not love of sport,
Sways the curled darlings of the Centre Court,
Fickle as film-stars, pitiable things
With nerves as thin and taut as racquet-strings.
Now even the conduct of the cricket-field,
Home of prescriptive chivalry, must yield
To the base manners of a crew that gauges
Worth not by sportsmanship, but averages;
Who, scornful of the game's unselfish pride,
Play for themselves alone, not for their side,
Pose for the groundlings, court the crowd's applause,
And measure merit by the 'gate' it draws.
"But these are trivial evils?" Rather say,
The subtler symptoms of a gross decay,
The taint of gangrene that corrupts the whole.
"Are there no doctors, then, for the sick soul?"
Only too many: sedulous to trace
The springs of decadence in a dying race:
Sly charlatans, whose prurient fingers probe
Beneath the veil of consciousness, disrobe
The vestal spirit's nakedness, and pry
In holier regions, where great Poetry

Is born, yet, fumbling in that magic dust,
Find naught but Fear and Hatred, Shame and Lust.
"Who then shall heal our sickness? Poets, Priests,
Prophets, Philosophers and Dramatists?"
A hope forlorn! Shut in her ivory tower,
Philosophy heeds not the passing hour;
Prophets preach not to them that neither stay
Nor hearken; the poor Priest has had his say
And can no more—while little's to be said
For Poets now, since all the best are dead,
And the shrill, tuneless singers that remain,
Consumed by rancour, jealousy and pain,
With mutual admiration roll along
Each others' logs as beetles roll their dung
Those lily-handed revolutionists
Who think that true modernity consists
In sloven prose laboriously spun
In metres sired by Hopkins out of Donne;
Who, when their images refuse to flow,
Drag in the tractor or the dynamo
To mechanize their Muse; too proud to pander
To Beauty: Poetry being Propaganda,
Far better written on a Five Year Plan,
(What were the politics of Kubla Khan?
But pray, proceed . . .) and communally writ
With spite for satire, vitriol for wit.
No help from these! For prose, you take your choice:
The aphasiac stutterings of Stein and Joyce;
The sullied spate of poor, tormented Lawrence,
That frail, hag-ridden Titan, whose abhorrence
Of Reason, frothed with ineffectual rage,
Flaws the pure crystal of a lyric page
Unmatched in power or beauty since he died,
Launching his Ship of Death on the dark tide
Of dear oblivion. He, at least, can give
More solace than the frigid, half-alive

Highbrows of Bloomsbury, who with eyes of stone
Stiffly disdain all talents but their own;
Strict snobs of letters, chary to admit
There's such a thing as wisdom, style or wit
Beyond the boundaries their pundits keep.
(*Dear God, the very houses seem asleep!*)
Cold comfort here. . . . Nor can the stage purvey
More genial fare; for, though some critics say
The Comedy of Manners is reborn,
The rapier's blunted, and the wig's outworn;
The bawdry's dull, the salt has lost its taste,
The gold's mere tinsel and the diamond paste;
The modish cracks sound sillier and sadder
Than dried peas rattling in a jester's bladder;
Yet frivolous fashion still prefers this raw
Slick stuff to the cathartic wit of Shaw,
Dreads his keen glance, rejects his wisdom mellow,
And butters up the tricks of Pirandello,
A nimble casuist who can prove by sleight
That black (especially in shirts) is white,
And with a deal of complicated trouble
Sees life unsteadily—and sees it double.
Such are our seers and prophets! Can you wonder,
Led by such guides, our race is going under,
Sinking in treacherous quicksands none can sound?
"Dig deeper, then! Surely there can be found
Some granite core?" However deep one delves
Tis vain—unless we strive to save ourselves.
Britain must steel her sinews, and forswear
The false gods of indifference and despair,
Refine her spirit's gold, reject the dross,
Or fall to dust like Hecatompylos.

Finale: alla marcia

Time will not wait. On every hand one sees
Monstrous rebirths of dead theocracies:
A new Olympus and a new Valhalla
Shall salve the wounds of unrequited valour,
And promise those who lost (or won) the war
Post-dated credits, well worth starving for,
Making but one condition to the deal:
Their creditors shall neither speak nor feel
Nor think, save as the sovereign will commands.
Thus idlers basking on Italian sands,
With no desire to think or feel or speak,
Acclaim the fat Dictator as unique;
Sleep in their own (or in each other's) beds
Unvexed by fears of the atrocious 'reds',
And murmur: "Mussolini's too sublime!
Would you believe it? The trains run on time.
Black shirts are so becoming, don't you think?"
Yes Ma'am: and castor-oil's the proper drink
To purge obstructors. If they still protest,
The blackshirt, with his bludgeon, does the rest.
Thus, from the underworld that seethes within
The festering stews of Munich and Berlin,
Haunted by pimps and perverts, the last lees
Of infamous depravity, one sees
The dreams of desperate, disillusioned men,
Debased, and yet resolved to rise again,
Take hideous shape: an iron monster, meet,
Like Frankenstein's, to serve, but, once complete,
Its makers' master: whose accustomed food
Is flesh and bone, whose drink is tears and blood;
Greedier than Syrian Moloch to devour,
Fiercer than Crete's bronze-bellied Minotaur,

[439]

P

Whose dark dominion summons from the foul
Hyrcanian forest of the Teuton soul
An atavistic longing to destroy
All human civilties, a sadic joy
In cruelty that would debase the beast,
The exaltations of a mind diseased:
A maniac cult—a madman its high-priest.
Hitler. . . . No darker angel ever fell
With Lucifer to rule the hordes of hell
Than he, nor yet with more infernal skill
Bent a strong race to his perversive will:
The selfless saint—whose venal deeds profaned
All sanctities; the ascetic, who maintained
The loftiest of ideals—yet inspired
The basest minds to win what he desired;
The upright man, who prated to his herd
Of Honour—and who never kept his word;
God-guided mystic, speaking in a trance—
Yet always with an eye on the main chance;
The cool brain—tortured by neurotic fears;
The man of ice—who melts in shameless tears;
The rigid moralist—who merely laughed
When half his henchmen lived by loot and graft;
The father of his folk, supremely human—
Who ne'er begat a child nor loved a woman;
True comrade, loyal to protect and keep
His friends—until he shot them in their sleep;
The steadfast mind—that's swayed by chance and change;
Magnanimous spirit—brooding on revenge;
Bold Siegfried, with high chivalry aglow,
Whose *heilige Nothung* is the Gestapo;
All, these and more. . . . What matter? 'Tis enough
That Germans love this stale Wagnerian stuff,
Hail their new master as a tribal god,
Fondle the blood-stained fist, and kiss the rod.

[440]

And England—God forgive her—half admires
Their cult! What restless Germany desires
Is equilibrium. Arson, loot, and murder,
Seem an odd price to pay for Law and Order;
But that's their way. To persecute the Jew
Is vile; but lots of us are Aryans too,
And understand. Meanwhile the storm grows nearer:
Hitler *Reichskanzler*—Hitler *Unser Führer*,
Champion of meek Germanity oppressed!
He strikes—and mangled Austria goes West.
Next the Sudetenland. . . . Why should we vex
Our consciences about these tiresome Czechs—
A tiny race, whose fate no man bewails,
Mere misbegotten offspring of Versailles?
We've far too many noisy cranks at home
To hear the braggart of bombastic Rome
Howl, like a dervish, from his gimcrack rostrum
"Eight million bayonets" or "Mare Nostrum":
Let him howl on! Our Nordic nerves are proof
Against such Bobadils of Opéra Bouffe
Or neo-Roman empires in Utopia.
What's this he wants? A slice of Ethiopia?
"Give him his head: perhaps 'twill keep him quiet,"
Says foul Laval. But England's in a riot,
When, figure-skating upon ice too thin,
The unlucky exhibitionist falls in.
Did the splash wake her? No, 'twas but a gleam
Of consciousness that broke her waking dream.
Within a year she's lulled to sleep again
By the naïve platitudes of Chamberlain,
Assuring her that nine times out of ten
The common sense of cautious business-men
Drives better bargains than the devious wiles
Of diplomats. Let threats give way to smiles,
Hard words to soft. Let's all get round the table,
Turn up our cards, and prove that we are able

[441]

To face hard facts with realistic eyes,
And close the meeting with a compromise
That leaves the lion sleeping with the lamb:
That's how we manage things in Birmingham!
Vain innocent, condemned to learn too soon
Who sups with Hitler needs a good long spoon,
He flounders into depths beyond the ken
Of even the most enlightened business-men,
Returning from his missionary caper
To Munich with . . . another scrap of paper!
Peace in our time, my friends! Sleep in your beds!
And, as he speaks, down many a spine there spreads
An ominous thrill of fear—not of relief.
Though, by the narrow lights of his belief,
He did his best, his was a craven creed:
No smaller man e'er failed a greater need.
Sleep in your beds! The Germans did not sleep:
The beast lay crouching for another leap:
In mine and foundry, factory and mill,
The hammers beat, the wheels are never still,
As from red furnace-throat and clangorous forge
Pale gangs of slavish Nibelungs disgorge
A weight of metal such as ne'er before
Armed a mad nation for aggressive war;
The crushed earth thunders 'neath their tracks; on high
The throb of engines shakes the crowded sky.
Though still that harsh, neurotic voice demands
Mere tutelage of German-speaking lands,
Men smile no more at Hitler's bluff or blague:
Danzig, they guess, will share the fate of Prague.
And then? "Ah then, in terrible rebirth
Our Reich shall claim dominion of the earth.
Who can withstand us? Can the Poles rely
On France or Britain? Let them only try!
Britain's too soft, too decadent to fight
We're told—and Ribbentrop is always right,

While France, corrupt and venal to the core,
Will bargain for her body like a whore.
And Russia? Who can fathom the Slav soul?
But one's thing sure: no Russian loves the Pole,
And Stalin's gang, whatever they may feel,
Are crooks, like us, and open to a deal."
   Now the mask's off—if ever mask there were
To eyes unprejudiced by *laissez-faire:*
The Panzer wolfpack strips the Polish plain
As Danzig falls—and Warsaw burns in vain.
Unready Britain and reluctant France,
Helpless to implement their word, advance
To fend the March of Flanders and the Rhine,
While Hitler, safe behind his Siegfried Line,
Taunting their impotence with derisive mirth,
Wipes the proud name of Poland off the earth—
And calls for Peace! No peace shall e'er be given
To that damned soul this side of hell or heaven!
Eight weary months, stretched on the Flanders plain,
We held our front, from Bailleul to Lapaigne;
Eight dreary months, four hundred thousand men
Kept guard, till Spring awoke the sodden fen,
And fierce as snow-fed torrents of the North,
Drunken with Polish blood, the beast broke forth.
The dykes of Holland crack; the grey-green flood
Drowns Ardennes' valleys once again in blood;
Westward it flows: the bridges of the Meuse,
Betrayed by guile or treachery, let loose
A more resistless spate than suffering man
Has known, and through the gateway of Sedan
Pours to the South beyond Scheldt's crumbling bank,
Spins like a whirlpool round the British flank,
And laps their rear. . . . But why should I repeat
This oft-told tale of undeserved retreat
And unavailing valour—save to claim
That those were days of spendour, not of shame,

When, through the moving battle's dust and murk,
Shone the bright names of Calais and Dunkirk?
Proud Calais—where the Rifles held their van
Four days and nights, and perished to a man:
Dunkirk, that nine days wonder, where the ghost
Of a great army, number'd with the lost,
Clung to that strip of sand whereon their sires
Once drove the Spaniard—caught betwixt the fires
Of the burnt city and the cruel sea,
Sodden, unsheltered, dazed, incessantly
Pounded by shell-fire hurled from far inland,
That plunged to soar in fountains of grey sand
And red-hot steel, dive-bombed from overhead
By waspish Stukas spitting sleet of lead,
Bleeding, forlorn and famished—yet sustained
By the unreasoning hope that lies ingrained
Deep in the soul of their mysterious race
That oft has looked disaster in the face
Yet seldom known despair, or harboured doubt
Of ultimate victory. This was no rout,
No lawless rabble, frantic in defeat,
But a calm multitude, resigned to meet
The worst unmoved, and patiently to wait
Doom or salvation at the hands of fate.
And lo . . . a wonder! The high seas subside,
And thin-spun veils of seaborn vapour hide
The glassy straits. A miracle no less
Of ready wits: from each remote recess
Of England's shores, from every uttermost
Cranny and creek of her indented coast,
Ports, sands and shingles, coves and estuaries,
The rescuing flotillas take the seas:
Sloops and destroyers, tiny rowing-boats,
Tugs, drifters, colliers—everything that floats—
Dutch skoots and trawlers, paddled pleasure-craft,
Wherries and lighters (and the less the draught

The handier for the shallows) they put forth,
Manned by brave souls that recked not of the wrath
Shed from the skies upon the bomb-froth'd sea:
Unmedalled sponsors of strange victory
Sprung from the fiery embers of defeat:
A full-fledged phœnix, fluttering to cheat
The fowler's springe: three hundred thousand men
Plucked from the toils of death to fight again!
While from the emptied beaches the foiled foe
Snarls to the world: "There are no islands now!"
What? No more islands? Let him tempt his fate
On our untameable seas, and learn too late
The landsman's lesson! Let the embattled skies
Answer his boasts and flout his prophecies!
Let him beware: his brutish legions face
The united will of an unvanquished race
Led by their chosen chieftain, whose grave voice
Offers no guerdon, promises no choice
In all their toil but blood and tears and sweat.
In Europe's ears that voice is ringing yet,
And like a trumpet warns the tingling air
That, once again, *Malbrouk s'en va-t-en guerre.*

XLVI

Two thousand years have passed
All but a lustrum since great Cæsar massed
His leathern-sailed flotillas in the loom
Of Griznez's hoary dome,
Where once the Norman and the Corsican
Mustered their might to span
The treacherous channel's narrow rift of foam:
Here now, in even more vindictive mood
Than theirs, a more malignant conqueror
Than ever was suckled by the wolf of Rome,
Spawned in fierce Corsica or crowned in Caen,
Gazes with lust upon the Kentish shore:
Last citadel of Freedom unsubdued,
Last refuge of the sanctities of Man.
Here, seaward staring,
Drunk with the zest of unresisted daring,
He stands—and sees, a cannon-shot apart,
England, the first antagonist to thwart
The illimitable greed of his black heart:
England, at last forsaken and unmanned!
This is his moment: now
Let the old score be settled, once for all,
And from the shaken bough
Let this, the ripest fruit of victory, fall
Of its own weight into his outstretched hand!

Others before had planned
Such dooms as these; yet none but he could boast
The overweening might his malice flings
High in the air above the British coast.
A fury of innumerable wings
Shall sink our furtive convoys, bomb to dust
Their sheltering havens; then a shrewder thrust

[446]

Strike at our seaward aerodromes and pound
Our fighter-planes to splinters on the ground,
Slaughtering the fledgeling squadrons where they nest;
Or, should vain valour dare
To put the hopeless issue to the test,
Challenge the irresistible and rise,
Then shall the power of swarming myriads wrest
From their weak wings the mastery of the air
And brush them from the skies;
While mustered in the dark,
And stealing through the sea-reek that enshrouds
The summer straits, his panzers disembark
And roll inland; while, headlong from the clouds,
Vast air-borne legions fill the secret ways
Of every southern shire
With havoc and confusion, to embrace
Imperial London in a ring of fire.
Such was his fell desire:
Yet, even as his wings were launched in flight,
Far beyond sound or sight,
Viewless antennae of sky-probing rays
Gave back their reflex: *Aircraft coming over*
A convoy off the Wight! . . .
Two hundred bandits heading straight for Dover:
Eleven waves in all! . . . Three hundred more
Nor' East by East, twixt Harwich and the Nore! . . .
Portsmouth, Southampton, Weymouth, Portland Bill! . .
Wave upon wave they come,
Fanned out from Flemish airfields; yet before
They sight their targets, every fighter-drome
Eastward from Gosport—Tangmere, Biggin Hill,
Lympne, Hawkinge, Manston—rumbles with the roar
Of revved-up Merlins, as our Hurricanes
And Spitfires take the air,
Upleaping to the flawless zenith where
Heinkels and Dorniers, wedged wing to wing,

Hang staggered heavenward in a golden stair,
Step above step, to the meridian sun:
And, higher still than these,
Their guardian Messerschmitts in mazy flight,
Like swarms of angry bees,
Stipple the vault with silvery specks of light,
Poised for the deadly stoop, outnumbering
Our scanty fighter-squadrons five to one.
Nine weeks, in icy realms beyond our ken,
That cold vindictive combat filled the skies,
While unadventurous men
Who sweated in their harvest-fields beneath
The August sun, or sweltered in the streets,
Recked little of its daily toll of death
Nor counted the incomparable feats
Of daring wrought above their heads—save when,
Raising sun-dazzled eyes,
They saw, perchance, mysterious vapour-trails,
Those evanescent scriptures that betrayed
The swirling vortex of invisible battle;
Or, resting in the shade,
Ears strained to catch the throbbing undertone
Of unseen engines, heard the vicious rattle
Of gunfire drowned by agonizing wails
Of helpless aircraft falling like a stone;
Saw the void heavens scattered near and far
With the charred shreds of Heinkels blown to bits
Or flaming carcasses of Messerschmitts
Plunge with the fury of a shooting-star,
Black smoke and wildfire streaming from their tails;
Gazed in bewilderment, yet never knew
That in the waning of that harvest moon
The deadlier reapers of the skies had won
A victory as immense as Waterloo,
A mastery unmatched since Trafalgar.

THE WINGED VICTORY, A.D. 1940

It had come at last: the proud climactic hour
Of the Winged Victory! How shall images
Mirrored by earthfast eyes aspire to reach
The dizzy patch of these
Remote, unvisioned conflicts that outsoar
Imagination? How shall halting speech
Snare in its weft of words such flashing speed
As theirs? the splendour of the breathless deed
Too swift for pen or tongue
To capture—poems that were lived, not sung,
In brief ecstatic moments that defied
Death in the air, by lads who lived—or died—
Fending the deadliest fate that could befall
The souls of mortal men? How shall we call
These heroes of our skies,
How symbolize
Their terrible swiftness—when the fiercest wind
That strips the sea seems but a breath behind
Their furious slipstream? How shall we compare
With theirs the fleetest wings that cleave the air,
Kestrel and Peregrine—when their Hurricanes
Revelled in regions where the gasping lung
Of any feathered thing would burst its breast
In spurts of crimson foam—or earthward flung
Outspeed the diving gannet; when the vanes
Of whirling Spitfires scornfully outsoar
The untrodden peaks of icy Everest
Five thousand feet and more;
Gliding through glacial deeps of purest light
Above the utmost bound
Of human sense or sight;
Snarling through silences that ne'er before
Knew any other sound
Than the death-roar of the spent meteorite?

Who were these paladins,

Anonymous and immortal? Whence this breed
Of heroes born to fend the direst pass
Our Island ever knew? They were the seed
Of the mild, unadventurous Middle Class:
Plain-sailing folk, who neither knew the need
That stunts the body nor the wealth that cankers
The spirit, moderate in dream and deed:
The sons of parsons, lawyers, doctors, bankers,
Shopkeepers, merchants, chemists, engineers,
Whose loftiest endeavour was to live
Within their calculable means, and give
These lads at least as good a life as theirs,
A better schooling, and the chance to rise
Above their native station: such were they
Who, in this desperate day,
Won for our wings dominion of the skies:
Theirs the resourceful brains
That launched into the air the warning ray
That saved our cities; shaped the fighter's vanes,
Tail, fuselage, and with inventive skill
Powered these dread implements to soar and kill.
Yet neither science, craft nor sacrifice
Had aught availed
Unserved by an inexorable will:
Were there not mingled in their moderate blood
The fierce ancestral strains
Of Caradoc's charioteers, who never quailed
Before Rome's armoured legions; those who stood
Round the thrawn crab at Hastings, when the mailed
Might of the Norman broke on the locked shields
Of Harold's housecarls; mariners who sailed
With Drake and Hawkins, when the Spaniard sought
To sweep our seas, and failed.
Theirs was the valour of the few that fought
Immeasurable odds at Agincourt,
And on the harvest-fields

Of Hougomont made good the shot-thinned squares.
Yet something more was theirs
Than heedless daring, stubborn fortitude:
A fervour of the spirit, which imbued
Their inmost being, uncontrolled, unknown
By conscious will or thought, that swept them on
To pinnacles of grandeur more sublime
Than ever yet were won
In all the annals of recorded time.

My lingering task is done;
My tale is told; the parting moment nears.
Much have I pondered through four slow-paced years
Upon our Island's storied palimpsest,
And read therein
Some chronicles of cruelty and shame,
Folly and stupid arrogance unconfessed;
Yet many a nobler page have I perused
Lit by bright flashes of the spirit's flame
And by a radiant gentleness transfused:
Records of selfless virtue that attest
The quenchless love of Liberty and Truth
In an old race that has not lost the zest
And buoyancy of youth:
And this I know full well:
Our anguished world would show a sorrier scene
If Britain had not been,
Or if, perchance, she fell.
And this again I claim:
In all my story there has been no page
Brighter than this: we have lived in a great age;
The ancient glory fades not from our name,
And goodly is our Island heritage.

Craycombe—Talland.
1940–1944.